My Turn

THE MEMOIRS
OF NANCY REAGAN

My Turn

THE MEMOIRS
OF NANCY REAGAN

by

Nancy Reagan

WITH WILLIAM NOVAK

Weidenfeld and Nicolson
London

Published in Great Britain in 1989 by
George Weidenfeld & Nicolson Limited
91 Clapham High St, London SW4 7TA

Grateful acknowledgment is made to the following for permission to reprint previously
published material:

American Express: Excerpt from a Ron Reagan, Jr., American Express commercial, "Do You
Know Me?" series. American Express Company is owner of the trademark "Do You Know
Me?" and the copyright owner of the "Do You Know Me?" series of commercials. These
materials are being used with the express permission of American Express Company.

Principal, Dixon High School: Excerpt from a poem by Ronald Reagan from his yearbook,
The Dixonian. Reprinted by permission.

The Gridiron Club of Washington, D.C.: A parody of the song "Second-Hand Rose," with
lyrics by the Officers of The Gridiron Club of Washington, D.C. Reprinted by permission
of The Gridiron Club of Washington, D.C.

William Morris Agency: Excerpt from an article written by Ron Reagan, Jr., which appeared
in *The Washington Post* on January 17, 1980. Reprinted by permission of William Morris
Agency on behalf of Ron Reagan, Jr.

The New York Times: A Margaret Truman Daniel quote which appeared in "Notes on
People" by Albin Krebs and Robert McG. Thomas, Jr., October 16, 1981; excerpts from "The
First Lady Stages a Coup" by William Safire, March 2, 1987; and an excerpt from "Whispering
in the President's Ear" (editorial), March 4, 1987. Copyright © 1981/87 by The New York
Times Company. Reprinted by permission.

Landon Parvin: A reprise of the parody of the song "Second-Hand Rose," lyrics by Landon
Parvin. Reprinted by permission.

The Saturday Evening Post Society: Excerpt from "Pretty Nancy" by Joan Didion. Reprinted from *The Saturday Evening Post*. Copyright © 1968 by The Curtis Publishing Company. Reprinted by permission.

The Washington Post: Excerpt from "Below the Belt" by Judy Mann from the March 6, 1987,
issue of *The Washington Post*. Copyright © 1987 by The Washington Post. Reprinted by
permission.

British Library Cataloguing in Publication Data
Reagan, Nancy,
    My turn : the memoirs of Nancy Reagan.
    1. United States, Social life, 1901 – Biographies
    I. Title II. Novak, William
    973,9'0924

    ISBN 0 297 79677 1

Printed and bound in Great Britain by
Butler & Tanner Ltd, Frome and London

To Ronnie, who always understood
And to my children, who I hope will understand

Contents

Contents

Foreword

IN 1981, when Ronnie and I moved to Washington, I never dreamed that our eight years there would be a time of so much emotion. But life in the White House is magnified: The highs were higher than I expected, and the lows were much lower.

While I loved being first lady, my eight years with that title were the most difficult years of my life. Both of my parents died while Ronnie was president, and my husband and I were both operated on for cancer. Before we had even settled in, Ronnie was shot and almost killed. Then there was the pressure of living under the intense scrutiny of the media, and the frustration of frequently being misunderstood. Everything I did or said seemed to generate controversy, and it often seemed that you couldn't open a newspaper without seeing a story about me—my husband and me, my children and me, Donald Regan and me, and so on.

I don't think I was as bad, or as extreme in my power or my weakness, as I was depicted—especially during the first year, when people thought I was overly concerned with trivialities, and the final year, when some of the same people were convinced I was running the show.

In many ways, I think I served as a lightning rod; and in any case, I came to realize that while Ronald Reagan was an extremely popular president, some people didn't like his wife very much. Something about me, or the image people had of me, just seemed to rub them the wrong way.

During our White House years, I said almost nothing about how I really felt regarding the controversies that swirled around me. While the first lady has a marvelous opportunity to speak out on important issues—I chose the drug problem—on a personal level she loses her freedom of speech. There were so many things that I longed to say but couldn't; it just wouldn't have been appropriate.

But now those years are over, and it's my turn to describe what happened. Although there is a certain dignity in silence, which I find appealing, I have decided that for me, for our children, and for the historical record, I want to tell my side of the story. So much was said about me—about astrology, and my relationship with Raisa Gorbachev, and whether I got Donald Regan fired, and what went on between me and my children, especially Patti. Ironically, I felt I could start rebuilding our private life only by going public on these and other topics—to have my say and then to move on.

I often cried during those eight years. There were times when I just didn't know what to do, or how I would survive. But even so, I wouldn't trade those experiences for anything. I did things I never dreamed I could do, went places I never imagined I'd go, grew in ways I never thought possible. In 1988, during the space of a single week, I stood in the Kremlin with the Gorbachevs, had tea in Buckingham Palace with Queen Elizabeth, visited with Mrs. Thatcher at 10 Downing Street, and stopped off at Disney World in Florida with some of my favorite people on earth, the Foster Grandparents. And always, there was the love and support of my husband.

Yes, almost from the day I met him, Ronald Reagan has been the center of my life. I have been criticized for saying that, but it's true.

It's impossible to cover everything, and so I have tried in *My Turn* to focus as much as possible on the topics that people ask me about most often. Although much of the book concerns the 1980s, I don't really intend this as a history of the Reagan years in Washington. This is a book about people rather than politics, except where political matters touched me directly, as they did during the long months of the Iran-contra affair, and during Ronnie's five election campaigns.

I kept a diary during our White House years, and I have drawn upon it often in this book. I experience the world through my intuitions and feelings, and you'll find out a lot about those in these pages.

My mother used to say, "Play the hand that's dealt you," and that is what I have always tried to do. And this, for better or worse, is how it seemed to me.

Acknowledgments

How do I begin to thank everyone I should for helping me to write a book I never intended to write? I think I should start with my husband, for his patience, support, and suggestions. Then comes the man who really persuaded me and gave me the final push—Mort Janklow, my agent. It was he who pointed out that people would be interested in my story (we'll see!), and that the first lady is often controversial—as I certainly was.

Thank you to Bill Novak, my collaborator, who kept pushing me patiently to go farther when I was reluctant, and to his wife, Linda, who urged him to "Just Say Yes" when he was first approached to help. Thanks, too, to Bill's agent, Steve Axelrod.

Bill interviewed many people who were especially helpful, including my son, Ron, and Maureen Reagan, who has the best memory of anyone I've ever known, as well as Martin Anderson, Joe Canzeri, Linda Faulkner, Peter Hannaford, Richard and Cynthia Helms, John Hutton, Jim Kuhn, Nancy Reynolds, Mark Weinberg, and Barbara Wyden. Also, David Abshire, Letitia Baldrige, Jim Billington, Mike Deaver, Kay Graham, Meg Greenfield, Peter McCoy, Lyn Nofziger, Richard Perle, Stu Spencer, Bob Strauss, Sheila Tate, Mike Wallace, Mary Jane Wick, and Richard Wirthlin.

Thank you to Kathy Osborne, who spent hours transcribing tapes, and to Mary Anne Fackelman-Miner, who was relentless in helping us track down pictures.

Also, the White House staff: dear Rex Scouten, Gary Walters, and Chris Emery, and my own East Wing staff, especially Jane Erkenbeck and Elaine Crispen, who saw me through some pretty tough times, but whom I could always rely on and trust. And most recently, Lisa Cavelier and my present staff.

I kept a lot of people at Random House busy, starting with Joni Evans, the publisher, and including publicity director Carol Schneider and her department; copy editor Virginia Avery; and editorial assistants Jonathan Karp, Amy Roberts, and Olga Tarnowski. Donald Altschiller and Colleen Mohyde helped with research.

I especially want to thank Kate Medina, my editor. Kate was there for me from the beginning, day after day, helping me tell my story my way. Kate helped me in so many ways . . . far more than I can ever put into words. And Associate Publisher Peter Osnos, who really went above and beyond the call of duty. I hope they know how enormously grateful I am.

Thank you, everyone. I hope I haven't forgotten anyone, but you'll all be deep in my heart, always.

My Turn

THE MEMOIRS
OF NANCY REAGAN

1

❖❖❖

"There's Been a Shooting"

It was early afternoon on March 30, 1981, only seventy days after my husband was sworn in as president of the United States. I had just returned to the White House from a luncheon and was talking in the third-floor solarium with Ted Graber, our decorator, and Rex Scouten, the chief usher.

Suddenly I saw George Opfer, the head of my Secret Service detail. He motioned for me to come down the ramp toward him.

What's George doing here, I wondered. Something must be wrong, or he would have come up to me.

"There's been a shooting at the hotel," George said. "Some people were wounded, but your husband wasn't hit. Everybody's at the hospital."

I had started moving at the word "shooting." By the time we reached the elevator I was getting panicky, and I told George I was going to the hospital. Although Ronnie was safe, I wanted to be with him, especially if anyone had been hurt.

"It's best if you stay here," George said. "It's a madhouse over there. The president is fine. They'll be bringing him back. There's no need for you to go."

"George," I said, "I'm going to that hospital. If you don't get me a car, I'm going to *walk*." A White House limousine pulled up to the Diplomatic Entrance, and we got in.

As we approached George Washington University Hospital, the

street was jammed—police cars, reporters, onlookers. Without a siren or a police escort, we just had to sit there. I was frantic. "If this traffic doesn't open up," I said, "I'm going to run the rest of the way."

"No, no," George kept saying. "You can't do that." Finally the traffic broke and we made it to the emergency entrance.

The Secret Service had radioed ahead that I was coming, and Mike Deaver met me at the door. Mike was Ronnie's deputy chief of staff, and a close family friend.

"He's been hit," Mike said.

The emergency entrance was crowded, but all I remember is Mike standing there, staring at me.

"But they told me he *wasn't* hit," I stammered.

"Well," Mike said, "he was. But they say it's not serious."

"*Where? Where* was he hit?"

"They don't know, they're looking for the bullet."

Looking for the bullet! "I've got to see him!" I said.

"You can't. Not yet."

"Wait a minute," I said, my voice rising. "If it's not serious, *then why can't I see him*?"

"Wait. They're working on him."

"Mike," I pleaded, as if it were up to him. "*They don't know how it is with us. He has to know I'm here!*"

Mike explained that the doctors were searching for the bullet, and that Jim Brady, Ronnie's press secretary, had been shot in the head, and it looked bad. Two others had been hit—a Secret Service agent and a D.C. policeman.

Somebody led me into an office, and Mike went off to find out when I could see Ronnie. John Simpson, the head of the Secret Service, came in with Agent Ed Hickey and Senator Paul Laxalt, our old friend. Ed squeezed my hand, but soon I had to comfort him, as he broke into tears.

It was a nightmare—the panic and confusion, the waiting, the not knowing. But something takes over at these times and somehow I held myself together. *They're doing what they can,* I told myself. *Stay out of their way. Let the doctors do their work.* My father, a doctor, had told me that so many times—it was like an echo in my head.

Around me, the hospital was bedlam. I still wake up at night remembering that scene—confusion, voices, sirens, reporters, doctors, nurses, technicians; the president's men, the Secret Service with their walkie-talkies. People running through the corridors, doctors barking orders, and the police shouting, again and again, "Get these people out of here!"

As my mind raced, I flashed to scenes of Parkland Memorial Hospital in Texas, and the day President Kennedy was shot. I had been driving down San Vicente Boulevard in Los Angeles when a bulletin came over the car radio. Now, more than seventeen years later, I prayed that history would not be repeated, that Washington would not become another Dallas. That my husband would live.

With three shooting victims to take care of—the fourth, Officer Thomas Delahanty, had been taken to another hospital—the doctors were working frantically. Nurses kept coming in with new reports, and the news they brought was increasingly alarming. Twice I was told that they couldn't find Ronnie's pulse: They were afraid he might go into shock. If that happened, I knew we might lose him.

Then another nurse came in to tell me that Ronnie's left lung had collapsed, and that they had him on a machine to help him breathe.

When Ronnie first arrived at the hospital, they thought he'd suffered a heart attack. It wasn't until two nurses cut off his clothes with special trauma scissors and a doctor lifted his left arm that they noticed the small bullet hole. There was no exit wound, which meant that the bullet was stuck inside him.

Until they found the bullet hole, the doctors and nurses hadn't understood what was wrong. All they knew was that the president of the United States was dying in front of their eyes.

Ronnie had been hit by a "devastator" bullet, which is designed to explode on impact. For whatever reason, this one hadn't. After striking a panel of the armored car, it flattened out to the size of a jagged-edged dime, bounced off, and then pierced Ronnie's body.

But they still didn't know where the bullet was.

Over and over I insisted, "I want to see my husband!"

"Soon," they told me. They said he had to be cleaned up and

stabilized. Later, I learned that they were afraid to let me in too early because they thought I'd be traumatized by what I saw. Considering what I did see, they were probably right.

Finally they said I could see him, and I flew down that hall. Dr. Theodore Tsangaris explained that Ronnie had a tube in his chest and was breathing through an oxygen mask. I was so frightened by what I was hearing that I could barely speak.

I walked in on a horrible scene—discarded bandages, tubes, blood. In the corner were the remains of Ronnie's new blue pin-stripe suit, which he had worn that day for the first time. I had seen emergency rooms before, but I had never seen one like this—with my husband in it.

Ronnie looked pale and gray. Underneath the oxygen mask, his lips were caked with dried blood. He saw me, and pulled up the mask and whispered, "Honey, I forgot to duck." I was fighting tears too hard to try to smile, so I just leaned over and kissed him. Then I pushed his mask back down again and said, "Please, don't try to talk."

When I came out, Mike Deaver took my hand. "Oh, Mike," I cried. "He's so pale!"

"I know," he said. "But if you think he's bad now, you should have seen him when he first came in." I nodded, but I really couldn't imagine what Mike meant.

Minutes later, Dr. Benjamin Aaron, the head of cardiothoracic surgery, came to see me. "He's losing too much blood," he said. "We need to operate. First we've got to check his stomach for blood. Then we'll look for the bullet and try to get it out of his lung. We have it on the X ray."

As they wheeled Ronnie toward the operating room, I walked along beside him, holding his hand. We were surrounded by a team of doctors and nurses, some of them in green surgical gowns. Bags of blood hung above the cot. Just before they took him inside, I kissed him on the forehead and told him I loved him.

John Simpson from the Secret Service accompanied Ronnie into surgery. He, too, was wearing a surgical gown, and he stayed at the president's side throughout the operation, as security required.

They gave Ronnie an injection of Pentothal to put him to sleep. Just before he went under, he managed to crack another joke: "Please tell me you are all Republicans," he said.

As Ronnie was wheeled into surgery, another patient was right behind him. It was Jim Brady, his head open and bleeding and grotesquely swollen. I had never seen anybody with a head wound, and it was monstrous. A few minutes later, when a nurse said, "We don't think Mr. Brady's going to make it," I believed her.

While Ronnie was being operated on, I was led into a larger waiting room. There was a television, and Frank Reynolds announced on ABC that Jim Brady was dead. Minutes later, when the report was corrected, he slapped the desk in frustration. "Can't we get things straight around here?" he snapped.

But it was chaos everywhere. NBC and CBS also announced that Jim was dead, and CBS observed a moment of silence in his memory. On NBC, Chris Wallace reported that Ronnie was given open-heart surgery.

Despite the mistakes, I was mesmerized by the television and took some comfort from the steady flow of words and pictures. At least it was something to hold on to.

With so little hard news to report, the networks kept showing a film of the shooting. Even now, if I shut my eyes, the scene flashes through my mind: Ronnie coming out of the hotel, smiling, waving to the crowd. And then that terrible sound—he later told me he thought it was firecrackers. The look of surprise on his face. Jim falling to the ground. Bodies on the sidewalk, and agents moving in on the gunman. And then Agent Jerry Parr grabbing Ronnie and pushing him into the car.

While Ronnie was still in the operating room, somebody from the hospital came to ask if I wanted to visit the chapel. When we got there, George Opfer took my hand and said, "All we can do now is pray."

Sarah Brady, Jim's wife, came in too, and we embraced. The Reagan administration was still so new that this was the first time Sarah and I had ever met. She hadn't yet seen her husband, so she had no idea how badly he was hurt.

"They're strong men," she said. "They'll get through this."

"Yes," I said. "Yes." But my voice lacked conviction. I wanted to be optimistic, but I couldn't get those horrible images of Ronnie and Jim out of my mind. Before we left the chapel, Sarah and I held hands and prayed together.

When I first walked into the larger waiting room, I went straight to the window and looked down at the crowds gathered on the street below. George immediately pulled me back. The shooting had occurred only a few hours before, and nobody could be sure it wasn't part of a larger conspiracy. Once again I thought of Dallas.

Every few minutes, nurses came in with news from the operating room. I was relieved when they told me that the doctors hadn't found any blood in Ronnie's stomach. But then another nurse said they still hadn't found the bullet. "They might have to leave it in," she told me.

"Leave it *in*?"

"Yes, sometimes we do that."

Finally, some good news: Just as they were going to close Ronnie up, they found the bullet and removed it. It had penetrated to the seventh rib, where it deflected to the left lower lobe of his lung.

It missed his heart by one inch. It doesn't come much closer than that.

Ronnie had lost so much blood that they had to replace almost all of it. He received five units before the surgery. It was the blood loss, combined with the chance that Ronnie could go into shock, that had everyone so frightened.

Our son Ron was the first of our children to reach the hospital. He'd heard the news in a coffee shop in Lincoln, Nebraska, and when he couldn't find a flight to Washington, he had chartered a plane so he and his wife, Doria, could get to us as fast as possible. The other children—Patti, Mike, and Maureen—were all in California, and their military plane didn't get in until early the next morning.

When Ron came in, I was in a stupor, staring at the television.

By then I was moving by rote: Somebody tells you to do something and you do it. Ron hugged me; I said, "I'm so frightened"; he said, "I know, Mom, but hold on."

Ronnie began to wake up around seven-thirty that evening. They took us through a back door into the recovery room and led us to his bed, which was fenced off with screens. When I saw him, his face drained of color, a tube in his throat to help him breathe, and all that equipment attached to his body, I just started to cry. "I love you," I said, holding his arm. For what seemed like a long time we just looked at each other. Then Ronnie reached for a pencil and paper. "I can't breathe!" he wrote.

"He can't breathe," I repeated. I understood the fear in his eyes. When I was pregnant with Patti, years ago, I would wake up in the middle of the night, unable to take in any air. Once I even saw myself in the mirror, turning green. It was frightening. All I could think about was where my next breath would come from.

Ronnie started to sit up.

"He can't *breathe*!" I shouted.

"Don't worry, Mrs. Reagan," one of the doctors said. "The respirator is doing it for him. He just has to get used to it."

Ron leaned over his father and said, "It's okay, Dad. What you're feeling is the tube down your throat. It's like the first time I went scuba diving. When I put the mask on, I thought I was choking. But it's okay, just relax. They're getting air to you, and you'll be fine."

Ronnie was so groggy from the operation that when I saw him the next morning, he had no recollection of any of this.

He drifted in and out of sleep. Then he wrote another note: "I'm still alive, aren't I?" He cracked a number of jokes in the hospital, but this wasn't one of them. The writing on that note was so faint and wobbly I could barely read it.

Later, he told me, "When I started to wake up and open my eyes, all I could see was white. The sheets, the walls, the coats on the doctors and nurses—everything was white. For a minute I wondered if I was in heaven and these were all angels."

I didn't want to leave the hospital, but the doctors and nurses had plenty of work to do on Ronnie, and there was nothing I could do to be helpful. I also knew that if I spent the night at the hospital, I'd be sending out a message to the world that Ronnie's condition was critical. It was, of course, but at that moment I didn't want people to know. It was Ron who talked me into leaving.

As Ron, Doria, and I left the hospital, George Opfer pointed out the parents of Agent Tim McCarthy, who were coming in. From the calm expressions on their faces, I could see they hadn't really grasped what had happened to their son, who had been shot in the stomach as he crouched in front of Ronnie to protect him. I went over to tell them how much I appreciated what Tim had done, that if he hadn't made himself a target in place of Ronnie, I would have lost my husband. But I could see that my words didn't register.

A few days later, Tim was well enough to visit Ronnie, who praised him for his courage. Ronnie said, "Someday I hope your children will know what a brave father they have." When he returned to the White House, Ronnie wrote a letter to Tim's children, saying just that.

Tim told me later that he'd been scheduled to do something else that day and wasn't even supposed to be at the hotel with the president. He and another agent had flipped a coin, and Tim lost.

As I left the hospital that night, everything was illuminated by bright television lights. People had hung sheets on the surrounding buildings with messages on them: GET WELL SOON and WE LOVE YOU and my favorite, TONIGHT WE ARE ALL REPUBLICANS.

Chris Wallace of NBC told me later that I had looked so drawn as I left the hospital that he decided not to ask me any questions. I can only imagine how I must have seemed if it was enough to silence a network reporter.

Back at the White House, Ted Graber and Rex Scouten were waiting for me on the second floor of the residence. Rex disappeared when I arrived, and Ted stayed with me. Phone calls were pouring in, but I didn't feel like talking, so Ted and the wonderful White House operators handled them for me. The staff offered us something to eat, and I ended up pushing some scrambled eggs around on a plate.

I felt cold, so the four of us—Ron, Doria, Ted, and I—went into the bedroom and lit a fire. Later, I tried to sleep, but it was hopeless. I spent the night glued to the television.

"Nothing can happen to my Ronnie," I wrote in my diary that night. "My life would be over."

The next morning I went back to the hospital. They had taken the tube out of Ronnie's throat, and his condition was slightly better. But after a night in intensive care, he still hadn't slept. Every four hours, they turned him over on his stomach so the nurses could pound on his back to shake out the fluids and keep them from building up in his lungs. The noise was so loud you could hear it in the next room; it sounded like somebody slapping a side of beef. I remember telling Mermie (Maureen), who had just arrived along with the other children, "That's your father they're doing that to."

Ronnie had been writing notes and asking questions about who else had been hurt. Dan Ruge, the White House physician, had told the doctors and nurses to put Ronnie off, to avoid upsetting him, but now Dan decided that we had to tell him. I knew Ronnie would take it badly, and I wanted to be there.

When Ronnie heard about Jim Brady and the others, his eyes filled with tears.

"Damn," he kept saying, hitting the bed with his fist.

"Was Jim hit in the head?" he asked.

I nodded. "Damn," he said again.

Later, I collected some of the notes Ronnie wrote to the doctors and nurses, and I was struck, although not altogether surprised, at the humor in many of them. Some of the best comments ended up in the newspapers. After waking up in the recovery room, Ronnie wrote, echoing W. C. Fields, "All in all, I'd rather be in Philadelphia." Another note quoted Winston Churchill, who had once said, "There is no more exhilarating feeling than being shot at without result."

The notes showed me that despite the harm done to his body, Ronnie's outlook was strong. "Can we rewrite this scene beginning at the time I left the hotel?" he asked. And later, in the recovery room, "Send me to L.A., where I can see the air I'm breathing!" When a nurse was combing his hair, and taking the opportunity to examine his roots, Ronnie wrote, "Now you can tell the world that I don't dye my hair." And when everybody was fussing over him in the recovery room, the note read, "If I'd had this much attention in Hollywood, I'd have stayed there."

Looking back on this whole period, I can see how these one-liners provided a great deal of reassurance to the nation. People reasoned, understandably, that if the president could be so good-natured in the hospital, his injuries must not be too serious.

But not all of the notes were amusing:

"What happened to the guy with the gun?"

"What was his beef? Was anyone hurt?"

"Can I keep breathing?"

"How long in the hospital?"

"Will I still be able to work on the ranch?"

While Ronnie slept, I talked with Sarah Brady and with the doctors. They were feeling a great deal of pressure, and I'm sure my questions didn't make it any easier. But I wanted to know everything.

I'm the type of person who needs as much information as possible, even if the news isn't good. And that was my real fear: that with the best of intentions, the doctors were withholding bad news. At the White House, the first thing I'd been told was that Ronnie wasn't hit. It was an honest mistake, but now, at the back of my mind, I wondered what else they weren't telling me.

The Academy Awards had been scheduled for March 30, but were postponed for two days because of the shooting. Ronnie had taped a greeting for the show, and on the night of April 1 we moved him out of intensive care and into a room with a television. He was still pretty groggy, but I thought the awards show would boost his morale.

Johnny Carson was the host, and when he mentioned Ronnie's name, the audience erupted with applause. I had hoped something like this would happen to cheer Ronnie up—and it did. The whole world was praying for him and sending messages of support, but Ronnie was cut off from all of it as he lay in his hospital room, drifting in and out of sleep.

From where he lay, Ronnie couldn't even see the sky. The curtains in his room were actually nailed shut, because there was still the possibility that John Hinckley hadn't acted alone. There was also a sudden rise in the number of threats against Ronnie, which is apparently a common pattern following an attack on the president.

I couldn't argue with the need for tight security, but my chief concern was Ronnie's recovery, and it saddened me that this man who so passionately loves the outdoors couldn't even see out his window. The cherry blossoms were in bloom and spring was bursting out all over Washington, but that little hospital room was dark and depressing—you couldn't tell day from night. I did my best to liven it up. We were receiving an enormous amount of mail, and I brought in some pictures from schoolchildren and tacked them up on the bare white walls.

Within days, the White House was bursting with gifts of jelly beans, chocolates, and enough flowers to fill a meadow. Soon we were delivering candy and flowers to every hospital in the Washington area. When a ten-pound box of chocolates arrived from King Hassan of Morocco, I gave it to the nurses and doctors.

A great many people wanted to visit Ronnie in the hospital. Some wanted to wish him a quick recovery. Others had pressing business. And still others, I suspected, just wanted to look important. But Dr. Ruge clamped down on visitors so Ronnie would have enough time to rest and heal. We had to keep reminding people that aside from being the president, Ronnie was also a patient who was trying to recover from a terrible physical and emotional trauma.

Many, many friends called to comfort me. My brother, Dick, a neurosurgeon, came down from Philadelphia and helped explain some of the medical procedures. Billy Graham came, as did Donn Moomaw, our minister in Los Angeles, and our old friends the Wicks, and their son, C.Z., who flew in from California. Frank Sinatra canceled a performance and flew to Washington. Elizabeth Taylor was in town with *Little Foxes,* and she canceled her show, too. I felt really grateful for all their help and support.

But ultimately I had to face these events on my own. One evening, after another long day at the hospital, I came back to the White

House and wrote a single line in my diary. As I look back on that brief entry now, it still evokes the immense loneliness I felt during that week: "It's a big house when you're here alone."

On the fifth day after the shooting, just as Ronnie seemed to be showing real improvement, we suffered a major setback when he began to run a fever of a hundred and three. The doctors couldn't explain it, and they thought he might need another operation. Fearing he might come down with pneumonia, they put him on antibiotics and Tylenol.

The Tylenol, incidentally, served to minimize the seriousness of Ronnie's condition. When the press asked what drugs Ronnie had been given to deal with the pain, Dennis O'Leary, the hospital spokesman, who was marvelous under pressure, told the truth: In the first two days Ronnie was given a small amount of morphine, but the rest of the time he had nothing stronger than Tylenol. In retrospect, I suppose people were fooled by that answer. But Ronnie withstands pain very well.

My anxiety increased when Ronnie's fever was accompanied by a sharp loss in appetite. I arranged for meals to be sent over from the White House, hoping he would find them more appealing than the hospital food. When that didn't work, I called Anne Allman, who had been our housekeeper in Los Angeles for many years, and asked her to send up Ronnie's two favorite soups: hamburger and split pea.

By this time, the doctors had Ronnie walking up and down the hallway, holding my hand. Every day we'd try to go a little farther. But even Anne's soups failed to revive his appetite, so one night I came into his room and announced, "We're going out to dinner."

"Out to dinner?" Ronnie said. "Where?"

"Just come with me," I said. "We're going to a little disco near the hospital."

"All right," he quipped, "but I won't be able to dance."

"That's okay," I said. "We can just hold hands."

When he stood up to put on his robe, I took his arm and walked him down the hall to another room, where I had set up two chairs in front of a television set. I thought that if he watched the news, as we often did over dinner at the White House, maybe I could get some food into him. Ronnie didn't eat much that night either, but at least he tried.

More than once, the doctors and nurses commented on what a considerate patient Ronnie was. One afternoon, when George Bush came to visit, he found the president on his knees in the bathroom, wiping up some water. Because of the fever, the doctors hadn't allowed Ronnie to bathe. But when he found his body covered with sweat, he had given himself a sponge bath.

"You should let the nurse clean that up," George said.

"No," Ronnie replied. "I'm the one who disobeyed orders. If the doctors see her mopping it up, she'll get in trouble."

The doctors mentioned that Ronnie was in excellent physical condition, and that although he was seventy, he had the body of a man in his fifties. His lungs were clean, and the fact that he had never smoked cigarettes made it easier to remove the bullet. Just three days before the shooting, Dr. Ruge, who is seven years younger than Ronnie, had said, "What can I tell a man who is seventy and in better shape than I am? He knows how to take care of himself."

Finally they said Ronnie could go home. He left the hospital in a red cardigan sweater, but underneath it was a bulletproof vest. The threats on his life were continuing.

The nurses and doctors all lined up to say goodbye. They had come to know Ronnie, and they obviously admired him. All I remember about the ride back is that it was raining, and that Ronnie and I were together, finally, going home.

Mike Deaver and Dan Ruge were in another car. Mike told me later that as they pulled away from the hospital, Dan, who usually kept his emotions firmly in control, turned to him with tears in his eyes. "You know," he said, "we could easily have been leaving here in a very different way."

When we arrived at the White House, Ronnie walked from the car into the Diplomatic Entrance and then to the elevator. There were reports later that as he did this, he was disoriented. He wasn't. Or that he had to use an oxygen tank. He never did. But he did receive some special home care. Dan Ruge spent the first few nights in the Lincoln Bedroom, and for a brief time Ronnie slept in a hospital bed. At first they gave him penicillin intravenously, coming into our bedroom at two A.M. and again at six, but he was soon switched over to pills.

Ronnie wasn't used to being incapacitated, and he thought he could do more than he was really able to. I showed him a letter I had received from Lady Bird Johnson, who wrote that Lyndon had needed a full month of his presidency to recover from his gall-bladder operation. During the next three weeks, I insisted that Ronnie follow the doctors' orders by doing as little work as possible. His schedule was drastically shortened. In the morning, he would meet with his close advisers, and then with the National Security Council. But that was it. He attended both meetings in his pajamas and bathrobe, and he spent the rest of the day resting.

While Ronnie was still in the hospital, I had tried to speed up the renovations in the private living quarters of the White House so that the solarium, at least, would be completed by the time he came back. He had been in a small, dark, enclosed space for almost two weeks, but in the solarium there were windows all around, the room got lots of sun, and Ronnie could once again see the sky. And in good weather, we could pull a chair outside and he could sit on the terrace.

They had removed part of Ronnie's left lung, so they explained that he would need a regular exercise program to recover his full lung capacity. A few days later, Mike Abrums, a friend of ours who runs a workout facility in California, flew to Washington and helped set up an exercise room in Tricia Nixon's old bedroom, across the corridor from ours. As soon as he was able, Ronnie started working out every day after work; I used the weight machine and the treadmill each morning.

That exercise room turned out to be valuable. Unless they make a special effort, presidents and first ladies don't get much exercise. Every possible chore was done for us, and we were never required to do anything more strenuous than walk from the door of the White House to the car, and from the car to another door.

Ronnie became so devoted to these workouts that he grew an entire size in the chest, while the biceps in his arms practically doubled. Before long, we had to buy him some new suits. "I'm proud of you," I said, "but slow down. This is getting expensive!"

Once we were home and I was able to reflect on what had happened to Ronnie, I began to realize just how close we had come to losing him. Hinckley had fired six shots in less than two seconds, and four people had been injured. In those two seconds Ronnie came within an inch of death, and I came within an inch of losing the man I love. I now understood that each new day was a gift to be treasured, and that I had to be more involved in seeing that my husband was protected in every possible way.

Also, there were so many people to thank for the fact that Ronnie survived. There were the doctors and nurses at the hospital, some of whom we were able to invite to a state dinner. There was Officer Delahanty of the Washington police force. There was Tim McCarthy, who had been willing to give his life for Ronnie. There was Jim Brady. And finally, there was Jerry Parr, the head of the White House Secret Service detail.

When the shots were fired outside the hotel, nobody knew that Ronnie had been hit. He himself didn't realize it. The first bullet hit Jim Brady in the forehead. The second hit Officer Delahanty, the third hit Tim McCarthy. The fourth shot hit the car window, right in front of Ronnie, and the fifth hit the car door and ricocheted into Ronnie. The sixth bullet missed completely. According to eyewitnesses, Hinckley continued pulling the trigger even after the gun was empty.

As soon as the shots rang out, Jerry Parr threw himself against Ronnie, crashing him down onto the floor of the limousine. Another agent pushed their feet into the car, slammed the door, and yelled, "Take off!" The whole procedure took only thirteen seconds.

As they drove away, Jerry remained on top of Ronnie to shield him.

"Jerry, get off me, you're hurting my ribs!" Ronnie said. Jerry had pushed him so hard that Ronnie's head hit the doorway of the car, and he landed face-down on the transmission hump in front of the rear seat. Neither man realized yet that Ronnie had been hit.

By then they were speeding back to the White House. But when Ronnie started coughing up blood, Jerry saw the bright red color and knew it had come from his lungs. Thinking that a rib had indeed been broken, and that Ronnie's lung might have been punctured, Jerry told the driver to turn right on Pennsylvania Avenue and to rush to George Washington University Hospital—less than a mile away. The entire drive from the hotel to the hospital took three and a half minutes. Although he didn't know it, for the second time in two minutes Jerry had saved Ronnie's life. If they had driven to the White House, we would have lost him.

When they arrived at the emergency room, Ronnie still didn't know he was hit. He insisted on walking in on his own—but the moment he entered the hospital, his knees buckled.

I'll always be grateful that Jerry insisted on bringing Ronnie straight to the hospital—even if it was for the wrong reason. Dr. Aaron said later, "He was right on the margin when he got here."

Fortunately, too, Ronnie arrived at the hospital just as a big staff meeting was ending, so all the doctors were on hand. And there was a shift change coming up, which would double the number of people there to help.

I also thought about the young man who pulled the trigger, and especially about his parents, who had sent me a moving apology. I could imagine how awful this must be for them. As a mother, I knew that although most of us do the best job we can, it doesn't always work out. But while I certainly felt compassion for John Hinckley's parents, I could not find it in my heart to feel compassion for their son.

Ronnie is different. On his first weekend home, Patti described how angry she felt toward John Hinckley. "You know," Ronnie replied, "when I was lying there in the hospital, looking up at the ceiling and wondering if I was going to die, I spent a lot of time praying, and I knew I couldn't just pray for myself. I had to pray for John Hinckley, too. And if God loves me, then in spite of everything, He must also love John Hinckley."

I couldn't help thinking about the fact that John Hinckley had been obsessed with the movie *Taxi Driver,* about a deranged man who stalks a politician. He had seen the movie repeatedly and had then started stalking President Carter. When Carter was defeated, Hinckley began to stalk Ronnie.

Movies make a powerful impression on people's minds—especially the minds of people who may be unbalanced. I think there's too much violence in films and on television, and it's one of the reasons for our terrible problems with crime. It used to be that when a character was shot on screen, the cameras didn't zero in and show you the blood pouring out of his wounds. People today are too accustomed to seeing violence.

The shooting also made me question my attitude toward gun control. Ronnie's position didn't change; he just doesn't believe this is where the problem lies—a point he repeated more than once while he was still in the hospital. He favors the California system, with a waiting period for anyone who wants to buy a gun. After what I saw in that hospital, I'm not sure I agree with him.

As for the Secret Service, I differ from some occupants of the White House, who have felt hemmed in by the agents and have resented the loss of privacy. No, I'm grateful to have the Secret Service around. If it weren't for them, I wouldn't have a husband.

Looking back now, I see that I was in a state of shock for much longer than I realized, and that the psychological effects of March 30 were more enduring for me than they were for Ronnie. Ronnie understood this better than I did; even in the hospital he remarked on how pale and drawn I looked and urged me to go home and get some sleep. "You don't need to stay here all day," he would tell me.

Later, he suggested that I attend Prince Charles's wedding because he thought the trip would be good for me. As close as we are, we both had to go through our separate traumas. His was mainly to the body; mine was to my spirit.

I expected that the memory of the shooting would fade with time, but it never has. For the rest of Ronnie's presidency—almost eight more years—every time he left home, especially to go on a trip, it was as if my heart stopped until he got back.

I was so shaken by the events of that spring that it took me a couple of years just to say the word "shooting." For a long time I simply referred to it as "March 30," or, even more obliquely, as "the thing that happened to Ronnie." For me, the entire episode was, quite literally, unspeakable.

I also felt guilty that I hadn't been with Ronnie at the hotel. Maybe I could have done something. I know this is irrational; I can't imagine what I could have done to change things. But for a long time I believed that if I had been with Ronnie that day, nothing would have happened.

In retrospect, I don't think I would have been quite as shocked had the shooting occurred when Ronnie was governor of California. He held that office, after all, during the late 1960s and early 1970s, which was a period of frequent demonstrations and a great deal of anger and hostility toward elected officials. But in 1981 there seemed to be so much good feeling from the American people that violence was the last thing I worried about. I knew in the back of my mind that something like this was always possible, but until it actually happens, you just don't think it ever will.

Although Ronnie recovered quickly, he continued to be upset that three other people had been hurt. He felt especially bad about Jim Brady, who was permanently disabled. (Under the circumstances, the fact that he was alive at all was a miracle. Today, Jim is vice chairman of the National Organization on Disability.) As soon as Ronnie could, he went to visit Jim in the hospital, and he promised he would hold the position of press secretary open until Jim was able to return. Although most of Jim's duties in the press office were taken over by Larry Speakes, as long as Ronnie remained in office, Jim retained his title. Ronnie knew that the bullets that struck the others had been meant for him, and he was tormented that they had been shot simply because of their association with his presidency.

A few weeks after the shooting, I told Ronnie I felt panicky every time he left the White House. He said, smiling at me, "I don't understand what you're worried about. I knew all along that I'd be fine." But I continued to be haunted by what had happened, as well as by what had almost happened.

2

⟡⟡⟡

Nothing Prepares You

WHEN we arrived in Washington, in January of 1981, I honestly thought I understood the demands and pressures of being the first lady. I had been married for almost thirty years to a well-known actor and television personality, and I had been a movie actress myself. I wasn't a newcomer to politics either, having spent eight years as first lady of California—the largest state in the nation and the most media-conscious place on earth. While I knew that Washington was different, I thought I was prepared for living in the public eye.

But I found out the hard way that nothing—*nothing*—prepares you for being first lady.

In those first few months, as controversy after controversy swirled around me, I often thought of what Helen Thomas, the veteran UPI reporter, had said to me shortly after the election. We were sitting together on the campaign plane, discussing the possibility that Ronnie would be elected, when Helen mentioned the enormous pressures on the first lady. I nodded and said, "I'm sure you're right, but there will always be a part of me that is private, that's mine."

"You may think so," Helen said. "But you have no idea what it's really like. I don't see how you *can* know until you get there."

Well, it didn't take me long to find out what Helen meant.

From the moment I walked into the White House it was as if I had no privacy at all. Everything I did or said, whether as first lady, wife, or mother, was instantly open to criticism—to interpretation, speculation, second-guessing. My clothes. My friends. My taste in decorating. My relationship with our children. The way I looked at my husband! My entire *life* was suddenly fair game for comment by the press and the public alike. Looking back, I think my own naïveté, and that of my staff, added to this, and perhaps even prolonged it. Washington can be a tough town, and I didn't know how to handle it. I suspect we all would do things differently if we had it to do over again.

Virtually everything I did during that first year was misunderstood and ridiculed. I sometimes had the feeling that if it was raining outside, it was probably my fault.

But the first big controversy was over the renovation of the White House.

I have always been a nester, and my first priority in any new house has been to get that house in order. That's just the way I am. I like to be organized, and I also like to provide a warm, restful, and welcoming home for my husband. I always did, but it seemed especially important now that Ronnie was president. And I think it made a big difference to him, whether he knew it or not.

I knew the White House needed work, but it wasn't until we moved in that I began to realize how *much* work was actually required—especially in the private living quarters. Some of the bedrooms on the third floor hadn't been painted in fifteen or twenty years! The floors hadn't been touched in ages. There were cracks in the walls. The long, wide Center Hall, which runs the entire length of the second floor, was virtually empty.

When I realized the magnitude of the job that faced me, I was overwhelmed. After all, this wasn't just *our* house; it was the White House. We would be living here for four years, or perhaps eight, but the White House belongs to *all* Americans. It's supposed to be something we're proud of, but I was dismayed by how shabby it was when we first moved in. I was sad and disappointed that it had come to this.

Most of the immediate problems were in the residence, but over in the Oval Office and elsewhere in the West Wing we actually found half-eaten sandwiches and empty beer cans in some of the drawers.

While I had no desire to turn the White House into an imperial palace, I did want to reclaim some of the stature and dignity of the building. I've always felt that the White House should represent this country at its best. To me, this was so obvious that I never dreamed that I would be criticized for my efforts. If anything, I expected to be applauded.

Nor did it ever occur to me to think in terms of a public-relations campaign. I just went ahead with the restoration without thinking about public opinion. I hadn't yet realized that my actions might provoke anger or controversy. Perhaps somebody on my staff should have, but they were as inexperienced in these matters as I was.

The White House is an important symbol in our country, and I thought—and *still* think—that people want it to look its best. Every morning, thousands of tourists line up for a brief look at some of the public rooms. I think they want to be impressed.

Whenever a new family moves in, Congress appropriates fifty thousand dollars for renovations and upkeep. Ronnie and I decided not to accept this grant: For one thing, it wasn't nearly enough to make up for years of neglect. For another, we thought it would be better if the money came from private contributions, not from the taxpayers.

Our goal was to raise two hundred thousand dollars, but we soon raised more than four times that much. It was true, as all the papers reported, that some of our wealthier friends were very generous. But so were many other Americans who were excited to be part of this historic project and who sent in smaller donations—twenty dollars, ten dollars, even one dollar. They didn't get their names in the paper, but I was grateful that they cared.

I was angry that so much attention was paid to the big donations. The media made it look as if the donors were some kind of exclusive, wealthy club, and it wasn't that way at all.

Without the help of Ted Graber, who had helped me decorate

our home in Pacific Palisades, I don't think I could have done it. I love decorating, and I've never worked harder than I did during the first three weeks after the inauguration. Ronnie and I normally go to bed early, but sometimes, at night, it would suddenly occur to me that a lamp or a painting might go better in some other spot. At eleven o'clock, Ronnie would call out, "Honey, where are you? It's late. Come to bed!" I would be down the hall in the Yellow Oval Room, moving an end table or wrestling with a chair.

I didn't want to redo the White House in my own image, but I did want to restore it. Some of the White House treasures were tucked away and out of sight—for instance, the lovely Persian rug with semiprecious stones that had been hanging on the back of a door on the first floor, where nobody could see it. I moved it up to Ronnie's study, where it could be enjoyed, and hung it behind his desk.

Many other items were in storage, so together with Rex Scouten and Ted Graber, I drove out to the White House storage facility in Alexandria, Virginia, near National Airport, which consisted of a World War II warehouse and two Quonset huts, with no temperature control. It broke my heart to see hundreds of historic pieces from the White House, some of them over a century old, deteriorating and in urgent need of restoration. I couldn't understand it: Why keep all of these beautiful objects sitting in a warehouse? Why not display them so they can be seen and enjoyed?

When Ted and I began taking pieces out of storage, the people at the warehouse were delighted. "Take more, take more," they kept saying. "These things shouldn't be *here.*" We selected dozens of chairs, desks, tables, and mirrors, had them restored, and moved them into the White House.

Because so much money had been raised, we were also able to refinish many of the mahogany doors and hardwood floors. We restored the marble walls on the State and ground floors, cleaned the floors with acid-etching, and cleaned all twenty-nine of the White House fireplaces.

We also took care of other problems in the residence that hadn't been touched since the Truman administration. Some of the original handmade plumbing fixtures for the bathrooms and kitchens had to be replaced with modern fixtures because those items hadn't been made in years, and it cost a small fortune to repair them. We embarked on a long list of mundane but essential improvements, including rewiring, replacing worn carpeting, repainting, and fixing the heating and air-conditioning.

The most dramatic and visible improvement was the newly renovated Center Hall. The walls were painted a light yellow to make it seem brighter, and we created several sitting areas by using items that had been in storage, including a reproduction Sheraton sofa and two bergère chairs, and a Chippendale-style bench, which was covered in rose fabric. To break up the long expanse, Ted inserted an eighteenth-century English octagonal writing desk that had been donated to the Kennedys by Jules Stein, the founder of MCA. When we came across it in storage, I recognized it, and I called Jules to tell him it was back in the White House. He was so pleased, and I was particularly glad I had made the call when I learned of his death shortly after.

I'll never forget the moment that made it all worthwhile. One evening, after most of the second floor had been finished, Ronnie and I were having dinner in the sitting area in the West Hall. We were served by one of the butlers, who had been there for thirty-seven years. As he was setting down the tray in front of me, he looked down the Center Hall, smiled, and said, "It's beginning to look like the White House again."

I felt as if I had just been awarded the Congressional Medal of Honor.

Around that same time, Ronnie convened a meeting of the congressional leadership in the Yellow Oval Room. After the group had left, Tip O'Neill came back up on the elevator to give Ronnie a message: "Please tell Nancy that I've never, ever, seen the White House look this beautiful!"

But the reaction outside the White House was very different, and I was totally unprepared for it. On television, reports of the renovation were contrasted with rising unemployment and homelessness. Some commentators suggested or implied that the renovation had been paid for with public funds. Other reports criticized the fact that many of our personal friends had donated money for the restoration, as though this were somehow inappropriate. But once the press started in on this theme, they kept on it like a dog with a bone.

I was particularly hurt by a column by Judy Mann in the *Washington Post*, who wrote that instead of helping all Americans, "Nancy Reagan has used the position, her position, to improve the quality of life for those in the White House."

This was so completely different from how I viewed my work that I was devastated. All I could think of was Clare Boothe Luce's famous line that no good deed goes unpunished.

When Judy Mann's column appeared, I was already planning the drug program that would soon occupy so much of my time. But I wanted to get the White House renovations completed before I undertook another big project, and I was reluctant to travel while Ronnie was still recuperating.

Now, it didn't help my image that most of the initial improvements took place on the residential floors, which were closed to the public, or that the White House renovation was featured first in the December 1981 issue of *Architectural Digest*, which sold for $4.95—a good but expensive magazine. That was a mistake that only added to the picture many Americans already had of me—that I was a fancy, rich woman who kept acquiring more and more expensive items.

If the renovations made people angry, the new White House china drove them crazy!

After our first state dinner, held in honor of Margaret Thatcher, the press reported that I had used a mixture of china patterns that had been selected by several past presidents, including Theodore Roosevelt, Woodrow Wilson, Franklin D. Roosevelt, and Harry Truman. This was true, but I hadn't done it to honor these past leaders. I did it because there simply wasn't enough china from any one pattern to go around.

One reason was breakage. Fine china is delicate, and when it's repeatedly handled and washed, a certain amount breaks. The cups and saucers are always the first to go because they're the most fragile.

Then there's the problem of theft. Although the great majority of guests behave themselves, there's always somebody who just can't leave the White House without taking home a souvenir. Back in the 1930s, Eleanor Roosevelt had to order new, larger-than-usual bread-and-butter plates because so many of her guests were sneaking the old ones into their pockets and handbags! And during the Kennedy administration, linen cocktail napkins could no longer be used for White House receptions because so many people were taking them home.

But the main reason we needed new china was that nobody had ordered a complete set since the Truman administration. The Johnsons had purchased new china in 1967, but it did not include serving platters, finger bowls, dessert bowls, and bouillon cups. And while the Johnson china was lovely, with the various state flowers around the edge, it was more suitable for a luncheon than a formal state dinner.

The new White House china was made by the Lenox Company in Pomona, New Jersey, the same people who had made china for the Wilson, FDR, and Truman administrations. With their help and advice, I chose a new design—ivory edged in red, with a raised presidential seal in gold on the serving and dessert plates.

But I did not buy the china. It was purchased, at cost, by the Knapp Foundation in Maryland, who donated it to the White House. This was originally done anonymously, but there was such a furor over the new White House china—and so many rumors, including one that it had been purchased by Texas oil tycoons—that Antoinette Vojvoda, whose grandfather had started the Knapp Foundation, called Rex Scouten and said, "Look, I think Mrs. Reagan is taking an unfair rap on this, so I'm going to announce that we were the ones who donated the china."

I was delighted, but nobody seemed to pay any attention to the announcement, and I rarely saw her name in print. To this day, I still read that I "bought" the china. I don't know how many times I have to say this, but let me say it yet again: I did not buy the china!

For the press, the china was a symbol of my supposed extravagance. Here, too, the timing was unfortunate: The new White House china was announced on the same day that the Department of Agriculture mistakenly declared ketchup to be acceptable as a vegetable for school lunches. As you can imagine, the columnists and the cartoonists had a field day with that one.

It was a Democrat who came to my defense. Margaret Truman Daniel, who had lived in the White House during her father's administration, told the *New York Times*, "I think it's too bad about this hassle over her doing something she should have done. It's really ridiculous. . . . As for mixing up place settings from different settings bought by different administrations, as some people suggest Mrs. Reagan should do, all I can say is that looks just awful. Anyone who's ever been a hostess knows that mixed china doesn't work. When the President and the First Lady give a state dinner, the china should match. It certainly did in our day."

There's something about White House china that seems to rile people. Back in 1933, when Eleanor Roosevelt ordered a new set, she had to call a press conference to defend herself. People want the White House to look great, but they don't want it to cost anything.

And then, of course, there were my clothes. Ah yes, my clothes.

The criticism began on Day One, with the inaugural gown: a beautiful white one-shouldered beaded dress made by James Galanos that the newspapers valued at $25,000. (I have no idea what it was worth, but that estimate seems pretty high.) Jimmy Galanos donated the dress, which was later given to the Smithsonian's collection of inaugural gowns.

I've always liked Jimmy's creations, and I've been wearing them for years. In fact, I've known Jimmy Galanos longer than I've known my husband. When I first came to Hollywood, a girl in the publicity department of MGM introduced me to Amelia Gray, who had a shop in Beverly Hills. Amelia knew Jimmy, and I bought one of his first designs, a black cocktail dress with a white collar, white cuffs, and a full skirt. The price was $125, which was a lot in those days. I hate to think what that dress would cost today!

After Ronnie was elected president, I called Jimmy, who was

thrilled at the opportunity to design the inaugural gown. He made a few sketches, and together we decided on a white beaded dress. I loved it, and I wore it proudly. And I wore it again a few weeks later to a White House reception for the diplomatic corps.

After I became first lady, I didn't dress any differently than I ever had. I've been interested in clothes for as long as I can remember— ever since I was little, when I loved dressing up in Mother's outfits.

So yes, I do enjoy wearing fine clothes. They make me feel good—the same way I feel when I get my hair done. Also, I come from the picture business, and in my day, at least, you didn't go out in public unless you were well dressed. In Washington, the stage was larger and the events were more numerous, but there, too, I was aware that people were looking at me, and I felt, and still do, that I should look my best. After all, I was representing our country.

For me, dressing well means dressing simply. Ginger Rogers used to overdress, and somebody at the studio once told her, "Before you leave the house, look at yourself in the mirror and take one thing off." I think that's good advice for lots of us.

I've never been on the cutting edge of fashion, and I don't go for the latest look. I try to choose clothes that look good today, but that will also look good tomorrow. As the old saying goes, "Fashion passes; style remains."

I hang on to things forever, and you practically have to use dynamite to get them away from me. Ronnie likes to tease me that I still have my gym bloomers from high school. When I first came to the White House, I brought a lot of dresses from California. At our first state dinner in 1981, I wore a dress by Galanos with a maroon velvet top and a black chiffon skirt. That dress was sixteen years old. I still have it, and I'll probably wear it again someday.

I'm a last-minute dresser, and I rarely decide in advance what I'll wear on a given evening. My press secretary would often call and ask what I was planning to wear, because the press wanted to know. "I don't know yet," I would tell her. "It depends on how I feel."

There were so many different occasions for which I had to dress that I don't know how I would have managed without the help of Chris Limerick, the White House housekeeper, and Liz Hagerty, her successor. Chris had organized Rosalynn Carter's wardrobe with plastic-covered tags listing the designer, the color, and the purchase date, and, most important, the occasions when that particular outfit had been worn. It sounded like a fine idea, and we continued it. It certainly made my life easier.

But despite the image that I wore expensive designer fashions twenty-four hours a day, the fact is that whenever I wasn't on display, I dressed as casually as possible. I always wore jeans at the ranch and at Camp David, and on long trips, the first thing I did on *Air Force One* was to change into my velour running suit, which was comfortable and warm. In the evening, if we weren't going out, I would generally be in my nightgown and robe before dinner.

I appreciate good clothes, but they certainly don't rule my life. And I think it's unfair to assume that when a woman dresses well, it means she's not doing much else. I really did have other interests—although in 1981 that wasn't yet clear to the press and to most of the public. During my first six months in Washington, Sheila Tate, my press secretary, told me, something like 90 percent of the inquiries she received had to do with fashion.

And they say *I'm* obsessed with clothes!

First ladies have different styles. But if you look back at some of my predecessors, you'll see that after a few months, even the first ladies who seemed not to care very much about fashion and appearance began to pay more attention to their hair and their clothing. As I write these words, this is happening with Barbara Bush. And it's only natural—once you find yourself representing the nation, on display and photographed all the time, not only throughout the United States but all over the world, you begin to dress more carefully. You realize that people *like* to see you in different clothes. They want to see you looking your best.

When I moved to Washington I needed a larger wardrobe than I did in Los Angeles or Sacramento. The first lady attends a constant stream of official luncheons, receptions, award ceremonies, conventions, formal dinners, and so on, and at each one she is stared at and photographed. Every time she leaves the White House she's making a personal appearance.

•

Then there are the state dinners, which take place almost every month. During our eight years in Washington, Ronnie and I hosted almost eighty of them. Even if you wear outfits more than once, as I did, that adds up to a lot of formal dresses.

And when I traveled abroad, I thought I should represent our country in the best possible light. A royal wedding in London or a state dinner in the Hall of Mirrors in Versailles is a far more elaborate affair than anything in Washington, New York, or Hollywood. I don't need such extra-dressy gowns anymore, but I certainly needed them then.

Because I needed more clothes—far more than I could afford to buy—I borrowed outfits for specific occasions from some of my favorite designers and old friends. And here I made a big mistake. No, not by borrowing, but by not announcing from the start that I was going to do this, and that I would return them.

But I honestly never expected that this would be seen as a problem. Borrowing designer clothes is such a widespread and accepted practice in the American fashion industry that it never occurred to me that I'd be criticized for it. With astrology, which I'll get to shortly, I knew there was a risk of embarrassment. But when it came to borrowing clothes, I couldn't imagine that anyone would object.

In Europe, first ladies borrow clothes all the time. In France, for example, the wives of the presidents and prime ministers routinely wear dresses lent to them by such designers as Yves St. Laurent, Pierre Cardin, and Christian Dior. The French government not only condones this practice but actually supports it as a way of helping one of the country's most important industries.

But many Americans were surprised when my borrowings were revealed in the press. I don't understand why. First ladies have often borrowed clothes, or have purchased them at less than full price. Shortly before I left the White House I was given a Lifetime Achievement Award by the American fashion industry. Barbara Walters, who introduced me, suggested that first ladies should be *encouraged* to borrow designer dresses because, as she put it, "it stimulates the fashion industry, it hurts no one, and it adds to our pride in American clothes."

I was also criticized in 1981 for wearing nice outfits during a recession. But if I had suddenly started dressing differently, how would that have helped the economy? On the contrary: I was told that because so many women look to the first lady as a fashion leader, I provided a great boost for American designers. The fashion business is our seventh-largest industry, and in New York City it employs more people than any other business. If anything, the case could be made that I *helped* the economy by putting so many people to work!

If the public really wants the first lady to look her best, why then was I attacked so strongly, and so often, for my wardrobe?

One reason may be that some women aren't all that crazy about a woman who wears a size four, and who seems to have no trouble staying slim.

No, I am not anorexic, and I never have been. (That's another rumor I had to endure, and I always hated it. Anorexia is a terrible illness, and it's not a condition that should be assigned frivolously.) The truth is far less dramatic: Despite the fact that I always eat three meals a day and don't skip desserts, I worry constantly. I'm not a big eater, and it doesn't take much to fill me up.

It may be hard to believe, but I used to be chubby. By the end of my freshman year at college, when I was living away from home for the first time, I had puffed up to 143 pounds. In addition to starchy food, we were given a tray of peanut-butter-and-jelly sandwiches at bedtime—and I used to eat about three of these a night! When I came home in June, my father said to me, "Nancy, you seem to have put on some weight."

Well, that's all it took, because any criticism from my father just mortified me. I started watching what I ate, and three years later, when I graduated, I was down to 125, which was still a lot for me. My problem now is keeping weight on, not taking it off. My current weight is 106 pounds.

During our final year in the White House, the fashion "story" broke again after an article in *Time* magazine noted that I was continuing to borrow dresses from leading designers after I had supposedly promised not to, and that I had kept them. I couldn't help but wonder about the timing of an old story that was brought back during the height of the 1988 campaign. At that time, Elaine Crispen, my press secretary, was widely quoted as saying, "She made a little promise and she broke it." I don't know why Elaine said that, but she was wrong, and I told her so. None of the clothes were given to me to keep. Some have gone to the Reagan Library; some have been committed to museums. The rest belong to the designers.

And I wonder: What would have happened if I *had* stopped borrowing dresses and had started wearing only the clothes that I could actually afford to buy? Before long, instead of calling me extravagant, the press would have started referring to me as "dowdy" and "frumpy." And the newspapers would soon have been keeping track of how many times they had seen me in the same outfit. I don't think I could have won this one.

In 1981, when the fuss over my clothing first erupted, I had very few defenders. But in 1988, when the same reports surfaced again, I had plenty of allies. By then, I guess, people knew me better. The *Chicago Tribune* actually suggested that perhaps I should have *charged* my favorite designers several hundred dollars an hour for modeling their latest creations.

The renovation, the china, the dresses—all of these criticisms reinforced an image of me that existed even before Ronnie and I moved into the White House. Katharine Graham once pointed out that a number of the articles about me before 1980 were written by younger women who were caught up in the feminist movement. "They just couldn't identify with you," she said. "You represented everything they were rebelling against."

It hadn't occurred to me at the time, but now I think Kay had a point. And I suspect that what may *really* have bothered some women was my decision to give up my career and devote myself to my husband and our family. Ronnie had never asked me to do this; it had been my own choice. I could have continued working regularly in movies. But I had seen too many marriages fall apart in the picture business because both partners had a career. I've always felt that I had the best of both worlds—a career, followed by a happy marriage. Still, some women have never forgiven me for making that choice, or for saying that my life really began when I married Ronnie. But for as long as I can remember, I have wanted to belong to somebody, and to have somebody belong to me. I never wanted to go it alone.

It's also possible that some of the reporters who wrote about me then felt that our marriage was at least partly an act. She can't *possibly* be that crazy about him after all those years, they seemed to be saying. And the way she looks at him when he's giving a speech. Come on! They're actors, after all, and for them this is just another role.

But it wasn't—and it isn't. Eventually people got used to our relationship and accepted it; I guess they came to think that nobody could be faking it that well—or for that long!

Another point that Kay Graham mentioned was that when Ronnie and I first moved to Washington, I was pretty much of an unknown quantity. "Just about the only thing we knew about you was that article by Joan Didion in the *Saturday Evening Post*."

I winced when I heard Kay say that. Back in 1968, Joan Didion had spent a day with me at our house in Sacramento. I thought our conversation had gone well, and I had enjoyed the time we spent together. But a few weeks later, when I read her article during a flight to Chicago, I was shocked to find that it was dripping with sarcasm: "Nancy Reagan has an interested smile, the smile of a good wife, a good mother, a good hostess, the smile of someone who grew up in comfort and went to Smith College and has a father who is a distinguished neurosurgeon (her father's entry in the 1966–67 *Who's Who* runs nine lines longer than her husband's) and a husband who is the definition of Nice Guy, not to mention Governor of California, the smile of a woman who seems to be playing out some middle-class American woman's daydream, circa 1948. The set for this daydream is perfectly dressed, every detail correct. . . . Everyone on the set smiles, the social secretary, the state guard, the cook, the gardeners."

Well, I was doing an interview, and yes, I had smiled when I opened the door to welcome Joan Didion. That, apparently, was my big mistake, for elsewhere in the article, my smile was described as "a study in frozen insincerity."

Well, I wasn't insincere. And I smile, I'm afraid, the way I smile. I couldn't help but wonder: Would she have liked it better if I had snarled? She had obviously written the story in her mind before she ever met me.

Twelve years later, in 1980, several other profiles of me followed similar lines. My biggest fault, it seems, was that I was too polite, too much a lady. Writing in the *Washington Post,* Sally Quinn attacked the way I sat and listened when Ronnie gave a speech: "She never seems to get an itch, her lips never stick to her teeth, she hardly blinks. Don't her legs ever go to sleep? Haven't they ever had a terrible fight just before the speech? Isn't she ever bored hearing the whole thing over and over and over?"

Julie Baumgold in *New York* magazine went a little further: "She does not provoke; she flatters and always suppresses the little touch of the bitch inside."

Wow!

It got worse as the campaign went on. In October, just two weeks before the 1980 election, the *Los Angeles Herald Examiner* ran a five-part series called "The Woman Who Would Be Queen." It was just awful! I still cringe when I think of it. Beneath a full-page hideous drawing of me—in regal clothes, wearing a crown, and towering over a chessboard—the author, Wanda McDaniel, portrayed me as a calculating, power-hungry manipulator who was just dying to move into the White House. Some of the stories she described were simply absurd: In one of them, she said that I wouldn't allow the actress Ruta Lee and another woman to ride in an elevator with Ronnie and me because they were too attractive and I was jealous. Ruta is very attractive, but she's also a friend, and no such thing ever happened.

Later in the article, Ms. McDaniel also quoted an old friend of mine, Rupert Allen, as saying that if Ronnie was elected, Nancy Reagan would make the White House comfortable and "all their non-Jewish friends would be there." Rupert never said that, and he was so angry that he threatened to sue the paper.

Wanda McDaniel also repeated a myth that I've heard hundreds of times: that my father was an extreme right-winger who was responsible for Ronnie's political shift from liberal to conservative. Or, in yet another article from that period, "They fell in love, and Nancy converted him to her father's politics, and out popped Ronald Reagan, the right-winger."

Well, these stories hurt.

Kay Graham was probably right to mention the influence of Joan Didion's profile, because it did seem that other women writers elaborated on the same themes, not only in 1980 but into 1981. With few exceptions, they described me as a woman who was interested only in rich friends and fancy clothes, a supercilious and shallow socialite, a lady who loved shopping and going out to lunch.

In another words, an airhead.

Writing in *Ms.*, Gloria Steinem called me "the marzipan wife," and "the rare woman who can perform the miracle of having no interests at all."

A few years later, of course, I would be criticized for having too many interests—especially in politics. But back in 1981, *Newsweek* predicted that "Nancy is not likely to be faulted for interfering in affairs of state." I wish!

And the *Chicago Tribune* surely deserved a prize for squeezing the greatest number of negative references into a single sentence, when it described me as "Queen Nancy the Extravagant, an aloof former debutante and movie star whose main concerns are fashion, decorating and lunching with rich girlfriends, whose idea of hard times is tablecloths that shrink, whose doe-eyed devotion to her husband leads to hard-eyed terrorizing of her aides."

I was called more names than I can remember. Queen Nancy. The Iron Butterfly. The Belle of Rodeo Drive. Fancy Nancy. The Cutout Doll. On the *Tonight* show, Johnny Carson quipped that my favorite junk food was caviar.

These stories not only hurt, they also made me damn mad. They usually mentioned my friends who were well known (and whom the press referred to as "The Group"), but they rarely mentioned my friends who are not well known. It infuriated me to read that

I had been part of the lunch bunch who spend their days shopping on Rodeo Drive. I *know* there are women who shop every day and who center their lives on going out for lunch, but I didn't do that then and I don't do it now. It would bore the daylights out of me.

When we lived in Pacific Palisades, Ronnie and I had small children, and I spent most of my time carpooling with them, driving the kids to the dentist, taking them to buy shoes, going to the market, serving on the board of the school, manning the hot-dog stand at the school fair—all the normal things that mothers do. Did I sometimes go out to lunch? Sure. Did I ever shop? Of course. But shopping and lunch were never my life.

I was also accused of being "Hollywood." Well, yes, Ronnie and I worked in Hollywood. We're proud of it. But we were never part of the glitzy Hollywood scene—the world of stars like Ava Gardner and Joan Crawford, or later, Elizabeth Taylor and Joan Collins. When we were married in 1952, we deliberately chose *not* to live in Hollywood—at that time, Pacific Palisades was considered a distant suburb. Our idea of a big evening was to watch a picture on television with the Holdens, or go out to the movies.

But by the time I became first lady, there was already a fixed image of me in the press. Then, during my first year in Washington, the White House renovation, the new china, and my wardrobe all were seen as confirming that image.

It's easy to blame it all on the press, but I now think that in fact there was fault on both sides. I wish the press had taken a little more time to get to know me better, rather than relying on old stories and images. And I also wish I had tried harder to communicate to them who I really was. I'm a very private person, and it has always been difficult for me to open up to people, especially reporters, and especially about personal matters. And in the beginning, when I did, it often backfired. When I'm hurt, as I was repeatedly in 1980 and 1981, I tend to retreat, a form of self-protection. Now I see that this might just have made things worse, by making me appear aloof and snobbish.

I'd like to think that by the time we left the White House, the press and I had come to know each other a lot better. I wasn't the first first lady to be attacked by the media, but nobody could remember anything remotely resembling the bad press I endured during that first year. Bess Truman and Mamie Eisenhower were criticized for their dowdy clothes and unglamorous friends. Jackie Kennedy fared somewhat better, although I'm sure she grew tired of the endless curiosity about her wardrobe. Mrs. Johnson was treated well—nobody objected to the fact that she had many wealthy friends who helped support her beautification project. I always thought Pat Nixon was maligned simply for being herself. Betty Ford received good press, but Rosalynn Carter was mocked for taking an interest in policy issues. But I won the unpopularity contest hands down. By the end of 1981 I had a higher disapproval rating than any other first lady of modern times.

It isn't often in life that one is lucky enough to enjoy a second beginning, but during one five-minute period in the spring of 1982, I was able to make a fresh start with the Washington press corps.

It happened at the annual Gridiron Dinner, which, as I soon learned, was one of the most important events in Washington. The Gridiron is a small, select club of sixty print journalists. Every spring they hold an elegant white-tie dinner, which is limited to six hundred invited guests. The program is always the same: Members of the press perform clever and (hopefully) funny skits that poke fun at both Democrats and Republicans. These skits are followed by two speakers—one from each party. The evening ends with a brief toast to the president—followed by his response.

For politicians and reporters in Washington, the Gridiron Dinner is the social event of the year. The guest list always includes the Speaker of the House, members of the Cabinet, top White House aides, justices of the Supreme Court, and leading members of Congress, along with a fair number of anchormen, publishers, columnists, diplomats, and other opinion leaders.

Every president since Benjamin Harrison has been to at least one Gridiron Dinner, and during our stay in Washington, Ronnie and I attended them all. Ronnie had a particularly good time at the 1984 dinner, where he got to tease several of the Democrats who were fighting it out for the honor of opposing him in the November elections. When he came to Senator Alan Cranston, who was a few years younger than himself, Ronnie said, "Imagine running for president at his age!" And he dismissed Gary Hart by saying, "This country would never accept a president who looks like a movie star." It was typical of Ronnie that both of these quips were really directed against himself.

A few weeks before the 1982 dinner, Sheila Tate realized that after the year I had just gone through, it was inevitable that the evening would include a skit about me. She thought it would be terrific if I appeared in that skit, in a surprise cameo role.

First, Sheila tried the idea out on several of Ronnie's advisers, including David Gergen, Larry Speakes, and Mike Deaver. After they had all given it their blessing, Sheila came to me.

It turned out that the Gridiron members were planning to have somebody sing a song about me. Someone suggested that I should respond with a song of my own that would attack the press.

"Forget it," I told Sheila. "I'm not willing to attack the press. If I'm going to do this at all, I think I should make fun of myself."

"Are you willing to sing?" she asked.

"Sure."

"Dance?"

"Absolutely."

"Would you be willing to smash a plate that was painted to look like the new White House china?"

"Of course! But only if it's a surprise. I don't want anybody to know in advance—not even my husband!"

To help us prepare a suitable response to their skit about me, the Gridiron officers provided us with the lyrics to their song, in which a singer pretending to be Nancy Reagan sang new words to "Second-Hand Rose," an old Fanny Brice hit song from the 1920s that had recently enjoyed a revival. Their lyrics went like this:

> Second-hand clothes.
> I give my second-hand clothes
> To museum collections and traveling shows.

They were oh so happy that they got 'em
Won't notice they were ragged at the bottom.
Goodbye, you old worn-out mess.
I never wear a frock more than once.
Calvin Klein, Adolfo, Ralph Lauren and Bill Blass.
Ronald Reagan's mama's going strictly First Class.
Rodeo Drive, I sure miss Rodeo Drive
In frumpy Washington.

Second-hand rings.
Donate those old used-up things.
Designers deduct 'em.
We're living like kings.
So what if Ronnie's cutting back on welfare.
I'd still wear a tiara in my coiffed hair.

Sheila then asked Landon Parvin, one of our best speech-writers, to work on a set of lyrics for my response. Meanwhile, we had to decide what I would wear. With the enthusiastic help of my staff, we put together a really ridiculous costume—it made me look like a bag lady on Halloween. I wore white pantaloons with blue butterflies, yellow rubber rainboots, a blue blouse with white dots, and over that a really ugly sleeveless red cotton print housedress. Over *that* I wore a blue print skirt pinned up on the side with a sequinned butterfly, a long strand of fake pearls, a mangy boa, and a red straw hat with feathers and flowers. I was gorgeous!

During dinner (dressed properly, of course), I was so nervous that I couldn't eat a thing. Maybe, just maybe, it was because six hundred of the most influential people in America were about to see the first lady make a complete fool of herself.

But it was too late to back out. When the singer on stage was singing "Second-Hand Clothes," I turned to Ronnie and told him I had to go to the ladies' room. Sheila Tate, who was even more nervous than I was (if that's possible), was sitting between two newspaper publishers. "Oh, boy," one of them said. "Mrs. Reagan has just left the head table. I bet she's really ticked off."

Backstage, I got into my costume. One of the stage props was a big clothing rack, the kind you see in the stock room of a store. I hid behind the rack where nobody could see me, while the Gridiron skit poking fun at me went on. When the song was over, I parted the clothes and walked out.

I was greeted by a thunderous silence. For a few seconds, nobody realized who this woman was, or why she looked so ridiculous in those silly clothes. But when it sank in, the audience rose and gave me a standing ovation before I even opened my mouth. When the room was quiet again, I sang Landon's lyrics to "Second-Hand Rose":

> I'm wearing second-hand clothes
> Second-hand clothes
> They're quite the style
> In the spring fashion shows.
> Even my new trench coat with fur collar
> Ronnie bought for ten cents on the dollar.
>
> Second-hand gowns
> And old hand-me-downs
> The china is the only thing that's new.
> Even though they tell me that I'm no longer Queen,
> Did Ronnie have to buy me that new sewing machine?
> Second-hand clothes, second-hand clothes,
> I sure hope Ed Meese sews.

When I was finished, the audience responded with another standing ovation. Even better, they had laughed at all the right places, and I began to relax and enjoy myself. The only snag came at the very end, when I was supposed to smash the "china" plate on the stage. I threw it down, but it didn't break!

When the audience yelled for an encore, I sang the whole thing over again, threw down the plate again, and this time it broke.

I was wondering what Ronnie's reaction would be to all of this, but when I got back to the table he was still laughing, so I knew he had thought it was all right.

I never dreamed that my appearance that night would be so influential. It was talked about for the rest of our years in Washington, almost as though it were an important political event—which in a way it was. This one song, together with my willingness to sing it, served as a signal to opinion-makers that maybe I wasn't the terrible, humorless woman they thought I was—regal, distant, disdainful. From that night on, my image began to change in Washington.

It had been a long time since I had received any favorable press, so I treasured the newspaper reviews of my performance. The Gridiron Dinner is supposed to be off-the-record, but I wasn't about to quibble when reports about it in the press were kind to me. FIRST LADY FLOORS 'EM WITH SONG AND DANCE, said the New York *Daily News*. SHE SINGS, SHE JOKES, SHE'S A HIT, said the *Los Angeles Herald Examiner*.

According to the *Washington Post*, "the sophisticated audience of journalists, politicians and their friends responded to her performance as though she had undergone a major change. A number of those image-makers left the ballroom saying that Nancy Reagan's song-and-dance number had transformed her image."

And the *New York Times* said: "President Nixon once played the piano and Betty Ford once danced, but the consensus was that no other First Lady had ever come so well prepared. . . . Socko!"

3

Astrology

THE criticism I faced during that first year of Ronnie's presidency was nothing compared with the eruption over astrology that occurred during Ronnie's last year in office. At the time I said nothing about it. But now it's my turn to explain exactly what I did—and why.

I was devastated after the shooting, as I've already explained. Ronnie recovered, but I'm a worrier, and now I really had something to worry about: that it might happen again, and that this time I would lose him forever.

Astrology was simply one of the ways I coped with the fear I felt after my husband almost died.

For a long time after the shooting, the world seemed to be inundated with violence. Six weeks after Ronnie was almost killed, the pope was shot and wounded—right in St. Peter's Square. Four months after *that*, President Sadat was shot and killed during a military parade in Cairo. Within nine months of my husband's inauguration, three world leaders had been shot.

Everyone said it was just a coincidence, and yet I worried. How could any public figure be protected from acts of violence? And what if these three events were somehow connected in a way that would become known only at some future time?

There was also the so-called twenty-year death cycle for American presidents. For more than a century, every president elected or reelected in a year ending in zero had died in office. This strange pattern had been written about during the 1980 campaign. Back then, I hadn't paid much attention—but it *had* stuck in my mind.

Now that my own husband was president and an attempt had been made on his life, the historical pattern became terrifying to me. President William Harrison, elected in 1840, had died in office. Lincoln, elected in 1860, had been killed, as had Garfield (1880) and McKinley (1900). Harding (1920) had died, and in my own lifetime, Franklin Delano Roosevelt (1940) had died, and John F. Kennedy (1960) was killed.

Was Ronald Reagan, elected in 1980, next?

Was the shooting in March 1981 merely an omen, an early warning that something even worse might lie ahead?

All *that* aside—if an assassination attempt had come so close to succeeding, what would prevent it from happening again? After Ronnie was shot, the threats against his life continued, something that apparently happens whenever a major public figure survives a shooting: His recovery serves as a kind of perverse challenge to other would-be assassins. According to the Secret Service, it was very possible that someone would try to complete the task.

What if March 30 was only the beginning? And how was I ever going to live through eight *years* of this?

Night after night, I lay beside my husband and tried to drive these gruesome thoughts from my mind. Ronnie slept, but I could not. When Ronnie was in the hospital, I would lie on his side of the bed at the White House as a way of feeling closer to him, but I barely slept. Now that he was home, I still kept waking up during the night.

I had no appetite for food. I tried to eat because I knew I should, to keep up my strength, but it didn't stay with me. When I came to Washington I weighed 112 pounds. After the shooting I slipped below a hundred. In most pictures from 1981, I look gaunt.

When you're as frightened as I was, you reach out for help and comfort in any direction you can. I prayed what seemed like all the time, more than I ever had before. I talked with religious leaders such as Billy Graham and Donn Moomaw. I talked a lot with my old friends, who called to offer support.

And when Ronnie wasn't around, I cried. Sometimes I also cried when he *was* around, but I would usually manage to slip away into the bedroom or the bathroom so he wouldn't see me and be upset by the fact that *I* was upset. I knew that if Ronnie saw me crying, he would be—and that's the last thing I wanted. He was recovering, but he still looked very fragile.

For instance, just a few days after Ronnie returned from the hospital, the circus paraded into Washington, marching down Pennsylvania Avenue. When they reached the White House, they stopped and put on a little performance to cheer Ronnie up in his recovery. I was in the exercise room when Ronnie came by to tell me how happy their performance had made him. He looked so frail standing there in his navy blue robe and pajamas, so different from the Ronnie I knew. I could barely control myself until he left the room.

One afternoon I was on the phone with Merv Griffin, an old friend from my Hollywood days, and he mentioned that he had recently talked with Joan Quigley, a San Francisco astrologer. I had seen her years ago on Merv's television show, where she was part of a panel of astrologers. Later, Merv had apparently introduced us, although I don't remember meeting her. Joan had then volunteered her advice during Ronnie's 1980 campaign, and had called me several times to talk about "good" and "bad" times for Ronnie. I was interested in what she had to say, and I was pleased when she told me that Ronnie was going to win—that it was in his chart and in mine.

I remember as if it were yesterday my reaction to what Merv told me on the phone. He had talked to Joan, who had said she could have warned me about March 30. According to Merv, Joan had said, "The president should have stayed home. I could see from my charts that this was going to be a dangerous day for him."

"Oh, my God," I remember telling Merv. "*I could have stopped it!*" I hung up the phone, picked it up again, and called Joan.

"Merv tells me you knew about March 30," I said.

"Yes," she replied. "I could see it was a very bad day for the president."

"I'm so scared," I told her. "I'm scared every time he leaves the house, and I don't think I breathe until he gets home. I cringe every time we step out of a car or leave a building. I'm afraid that one of these days somebody is going to shoot at him again."

Joan was a good listener, and she responded with the warmth and compassion I needed. Before long I found myself telling her about other problems I was having, including problems with two of our children, Patti and Michael, and concerns over my aging parents, both of whom were sick. On all these matters, Joan was helpful and comforting. We had a professional relationship, but I came to view her as a friend. I now see that she was also a kind of therapist.

My relationship with Joan Quigley began as a crutch, one of several ways I tried to alleviate my anxiety about Ronnie. Within a year or two, it had become a habit, something I relied on a little less but didn't see the need to change. While I was never certain that Joan's astrological advice was helping to protect Ronnie, the fact is that nothing like March 30 ever happened again.

Was astrology one of the reasons? I don't *really* believe it was, but I don't *really* believe it wasn't. But I do know this: It didn't hurt, and I'm not sorry I did it.

Joan and I had talked several times when she finally said, "Why don't you let me know when the president plans to go out? I could tell you if those are good days or bad days." Well, I thought, what's the harm in that? And so once or twice a month I would talk with Joan (sometimes by appointment, sometimes not). I would have Ronnie's schedule in front of me, and what I wanted to know was very simple: Were specific dates safe or dangerous? If, for example, Ronnie was scheduled to give a speech in Chicago on May 3, should he leave Washington that morning, or was he better off flying out on the previous afternoon?

People seem to be fascinated by the logistics of all this, but it was really quite simple. As with other friends, I placed the calls to Joan myself, on my private line. If she had to call me back, the White House and Camp David operators knew her as a friend of mine, and put the calls through.

When Joan got back to me with her advice on specific dates, I would, if necessary, call Michael Deaver, who was in charge of Ronnie's schedule. Sometimes a small change was made. Beginning in 1985, I would do the same with Donald Regan, who became

Ronnie's chief of staff then. If a change wasn't possible, I deferred to Mike or Don. While astrology was a factor in determining Ronnie's schedule, it was never the only one, and no political decision was ever based on it.

I knew, of course, that if this ever came out, it could prove embarrassing to Ronnie—although I never imagined just *how* embarrassing. But as long as I worked with Mike Deaver, I knew my secret was safe. Mike was discreet. He had known Ronnie and me for years and was one of my closest friends. I never even thought of asking him to keep a confidence; I just knew he would.

And about astrology, Mike understood. He too had been traumatized by the shooting—one of the bullets aimed at Ronnie had whistled over Mike's head, missing him by inches. If he hadn't ducked at precisely the right second, he would have been killed. And so, partly because of this, Mike seemed to think it was a good idea to get Joan's input. Like me, he thought: Why not? Why take chances? It may be nonsense, but does anybody *really* know? And people have certainly been fascinated by astrology for thousands of years. It's one of those mysteries that just don't seem to go away.

Later, because I didn't know Don Regan very well, I was a little more careful—an instinct I now wish I had taken more seriously. With Regan, for example, I never used Joan's name, referring to her only as "my friend." Don never commented on the information one way or the other. He never challenged my practice, or discouraged it, or mocked it. He certainly never said, "Let's not do this. I don't think it's a good idea." When people are direct with me in voicing their opinions, I can deal with that, but I can't if I don't know what they're thinking. What I was thinking about most was Ronnie. I now believe that what Don was more interested in was Don.

Don also never implied, however, as Mike did, that he thought consulting Joan was a good idea. I could tell Don didn't approve of Joan, but it wasn't clear whether this wasn't partly because he always wanted things done his way—and on his schedule.

Don Regan has said that he kept a color-coded calendar on his desk to keep track of Joan's advice. If he did, I certainly didn't know about it. I learned about it the way everybody else did: from press reports about his book. As far as I can remember, Don and I never discussed astrology directly. Nor did we discuss my relationship with Joan Quigley.

When I first started talking to Joan, I hoped she would volunteer her services, as she had during the 1980 campaign, but no such luck. I don't think it's fair to say how much she charged me, any more than I would disclose how much I paid my doctor. But it wasn't cheap! Joan sent me monthly statements, and I asked her to write my personal five-digit code on the envelope—a White House convenience so that personal mail addressed to the president and first lady doesn't get lost in the mountains of general mail sent to the White House.

You learn *something* from living in the White House, and I didn't think an astrologer should be sent checks signed by the first lady. And so I asked a friend back in California to pay Joan, and I reimbursed her each month.

I want to state one thing again, and unequivocally: *Joan's recommendations had nothing to do with policy or politics—ever. Her advice was confined to timing—to Ronnie's schedule, and to what days were good or bad, especially with regard to his out-of-town trips.*

Although the shooting had occurred only a mile from the White House, I was less frightened about Ronnie's appearances in Washington, partly because I could see with my own eyes that security arrangements there had clearly been improved since March 30. Now, for example, whenever we drove to a hotel where Ronnie was speaking, the Secret Service would have erected a large canvas sheet over the entrance to the building so the president was no longer visible from the street. It was a simple change, but just seeing that piece of cloth was a big comfort to me.

Security had been improved in other ways as well—especially after American security agencies began receiving reports that Libyan hit squads would soon be operating in the United States, and that Ronnie and I were among their principal targets. At the time these warnings were taken so seriously that concrete barriers were installed around the White House. As if I weren't feeling vulnerable enough already!

But it was Ronnie's trips outside Washington that worried me the most, and this is where I found Joan's advice particularly reassuring. The hardest times of all were when Ronnie went on trips without me—because, illogical though it is, I never got over feeling that if only I had been with him on March 30, the shooting would not have happened.

I should say, too, that the idea of consulting an astrologer never struck me as particularly strange. I used to look at my horoscope every morning as I read the paper, although fifteen minutes later I usually forgot what it said. And although I'm far from a true believer, I do think there are certain characteristics that tend to be true of individuals born under a particular sign. But I don't run my life by astrology, and no, I don't go around asking people what sign they were born under!

I was born on July 6, which makes me a Cancer. It is often said that people born under the sign of Cancer are above all homemakers and nesters, which is exactly how I would define myself. Cancers also tend to be intuitive, vulnerable, sensitive, and fearful of ridicule—all of which, like it or not, I am. The Cancer symbol is the crab shell: Cancers often present a hard exterior to the world, which hides their vulnerability. When they're hurt, Cancers respond by withdrawing into themselves. That's me, all right.

Then too, when I lived in Hollywood, almost everybody knew Carroll Righter, an astrologer who wrote a column for the *Los Angeles Times*. He was a nice elderly man who would tell everyone their good and bad days—so I was familiar with those categories.

Another reason I was open to astrology was that I have spent most of my life in the company of show-business people, where superstitions and other nonscientific beliefs are widespread and commonly accepted. Maybe it's because the entertainment business is so unpredictable and impervious to logic, but starting with my mother, who was an actress, just about every performer I have known has been at least mildly superstitious. For example: It's bad luck to whistle in the dressing room. Never throw your hat on the bed. And never keep your shoes on a shelf that's higher than your head.

I don't think actors and performers literally *believed* these things, but you went along with them as a way of hedging your bets. When someone consulted an astrologer, nobody thought much about it.

After March 30, 1981, I wasn't about to take any chances. Very few people can really understand what it's like to have your husband shot at and almost die, and then have him exposed all the time to enormous crowds, tens of thousands of people, any one of whom might be a lunatic with a gun. I have been criticized and ridiculed for turning to astrology, but after a while I reached the point where I didn't care. I was doing everything I could think of to protect my husband and keep him alive. Living without Ronnie was unthinkable: I was willing to do anything I thought might possibly keep him safe. Everyone reacts differently, but this was what *I* needed to do. Astrology helped me cope—and nobody has ever shown that it caused any harm to Ronnie or to the country.

And all during those years, Joan Quigley was there for me. As I look back on that period, it's not her advice about specific dates that I remember so much as her personal concern and support. Joan was somebody I could turn to with my anxieties and fears.

It wasn't until 1985 that I finally met her. Joan had always wanted to attend a state dinner at the White House. As soon as she came through the receiving line and her name was announced, I remember thinking, So that's what you look like! We only said a quick hello because of my responsibilities as hostess. But on the telephone, where we had more time, Joan was always sympathetic and never rushed. She commiserated with me. She sent me inspirational texts in the mail. She was so supportive—not only about Ronnie and the job he was doing as president, but also about my parents and the problems I was having with Patti.

At first Ronnie knew nothing about my conversations with Joan. He didn't know that Mike Deaver and I might have discussed changing a certain departure time or an appointment, based on Joan's advice. I wanted to tell Ronnie about it, but I wasn't exactly *dying* to tell him, and I kept putting it off. Then one day, after I'd been talking to Joan on and off for quite a few months, Ronnie walked into the bedroom while I was on the phone to her.

"Honey, what was that about?" he asked.

When I told him, he said, "If it makes you feel better, go ahead and do it. But be careful. It might look a little odd if it ever came out."

Normally, I'm the one who sees a potential trouble spot. This time it was Ronnie who foresaw that my involvement with Joan could have serious consequences for us. Boy, was he right. Politically, I made a terrible mistake when I started calling Joan, and what I regret most is the enormous embarrassment I caused Ronnie. And now, of course, I realize that I was foolish to think it was possible to have any secrets in the White House.

When I first began working on this book, I never imagined that I would be writing about astrology. But then I also never imagined that my confidential relationship with Joan would be betrayed by Ronnie's former chief of staff. I had heard that Donald Regan was writing a book about his two years in the White House. He and I had had our differences, and I didn't expect to be treated kindly in his memoirs.

But it never, *ever,* occurred to me that Don Regan would do what he did—that he would take this information about my interest in astrology and twist it to seek his revenge on Ronnie and me. As I watched him on the talk shows, I fumed. How long had he been planning this? When did he first come up with the idea?

When Don lost his job, he must have been so angry that he was determined to strike back in any way he could. And obviously my relationship with Joan presented an easy target.

At first, Don's disclosure didn't seem too serious. A week before his book was serialized in *Time,* the "Periscope" page of *Newsweek* carried a brief mention of the book, with a reference to astrology in the last sentence, almost like an afterthought. I wasn't happy to read it, but I wasn't too upset, either. After all, my interest in astrology seemed to merit only a single line in *Newsweek.*

But that was just the beginning.

Within a few days, it became the biggest story in town. When the news media started in on me, I felt a terrible cold rush to the heart and a sinking feeling in my stomach. Even so, I thought the whole thing would blow over in a day or two.

But for several weeks the entire country seemed to talk of little else. Donald Regan had not claimed that the United States was being run by Joan Quigley, but such subtleties seemed lost during the media frenzy in May 1988. ASTROLOGER RUNS THE WHITE HOUSE read the headline in the *New York Post,* and millions of people believed it.

It didn't seem to matter that nothing other than Ronnie's schedule was affected by astrology. Or that tens of millions of Americans really believed in astrology. Or that almost every newspaper that ridiculed me for taking astrology seriously also featured a daily horoscope column.

I felt shocked and humiliated that my relationship with Joan was portrayed as a great and terrible secret. I had always considered it a private project, something I did to hedge our bets, to try to keep Ronnie from getting shot again—and to keep me from going mad with worry. At least by consulting with Joan I was *doing* something. I knew it might not be effective or the smartest thing to do, but given my temperament, it was a lot better than just sitting there. If I hadn't taken every step I could think of to protect my husband, and Ronnie *had* been shot again, I would never have been able to forgive myself.

What it boils down to is that each person has his own ways of coping with trauma and grief, with the pain of life, and astrology was one of mine. *Don't criticize me,* I wanted to say, *until you have stood in my place. This helped me. Nobody was hurt by it*—except, possibly, me.

In the midst of the furor, what I felt worst about was Ronnie, and I apologized to him. "I feel terrible about this," I said. "I've put you in an awful position."

"No, honey," he kept saying, "it's all right. I could see what you were going through. It's all right."

Of course Ronnie easily could have said "I told you so"—but that just isn't like him. He was angry, but not at me.

I don't think he will ever forgive Don Regan for writing that book.

By 1988 I had grown used to criticism, but this was different: I had become the national laughingstock. I was the butt of countless jokes on television, radio, and in the press. It was like a long nightmare.

From the moment I got dressed in the morning until the time I got ready for bed, no matter what channel I turned to, there was Don Regan, talking about me and astrology. The man was *everywhere.* It was almost as if he had put a hit out on me.

Each time I saw him on television, I felt like standing up and shouting, *Wait a minute! That's not the way it was!* The charges being reported about me were so distorted that I ached to respond, to explain what really happened, and why. I was especially angry at things Don Regan had just *assumed:* for example, that Ronnie's operation in July 1985 had been delayed because of Joan. There was *no* delay—the operation took place the morning after cancer was suspected. As far as I was concerned, if Ronnie had a cancerous growth, it had to come out. Immediately.

During this time, I made no public comment. I had learned long ago that sometimes the best response to a negative story is to keep your mouth shut. It wasn't easy, but I knew that anything I said would only call more attention to the whole controversy and pro-long it. At one point I allowed myself to give what I thought was a funny answer: "It's managed to come through to me that Donald Regan doesn't like me very much." But when that only provoked another blast from Don, I resumed my silence. Donald Regan seemed to be working around the clock to promote his book, and he didn't need any help from me.

Joan had been on vacation when the story broke, but as soon as her plane landed in San Francisco she was met by a crowd of reporters. She was unprepared for them, and she said more than she should have. When she called me I said, "The best thing you can do is to say nothing. Have your sister answer the phone and don't take any calls. Let's treat this like a doctor-patient relationship."

At the time, I was upset that Joan had said anything. But looking back, I admire the way she handled herself. "I don't make decisions for them," she told *Time* magazine. "An astrologer just picks the best possible time to do something that someone else has already planned to do. It's like being in the ocean: You should go with the waves, not against them."

Exactly.

4

First Lady, Dragon Lady

By 1988 I had learned the hard way that when it comes to press coverage of the first lady, anything is possible. And yet throughout my years in the White House I was continually astonished and hurt by what I read about myself in the papers. Even before Ronnie's inauguration, for example, I read that I had asked the Carters to leave the White House early so I could get started on redecorating, and that I planned to tear down a wall in the Lincoln Bedroom. *The Lincoln Bedroom!*

What surprised me the most was that people actually believed these reports. But then, how could they know? I also wondered how they could reconcile these often contradictory accounts. For example, in October 1988, three months before Ronnie and I moved out of the White House, two very different stories appeared in the press. One said that I couldn't wait to leave the White House, and had already shipped everything back to California. The other said, "It's curtain time, and to put it simply, Nancy Reagan does not want to get off the stage." I had to laugh, and yet I knew that some people would find a way to believe both views of me.

No matter what I said or did, the stories never stopped. Some of them were amusing, others were maddening, and a few are still deeply offensive. Over eight years, I never stopped being hurt, although eventually I stopped being very surprised.

But it was always disheartening to see how influential these articles could be. Three or four years into Ronnie's first term, I was having lunch one day with Robert Strauss, the former chairman of the Democratic National Committee, who had become a close friend. Bob is one of the more candid men in Washington, and just before dessert, he leaned over the table and said, "When you first came to town, Nancy, I didn't like you at all. But after I got to know you, I changed my mind and said, 'She's some broad!' "

"Bob," I replied, "based on the press reports I read then, I wouldn't have liked me either."

I said earlier that nothing prepares you for the job of first lady. The experience of having not only your public appearances but your private life scrutinized and examined by the entire country, by the entire *world,* is almost too intense to describe. Although I lived with it for eight years, I still have trouble believing it.

For me, the biggest shock of all was that even the most intimate details of our medical treatment became a matter of public discussion. I agree that the public has a right to know in some detail about the president's health, especially after several previous presidents have concealed important information. But when that right to know clashes with the president's right to some privacy and dignity, the situation calls for discretion—and some limits.

As far as I'm concerned, those limits are violated when the news media show diagrams of the president's insides, or find it necessary to inform the country how many times he urinated during his first day in the hospital. I didn't like it any better, by the way, when diagrams of my 1987 breast cancer surgery were shown on television. Was *that* really necessary?

In the summer of 1985, two days after Ronnie was operated on for cancer of the colon, I turned on the television in his hospital room so we could see the evening news. And there was a doctor pointing to a diagram of Ronnie's bowel and intestines. How unprofessional, I thought. This man isn't connected with the case, and he's never even met the patient.

But soon it got worse—much worse. After summing up his diagnosis, the doctor said, "I give him four or five years."

I didn't dare look at Ronnie.

Didn't it occur to anyone that we might be watching? Or our children? Or our friends?

We've reached the point where there is so much interest in the president as a symbol and a celebrity that people sometimes forget he's also a human being.

During Ronnie's first term, I was portrayed as caring only about shopping, beautiful clothes, and going to lunch with my fancy Hollywood friends. During his second term I was described as a power-hungry political manipulator, a vindictive dragon lady who controlled the actions and appointments of the executive branch.

As my son, Ron, said, "Yeah, Mom, that's you all right!"

Part of the problem is that while the president's job is clearly defined, nobody really knows exactly what the first lady is supposed to do. The Constitution doesn't mention the president's wife, and she has no official duties. As a result, each incoming first lady has had to define the job for herself.

Once upon a time, the president's wife was seen and not heard. But there have always been exceptions, and ever since Eleanor Roosevelt, the first lady has become not only more visible but more active as well.

I realized early on that I would be the object of enormous attention no matter what I did. And soon after I moved to Washington, I began to try to find ways to focus some of that attention on the problem of drug abuse among young people. Here, too, I was remembering something Helen Thomas had told me during our talk on the campaign plane. "If your husband is elected," she said, "you will have a platform that is given to very few people. You should think about what you want to do with it. You'll never be given this kind of opportunity again."

That was one part of the job, and now that I'm back in Los Angeles, I'm continuing to work on the drug problem through the Nancy Reagan Foundation.

Then there's the ceremonial role of the first lady. I soon found that this in itself is practically a full-time occupation. In eight years, I hosted close to a hundred Christmas parties—not to mention dozens of official dinners, lunches, meetings with wives of foreign dignitaries, receptions, arrival ceremonies, awards, speaking engagements, political dinners, fund-raisers, and dozens of trips.

Every first lady makes her own choices, and mine was to become very involved in planning White House events, right down to the details: the menu, table settings, flowers, and entertainment. I always loved doing this, but it took an enormous amount of time.

Then there were the mostly invisible parts of the first lady's job: meeting with my staff, working with my press secretary, answering the mail, signing autographs, and meeting with some of the many people who, for a variety of good reasons, ask for "just five minutes of your time." I never worked harder in my life—and I liked doing most of it. Mostly, I liked being useful—to Ronnie, to individual people, and to the country, in helping address the drug problem.

Through it all, I didn't want to neglect my friends. I knew how intimidating and isolating the White House could be, and how easy it could be for us to lose touch with people, so right from the start I made it a practice to stay in touch with our friends back in California. Thank heaven for the telephone, which is really the only way you can do it. That's one media image of me that I can't object to. When they come to bury me, I'll have a receiver in one hand and my personal phone book in the other.

One thing that surprised us was how difficult it became for our friends in Washington to invite us to dinner. Ronnie and I looked forward to these invitations as a relief from formality, and from our point of view, these evenings were simple. All *we* had to do was get dressed and walk out to the car. It wasn't until we returned to California in 1989 that I began to discover just how complicated these events were for our hosts.

I hadn't known, for example, that if you invite the president to dinner, the Secret Service shows up at your house *two weeks* in advance to install extra telephone lines, or that they review your seating plan to ensure that the president cannot be seen from any of the windows, or that all wine and liquor must be poured from new, sealed bottles which must be opened under the sharp eyes of the Secret Service. And it must be an amazing experience to have your home suddenly transformed into the command post of the free world. I'm not so sure I would ever have asked us to dinner!

The publicity and the security at the White House are so intense that we soon started spending most of our weekends at Camp David. This became even more necessary after the shooting, when even a simple walk on the White House grounds became a major security problem. Camp David gave us a chance to enjoy a little privacy, and we relished it. It was also a place where we could spend time outdoors without anyone staring at us, shouting at us, or taking our picture.

I had expected we would enjoy a similar degree of privacy at our ranch near Santa Barbara, and for the first two or three years we did. But two miles from our ranch house there's a mountaintop, and pretty soon the television networks installed cameras there. By 1984, with the benefit of telescopic lenses, they were actually able to show Ronnie sitting at the breakfast table. To my mind that's just as bad as being a Peeping Tom—and Peeping Toms are arrested. We were on our own private property, but because the cameras were mounted on public property, there was nothing we could do about them. I felt a little better when we learned that the people operating those cameras were genuinely embarrassed to be doing this. But they had their orders.

When we're at the ranch, Ronnie and I usually go riding in the morning. One day, for reasons I no longer remember, I rode a different horse than usual and came back early. The press immediately wanted to know why I had cut the ride short. I answered the question, but later, I realized I was angry. What business was it of theirs? Maybe I didn't feel like riding that day. Maybe I wanted to read a book. Maybe I wanted to lie down, or work on a speech, or talk to a friend. Maybe I wanted to do nothing at all! This was supposed to be our *vacation*.

The next morning, I made up a sign saying JUST SAY NO. Then, as Ronnie and I rode by a clearing where we knew the cameras had a good view of us, I held up the sign. As long as we were going to be on TV, I thought I might as well make the most of it.

It was hard not to take it personally that our privacy was invaded so constantly. I repeatedly had to remind myself that this is an age of enormous curiosity about famous people, and that the president and his wife are celebrities. But I don't believe that the privacy of any other president has been invaded to this extent. I wondered—and still do: Is there something about Ronnie and me that prompts this endless curiosity?

I threw myself into these various first lady roles—spokeswoman, hostess, manager, and friend. I thought all of them were important. But there was one part of the job that outranked them all. Above everything else, the first lady is the president's wife. After all, that's the only reason she's there. Throughout Ronnie's presidency, there was an ongoing public discussion as to how much influence the first lady should have on the president. It's hardly a new problem. As long as mankind has lived in groups, there's always been a question as to how to handle the boss's wife.

I got used to all the comments, and sometimes I even was able to enjoy them. Ronnie and I once attended a reception at the Ford Theater which featured a particularly good ventriloquist. "Do you know who's sitting out there?" he asked the dummy. "It's the leader of the free world."

"Yes," replied the dummy, "and I see she's got her husband with her!"

I had no problem laughing at that one. But no, I was not the power behind the throne.

Did I ever give Ronnie advice? You bet I did. I'm the one who knows him best, and I was the only person in the White House who had absolutely no agenda of her own—except helping him.

And so I make no apologies for telling him what I thought. Just because you're married doesn't mean you have no right to express your opinions. For eight years I was sleeping with the president, and if that doesn't give you special access, I don't know what does!

So yes, I gave Ronnie my best advice—whenever he asked for it, and sometimes when he didn't. But that doesn't mean he always took it. Ronald Reagan has a mind of his own.

Most of my suggestions were about personnel. I don't know

much about economics or military affairs, but I have strong instincts about people, and I'm a good judge of character. As much as I love Ronnie, I'll admit he does have at least one fault: He can be naïve about the people around him.

Ronnie tends only to think well of people. While that's a fine quality in a friend, it can get you into trouble in politics. I don't think Ronnie always saw that some of the president's aides were motivated not by loyalty to their boss or to his policies but by their own agendas and personal ambitions.

For example, in November 1981 I was furious when David Stockman, Ronnie's budget director, revealed in a magazine interview that he didn't really believe in the economic plan he was supposed to be implementing. Had it been up to me, Stockman would have been out on the street that afternoon. I saw him as a shrewd and crafty man who knew exactly what he was doing. There's an implied trust when you're working for the president, *any* president, and David Stockman clearly violated it. He violated that trust a second time, five years later, when he wrote a self-righteous book about Ronnie's first term as president.

Ronnie didn't ask for my opinion about Stockman, but I told him anyway. So did Michael Deaver, Ed Meese, and what seemed like half the Republicans in the Senate. But Ronnie can be stubborn, and he insisted on keeping Stockman. Later, he admitted to me that he wished he *had* let him go but at the time he trusted Stockman's judgment and thought he needed him. I believed then, and I believe now, that this was a serious mistake.

If Ronnie had thrown Stockman out when that story appeared in *The Atlantic Monthly,* he would have made an example of him. It would have been a signal to everybody else who worked for Ronnie that he expected their loyalty. And who knows? Maybe we wouldn't have had so many kiss-and-tell books about the Reagan years.

Later, Ronnie and I had a similar disagreement about Raymond Donovan, the secretary of Labor. This case was much more complex because, unlike Stockman, Donovan hadn't done anything wrong. But he was being investigated for fraud and grand larceny, and in politics even the appearance of wrongdoing can be enormously damaging. I could see that this was going to be a long, drawn-out ordeal which would severely limit Donovan's effectiveness in the Cabinet. The Donovan affair, which dragged on for months, was draining both to Ronnie personally and to the office of the president. Donovan resigned when the indictment was handed down, but as I told Ronnie on any number of occasions, it would have been better for everyone if he'd stepped down earlier.

I felt terribly sorry for Ray Donovan then, and I still do. In 1987, when he was acquitted, he asked, quite properly, "Who do I have to see around here to get my reputation back?" What a sad question to ask!

But when a political appointee turns out to be more of a problem than an asset, even if it's not his fault, he should step aside.

There were a few other times when I thought that Ronnie was not being well served by some of his senior appointees. When James Watt, secretary of the Interior, banned the Beach Boys from performing near the Washington Monument on the Fourth of July because they would attract the wrong crowd, I thought that was dumb, and I said so publicly. I knew the Beach Boys from California, I knew they were popular, and they seemed perfectly fine to me.

When Donald Regan became a serious liability for Ronnie, I told Ronnie repeatedly that he should be fired. But it was many months before Ronnie took that advice. There were also times when I felt that people who had known Ronnie for years were taking advantage of his friendship to pursue their own agendas. Here too, if I thought so, I said so.

Once or twice I even took a stand on an issue of policy, such as the time in May 1985 when Ronnie was supposed to lay a wreath at a military cemetery in Bitburg, Germany. Months earlier, when our advance team had gone over there, the graves in the cemetery had been covered with snow, and our people had been unable to read the inscriptions. When they asked whether any Nazi war criminals were buried in this cemetery, they were assured by the Germans that this wasn't the case.

Ronnie's visit to Bitburg was supposed to be the symbol of our reconciliation with the Germans on the fortieth anniversary of the allied victory in Europe. But after the entire trip had been arranged and announced, we learned that among the two thousand German soldiers buried in Bitburg were forty-seven members of the Waffen SS.

Many Americans, and especially war veterans and members of the Jewish community, were understandably outraged. So was I. I pleaded with Ronnie to cancel the trip.

He too had strong reservations about going to Bitburg. Two days before we left for Europe, he called Chancellor Helmut Kohl and asked him to consider an alternative site—a fortress on the Rhine with no SS connections, which would have served the same symbolic purpose. But Kohl adamantly refused to cancel the Bitburg visit. He insisted that such a change would make him look like an American puppet and would cause the collapse of his government.

I was furious at Helmut Kohl for not getting us out of it, and again I urged Ronnie to cancel the visit. I wasn't alone: Fifty-three senators and almost four hundred members of the House asked Ronnie not to go. But the previous November, in the Oval Office, Ronnie had given his word to Kohl, and he felt duty-bound to honor his commitment. He also felt strongly that it was time to put the past behind us—not to forget what had happened, but to move forward into a new era.

In the end, of course, Ronnie went to Bitburg, and I went with him. We stayed there for only a few minutes, but even so, it seemed like an eternity.

And yet I was also proud of Ronnie for following his conscience, for doing what he believed was right. Bitburg was a gesture of reconciliation, and he was determined to go through with it.

I was somewhat more successful in encouraging Ronnie to consider a more conciliatory relationship with the Soviet Union. For years it had troubled me that my husband was always being portrayed by his opponents as a warmonger, simply because he believed, quite properly, in strengthening our defenses. Jimmy Carter had made this charge in the 1980 campaign, and it stuck to Ronnie for years.

Now that Ronald Reagan is out of office, even his critics acknowledge that his policy of peace through strength turned out to be an enormous success.

I knew that "warmonger" was never a fair description of Ronnie's position, but I also felt that his calling the Soviet Union an evil empire was not particularly helpful in establishing a dialogue with the other side. The world had become too small for the two superpowers not to be on speaking terms, and unless that old perception about Ronnie could be revised, nothing positive was likely to happen. Some of his advisers wanted him to keep up the tough rhetoric, but I argued against it and suggested that he tone it down. As always, Ronnie listened to various points of view and then made the decision that he thought was best.

In most good marriages that I know of, the woman is her husband's closest friend and adviser. There are limits to that role, of course. But when the president returns each afternoon from the West Wing, it's only natural that he'll talk things over with the person he's closest to, and that he'll take her viewpoint into consideration.

Historically, there has always been a certain amount of tension between the West Wing, where the president works, and the East Wing, where he and his wife live, and where the first lady has her office. The West Wing has traditionally seen itself as the sole center of power, and the men surrounding the president have resented any assertion of independence and autonomy on the part of the first lady.

But it doesn't have to be that way. It would be far better, and more realistic, if the president's men included the first lady as part of their team. After all, nobody knows the president better than his wife. The president has a host of advisers to give him counsel on foreign affairs, the economy, politics, and everything else. But not one of these people is there to look after him as an individual with human needs, a man of flesh and blood who must deal with the pressures of holding the most powerful position on earth.

And if my experience was typical, the first lady is often exposed to perspectives and viewpoints that the president never gets to hear. Time after time I was approached by White House aides and elected officials who gave me valuable information, warnings, and insights.

"I wish you'd go in and tell my husband," I'd say. But something happens to people when they walk into the Oval Office. They just freeze up, and they tell the president only what they think he wants to hear. There are times when his wife may be the only person who can be honest with him. If he's lucky, and when it's necessary, she'll be able to tell him the bad news. Or at least give him another point of view.

Every situation is different, of course, and every couple living in the White House must work out its own arrangement. President Carter liked to have Rosalynn sitting in on Cabinet meetings, whereas Ronnie and I would have found that embarrassing. And yet I learned only recently that it was Rosalynn Carter who suggested to her husband in 1978 that he invite Prime Minister Begin and President Sadat to meet with him at Camp David. I wouldn't be surprised to discover that other recent first ladies were far more helpful and involved than the public ever knew.

But however the first lady fits in, she has a unique and important role to play in looking after her husband. And it's only natural that she'll let him know what she thinks. I always did that for Ronnie, and I always will.

5

Nancy Davis

I LEARNED a lot about how to be a wife, and about many other things, from my mother, Edith Luckett Davis. She had a profound influence on the woman I turned out to be, as did her second husband, Dr. Loyal Davis, whom I have always considered my true father.

They were very different—opposites, really—and the different worlds they represented made for great contrasts and enormous changes during the first ten years of my life. My mother's world was the theater; she was an actress and a real character—fun-loving, social, irrepressible, and irresistible. Loyal Davis, a prominent Chicago neurosurgeon, was serious, dignified, and principled.

Before I was ten, I had lived in three completely different environments: as a baby, going from theater to theater with my mother; then living a small-town life as a little girl, with my aunt and uncle in Bethesda; and finally, moving into the socially prominent world of Loyal Davis in Chicago. Every period of my life has been marked by dramatic changes, and as I'll explain, these early years were no exception.

Mother always said that I was supposed to be born on the Fourth of July, but the Yankees were playing a doubleheader that day (Mother was living in New York), and she was such a passionate baseball fan that she delayed my birth until July 6.

In 1917 she had married a man named Kenneth Robbins, a Princeton graduate from a well-to-do family that had lost its money. He wasn't very ambitious, and he worked as a car salesman in New

Jersey. It wasn't a good marriage, and by the time I was born their relationship was so tenuous that Kenneth Robbins wasn't even at the hospital. They were soon divorced.

When Mother arrived at the hospital to give birth to me, they told her there were no rooms.

"No rooms?" she said. "Then I guess I'll have to lie right down on the floor of this lobby and have my baby here!"

They found her a room.

I was christened Anne Frances Robbins after my two grandmothers, but for some reason I was always called Nancy.

I don't remember the name of the hospital where I was born. It burned down years ago, but there's no truth to the rumor that I set that fire to destroy any records that might reveal my age. When Ronnie was president, every year on July 6 there would be a story in one of the papers about how Nancy Reagan *says* she was born in 1923, but we all know she was *really* born two years earlier.

When, exactly, was I born? I still haven't made up my mind. Besides, as Mother used to say, "A woman who will tell her age will tell *anything.*"

The age game actually began when I moved to Hollywood in the late 1940s and signed a film contract with MGM. In those days, almost no actress in the entire studio admitted to being over twenty-five. Years later, when Ronnie and I had to fill out some forms, I realized that I had actually forgotten my true age, and I had to ask him what it was.

According to Mother, I was born on a very warm day—before air-conditioning. The last thing my mother remembered hearing before they put her out was the doctor saying, "My, it's hot in here. Let's finish up so I can go out and play some golf."

It was a forceps delivery, and maybe the doctor did rush a little. When they brought me in, Mother was horrified: The skin on my right temple was broken, and my right eye was still closed.

"If it doesn't open in two weeks," the doctor said, "your child could be blind in that eye."

"Listen," Mother replied. "I heard what you said. You rushed through the delivery so you could go play golf. If my little girl's eye doesn't open, so help me God, I'm going to kill you!"

Knowing Mother, I wouldn't have put it past her.

Fortunately, my eye did open, but to this day I have a tiny scar from the forceps on the right side of my face.

Mother had been born in Petersburg, Virginia, the youngest of nine children. Her father, Charles Edward Luckett, worked for the Adams Express company, which later became the Railway Express. He was transferred to Washington, but his wife, Sarah, was such a staunch Southerner that each time she became pregnant, she went back to Virginia to have the baby, saying, "I refuse to give birth to any damn Yankees!"

Mother's career on the stage began in 1900, when she was three. Her brother Joe was the manager of the Columbia Theater in Washington, and when a child in one of the productions became ill, Uncle Joe put his baby sister in as the substitute. Little Edith had no speaking lines, and her only task was to die on stage. But she did it so convincingly that the audience was in tears. As the curtain came down, she stood up and waved to the crowd, to let them know she wasn't really dead.

Mother claimed that when the audience responded with great applause, she decided on the spot to devote her life to the theater.

Her next big break came ten years later, when Chauncey Olcott, the very popular singer and composer of the classic "My Wild Irish Rose," came to town to perform in Uncle Joe's theater. Olcott's accompanist fell ill the day before the concert, and Uncle Joe asked Edith if she could accompany Olcott in "My Wild Irish Rose." Mother was beside herself with excitement—even though she didn't know how to play the piano. She bought a toy piano and stayed up all night learning to play the song. Eventually she quit school and spent the rest of her teenage years working in stock companies that traveled up and down the East Coast, going on to perform with many of the great actors and actresses of the day: with George M. Cohan in *Broadway Jones,* with Spencer Tracy in *The Baby Cyclone,* and in other productions with Walter Huston and Louis Calhern. They were all her friends, but none more than Alla Nazimova, a legendary star of the silent movies, who had studied in Moscow with Stanislavski himself before she came to America, and who became my godmother.

Many of Mother's friends left the stage to work in Hollywood, but Edie continued on the stage and became the leading lady in several out-of-town stock companies. She gave up her career when she married, but after the divorce she went back on the stage, and I spent the first two years of my life as a backstage baby.

Mother took me everywhere. Her friend Colleen Moore once described how she met my mother—at a big party on Long Island at the home of Dick and Daisy Rowland. (Rowland was head of First National Studios, and Colleen was one of his stars.) "One of the women caught my eye," Colleen said. "She was a beautiful blonde, and she had the biggest blue eyes you ever saw. And she was carrying a tiny baby in her arms."

Colleen asked Rowland who the woman was, and then said, "Does she always go to parties with a baby in her arms?"

"She has no choice," Dick replied. "She just got divorced and she doesn't have a penny."

Colleen was impressed. "I made a point of getting to know your mother," she said, "and we have been friends ever since." And they were—such good friends that I later asked Colleen to be godmother to my own daughter, Patti.

Mother decided that traipsing around with me from show to show wasn't a good idea; she wanted me to enjoy a more normal childhood. And so, when I was out of diapers, she brought me to Bethesda, Maryland, to live with her sister Virginia, Virginia's husband, Audley Galbraith, who worked as a railroad shipping clerk, and their daughter, Charlotte. The Galbraiths had a warm, stable, and happy household, and they quickly accepted me as part of the family. Charlotte was three years older than I, and before long we were as close as any true sisters.

I've always been annoyed at the armchair psychologists who claim that I was "abandoned" by my mother when she brought me to live in Bethesda. It nearly killed her to do it, but she had to make a living, since she wouldn't accept alimony. As long as Mother had to work, this was the best possible arrangement.

Even so, it was a painful period for both of us. Years later I came across Mother's diary from those years, and at the bottom of every page she had written, "How I miss my baby!"

And I missed her—terribly. No matter how kindly you are treated—and I was treated with great love—your mother is your mother, and nobody else can fill that role in your life.

Maybe our six-year separation is one reason I appreciated her so much, and why we never went through a period of estrangement. It may also explain why, years later, during the 1960s, I couldn't really understand how children—including my own—could turn against their parents. I always wanted to say, "You don't know how *lucky* you are that we had all those years together."

At the age of five, I came down with double pneumonia—or "double ammonia," as I called it—which in those days was often fatal. My aunt and uncle took wonderful care of me, but I was angry that Mother was a thousand miles away in a touring company. I remember crying and saying, "If I had a little girl, I'd certainly be there if *she* was ever sick."

For some reason, my aunt repeated that comment to my mother. Later, when I had children of my own, I realized how much my words must have hurt her.

In terms of age, Virginia was Mother's closest sibling, but in almost every other respect the two sisters were classic opposites. Mother was not only outgoing and gregarious; she was also capable of uttering words that would shock a sailor, and was one of the few women I've ever known who could tell an off-color joke and have it come out funny. My aunt, on the other hand, was so modest that I'm sure she went into the bathroom to undress at night, and so proper that she called her husband "Mr. Galbraith" until the day he died.

Despite the pain of being separated from Mother, I was happy living with the Galbraiths. Aunt Virgie and Uncle Audley were good to me, and Charlotte and I were always close. I even had a boyfriend, who came to the house each morning while we were eating breakfast, and who used to pull me around the block in his little red wagon.

We lived in Battery Park, a modest section of Bethesda, in a typical suburban house—three small bedrooms and a screened-in porch with a lumpy old couch where we'd all sit on warm summer

evenings. One of our neighbors had a cinder driveway, and I fell
down there so often that my aunt had to make me kneepads. I was
chubby, and with those kneepads, I must have been quite a sight.
But that little boy with the red wagon didn't seem to mind!

I was a real little girl. I loved to play with dolls and to give them
tea parties on the front steps of the house. I wonder whether I was
preparing even then for the life I was someday going to lead as first
lady—half a century later, of course, but less than ten miles away.
I'm told I was taken to the White House for the Easter egg roll, but
I have no memory of that.

My favorite times were when Mother had a job in New York, and
Aunt Virgie would take me by train to stay with her. Although I
saw her productions over and over, I was never bored. In one of the
first plays I ever saw, the other characters were so mean to my
mother that I burst into tears. Later, when I went backstage, I
refused to talk to anybody in the cast because I thought they had
been so mean to Mother. Finally, she had to take me aside and
explain, "Nancy, it's just make-believe. The other actors were only
pretending not to like me."

I quickly came to love the special feel and the musty smell of
backstage. One of the stagehands built me a doll house, which I
brought back to Bethesda on the train and used as a backdrop to act
out my own little plays.

On those visits with Mother, I loved to dress up in her stage
clothes, put on makeup, and pretend I was playing her parts. I
would have given anything to have long blond curls, and when
Mother bought me a Mary Pickford wig I was in heaven. Between
the wig and those kneepads, I must have been gorgeous.

I always dreaded the end of my visits, when I had to leave Mother
again. When she wasn't staying in a residential hotel, she would live
in the brownstone apartment of a friend who was traveling with
some other show. To this day, I still get a sinking feeling in my
stomach whenever I'm in New York and pass one of those buildings. Strange, how little things can trigger memories buried deep
inside.

Sometimes Mother would visit me in Bethesda. Whenever she

swooped in on us, it was as if Auntie Mame herself had come to town. We all sat around the living room while she held forth about New York, or Atlanta, or wherever she had just been. On one of these visits she taught Charlotte and me the latest dance, the Charleston. Another time she brought us an adorable little wire-haired terrier named Ginger.

Mother loved to tell a story about an actor friend of hers named Spence. Once, when they were in a play together, Mother had bought a new girdle. She wanted to look especially beautiful because a man she liked very much was coming to the performance that night, and he had never seen her on stage.

A few minutes before the show began, she was in her dressing room getting into the new girdle and it got stuck halfway up. She called over to the next dressing room, "Spence! Get in here now and help me!"

Spence rushed in, and when he saw what the problem was, he started laughing.

"Goddamnit, Spence," she said. "Stop laughing and help me out."

"I can't, Lucky," he said, pretending to struggle with the girdle. "I'm trying, but I can't make it budge."

Mother got angry and started yelling, and finally, just as the curtain went up, Spence gave a yank and everything fell into place.

There are two reasons why this story stayed with me. One is that the man Mother wanted to impress that night was Loyal Davis, her future husband—although she didn't tell me that until years later. The other was that Spence, whose full name was Spencer Tracy, became an important friend of our family and a special help to me in my acting career.

I was thrilled when Mother came to visit and miserable when she left. I understood that she had to work, and I knew that as soon as she could manage it, we would be together. I realized that living with Aunt Virgie and Uncle Audley was only temporary. But I had been with them as long as I could remember, and I yearned for the day when Mother and I could be together again.

Early in the spring of 1929, Mother came to see me in Bethesda.

"Come out on the porch with me," she said. "There's something I want to tell you."

Mother and I sat down on the couch, and she told me she had fallen in love with a wonderful man. His name was Loyal Davis, and he was tall, handsome, and very kind. He was a doctor from Chicago, and he wanted to marry her, but Mother had told him that she would never get married unless I said it was all right. If I said yes, she would stop being an actress, and we would both move to Chicago, where we would live together as one happy family.

"It's up to you," she said. "I won't marry Dr. Davis unless you think I should."

I wasn't sure what to say. My life in Bethesda was happy, but living with Mother would be my greatest wish come true.

I have often looked back at that moment and wondered: What if I had objected? But knowing Mother, I'm sure she would have found a way to bring me around.

I had no way of knowing it, of course, but Mother's announcement eventually changed my life just as much as it changed hers. I can't imagine what my life would have been if they had never met.

They were married in a chapel at the Fourth Presbyterian Church in Chicago. The best man was Dr. Allen Kanavel, my new father's mentor. I was the bridesmaid, and I wore a blue pleated dress and carried flowers. I was happy for Mother, but I can remember, even then, feeling twinges of jealousy—a feeling I was to experience years later, from the other side, after I married a man with children. Dr. Davis was taking part of her away from me, and after being separated from Mother for so long, I wanted her all to myself.

On their honeymoon, they went to a medical convention and then toured the battlefields of the Civil War—Dr. Davis was a Civil War buff. Years later, my own honeymoon with Ronnie turned out to be about as romantic: We drove to Phoenix, and along the way my new husband stopped at roadside animal places which featured rattlesnakes and similar creatures.

"We've got a ranch now," he kept saying. "You'll have to learn what these things look like."

Sure. But on my *honeymoon*?

. . .

Loyal Davis was a man of great integrity who exemplified old-fashioned values: That girls and boys should grow up to be ladies and gentlemen. That children should respect and obey their parents. That no matter what you did, you should never cheapen yourself. And that whatever you worked at—whether it was a complicated medical procedure, or a relatively simple act like sweeping the floor—you should do it as well as you could.

Although I came to love this man, the transition to my new life in Chicago was neither smooth nor easy. He seemed formal and distant, and at first I resented having to share my mother with him. I was jealous of their close relationship. I remember one particularly embarrassing moment, when the two newlyweds were sitting together on a couch, and I squeezed in and forced myself between them.

But Dr. Davis understood, and he never pushed me into accepting him. Perhaps it was because he had a child of his own from a previous marriage, a boy named Richard, who was a little younger than I and who lived with his mother. (When she died, Richard, my brother, Dick, moved in with us.) But whatever the reason, Dr. Loyal Davis allowed me to come to know him at my own pace.

Soon after I arrived in Chicago, he sat me down and explained that he and my mother were in love, and that he would be good to her. He didn't think it was quite right to adopt me as long as my birth father was alive, but if I ever wanted him to, he would—and that nothing would make him happier. He hoped that he and I would come to love each other, and that we would all become one happy family. But both of us knew it would take time.

And it did. For more than twenty years I called him Dr. Loyal. I knew he would have loved it if I had called him Dad, and in retrospect I wish I had. But at the time I just couldn't. Although we became very close, it wasn't until my own daughter was born that I finally dropped his formal title. When Patti was too young to say "Grandpa," she called him Bapa—and so did I.

He detested the name Loyal, but I always thought it suited him perfectly, for he was nothing if not loyal—to his family, his students, his profession, his patients, and above all, to his values. He was the strong, silent type, reserved and sometimes gruff on the outside, but warm and tenderhearted underneath. Most people never saw his tender side—the man who wrote poetry and slipped it under my door, or who sent me silly limericks when I was in college.

As a teacher, he was known for being strict. And so, for example, his students were always required to wear a tie and jacket to class. He thought that if you were going to be a doctor, you should dress like one. Even today, when people talk about him, they often say that Loyal Davis was a tough teacher and a hard man to work for. But he made his students stretch to heights they hadn't always known they could reach.

He was a stickler about punctuality. When he said six o'clock, he didn't mean two minutes after six. If you were late, he'd let you know. When I started going out at night, I always had a curfew. But although he was a strict father, he was always fair. He was, I felt, what a real father ought to be.

After Bethesda, Chicago was a whole new world for me, and the Davis household was stimulating and challenging. My father loved to discuss serious topics, and I can remember more than one conversation about whether there was really such a thing as a human soul. I don't remember our answers, but I recall that, unlike my mother, Loyal wasn't religious.

I once asked him what happiness was. "Nancy," he said, "the answer to that question is almost twenty-five centuries old, and it's basically what the Greeks said. Happiness is the pursuit of excellence in all aspects of one's life."

Loyal Davis was the classic self-made man, but as I mentioned, I want to correct the impression that he was a rich ultraconservative crusader who turned me, and later Ronnie, into Republicans. I don't doubt that Bapa was both conservative and Republican, but if he had any real interest in politics, I wasn't aware of it. And I know that he didn't influence Ronnie's views. In fact, when Ronnie first decided to go into politics, my father cringed at the prospect of his beloved son-in-law stepping into what he called "a sea of sharks."

It wasn't politics he cared about; it was medicine. He loved his work, and I was thrilled when he finally allowed me to watch him perform an operation. I usually sat up in the gallery, and when he allowed me into the operating room, I felt I had passed the ultimate test. I'm not sure I could have watched any other kind of operation, but brain surgery is so precise, and everything is covered up except for one small area. He would work with tiny nerves that you could barely see.

I was so proud of him. Here was this wonderful, handsome, accomplished man—and he was my father!

My parents had a wonderful marriage, despite—or perhaps because of—their obvious differences. My father was tall and dark; my mother was short and blond. He was a Republican; she was a Democrat. He was often severe; she was always laughing. He was an only child; she came from a large family. He was reserved; she knew everybody.

They complemented each other beautifully. I once returned home from college with an assignment to learn several sonnets by Shelley and Keats. My father sent me upstairs for my English literature textbook, and when I came down again, Mother was doing a little soft-shoe dance, reciting a rhyme about Mr. Sheets and Mr. Kelly.

When my parents had company, she would tell the latest off-color joke. If I was in the room, she would turn to me and say, "Nancy, would you go to the kitchen and bring me an apple?" It took me quite a while to realize that this was a ruse to get me out of there until she had finished the joke. She ate a lot of apples in those years!

At first Mother wasn't accepted by the other doctors' wives in Chicago. I once found her crying in her bedroom because she'd overheard another woman make a disparaging remark about this *actress* who had married that nice, handsome, highly eligible doctor. In the circles my father moved in, actresses were not looked on very kindly.

I had never seen my mother as a wife before, but she was terrific at it. She cared for her husband, she expanded his social circle—she helped him in every possible way. "Now, Nancy," she used to say, "when you get married, be sure to get up and have breakfast with your husband in the morning. Because if you don't, you can be sure that some other woman who lives around the corner will be perfectly happy to do so."

Within a year, she knew more people in Chicago than he did. She loosened him up, introduced him to her friends, and exposed him to the arts. He, in turn, provided her with a security she had never known.

She did a lot of charity work. For twenty-five years she was chairman of the women's division of the Chicago Community Fund. She was involved in the Art Institute, helped set up the Passavant Hospital gift shop, and even organized an annual musical skit for my father's students. During the war, when he was overseas, she started a servicemen's center. There was a navy yard nearby, and when she learned that some of these young kids were being picked up by prostitutes and infected with venereal diseases, she had herself sworn in as a policewoman so she could go out on the streets of Chicago and protect those boys.

Mother gave up her career when she got married, but she didn't stop working. Chicago was the capital of the radio soap operas, and Mother was part of an NBC drama called *Betty & Bob,* in which she played two completely different roles: Bob's mother, a society grande dame, and Gardenia, the black maid. (In one episode, Bob's mother came to the door and Gardenia opened it to let her in.) She was also the only woman to appear on *The Amos and Andy Show.*

She worked at WGN and at WBBM, which is where I first met Mike Wallace, who was doing radio in Chicago then. In 1987, when Mother died, Mike published a moving column in the *Washington Post* in which he described how my interest in the drug program stemmed from the values that Mother had embodied.

All through these years, my mother kept in touch with her ex-husband and with Patsy, his new wife. Although I never had much of a relationship with my birth father, I did visit him a few times during my adolescence. He couldn't relate to me as a very young child, but as I grew older and became more of a person, he'd want

to see me more. He once made a disparaging remark about Mother—
I no longer recall what it was—which enraged me to the point
where I screamed at him that I wanted to leave. He got upset and
locked me in the bathroom. I was terrified, and I suddenly felt as
if I were with strangers.

Patsy felt terrible and wrote a letter of apology to Mother, but
there were no more visits. And to this day I can't stand to be in a
locked room. Years later, when Ronnie and I were staying in a hotel
suite during a campaign trip, I had to ask him to unlock the bedroom
door. He couldn't understand why, until I explained that the memory of being locked in that bathroom had never entirely disappeared.

Soon after my mother remarried, we moved to the fourteenth floor
of a lovely apartment building on Lake Shore Drive. One of our
neighbors was a retired judge, and a few years later, in the elevator,
I asked him, "How can I go about getting adopted?"

The judge called my mother, and she must have approved because
he volunteered to help me with the paperwork. I already knew that
according to Illinois law, a child who reached the age of fourteen
could make her own decision on matters of adoption. By then there
was no longer any question in my mind, and I finally made it official
by going to see Kenneth Robbins in New York.

He came with my grandmother to meet me under the clock at the
Biltmore Hotel. I explained what I wanted to do, and they agreed,
reluctantly. I'm sure it hurt my grandmother terribly.

When Kenneth Robbins signed the papers, I sent a wire to Chicago to tell my family that the adoption had gone through. I didn't
have much experience with telegrams, but I knew they had to be
brief. This one read: HI DAD.

Whenever Mother's old friends from the theater passed through
town, they would stay with us. When I came home from school in
the afternoon, it wasn't unusual to find Mary Martin in the living
room, or Spencer Tracy reading the newspaper, or the breathtaking
Lillian Gish curled up on the sofa, talking with Mother. Spencer
Tracy stayed with us so often that he became practically a member
of the family.

Spence was the most charming man I have ever known. He suffered from insomnia, and when I came home late from a date or a night out with friends, he would be up, eager to have a long talk. But he was also very shy. There are actors who will enter a room and immediately take possession of it, but not Spence. He'd always head for a corner and stay there.

He hated serious and high-toned discussions about dramatic technique, and he regarded the "method" actors as pretentious. His own approach was quite simple. When I told him I was thinking of a career in the theater, his advice was "Just know your lines and don't bump into the furniture."

Katharine Hepburn was another regular visitor. When I told her I wanted to be an actress, she sent me a long letter warning me that acting was a very difficult profession and that I had seen only the glamorous parts. Mother's friends were stars, she reminded me, but most would-be actresses ended up as waitresses and receptionists. It was sobering advice, but I wasn't put off.

When I moved to New York in 1946, Kate often invited me to her house, which was just around the corner from my apartment. That was the only place I ever saw her because she had a terrible aversion to going out. She once explained to me in that distinctive Hepburn voice that even going to dinner in a restaurant would make her unbearably nervous and sick to her stomach.

Kate and I were close for years, but something happened to our friendship around the time Spence died, in 1967. Suddenly it just ended, and to this day I don't understand why. I made several attempts to revive our relationship but got nowhere. Once, when I called her on the phone, she said, "I'm terribly busy, and besides, I don't know what we'd have to talk about. After all, you're a staunch Republican and I'm a staunch Democrat."

"What difference does *that* make?" I replied. "I have lots of friends who are Democrats. I even married one!"

I still feel bad about it, but I'm glad she was part of my life, and I have great admiration for her.

Of all my mother's show business friends, we were closest to Walter and Nan Huston. Walter is probably best remembered today for his role as the old man in *The Treasure of the Sierra Madre,* starring Humphrey Bogart, and directed by his son, John Huston.

To me, he was Uncle Walter. When I was a teenager we spent a good part of several summers at his magnificent vacation home on Lake Arrowhead in the San Bernardino mountains. After dinner, we would gather in the living room, where Uncle Walter would read to us.

One summer we wrote and produced our own little home movie. There I was, *acting*—and with real professionals like Mother, Uncle Walter, and Nan (who had played Desdemona to Uncle Walter's Othello on Broadway). My brother, Dick, was behind the camera, and Uncle Walter and I were the stars.

My father spent most of that summer working on a biography of John B. Murphy, the physician who had attended Theodore Roosevelt when Roosevelt was shot in 1912.

"Loyal," said Uncle Walter, "tell me about the day that Roosevelt was shot."

"But you've already read the manuscript," my father said.

"I know," said Walter. "But I'd still like to hear about it."

After my father described the scene, Uncle Walter said, "Loyal, go back and write it down exactly the way you just told it. The version you wrote is too stiff."

My father ended up rewriting the entire book. He didn't take criticism easily, but Walter Huston was his dearest friend.

One weekend, when I was fifteen, Joshua Logan, the great director, drove up to Lake Arrowhead to try to interest Uncle Walter in a musical comedy called *Knickerbocker Holiday*. What interested *me* about the visit was that Logan had brought along his friend Jimmy Stewart. I developed an instant crush on this tall, handsome man with that boyish charm, a charm so many sophisticated Hollywood women found irresistible. That night after dinner, when we were seated outside under the stars, he took out his accordion and sang "Judy," and I almost fainted.

The next day we sat around the pool while Josh read the script of *Knickerbocker Holiday*. Uncle Walter promised to consider it. Later, he asked each of us for our opinion. I was thrilled to be asked, and I said, "Oh, Uncle Walter, I wouldn't do that play. It would be a big mistake."

I remember feeling very important that I had been consulted. And then, without a word to me, he signed up for the part.

Need I add that *Knickerbocker Holiday* became a Broadway hit?

Or that Brooks Atkinson wrote that the decision to cast Walter Huston in the lead role was "a stroke of genius"?

Or that Uncle Walter's rendition of "September Song" became a classic of musical theater?

So much for *my* opinion!

Years later, Uncle Walter sent me a copy of a book that was made of *Knickerbocker Holiday,* inscribed, *To Nancy, who advised me to do this play?*

As Jimmy was leaving, he asked me to come down to Hollywood to go dancing at the Palladium. My heart was pounding, but my father said no, and that ended it. (Much as I love him, I found out years later that Jimmy Stewart is just about the worst dancer I know.)

My father was secretly infuriated that Walter made so much money as an actor. Loyal earned a good living, but even the most successful surgeon made only a fraction of what a Hollywood or Broadway star was paid. After years of training, my father was performing delicate brain surgery and saving lives. Sometimes he worked for nothing, and at most he received a fee of five hundred dollars. As my father saw it, Uncle Walter was being paid thousands of dollars simply to recite lines that somebody else had written. How difficult could *that* be?

One day, when Mother and Nan had gone off to do some shopping in Los Angeles, Uncle Walter suggested that we record a radio play to surprise the girls when they got back. My father jumped at the idea. With Uncle Walter directing, my father and I recorded a scene from *Dodsworth,* a play that Walter and Nan had both starred in. Then we moved on to *Othello,* with my father as Iago, myself as Desdemona, and Uncle Walter in the title role.

Uncle Walter in action was amazing to see. Dressed in his usual summer outfit—a bathing suit and an old T-shirt—he *became* Othello before our eyes, transforming himself into a dark-skinned nobleman with a gold earring. My father had done well enough in *Dodsworth,* but in *Othello* he made the mistake of trying to compete with Uncle Walter, and he sounded ridiculous.

The next evening we played the tape for Nan and Mother. *Dods-worth* was a hit, but just as I feared, *Othello* was a disaster. Next to Othello, Desdemona sounded like a child, while my father came off like a pompous amateur. Nan and Mother started teasing my father and accused him of hamming it up, but Uncle Walter didn't say a word.

Several days later, the two men were sitting out on the patio before dinner when Uncle Walter suddenly put his hand on my father's knee and said, "Kid, I remember sitting in the operating theater in Chicago and watching you work. And you know what I thought? *That* doesn't look so tough!"

Uncle Walter had known all along what was on my father's mind, and the tactful and sensitive way he responded to my father's feelings made a great impression on me.

I can't remember a time when I wasn't interested in the theater, and in school my main interest was drama. I was only an average student at Girls' Latin School in Chicago, but I was class president two or three times, and I acted in all the school plays.

In my senior year, I played the lead in *First Lady*, by George S. Kaufman. I don't recall much about the story, but I do remember that I wore a black dress with a white collar, and that when my classmates forgot their lines, I was able to jump in and start talking until we got back on track. Everyone was terribly impressed—including me.

After high school, I went to Smith College, where I majored in English and drama—and boys.

During this time I had my first serious boyfriend. We met in Chicago, where I had a modest coming-out party during Christmas vacation of my freshman year. It was an afternoon tea dance, and I wore a white gown with silver bands.

The party was scheduled to begin at four o'clock, but not everybody was as punctual as my father, and at four, the place was still empty. I waited, wondering if anybody was going to show up.

The first guest to arrive was a Princeton student named Frank Birney. (The Princeton Triangle Show was in town, and to be sure there would be enough eligible men, Mother invited the entire cast.) Frank must have sensed my discomfort, because he went through the receiving line over and over, each time using a different voice and pretending to be somebody else. He had us all laughing, and he put me at ease until the other guests arrived.

Frank was charming, funny, and bright, and when I returned to Smith, we started seeing each other. I went to a few football games and dances at Princeton, and he came to Smith for parties. Sometimes we'd meet in New York, under the clock in the lobby of the Biltmore Hotel, for a weekend in the city. But don't let that "weekend" business fool you. I stayed on the girls-only floor of the hotel, where men were not allowed—ever. There was even a chaperone to enforce the rules.

Shortly after Pearl Harbor, Frank was planning to go to New York. He must have been late, because he ran across the tracks to catch his train, not realizing how fast that train was moving. The engineer pulled so hard on the emergency brake that he broke it, but he couldn't stop the train and Frank was killed instantly.

It was the first time that anybody I was close to had died, and it was a tremendous shock. My roommate forced me to go out and take long, brisk walks. Frank and I had skirted around the subject of marriage, and even though I doubt it would have worked out, he was a dear friend and I felt a great loss. His mother gave me his cigarette case as a memento—a silver case I had given him the previous Christmas with his name engraved on it. He had been carrying that case when he was killed, and I still have it.

I acted in several plays at Smith, but my real experience in the theater came during summer vacations, when I worked as an apprentice in the old summer stock theaters of New England. Apprentices did everything: We ran errands, cleaned the dressing rooms, painted scenery, sold tickets. Sometimes we even got to act. But mostly we learned, by sitting in on rehearsals and watching the actors and directors. Stock companies were a terrific place to learn your craft, and I feel sorry for today's younger actors who don't have these opportunities.

Being an apprentice was far from glamorous. Sometimes we were relegated to a separate section of the hotel dining room and weren't even entitled to the same food as the other guests. But then, acting wasn't everybody's idea of respectable work. One evening, as I was rushing over to the tiny run-down theater across from the hotel, an elderly woman stopped me and said, "My dear, I hope you won't let this experience ruin you for the rest of your life."

Only once in those summers did I actually appear on stage, in a play with Diana Barrymore. I played the maid who announced, "Madam, dinner is served." It wasn't much of a part, but I made sure to follow Spence's advice: I knew my line and I didn't bump into the furniture.

My first professional role came after the war, when Mother's old friend Zasu Pitts offered me a part in a play called *Ramshackle Inn*. I joined the cast in Detroit, replacing an actress who had dropped out. It was a tiny role—that of a girl who is kept in the attic during the entire play, except for one brief moment when she runs down the stairs and says about three lines before they whisk her right back up again. But it was a start!

This wouldn't be the last time that I benefited from Mother's network of friends in show business. Many children of well-known individuals, including my own children, are embarrassed about using contacts that their parents have made. But all a contact can do is open that first door. The rest is up to you.

I don't think I would have had much work as a stage actress if it hadn't been for Mother. There was just too much competition, and I didn't have the drive that Mother had.

Ramshackle Inn eventually wound up in New York, and when our run was over, I decided to say there. I found a fourth-floor walkup at 409 East Fifty-first Street, not far from several of Mother's friends: Walter and Nan Huston lived around the corner, Kate Hepburn was on East Forty-ninth, and Lillian Gish was up on Fifty-seventh. Sometimes I would watch Spence rehearse for a play he was opening in, *The Rugged Path*. He was nervous about returning to the stage, but, as always, he was excellent.

Mother's friends looked out for me and invited me to their houses for dinner, so I was rarely alone. Besides, New York in the 1940s was an exciting place for a career girl to be. I felt safe, and I wasn't afraid to walk home late at night from the theater. The crosstown bus went across Fiftieth Street, and I walked a block uptown to my apartment.

By now I had joined the ranks of unemployed actors, going from one audition to the next, looking for work. These were known as cattle calls, and I hated them!

If you were lucky enough to land a part, for the first five days of rehearsal you were on trial. When I was starting out, actors were routinely fired without pay during the trial period.

It happened to me once. On the third day of rehearsal, the director took my arm and led me out through the stage door and into the alley. "I'm sorry to tell you this," he said, "but it's just not working. You aren't right for the part and we'll have to let you go."

I was so humiliated that I couldn't make myself go back inside to face the rest of the cast. Fighting back tears, I asked the director if he would please go in and pick up my coat and purse while I waited in the alley.

This was the first time in my life that I had ever been fired, and I took it very badly. "It's just not working," the director had said, but I believed he was simply being kind. What he was obviously *thinking* was, You're no good. What ever made you think you were an actress?

Or so I imagined. It's a terrible blow to your ego, and it helps when your friends describe their own firings and rejections—as mine did.

Eventually I appeared in *Lute Song,* a musical about the Orient starring Mary Martin and Yul Brynner, directed by John Houseman. After a long and unproductive series of tryouts, I was astonished to hear those magic words "You've got the part." "You look like you could be Chinese," said the producer. Nobody had ever told me *that* before. But Mary Martin and my mother were old friends.

It was Yul's first major role, and all the girls were swooning over him—except me. And yes, in those days Yul Brynner had hair.

Years later I learned that John Houseman had intended to let me go, and that Mary had intervened to save my job. As John told the story in his memoirs, *Lute Song* included "the usual nepotistic casting. . . . At Mary's behest, to play the princess's flower maiden, we engaged a pink-cheeked, attractive but awkward and amateurish virgin by the name of Nancy Davis."

I've always chosen to believe that John meant that as a compliment!

Lute Song was my first and only Broadway role, and opening night was terrifying and thrilling. My parents came in from Chicago, and following the time-honored tradition, the entire cast went to Sardi's for a party. The reviews were good enough to keep *Lute Song* at the Plymouth Theater for six months.

One fall evening, Mother called to say, "Nancy, if you hear from a man who tells you he's Clark Gable, be sure not to say, 'Sure, and I'm Greta Garbo.' It could very well *be* Clark Gable."

Gable was coming to New York and Spence had given him my number. Then, nervous that he hadn't done the right thing, he called Mother and told her that "The King" might be calling me.

I wasn't holding my breath—it was hard to imagine Clark Gable climbing three flights of stairs in an ordinary brownstone to call on an unknown actress. After the release of *Gone With the Wind* he was the most popular actor in Hollywood, which made him just about the most glamorous and desirable man in the entire world. But he did call and invited me to dinner!

I had met famous actors before, but Gable was in a category all his own. He was so handsome, and he had that intangible quality called charisma.

He was there for a week, and we went out every day and night—to baseball games during the afternoon and a play or whatever at night. It was my first experience with somebody that famous; there were times when we had to have police protection to get in and out of theaters and World Series games. When we went to the theater, the audience refused to sit down until Clark acknowledged them with a wave. But he never signed autographs, and I believe that, like Spence, he was never entirely comfortable with stardom.

He had a quality that good courtesans also have—when he was with you, he was really *with* you. One night he took me to a party he had promised to go to, and I was afraid I'd be left standing in a corner while Clark talked to dozens of beautiful actresses and models. But when we arrived, he never took his eyes off me; he made me feel I was the most important person in that room.

Clark was sexy, handsome, and affectionate, but I found him less the seducer he was reputed to be than a kind, romantic, and fun-loving man. He sent me flowers and we held hands, but I think that in his case the lover image had been so built up that it was a relief for him to be with someone like me, who made no demands on him.

We usually ended up at the Stork Club, which was the place to go in those days. Each time we went, a flood of women just happened to walk by our table on the way to the powder room! When we got up to dance, I never knew I had so many friends. "Nancy! How nice to see you!" And then, of course, I had to introduce them to my date.

When you spend that much time with Clark Gable, people notice. The gossip columnists were busy, but although Clark and I were more than casual friends, our relationship never developed into a big romance. But there was enough in the papers to prompt a call from Mother, who asked, "Nancy, what exactly is going on with you two?"

I replied that there wasn't much to tell, but I'm not sure she believed me.

We were together only a week, but the fan magazines had a field day. I still have one of the clippings, which asked, in the style typical of those publications, "Has something at last happened to Clark Gable, something in the form of a slim, brown-eyed beauty named Nancy Davis—that is changing the fitful pattern of his romantic life? Has he, in other words, finally found the Gable woman, for whom he is more than willing to give up the Gable women? The answer seems to be yes—even though, if it is a love at all, it is so far a love in hiding."

Deep in hiding, I would have said. But perhaps I missed some of the signals he was sending out. He lived in Encino, and he referred to his house as a ranch. One night, at dinner, he asked me, "How would you feel about living on a ranch?"

I mumbled something foolish like "Gee, I don't know, I never have." But I have often looked back at that moment and wondered: Was Clark Gable sounding me out about a possible future together? And if so, how should I have responded? I wasn't in love with him, but if we had seen more of each other, I might have been. I was certainly taken by his attentiveness and his kindness, and by his modesty. It just wasn't what you would have expected from such a star.

After *Lute Song,* I played in two more productions with Zasu Pitts and did a little television. All I remember from my first TV show was that I had to wear green makeup and black lipstick! TV was still very new, and you had to wear some pretty strange colors if you wanted to look good on those early, primitive black-and-white sets.

I played in a TV production of *Ramshackle Inn,* again with Zasu, which was followed by a minor drama called *Broken Dishes.* I don't remember much about that one, except that it led to the biggest career break in my life. Somebody from Metro-Goldwyn-Mayer saw me in *Broken Dishes* and suggested to my agent that I come out to Hollywood and make a screen test.

As soon as Mother heard the news she called Spence, who called George Cukor to ask him to direct my test. Well, you couldn't ask for better than that. George was one of the top directors in Hollywood and was known for being especially good at working with women. Howard Keel assisted in the test, and George Folsey, one of the top cameramen, photographed the scene.

Soon I heard from my agent that I had been offered the standard beginner's contract: seven years with options. In other words, the studio could terminate the relationship at any point, but I was locked in. They paid me $250 a week for the studio year, which consisted of forty weeks, with twelve vacation weeks.

I was beside myself with excitement. Not only was Metro the greatest studio in Hollywood, but I was finally earning a regular paycheck, which meant that I would no longer have to accept money from my parents. Until then, my family had helped support me, just as, years later, Ronnie and I helped support our son, Ron, during the early stages of his career.

Joining Metro was like walking into a dream world. In the MGM commissary I'd see stars like Fred Astaire, Lana Turner, June Allyson, Judy Garland, Elizabeth Taylor, Deborah Kerr, Esther Williams, Robert Taylor, Van Johnson, Gene Kelly, and Frank Sinatra. You could get a severe case of insecurity when you came into makeup in the morning and found yourself seated between Elizabeth Taylor and Ava Gardner.

Louis B. Mayer was head of MGM at the time, and when he threw a party, the stars would all be there. Years later, during Ronnie's second term as president, I began house-hunting in Los Angeles for a place to live when we returned to California. One of the homes I was shown had belonged to Mr. Mayer, and I had been looking forward to seeing it again after almost forty years. But when I walked inside, I couldn't shake the feeling that something was missing. Without Loretta Young, Vivien Leigh, and all the others in their finery, and Judy Garland providing the entertainment, that once-magnificent living room seemed empty and depressing.

I never became a big star, but I was far more successful in films than I had ever been in the theater. In the theater, you had to project "big," and exaggerate to the point where even the most subtle gesture or expression could be seen and understood in the very last row. In pictures you could play "small" and still be effective. Another thing I liked about pictures was that you would work on a scene over and over again, until it was as good as it could possibly be.

And I preferred the studio system to the anxiety of looking for work in New York. Metro was like an intimate little city, and even, at times, a large, extended family. Time and again, older and more established performers went out of their way to be supportive and encouraging to newcomers.

Ava Gardner, who was so beautiful she took my breath away, came up to me at a newsstand on the Metro lot. She wasn't wearing any makeup, but even so, her beauty was radiant. She told me that she had just seen one of my films, and she thought it was excellent. I was a nobody, and she certainly didn't have to do that. But this wasn't unusual; in those days, at least, it seemed that the bigger the star, the nicer and more down-to-earth he or she was.

I don't mean to suggest that Metro was free of troubles. Some of the stars had serious conflicts with the studio, and everybody knew when Judy Garland was replaced by Betty Hutton during the shooting of *Annie Get Your Gun.* But at that time nobody realized that Judy was addicted to pills.

As a newcomer at Metro, I was nervous and gullible. On my first day on the set of my first picture, Bill Tuttle, the head makeup man, came by to introduce himself. "We'll have to do something about those eyes," he said. "They're obviously too big for pictures." He was joking, of course, but I didn't know that. So for the rest of the day I went around with my eyes half-shut, trying to make them look smaller.

Finally, George Folsey took me aside and said, "Nancy, what's the matter with your eyes?" When I told him what Bill Tuttle had said, I thought George would never stop laughing. "Too big for pictures?" he repeated. "Believe me, Nancy, there's no such thing."

But on that first day, I was so anxious and confused that I didn't know *what* to believe.

I made about a dozen pictures in all, most of them at Metro before I was married. I loved the work, although it was a lot less glamorous than most people think. Although I knew actors who could stay up half the night at parties, most of us went to bed early in order to be up in time for an early-morning call.

I had always heard stories about the wild side of Hollywood, but I never saw much evidence of it—the heavy drinking, the drugs, promiscuity, and all the rest. I'm not so naïve as to think that such things never went on; they do in every town. But it wasn't part of my life. I wasn't a starlet either on or off the screen, and nobody ever chased me around the casting couch. I dated working actors or writers, and I was attracted to slightly older men with a sense of humor. I was always interested in falling in love with a nice man and getting married, and I also never minded spending evenings alone.

Actors tend to play the roles they're suited for, and unlike many young actresses, I just wasn't the big-bosomed sweater-girl type. As a result, I was usually asked to play a young mother or a pregnant woman.

Most of my films are best forgotten, but two or three still stand out in my mind. When Dore Schary came over to Metro, one of the first pictures he made was *The Next Voice You Hear,* in which I starred with Jim Whitmore. The director was Wild Bill Wellman, who told me when we met that he hated to direct women—as if I weren't nervous enough! But we ended up as close friends.

This was my first starring role, and I believe it was also the first time a character in a movie had ever been visibly pregnant on the screen. Until then you just wore a smock to indicate your condition. But because this picture was supposed to be highly realistic, I was fitted with a special pregnancy pad. I wore no makeup and had no hairdresser. When Sydney Guilaroff, head of the hairdressing department at Metro, came to the set the first day to wish me luck, Wellman, thinking he was there to comb my hair, threw him off the set.

The Next Voice You Hear had its premiere at Radio City Music Hall in New York in 1950, and the studio sent me East to promote it. Although it was only my second picture, my name was listed above the title! After years of minor roles in the theater, it was a great thrill to see NANCY DAVIS on that grand marquee, wrapping halfway around the theater. That picture brought me my first fan letter, and I was so proud of it that I pinned it to my dress and wore it around the studio all day.

I made a few other pictures, including *Night into Morning,* which I always thought was my best, and *Donovan's Brain,* a science-fiction story that still appears from time to time on late-night television. I also had a small part in *East Side, West Side,* starring Ava Gardner, Cyd Charisse, Van Heflin, James Mason, and Barbara Stanwyck. Barbara was a very big star, and I was nervous about working with her. Like Mary Martin, she was known as a real pro who always knew her lines—and who expected you to know yours. We had one long scene together, in which I had all the lines, and when I got my part right on the first take, the crew broke into applause and Barbara congratulated me. That was probably my greatest moment in pictures—I felt I had really passed the test.

Looking back on that film, I didn't do too badly, and I think I could have gone on and made a good career for myself. But after I met Ronnie, developing a career was no longer important to me.

For me, *East Side, West Side* was significant in one other respect. While we were shooting it, Mervyn LeRoy, our director and an old family friend, introduced me to an actor over at Warner Brothers whose name was Ronald Reagan.

6

Ronnie

I'VE said it before and I'll say it once again: My life didn't really begin until I met Ronnie.

This is how it happened.

One evening in the fall of 1949, I was in my apartment, reading one of the Hollywood papers, when I noticed a name—*my* name— in a list of Communist sympathizers in Hollywood. In those days I didn't know much about politics, but I knew that my name did not belong on that list. In New York I had also been mistaken for another Nancy Davis and had received her mail and even some of her phone calls. But it's not exactly an uncommon name.

When I came to Mervyn LeRoy with my problem, he had the studio arrange for an item to appear in Louella Parsons's widely read gossip column in the *Examiner,* pointing out that the Nancy Davis who was listed in the paper was not the actress who was under contract to Metro.

"Feeling any better?" he asked me the next day.

"A little," I said. "But my parents would die if they heard about this. What else can I do?"

"Maybe I should call Ronald Reagan," he said. "This might be something the Guild should look into."

Ronald Reagan was president of the Screen Actors Guild. I had seen some of his pictures, and on screen, at least, he seemed nice and good-looking—someone I thought I'd like to meet.

"Mervyn," I said, "I think that would be a *very* good idea."

"Come to think of it," he said, "you two might really hit it off. I'll have Ron call you."

I spent that evening waiting for the phone to ring. The longer I waited, the more I liked the idea of meeting Ronald Reagan. But he didn't call.

The next morning, Mervyn took me aside to say that he had spoken to Ronald Reagan, who had told him there were at least three other Nancy Davises in Hollywood. "If there's ever a problem," Mervyn said, "the Guild will defend you."

That was reassuring, but it wasn't exactly what I wanted to hear. So I put on a *very* unhappy face. "I'm really worried," I said. "I'd feel a lot better if Mr. Reagan explained it to me himself."

Late that afternoon, the phone rang. "Nancy Davis? This is Ronald Reagan from the Screen Actors Guild. Mervyn LeRoy asked me to look into your problem, and I have some answers for you. If you're free for dinner tonight, perhaps we could talk about it then."

"Well," I stammered, "I think I could manage it."

"How about seven-thirty?" he said. "It can't be a late night, because I have an early call in the morning."

I smiled when he said that. Everyone in Hollywood who went out on a blind date knew enough to mention an early call. If the evening turned out to be a disaster, you had an excuse to end it early.

"Fine," I said. "I have an early call too." (I didn't, but a girl has her pride!)

Two hours later, my first thought when I opened the door was, This is *wonderful.* He looks as good in person as he does on the screen! (That wasn't something you could take for granted in Hollywood.) My visitor was propped up on a cane, and he explained that he had hurt himself in a charity baseball game and had just spent eight weeks in the hospital with a broken leg.

We went to LaRue's, one of the best restaurants on Sunset Strip. In those days, the Strip was still the place to go and to be seen. By the time we sat down to dinner, we had finished discussing the Nancy Davis problem, and my date, who was more familiar than I with the mores of Hollywood, had come up with what he thought was the ideal solution.

"Have the studio change your name," he said. "You would hardly be the first."

He had no way of knowing how long I had waited to be called Nancy Davis, and how much that name meant to me.

"I can't do that," I told him. "Nancy Davis is my *name.*"

I had known Ronald Reagan only ten minutes when he suggested that I change my name. More than two years later, when we came back to this topic, I would be all too happy to change my name—to his.

One of the things I liked about Ronnie right away was that he didn't talk only about himself. I had been out on dates with a number of actors, and all the conversations were pretty much the same: his first picture, his second picture, his most recent picture, his current picture, his next picture.

But this man was different. His world was not limited to himself or his career. He told me about the Guild, and why the actors' union meant so much to him. He talked about his small ranch in the San Fernando Valley, about horses and their bloodlines; he was also a Civil War buff, and he knew a lot about wine.

When he did talk about himself, he was personal without being *too* personal. The whole world knew that he had recently been divorced from Jane Wyman, but he didn't go into details, and I wouldn't have liked him if he had. To this day Ronnie has never talked about his divorce to anyone except me, and I respect him for that.

He had a wonderful sense of humor, which came out when he told me about his trip to England, where he had recently spent four months making *The Hasty Heart* with Richard Todd and Patricia Neal. Ronnie had hated London. He had arrived to find the worst fog in a hundred years, a fog so thick that it rolled in through the doors and windows of his hotel. To make matters worse, the austerity program meant that no marquees or window displays were lit, and the whole city was gloomy and dark.

He also hated the food; he was served so many brussels sprouts that to this day he refuses to eat them. He finally sent over to "21" in New York for a dozen steaks, but he got to eat only two of them—the others were spoiled by the hotel's poor refrigeration system. "At least that's what they told me," he said with a smile. "But remember, the English were hungry, too!"

As I listened to him, I kept thinking of Mother. Like her, he told funny stories, and he really enjoyed them. When you laughed, he laughed along with you.

But he didn't do *all* the talking. I told him about my parents, and I probably bragged a little about my father's skills as a surgeon. I described our summers at Lake Arrowhead with Uncle Walter.

"Uncle Walter? You mean Walter *Huston*?"

I explained that he had acted on Broadway with Mother, and I told him about the time Uncle Walter was visiting us in Chicago and his son John called to offer him a part in *The Treasure of the Sierra Madre.* John insisted that his father play the role without his false teeth, and I had fond memories of Uncle Walter taking out his upper plate and learning how to talk without his dentures while we all laughed at him.

Ronnie told me that he had been offered a part in that same picture, where he could have played together with Humphrey Bogart and Walter Huston. He was dying to accept, but he was under contract to do *The Voice of the Turtle,* and Warner Brothers, which produced both pictures, made the decision for him. Ronnie regrets it to this day.

As we were finishing dinner, he said that Sophie Tucker was opening at Ciro's that night, together with Xavier Cugat and his band, and suggested that we drive over there "just for the first show."

"Fine," I said. "Just for the first show."

Of course we stayed for both shows, and by the time Sophie Tucker had finished, we had admitted that neither of us really had an early call. It was almost three in the morning when Ronnie brought me home.

I don't know if it was exactly love at first sight, but it was pretty close. We had dinner together the next night. And the night after that. And the one after *that.* For the first month or so we must have gone to every restaurant and nightclub in Los Angeles.

Almost as soon as we started dating, the press began to write about us and to speculate about marriage.

We realized early on that neither of us was the fast-lane type, and so instead of going out every night, we started spending most of our time alone in my apartment, watching movies on television and making popcorn. Sometimes we would spend the evening with Ronnie's close friends Bill and Ardis Holden, who lived in a charming Tudor house in the valley. (Ardis was better known by her stage name, Brenda Marshall.) We also became regulars at Chasen's restaurant, especially on Tuesday nights, when the special was Beef Belmont.

I wish I could report that we saw each other exclusively, and that we couldn't wait to get married. But Ronnie was in no hurry to make a commitment. He had been burned in his first marriage, and the pain went deep. Although we saw each other regularly, he also dated other women.

I remember sitting in the commissary at Metro, eating lunch with some of the other contract actresses, when one of them started talking about a gift that Ronnie had recently given her. That hurt. I didn't have one specific rival, but it did occur to me that perhaps I was just one girl among many.

I also knew that a divorced man needed time before he was ready to marry again. My mother reminded me that Loyal Davis had been badly burned in his first marriage. He had been terrified of making another mistake, and she had had to wait until he was ready.

Ronnie had been so deeply hurt by his divorce that it took a lot of time before he could even consider getting married again. Like most of his generation, he had been brought up to believe that you married once, and that was it. For better or for worse. And if you made a mistake and your marriage wasn't what you hoped it would be, you suffered in silence. No matter what, marriage was forever.

His divorce had come about suddenly, and he was totally unprepared for it. He also had nobody to confide in when it happened: Nobody he knew well had ever been separated from his children. He spent a week or so living with the Holdens, but he was really lost, and he missed the children terribly.

Ronnie took a lot of trips for the Guild. I would drive him to the station, and when the train pulled out, I would run alongside it for a few yards, waving to him. Then I would drive home and start knitting him a pair of argyle socks, feeling very sorry for myself.

Ronnie would stop in Chicago on his way to New York, and Mother would be there to greet him. They had already "met" over the telephone; I called my parents every Sunday, and Ronnie would get on and say hello. Just as I expected, Ronnie and Mother hit it off. Before long, my part of the conversation got shorter, while theirs got longer and longer. I soon had the feeling that if anything went wrong between Ronnie and me, he and Mother would be perfectly happy together.

Mostly, they told each other stories. One evening, Ronnie took a chance and told Mother a joke that was more risqué than usual. Although he seemed to have second thoughts along the way, he took a deep breath and plunged ahead. When the punch line was greeted with dead silence instead of Mother's familiar laugh, Ronnie was afraid he had gone too far. A moment later, when Mother still hadn't reacted, Ronnie said, "Hello, Edie? Are you still there?"

Then came a cool, distant voice that he didn't recognize. "To whom were you speaking?"

It was the long-distance operator. The call had been cut off, but before the operator told Ronnie, she had let him finish the story so she could hear the punch line.

Later, Ronnie's only complaint about Mother was that she had ruined one of his favorite jokes. For years, he liked to open his speeches by telling his audience, "I face you today with mixed emotions." Then he would define "mixed emotions" as the feelings a man has as he watches his mother-in-law drive over the cliff in his new Cadillac.

I decided that he was getting serious when he invited me to come with him to his ranch. Eventually I spent a number of Saturdays and Sundays there, which means that I painted a lot of fences. One Monday morning at the studio, the makeup man told me that I was the first actress he had ever worked with who had to have the paint removed before she could get her makeup on. Later, I accused Ronnie of marrying me just to get his fences painted.

But I also remember my disappointment when, driving to the ranch one day, Ronnie said, "You know, you really should buy a house. It would be a terrific investment, and you're just throwing away your money by paying rent."

Well! I had been thinking along the lines of *joint* ownership, and I just about died!

A few weeks later, Ronnie had to drive to San Diego to give a speech, and suddenly, for the first time, he realized that he didn't want to make that drive alone anymore—and that the only person he wanted to share it with was me. (He told me this much later.) I remember being so happy when he asked me to go with him.

Eventually he invited me to the ranch with his children, and I began to believe that we really would get married. By then we were spending most of our time together, but we tried to downplay our romance because of the press. Still, we were written about all the time, and I still have the clippings in my scrapbook. A clipping from March 1951: "Another date, this time for dinner, at Hollywood's Restaurant LaRue, added fuel to the fires of romantic gossip raging around Ronald Reagan and Nancy Davis. Their Movieland friends expect announcement of their marriage any day now." (In fact, we got married a year later.)

THE NEXT MRS. REAGAN? a headline read, and the article went on to say, "Nobody's seen an engagement ring, but Ronnie is wearing his heart on his sleeve, and there's a twenty-karat sparkle in Nancy Davis's eye."

And in *Modern Screen*: "Don't look now, but here comes the bride. Nobody's going to do a double-take when Ronnie and Nancy walk down the aisle. They've had that 'about to be married' look for over a year."

And another, "Reagan never shouts from rooftops. . . . He keeps out of the columns. . . . But one look at him and Nancy Davis gives the story away."

The hounding bothered Ronnie because he'd gone through so much of it with his first marriage and divorce. Every time we went out, the press was there, asking, "When are you going to get married?"

Ronnie had recently bought a larger ranch near Lake Malibu, and on Saturday mornings we'd pile Maureen and Michael into the car, together with their friends, and drive up for the day. Maureen and Michael lived with their mother, and Ronnie would often drive over to Jane's big house on Beverly Glen to see them—especially on holidays. Sometimes he'd ask me to come along, and I did, although this wasn't exactly my idea of pure joy. Jane was perfectly nice to me, but these visits were awkward. Not only had she been married to Ronnie, but she was very much The Star, and it was her house and her children. I felt out of place, and I was a little in awe of her.

I could see that Jane knew how to play on Ronnie's good nature. She had convinced him that he shouldn't get married again until she did. It took me a little time, but I managed to unconvince him.

Around the end of 1951, he told me that it wasn't so much that he hungered for someone to love him, but that he really missed having somebody to love. When I heard that, I knew he had recovered from the trauma of the divorce.

In previous years I had returned home to spend Christmas with my family in Chicago, but in 1951 I stayed in Los Angeles to be with Ronnie. We had been going together for two years, and we were so happy and comfortable together—he with me, and I with him. I had dated a number of men, and I knew Ronnie was the right one for me. He was all I had ever wanted in a man, and more, and he was different from anyone I had ever known.

Even then, Ronnie could see that I was totally supportive of him, and that he could trust me. Ronnie's interest in the Guild and in politics had been a source of irritation in his first marriage, and Jane had said publicly that she was bored by all of his talking. But I *loved* to listen to him talk, and I let him know it.

That Christmas, Ronnie brought over a small tree for my apartment, and on Christmas Eve I finally got up the courage to ask him what was, for me, a very bold question: "Do you want me to wait for you?"

And he said, "Yes, I do."

Before long, marriage just was inevitable.

He wanted to be with me all the time, but he still hesitated to get married. The press continued to write about us. I felt the pressure and was more than ready to move things along. And so a few weeks after Christmas, I told Ronnie that I had asked my agent to get me a play in New York.

We announced our engagement on February 21, 1952, and planned the wedding for early March. The columnist Louella Parsons wrote, "The long-expected marriage of Nancy Davis and Ronald Reagan has now been set for early next month." We were thrilled, and so were our parents. But Ronnie still wanted to keep things low-key. We had already agreed on a very small wedding, with absolutely no press. I would have preferred a bigger one, with all our friends, but I understood how Ronnie felt, and if he thought a private ceremony was more appropriate, that was okay with me. By then we felt we were already married, and it was time to make it official.

One evening, Ronnie and Bill Holden were sitting together at a meeting of the Motion Picture Industry Council when Ronnie scribbled a note to Bill: "To hell with this. How would you like to be the best man when I marry Nancy?"

"It's about time!" was Bill's response, echoing our own attitude. Whereupon they both stood up and left the room without a word of explanation.

We were married very simply, on March 4, 1952, at the Little Brown Church in the Valley. We didn't invite anybody—no press, no family, no fuss. Our only witnesses were Ardis, who was the matron of honor, and Bill, our best man. After the ceremony, we went back to the Holdens' for wedding cake and dinner. Bill had arranged for a photographer, and our wedding picture ran everywhere. Bill and Ardis had offered to have a reception for us, which in retrospect I wish we had done. But again, Ronnie wanted to avoid publicity.

For the wedding, Ronnie gave me a bouquet of flowers, and I wore a gray wool suit with a white collar and a small flowered hat with a veil. I still have my wedding suit, which turned up again in the fall of 1988, as I was unpacking boxes in our new house in Los Angeles. It didn't look bad, either, and it still fit! I also have the wedding bouquet, and of course I saved the plastic bride and groom from the top of the cake.

I spent the entire day in a happy daze and didn't notice that Bill and Ardis had been fighting and weren't speaking to each other. I was so blissfully unaware that I hadn't even seen that they were sitting on opposite sides of the church! Nor can I remember hearing the minister say, "I pronounce you man and wife."

All I recall is Bill coming up to ask, "Can I kiss the bride?"

"Not yet," I replied. "It's too soon."

He laughed. "No, it's not!" and he kissed me. But I don't remember Ronnie kissing me, and I don't recall either of us saying "I do." Ronnie swore to me that it all happened, and that we really were married.

We spent the night at the Old Mission Inn in Riverside, and I still remember standing there and feeling so excited when Ronnie signed the register "Mr. and Mrs. Ronald Reagan." The next day we drove to Phoenix, where my parents met us for a happy celebration. When we got to our room at the Biltmore Hotel in Phoenix, where I had been going for years with my parents during Easter vacation, I picked up the phone and called room service.

"This is Mrs. Ronald Reagan," I said proudly, using my new name for the first time.

When the voice at the other end said, "Nancy, how *are* you?" I was absolutely crushed! Ronnie said I suddenly looked as if I were twelve years old again.

When we got engaged, Ronnie had called my father in Chicago to say we wanted to spend our lives together and to explain why we wanted a quiet ceremony. But for years afterward I teased him that I missed out on the proposal of my dreams. I had envisioned that Ronnie would take me out in a canoe as the sun was setting and would strum a ukulele as I lay back, trailing my fingers in the water, the way they used to do in the old movies I saw as a little girl.

Twenty-five years later, on our silver anniversary, he gave me a canoe called *Tru Luv* and took me out on the little lake at our ranch.

"I didn't bring a ukulele," he said. "So would it be all right if I just hummed?"

I know it sounds unbelievably corny, but I loved it.

We were so happy on our honeymoon, but the first year of our marriage was difficult. During that year we had our first child, Patti, who was born—go ahead and count—a bit precipitously but very joyfully, on October 22, 1952. I didn't know much about being a parent, and I was an insecure mother. Then too, Ronnie's career in Hollywood had trickled to a standstill; he just wasn't offered any good parts. I had said I wouldn't be a working wife and mother, but I went back to work and made some films because we needed the money. I'll get into these and other matters shortly, but although the course of our lives together hasn't always been smooth, I have never doubted for one single instant that Ronnie and I belong together.

7

Ronald Reagan

WHAT is Ronald Reagan really like? We have been married for almost forty years, so I think that makes me an expert.

The secret to Ronald Reagan is that there really is no secret. He is exactly the man he appears to be. The Ronald Reagan you see in public is the same Ronald Reagan I live with.

I realize that is the sort of line that some people will sneer at. After all, some of our recent presidents turned out, in hindsight, to be different men than we thought they were. But I honestly don't believe that will happen with Ronnie. There aren't any dark corners to Ronald Reagan's character that will be revealed twenty years from now, no desperate moments of anguish, indecision, and self-doubt. Of course he has his moods and his disappointments, but on the whole, Ronnie is the most upbeat man I've ever known.

There is also a common assumption that because Ronnie used to be an actor, everything he does must be an act. It's not. Ronald Reagan is not a fraud or a phony. He is what he seems to be. And ever since I've known him, this cynicism about Ronnie's good nature has led people to underestimate him.

I've always known that I am a classic Cancer, but it wasn't until we moved back to California, when a friend sent me an article describing the Aquarian personality, that I realized how closely that description fit Ronnie. "He has no affectation or snobbery," the article said, "and he hates all forms of hypocrisy." And "Aquarians are capable of love, but their version is somewhat impersonal. Much of their energy is likely to go into public life." If Aquarians have a fault, it's that they are "too tranquil, too gentle and kindly in disposition." They are "incapable of petty tyranny." Their attitude toward the world is "kindly and humane." The article even mentioned that Aquarian men are often slow to get married!

I'll come back to some of these traits shortly. But as with most people, the place to begin in understanding Ronald Reagan is with his past—his roots, his parents, and the way he was raised. .

He grew up in Dixon, Illinois, where life was wholesome, where people trusted each other, and nobody locked his door at night. People in Dixon stuck together and helped each other. To this day, Ronnie thinks that's the way it should be, and it's one reason he bristles at the idea of a large, impersonal government that takes care of the things neighbors once did for each other.

Ronnie's father was an alcoholic, which meant that Ronnie and his older brother, Neil, had to become self-reliant more quickly than many other boys. One of Ronnie's most powerful memories is of coming home from school one snowy afternoon when he was eleven and finding his father dead-drunk on the front steps. His mother and his older brother were out, so Ronnie dragged Jack Reagan upstairs, undressed him, and put him to bed. Years later, when he told this story, he said it marked a turning point in his life. He had wanted to go straight to bed and to pretend his father wasn't there. "I wasn't ignorant of his weakness," he wrote. "I don't know at what age I knew what the occasional absences or the loud voices in the night meant, but up till now my mother or my brother handled the situation and I was a child in bed with the privilege of pretending sleep."

Ronnie's mother used to tell the boys that Jack suffered from an illness, and that he couldn't always control himself. "Your father may sometimes say or do things that we don't understand," Nelle said. "He's sick, and he needs our help and love."

Jack had trouble keeping a job, and the family moved around a great deal. Ronnie spent his first five years in Tampico, Illinois; they lived above the general store where Jack worked as a shoe salesman.

From there they moved to Galesburg, where they stayed for two years, and then on to Monmouth; a year after that they returned to Tampico, and the following year they moved to Dixon, where Ronnie stayed until college—although even there Jack had to move his family to a less expensive house after three years.

It's hard to make close friends or to put down roots when you're always moving, and I think this—plus the fact that everybody knew his father was an alcoholic—explains why Ronnie became a loner. Although he loves people, he often seems remote, and he doesn't let anybody get too close. There's a wall around him. He lets me come closer than anyone else, but there are times when even I feel that barrier.

Ronnie's closest friends and advisers have often been disappointed that he keeps this distance, especially when he seems more open and candid with a complete stranger than with the people he sees every day. As president, Ronnie loved to answer some of the thousands of letters that poured in every week, and his replies were invariably warm and personal. Sometimes it's easier with people you don't know.

Ronnie is an affable and gregarious man who enjoys other people, but unlike most of us, he doesn't need them for companionship or approval. As he himself has told me, he seems to need only one other person—me.

Jack Reagan was a Catholic who felt very strongly about prejudice. Ronnie loved to go to the movies as a boy, but when *The Birth of a Nation* came to town in a revival, the Reagan boys were forbidden to see it. "The Klan is the Klan," said Jack, "and a sheet's a sheet, and any man who wears one over his head is a bum."

Ronnie's proudest story about his father is of the time Jack was on the road one winter's night and checked into the only hotel in a small town. "You'll like it here, sir," said the clerk. "We don't permit Jews."

Jack was outraged. "I'm a Catholic," he said, "and if you don't take Jews, I guess you don't want Catholics either." He walked out and spent the night freezing in his car. He soon developed pneumonia, which led to his first heart attack.

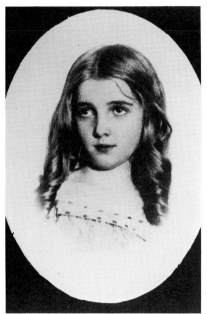

1 and 2. *My mother when she was a girl. I have this picture on my dressing table, along with this one of my father.*

3. *Mother and me with my natural father, who doesn't look too enchanted with me.*

4. *Mother and me with her father, who died not long after this picture was taken.*

5. Mother and me in New York shortly after I was born.

6. At the beach with Mother. The times when we could be together— when she had some time off—were few.

7. *With Charlotte and Loyal. I had lost my two front teeth.*

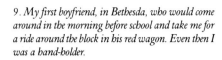

9. *My first boyfriend, in Bethesda, who would come around in the morning before school and take me for a ride around the block in his red wagon. Even then I was a hand-holder.*

8. Top left: *Serving tea to my doll in Bethesda. Little did I know this was preparing me for things to come.*

10. *The house in Bethesda where I lived with Aunt Virgie, Uncle Audley (whom she called Mr. Galbraith until the day she died), and Charlotte. When I went back to see that house, I was amazed at how small it was.*

11. *Aunt Virgie and Uncle Audley, who were so kind to me and treated me as their own.*

12. *Me at age six.*

13. *At Girls' Latin in Chicago. Here I am in the senior class play,* First Lady. *I never dreamed what that title was going to mean to me.*

14. *When my father was dying in the hospital, he asked me to bring him this photo of Mother. I put it on the wall at the end of his bed so he could lie in bed and look up and see her.*

15. *Better than the first letter I got from Ron when he went to camp! My writing was better then than it is now. I see I forgot the comma after "Love"...*

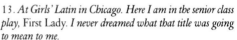

CAMP KECHUWA
MICHIGAMME, MICHIGAN

Dear Doctor Loyal:
    Please excuse my writing. It is hard to write sitting up in bed. I think I told mother that I passed my red cap. So I am working on my green cap now. Will you please tell mother that I wove a rug for the guest bath room. How do you like my book plates I made? I hope you like them. I passed a safty test for canoeing so I can go out in a canoe alone. I have learned how to paddle. Are you and mother coming down to see me? I hope so. Doctor Loyal there were a lot of girls from school that come here that I know so I know more then I thought. I miss you and mother a lot.
                    Love your daughter
                        nancy.

16. *Me with Clark Gable at the Stork Club during an unexpectedly exciting week.*

17. *At MGM, I was trying so hard to get out of playing roles that required wearing the pregnancy pad that I had some photos taken to show a little different side of me.*

18. *I don't like people who don't look at me when I'm talking, and I can't not look at people when they're talking to me! Me in a picture called* Night into Morning.

19. *MGM sent me to New York to promote* The Next Voice You Hear *and I was so impressed with having my name on the marquee that I took pictures of it. I also pinned my first fan letter to my dress and wore it to the studio.*

20. *After our wedding at the Little Brown Church in the Valley, we went back to the Holdens'. They had arranged to have a wedding cake and a photographer. I still have the bride and groom from the top of the cake.*

21. *At the Stork Club, on my first trip to New York as Mrs. Ronald Reagan. I thought I had packed everything so carefully —and it turned out that I was so excited that I forgot to pack the skirts to all of my suits.*

22. *The family together in Pacific Palisades —Ronnie, Ron, me, and Patti.*

23. *Ron and his father having fun in the treehouse Ron built with a friend.*

24. *At Ron's christening—Ronnie; me holding Ron; my mother; Patti with Ronnie's mother, Nelle; my sister-in-law Bess and Ronnie's brother, Moon; and my father.*

It's home and a moment of peace after another party.   *On the trail: This time, it's a GOP rally in Washington.*

CALIFORNIA'S LEADING LADY

Nancy Reagan, who never expected to be a governor's wife, is a hit. Even Democrats like her.

Mrs. Reagan is ready to try her skill as a decorator in the Governor's conference room at the Capitol. She redid her husband's inner office (in background) to make it more homelike.

The first impression is dignity—then the quick smile, the brisk, businesslike walk, the low-pitched voice, warm and friendly. Men like her femininity, women her clothes (Galanos). Nancy Reagan's taste and style, in her first ten months in Sacramento, have won professional admiration: even from California liberals who dislike her husband's politics. Her capital success started a rumor that she had secretly taken lessons in "How to Be a Governor's Wife." "Not true," rebuts Mrs. Reagan. "Unfortunately, no such school exists, nobody can teach you. It's like motherhood. You just do your best and hope you'll learn as you go along."

PRODUCED BY STANLEY GORDON
PHOTOGRAPHED BY STANLEY TRETICK

continued
LOOK 10-31-67 **37**

25. Look *magazine, 1967: a nice article about me as "California's Leading Lady." Stories like this one from the sixties made it more difficult for me to understand the press that I later got in Washington.*

26. On the campaign plane I'm always cold, and Ronnie's usually in his shirt-sleeves.

27. Ronnie taking the oath of office in 1981.

28. *Just before the inauguration in 1981, at the White House with the Carters for coffee.*

29. *Watching the inaugural parade. Jerry Parr, seated behind me, is the Secret Service man who pushed Ronnie into the car after the shooting.*

30. *At the last of the inaugural balls we attended in 1981, when Ronnie said, "I haven't had a chance to dance with my lady yet, so do you mind if we take a few steps up here on the stand?"*

31. *At Versailles, with the Mitterrands, for dinner in the beautiful Hall of Mirrors.*

32. *Leaving the hospital after the shooting, with an obviously concerned George Opfer, head of my Secret Service detail.*

33. Top: *At the hospital after the shooting, when Ronnie and I were making one of our walks down the hall.*

34. Center: *You wouldn't think, looking at this picture, that my heart was in my throat as I was getting ready to go on stage to sing, "Second-Hand Clothes" at the 1982 Gridiron Dinner.*

35. Bottom: *Heaven! An evening at home. Dinner in Ronnie's study.*

36. Top: *With Patti at the ranch in 1983 at the time of my birthday party.*

37. Center: *A last few special moments with Patti, before she got dressed for her wedding ceremony.*

38. Bottom: *With Paul Grilley and Patti on their wedding day in 1984. I was a happy mother and mother-in-law.*

39. *Christmas at the White House, 1983. Patti, Paul, Doria, and Ron.*

40. *Thanksgiving at the ranch, 1985. Bess, Patti, Paul, me, Ronnie, Colleen, Mike, Moon; Cameron in front of me; Ron, Doria, and Ashley.*

A lot of lies are told about people who go into politics, but the only one that ever got Ronnie steamed up was the occasional allegation that he was a bigot. Jack Reagan had his problems, but prejudice was one thing that was never allowed in the Reagan home.

These stories about Ronnie's father are well known because Ronnie has told them so often, and they're true. Ronnie is a conservative Republican, and to a lot of people that means he's probably a bigot. But that's ridiculous. He just doesn't believe that social problems should—or can—be solved by government.

When Ronnie came to Hollywood, he moved his parents out there too, and bought them a house on Phyllis Avenue, not far from where he was living. Ronnie didn't want his father to feel like a freeloader, so he gave Jack a job taking care of his fan mail.

Jack died in 1941, when Ronnie was away in New York. Ronnie didn't fly in those days, and when Nelle called him, she said, "Don't get on a plane, because if something happened to you I couldn't take it." Ronnie returned by train, and Nelle delayed the funeral until he arrived.

It wasn't until our final year in the White House, as Ronnie and I lay in bed one night, that he told me about his father's funeral. Ronnie was sitting in the chapel, feeling terrible, when it seemed he heard his father's voice saying to him, "I'm okay, I'm happy, don't worry about me. I'm doing fine here." When he told me that, I thought, Lord, how I would have loved to have had that happen to me when *my* parents died. I envied him that peace of mind.

Ronnie is a great deal like his mother. Jack Reagan could be cynical, but Nelle believed that people are basically good. She used to visit patients at sanatoriums and mental hospitals and bring cookies and Bibles to prisoners. After the men were released, she often took them into her house until they found a job. Nelle never saw anything evil in another human being, and Ronnie is the same way. Sometimes it infuriates me, but that's how he is.

She was a very religious woman whose faith saw her through bad times. She was also an incredible optimist—a trait her son shares. Ronnie once said, "We were poor, but I never knew it."

Nelle used to tell her boys that everything happens for a reason, that they might not understand the reason at the time, but eventually

they would. Ronnie still believes that. Nelle told him this repeatedly, especially after Ronnie's divorce from Jane Wyman. The divorce had happened suddenly, with absolutely no warning, and
Ronnie was shattered and ashamed. But later, he would say to me,
"You see, my mother was right. If I hadn't been divorced, I never
would have met you."

Because Ronnie really believes what his mother taught him, that
everything happens for a purpose, he doesn't let setbacks or disappointments get him down. At the age of seventeen he described his
optimistic outlook in a poem that was published in *The Dixonian*,
his high-school yearbook. It began,

> I wonder what it's all about, and why
> We suffer so, when little things go wrong?
> We make our life a struggle,
> When life should be a song.

This attitude is why, in my next life, I'd like to come back as
Ronald Reagan.

If he worries, you'd never know it. If he's anxious, he keeps it to
himself. Depressed? He doesn't know the meaning of the word.
He's really as relaxed and hopeful as he appears.

I've almost never heard him complain. If something is bothering
Ronnie, he'll rarely mention it. And he never tells anyone, not even
me, if he's not feeling well.

Ronnie is not impervious to events, but he is very resilient. In
difficult times, the people around him, including me—all right,
especially me—may become nervous and impatient. Ronnie stays
calm, and it usually turns out that he was right. Looking back, I
see that I have spent a lot of time worrying when I really didn't
need to.

But it can also be difficult to live with somebody so relentlessly
upbeat. There have been times when his optimism made me angry,
or when I felt Ronnie wasn't being realistic and I longed for him
to show at least a *little* anxiety. And over the years I think I've come
to worry even more than I used to because Ronnie doesn't worry
at all. I seem to do the worrying for both of us.

Every marriage finds its own balance. It's part of Ronnie's character not to confront certain problems, so I'm usually the one who brings up the tough subjects—which often makes me seem like the bad guy. During the White House years, if we were at a party, Ronnie would be having a wonderful time, but I'd be thinking, We'd better be leaving soon, because he's got an early meeting tomorrow morning.

Anyone can be optimistic when times are good, but Ronnie remains hopeful even in the worst of times. When the space shuttle *Challenger* was destroyed, he could reassure the nation that the seven astronauts had not died in vain, and that this tragedy would not mark the end of our scientific progress. When his meetings in Reykjavik in 1986 with Mikhail Gorbachev ended without an agreement, Ronnie was able to set aside his anger and continue talking to the Soviets. After his disastrous first debate with Walter Mondale in 1984, he recovered in time for the second debate. When he was shot in 1981, and again when he had surgery for cancer four years later, Ronnie's positive attitude helped him make a fast recovery.

Politically, the most difficult period he ever went through was during the long months of the Iran-contra affair in 1986 and 1987. Not only was Ronnie under attack from all sides, but for the first and only time in his life, the polls showed that millions of Americans had begun to doubt his integrity. I'll never forget the horror I felt when a panelist on a television talk show started speculating about impeachment. *Impeachment!*

In May 1987, just before the congressional hearings began, Ronnie and I were invited to a small dinner party in Washington. Ronnie was in fine spirits, which amazed even me. That night, in the privacy of our bedroom, I asked him if he was really as unperturbed about the hearings as he seemed to be. "Are you doing this for my sake?" I asked.

"No," he replied. "I don't believe I did anything wrong. I realize there will be some unpleasant times coming up, but no, I'm not worried."

I was so struck by his response that I wrote it down in my diary. I knew he done nothing wrong, but I was miserable that so many people didn't believe what Ronnie had been saying. And now that the hearings were about to begin, who knew what lay ahead?

Earlier that evening, as we were dressing to go out, Tom Brokaw said on the *NBC Nightly News* that Ronald Reagan was about to enter the most difficult week of his presidency. My heart sank when I heard that.

Ronnie recognized there was a problem, but he refused to let it get him down.

The presidency may be the most pressured job in the world, but Ronnie didn't get grumpy or yell at his staff. It takes a lot to make him angry, although now and then he does lose his temper. When it happened in the Oval Office, he would take off his glasses and throw them down on his desk. I never actually witnessed this, but apparently that was a signal—when the glasses go down, stand back!

Frankly, it sometimes made *me* angry that Ronnie didn't get angry more often—especially at some of his advisers who let him down. There were times when his optimism led to problems, and when a more suspicious person might have asked important and tough questions. Ronnie trusts people, often before they have earned that trust. And he was sometimes slow to realize that not everyone who worked in the White House shared his goals.

Some presidents have changed in office, but Ronnie hasn't changed since the day I met him. One morning, during the 1980 campaign, Ronnie complained to an aide that the day was starting a little too early. "You better get used to it, Governor," the aide replied. "If you become president, that fellow from the National Security Council is going to come in to brief you at seven-thirty each morning."

"Oh yeah?" said Ronnie. "Then he's going to have a hell of a long wait!"

As president, Ronnie never felt the need to arrive at the Oval Office at the crack of dawn, or to remain at his desk until late at night. He also never pretended to work longer than he actually did. Most nights, however, he would work in his study after dinner. And he always put in extra hours on weekends. I rarely saw him when he wasn't carrying a pile of papers.

. . .

My husband loved being president. He *enjoyed* it, all of it—the decision-making, the responsibilities, the negotiating, as well as the ceremonies, the public appearances, and the meetings. As George Will has said, Ronald Reagan has a talent for happiness.

I believe one reason people have misunderstood Ronnie is that they look at his profession instead of at his character. This is a man who didn't run for public office until he was fifty-five years old. And even when he went into politics, he never became a politician.

He has good political instincts and skills, but he lacks the cynicism that is so common in politics. When he held office, the worst thing his advisers could say to him was "This will be good for you politically."

He never fully understood how most politicians' minds worked. Shortly after he became governor of California, he came home one evening and said, "It's so damn frustrating! I'll make a statement, and an hour later, the press or the legislators will say, 'Sure, that's what he *says*. But what does he *mean*?'

"I don't get it," he said. "If they could only accept that what I say is what I mean, it would save so much time!"

Ronnie has never been one of the boys. I've heard people say that a basic rule of American politics is "To get along, go along," but Ronnie has never operated that way. One of the first things I noticed about him when we met is that when the day's shooting was over, he never stayed behind to have a drink with the fellows in the dressing room. He preferred to come home. Later, on the campaign trail, during the rare times when we had an early evening, he didn't sit around and chat with the staff. He would smile, say good night, and come back to our room.

As governor, Ronnie came straight home after work rather than going out for a beer with the legislators or the press. They had never seen anyone like him in Sacramento, and some of the old pols didn't like the fact that Ronnie didn't behave like one of their own.

In Washington, socializing is regarded as part of the job, an extension of the business day, but that went against Ronnie's grain. He believes that parties and dinners are for fun, not work, and in most social situations he prefers to tell stories. That would always put a gathering on a more informal plane, where political talk—or gossip, which Ronnie hates—seemed like an intrusion.

But the most striking difference between Ronnie and many other politicians is that he has never been interested in power for its own sake. When friends would ask, "How does it feel to be the most powerful man in the world?" Ronnie would always say, "Who, me?" It wasn't false modesty. He just didn't see himself in that way.

Before he was elected, Ronnie had always regarded the presidency with great respect, even with awe. But when he became president, he had trouble believing that other people could be in awe of *him*. Unlike, say, a Lyndon Johnson, he never looked at his position in terms of "I am president." Instead, he would refer to the presidency as "the office I now hold," or even "this job." Some people saw this as an affectation, or even a calculated pose that allowed him to appear distant from government while he was still part of it. But it was genuine. For Ronnie, it would have been presumptuous to view his job in any other way.

Perhaps the fact that Ronnie never equated the presidency with himself helps to explain why he wasn't worn down by the pressures and disappointments of the office. Even during difficult periods, he never saw the presidency as a burden, or as "the loneliest job in the world," as it's often described.

Two or three times during our White House years there were rumors on Wall Street that Ronnie had suffered a heart attack. Each time it happened, the stock market took a dive, but it always came as a surprise to Ronnie that rumors about his health could be that important.

And to the very end, whenever we left the White House to attend a dinner or a speaking engagement, Ronnie would turn around and shake his head: "I'll never understand why we need so many cars for a five-minute drive."

And yet he loved the ceremony of the office and the band playing "Hail to the Chief." Ronnie and I always remembered what Frank Reynolds of ABC News had once said to us about President Carter. "People *want* to hear 'Hail to the Chief.' They *want* to look up to the president. They don't like it when he goes on television wearing a sweater." Ronnie agreed with that assessment, and so do I.

. . .

Ronnie didn't seek the presidency in order to become somebody; he already was somebody. And he came into office with a clear idea of what he wanted to accomplish.

Maybe that's why he didn't seem to age in office. A president grows old when he's constantly forced to react to events, without a broad plan or an overall philosophy. Whenever something happens, he has to ask himself: My God, what am I going to do about this? Where do I stand?

But if he already knows what his principles and values are, and where he stands on the issues, the job becomes easier.

Ronnie knew exactly what he wanted to achieve in the Oval Office. His goals had been honed over a twenty-year period, and people knew exactly where he stood. Economic recovery. Greater economic freedom. A stronger defense. Less government. Those were his top priorities, and other things had to wait. He understood that if you try to accomplish everything, you run the risk of achieving nothing.

Now that Ronnie is out of office, it's easy to forget that when we first moved to Washington, most of the "experts" didn't expect him to be an effective president. Many people thought he was bound to fail. Some overlooked the fact that for eight years he had been a successful governor of the most populous state in the nation—a state that is larger and more prosperous than many countries. Others were convinced that the presidency had grown so large and complicated that nobody could manage it. Even some of Ronnie's supporters were skeptical. After all, it had been twenty years since *any* president had completed two successful terms in office. Why should Ronald Reagan be able to accomplish what other men could not?

But then, as long as he has been in politics, people have underestimated Ronnie. I remember the first time he ran for governor, and people said, "Ronald Reagan? He's just a washed-up actor. He'll never win."

And when he ran for president, they said, "Here's this actor. He may have been governor of California for eight years, but he really doesn't know anything."

In 1966, Governor Pat Brown was hoping that Ronnie would win the Republican primary because Ronald Reagan looked like an easy opponent. In 1980, Jimmy Carter, Walter Mondale, Tip O'Neill, and Ted Kennedy felt the same way.

After the 1984 election, when Ronnie was reelected by the largest electoral vote in history, most of that talk finally stopped. By then it had become difficult to explain Ronnie's success in terms of good luck, his handsome face, his charm, his staff, or his sense of humor.

Why did so many people underestimate Ronnie for so long? Part of it, as I've said, was due to his personality. People find it hard to believe that such a nice man could be effective, and that he could also be tough when he had to be.

But Ronnie's easygoing manner is deceiving. Although he isn't as driven or as intense as some of his predecessors in the White House, underneath that calm exterior is a tenacious, stubborn, and very competitive man. Just look at the record: Ronnie rarely loses.

Another key to Ronald Reagan is that he's a team player who has always been more comfortable as an ally than as an adversary. After the 1980 election, he was eager to meet with the local power establishment in Washington. Among other things, Ronnie wanted to let them know who we really were—that despite our images in the Eastern media, the president-elect wasn't a shoot-'em-up cowboy, and his wife wasn't a fluffhead.

And so, just two weeks after the election, Nancy Reynolds and Bob Gray, two of Ronnie's old friends and supporters, put together a dinner for fifty people at the F Street Club. They invited a diverse and unusual group that included the mayor, several businessmen, religious leaders, university presidents, cultural leaders, philanthropists, and so on. Just about the only thing these people had in common was that most of them were Democrats.

Because time was short, Nancy and Bob sent the invitations by telegram. To their surprise, about half of the people they invited didn't even respond. When the guests were called, most of them said, "Were you serious? I thought this was a *joke*."

These people were used to a very different style of politics. They were shocked but also delighted that the Republican president-elect wanted to meet *them*.

After dinner, everybody gathered around the fireplace as Ronnie told some of his favorite stories about Hollywood. But first he welcomed the guests. "You know," he said, "there's only one letter's difference between 'president' and 'resident.' And Nancy and I hope that you'll come to think of us as residents."

A few weeks later, we were invited to a dinner party at Katharine Graham's house in Georgetown. We had both known Kay for years, and when we drove up to her house, she was there to greet us. Ronnie was especially glad to see her, and he gave her a kiss. Kay's longtime housekeeper was watching all this from the second-floor window. When Ronnie kissed Kay, she turned to the woman beside her and said, "Well, I hope Mrs. Graham enjoyed it, because I can promise you, that's the last time *that* will happen."

But it wasn't. Although Kay owns the *Washington Post*, Ronnie and I never allowed politics to stand in the way of our friendship with her.

We felt the same way about Tip O'Neill. When Ronnie and Tip first met, the Speaker of the House told him, "You're playing in the big leagues now." Tip was Ronnie's toughest critic, and some of his bitter attacks on the administration's economic policies made Ronnie wince. But Ronnie and Tip remained friends until Tip's retirement in 1987. No matter what was going on in their political lives, they were always able to swap Irish stories or talk about baseball.

I liked Tip, and also Millie, his wife, who was always friendly and easy to talk to. I remember hosting a luncheon in 1981, when I was getting a daily dose of bad press. Tip looked at me across the table in the State Dining Room and said, "Don't let it get you down." Coming from my husband's chief political opponent, it meant a lot.

One of the hardest things for a political wife—or for any wife—to take is criticism of her husband. Anyone in politics is bound to be criticized, and I don't mind fair and honest disagreement. But when the criticism is unfair, dishonest, or simply wrong, it can hurt terribly. Ronnie has always been fairly thick-skinned about criticism, whereas I have often been vulnerable. I'm tougher than I used to be, but not tough enough.

To this day I am annoyed by a handful of misconceptions about Ronnie which have been repeated incessantly over the years.

For example, despite everything you've heard or read, Ronnie does not take naps. On a long flight on *Air Force One*, it was a struggle just to get him to stretch out on the couch. And despite all the jokes, including his own, Ronnie never came back to the residence to take a nap after lunch. I could never understand where this idea came from, because the press received a copy of his schedule every day, and they *knew* he didn't come back for a nap. Kennedy and Johnson did, but not Ronnie.

Ronnie is usually asleep by eleven, and he sleeps soundly. On the rare occasion when he wakes up at night, instead of counting sheep, he gets himself back to sleep by silently reciting "The Cremation of Sam McGee," by the Canadian poet Robert Service.

For years, Ronnie has enjoyed reciting another Robert Service poem, "The Shooting of Dan McGrew." One scene I'll never forget is of Ronnie at a state dinner in England, where he was seated between Queen Elizabeth and the queen mother. Apparently, "The Shooting of Dan McGrew" is also a favorite of the queen mother's. I don't remember how it began, but before I knew it the two of them were reciting that poem together—all eleven stanzas—back and forth at the table!

It *is* true that Ronnie nodded off during a public meeting with the pope in 1982. We had left for Paris on June 3, arriving for the economic summit on June 4. That day, Ronnie met with Margaret Thatcher and François Mitterrand. On June 5, he was in Versailles for talks with the leaders of Japan, Canada, Italy, and West Germany, as well as Thatcher and Mitterrand. On June 6, we attended a banquet at Versailles that ended after midnight. When it was finally over, Ronnie went directly into a meeting with his advisers to discuss the Israeli invasion of Lebanon, which had occurred a few hours earlier. He got almost no sleep that night, and early the next morning we flew to Rome, where we drove straight to the Vatican for the meeting with the pope.

It was held in the papal library, and Ronnie was seated next to the pope. The room was very warm. As the pope started speaking in his soothing voice, I saw Ronnie's eyes begin to droop. I started coughing and shuffling my feet as loudly as I could, but no luck. It's funny, looking back on it, but it was agonizing at the time—and in front of the *pope,* of all people. I kept hoping he would lean over and nudge Ronnie with his elbow, and say, "You know what I mean, Ron!"

Naturally, the press made a big deal about it, and that photograph of Ronnie with his eyes closed was shown everywhere. Mike Deaver normally did a terrific job, but he certainly overscheduled Ronnie on that trip. And it didn't help when Mike tried to explain it by telling Chris Wallace of NBC that Ronnie occasionally nodded off during Cabinet meetings! Actually, everyone at one time or another had a hard time keeping his eyes open at Cabinet meetings.

Then there's that old myth that Ronnie dyes his hair. Lord, I got sick of hearing that one! Once, in California, two reporters actually followed Ronnie into the barbershop, picked up some of his hair from the floor, and had it analyzed for traces of dye. They didn't find any.

In fact I've never known anyone who was as happy to get a few gray hairs as Ronnie was. He said, "Now, maybe they'll stop saying that I dye my hair." But the stories continued.

I still come across references to the "fact" that Ronnie never reads. He reads constantly. In Sacramento, and also in Washington, he would bring home a big pile of documents to read at night; his aides and advisers had to be reminded not to give him anything that wasn't important, because Ronnie's tendency is to read everything. He concentrates so hard that sometimes, when I talk to him, he doesn't hear me.

Ronnie remembers that at night, when he was young, Nelle would sit on the bed between the two boys—they shared a bed—and read to them. She used to move her finger under the words, and one evening, he recalls, all those funny little black marks clicked into place. This was a year or two before he started school.

When Ronnie was five, Jack came home one day and found his son sitting on the floor, reading the newspaper.

"What are you doing?" said his father.

"Reading," answered the boy.

"Oh yeah? Then read me something."

And Ronnie did. As he tells it, Jack went running out of the house, yelling, "My son can read! My son can read!"

When we lived in the White House, there were always magazines and books piled on his night table, and at night we'd both read in bed until it was time to fall asleep. Ronnie especially enjoys history, biography, and the novels of Louis L'Amour and Tom Clancy. During his final year in office, he was engrossed in a two-volume work called *The President's House,* and it inspired him to explore the White House, room by room, seeing it all through new eyes.

Ronnie is also a pretty good writer, and until he became president he wrote his own speeches. Anyone who has ever traveled with Ronnie on a campaign plane knows how much time he would spend on each one. He would start by writing the speech on a yellow legal-size pad. Then he would transfer it to note cards, using his own form of shorthand, which nobody else could understand. He would print the key words in dark ink and bold block letters so they would be easy to read.

He was always going through newspapers and magazines and clipping out little anecdotes or statistics that caught his eye and helped him make a point. That's one reason he became such a good speaker: Because he wrote his own material, he could deliver it with total conviction.

When he became president, there was simply no time for him to write his own speeches or to transfer them to note cards. Since 1981, he has been using a TelePrompTer; the text of his speech is scrolled across a glass panel by a projector—like credits at the end of a movie.

Before every speech, he removes the contact lens from his right eye, which allows him to see the audience with one eye and the TelePrompTer with the other. Ronnie started wearing contacts early, back in the days when they covered the entire eye. When we first started going out, he would sometimes pop out a lens at a red light, wet it with his tongue, and stick it back in. The first time he did it, my heart stopped. I was sure he wasn't going to get it back in before the light changed. But he did, and from then on I learned to trust his timing.

. . .

One thing that's true about Ronnie is that he lives a balanced life. He sleeps six or seven hours a night, eats properly, and makes time for daily exercise. He doesn't smoke, and on the rare occasion when he takes a drink, it's usually a glass of wine—or, at Camp David, a screwdriver before dinner.

Both of us stopped drinking coffee years ago, after Ronnie's doctor told him that he could probably prolong his life by a couple of years if he gave up caffeine in the morning. (We had already stopped drinking coffee at night because it kept us awake.) At the White House we always served decaffeinated coffee, and nobody ever seemed to know the difference. If guests turned the coffee down, I would mention that it was decaf and they'd usually change their mind.

Ronnie has never been a fussy eater. He'll enjoy a good steak, but this man, who as president was served some of the finest and most elaborate meals in the world, would just as soon have a hamburger. He adores macaroni and cheese and would be perfectly happy eating it for breakfast. Basically, he's a meat-and-potatoes man.

But he hasn't eaten a tomato in seventy years. When Ronnie was a boy, a neighbor brought over a bushel of tomatoes and told him they were apples. Ronnie liked apples a lot, so he took a big bite out of one. He hated the texture so much that he never looked at a tomato again.

Ronnie is also a big dessert man, and here you can forget about moderation. In fact, as long as you give him dessert, you can forget about the rest of the meal. When he's speaking at a luncheon or a dinner, he's always nervous just before they introduce him, but not because of the speech. No, he's afraid he'll be called upon to start speaking before they serve dessert! God forbid a piece of cake should go by and Ronnie not be able to eat it.

His other weakness, as everybody knows, is jelly beans. He doesn't eat as many of these as he used to, and he never ate as many as people said. But he does like them.

Ronnie often appears on the best-dressed list, but that's an honor he doesn't deserve. He pays little attention to clothes, and he'd be perfectly happy with one pair of jeans and a plaid shirt. It never occurs to him to buy anything new. We both hang on to clothes a long time, but I really have to tie him down before he'll get a new suit. (He orders them from Mariani in Beverly Hills, where he's been buying suits since long before I met him.) He still has the same white tie and tails that he had made when he was invited to a command performance for the king and queen of England back in 1948.

But Ronnie has picked out some of the worst ties over the years, and there have been times when those ties have just disappeared! There was also a particularly unsightly pair of slacks that mysteriously vanished during the move from the White House to Los Angeles. Amazing how these things happen, isn't it?

Once, early during Ronnie's first term, I ordered a suit for him from a fine English tailor who had his measurements on file. It was a blue-and-gray plaid that looked terrific in the swatch. But a few weeks later, when the package arrived from London, I was horrified. The suit came out loud and ugly, a real eyesore.

Foolishly, I gave it to Ronnie anyway, and of course it became his favorite suit. It wasn't long before I just couldn't stand to look at it anymore. He was wearing it one day as we boarded *Air Force One,* and I turned to him and said, "Honey, please. I want you to give that suit away. Otherwise, I might just have to burn it."

Ronnie was incredulous. "You don't like this suit?"

"You know I don't," I replied. "I've told you that a hundred times."

Mike Deaver was with us. "Let's ask Mike," said Ronnie. "Mike, what do you think of my suit?"

Mike just smiled.

"Come on, Mike," I said. "Tell him what you think."

"Do you want me to be honest with you?" he asked Ronnie.

"Of course I do."

"Well, then," said Mike, "around the office we refer to it as your Mutt-and-Jeff suit. Whenever you wear it, people say, 'If he had to be shot, why couldn't he have been wearing *that* suit?' "

So he's not the world's best dresser, and he doesn't appreciate fine dining. But he certainly has a flair for romance!

Ronnie doesn't wait until he's going away on a trip to be affectionate; sometimes he kisses me when he's only leaving the room. He says "I love you" frequently, and so do I. We are physically affectionate with each other, both in public and in private, and we're always holding hands. A reporter once told me that he and his colleagues were sometimes embarrassed to look at us, especially when I was meeting Ronnie's plane after a trip, because instead of a peck on the cheek, we would really kiss.

Although Ronnie doesn't show his feelings easily, he has always been sentimental. He used to send flowers to Mother on my birthday—to thank her for giving birth to me.

And I loved it when he told an interviewer that coming home to me was like coming out of the cold into a warm room with a fireplace. Or that being married to me was what he dreamed as an adolescent that marriage should be.

Does that mean we share everything? Of course not. As close as we are, we're still separate people. When we lived in the White House, I had a life that was completely different from his. As first lady, I was meeting and talking with people he didn't know anything about. And of course it was much easier for me to go out for lunch, which I did as often as I could—especially with George Will, and with Kay Graham and Meg Greenfield.

We don't often fight, but we have certainly had our disagreements—especially around raising children and about money. "Never go to bed mad," Mother used to say, and we never have. Sometimes after an argument we'll kiss and say good night. Ronnie will drop right off to sleep, but I'll be so stirred up that I'll lie awake for hours and get mad at him all over again.

Fortunately, our fights don't last very long. Years ago, when we were on vacation with my parents at the Arizona Biltmore in Phoenix, Mother described a pair of newlyweds she had overheard at the pool. The bride was crying, and her husband swam over to see what the problem was. "You were cool to me in the pool," she said.

Somehow, that line stuck. Whenever something isn't quite right between Ronnie and me, one of us will say, "You were cool in the pool." That's a signal that we have some repair work to do, to fix whatever small problem has come up before it has time to grow into a large one.

Whoever said that marriage was a fifty-fifty proposition didn't know what he was talking about. There are many times when you have to give 90 percent, or when both of you have to give 90 percent. If our marriage has been successful, it's because Ronnie and I have both worked very hard at it. Maybe we tried extra hard because Ronnie had been divorced, and he didn't want to go through *that* again. Both my parents had been divorced, so I too had some idea of what that meant.

Like Mother, I gave up my career when I got married. When I first signed up at Metro, I was asked to fill out a questionnaire for the publicity department. Under "Ambition," I wrote, "to have a successful marriage." That was always my goal, and I knew I would give up acting when the right man came along.

Times are different now, and I'm certainly not advising young women to give up their careers. But I had seen too many movie marriages founder, and I didn't think I could handle both a career and a husband. I believed that something would suffer, and I was afraid it would be the marriage—especially in Hollywood, where everybody is always telling you how dear and darling you are. Then, when you come home at night, it's hard not to expect your husband and children to treat you with that same adulation. Instead, it's "Hey, Mom, what's for dinner?"

Ronnie didn't ask me to give up my career, but he told me later that he thought it was wonderful that I was willing to. When he said that, he was probably thinking back to his first marriage.

Ronnie has always been there for me, even during the years when the world was on his shoulders. At the time of the shooting, he comforted me as much as I comforted him. When I had my mastectomy, he said, "This makes no difference to us. That's not why I married you." I knew that, of course, but it meant so much to hear him say it. It must be terrible to be married to a man who turns away from you at such a time, or who doesn't want to deal with it, to face it. But I've never felt there was anything that happened to me that Ronnie couldn't handle.

He takes care of me. If I'm going away for a couple of days, he'll count out the right number of vitamin pills and he'll put them in a bottle for me. And after all these years, he still leaves me notes on my desk saying "I love you." Ronnie doodles, and he once drew a picture of Jiggs from the *Maggie and Jiggs* comic strip and left it on my desk. It was inscribed, "Dearest wife, A portrait of Jiggs, who was a husband who couldn't begin to be as happy as you've made me."

On Valentine's Day, my birthday, or our anniversary, I'll find half a dozen cards from Ronnie waiting for me at breakfast—even during the White House years. Often he writes at the bottom, "I.T.W.W.W.," which stands for "in the whole wide world." As in: "I love you more than anything I.T.W.W.W."

During Ronnie's first term, we were at a dinner one night at Mark Hatfield's house, together with a small group of presidential biographers and historians. Like it or not, they told us, you are now part of history, and it's important for future generations that both of you keep a personal record of everything that happens to you in the White House.

Then Daniel Boorstin, who was Librarian of Congress, made a beautiful comment. "We have never had a presidential couple like the two of you, and that alone is an important historical fact. The love and devotion you show to each other isn't seen much around here these days."

"You know," Ronnie replied, "if Nancy Davis hadn't come along when she did, I would have lost my soul."

8

I Thought I Married an Actor

WHEN I married Ronnie, I thought I married an actor. But looking back now, I really should have known that acting wasn't fulfilling enough for him. He had already served five terms as president of the Screen Actors Guild and two more as president of the Motion Picture Industry Council. And he had always been active in supporting candidates for public office. All that should have been a signal to me, but somehow I missed it.

Shortly after we were married, the Democrats came to Ronnie to ask if he'd run for Congress, but he turned them down. He said he preferred to make his contribution by working in behalf of somebody else, and I just assumed it would always be that way.

Looking back now, I'm amazed at my own naïveté. But I honestly never expected that Ronald Reagan would go into politics.

Not only did I think I'd married an actor, I thought I'd married a successful actor. But after the war, Ronnie's career started slowing down, and soon after we were married we found ourselves with financial problems. Ronnie had been well paid for some of his films, but he was in the 91 percent tax bracket when he made his money—which certainly influenced his views later on taxes.

For the first few months of our marriage, we had two apartments. We lived in mine, but because it wasn't big enough to hold all our possessions, Ronnie held on to his. Soon we settled down in a house on Amalfi Drive in Pacific Palisades, which at the time was an affordable and quiet neighborhood. (We paid $42,000 for the house.)

At the time, nobody could understand why we were moving way out there—"in the country," as it was thought of then.

But Ronnie wasn't getting any good picture offers, and what with the mortgage on the house, child-support payments, and quarterly tax payments on money he hoped to earn later in the year, we quickly found ourselves in debt. It was a year and a half before we could afford to furnish our living room, but when we put up our Christmas tree, it seemed beautiful to me.

In 1953, five months after Patti was born, and despite my decision not to be a working wife, I went back to work for one picture. Quite simply, we needed the money. This was a blow to Ronnie, but we had to face facts, and face them together. I could get work, but his movie career was at a standstill.

The picture was *Donovan's Brain*, a low-budget film about a scientist, played by Lew Ayres, who keeps the brain of a dead man alive and then becomes dominated by it. The shooting took six weeks. It wasn't a classy picture, but it did pay some bills.

The phone continued to ring for Ronnie, but now he was being offered bad roles in bad films—pictures he described as "They don't want them good, they want them Thursday." He had made a few clunkers in the early years of his career, and he wasn't willing to do that anymore. We waited for over a year, and we got by only because Ronnie was able to guest-star on *Burns and Allen* and other television shows. Neither of us realized it, but Ronald Reagan's Hollywood career had pretty much come to an end.

There's no question in my mind that Ronnie's political involvements had begun to hurt his prospects for work. By the time I came along, he had become so identified with the Screen Actors Guild that the studio heads had begun to think of him less as an actor than as an adversary. In a small community like Hollywood, an actor's reputation has a lot to do with his off-screen image, and the men who made pictures had come to see Ronnie primarily as a negotiator. He used to say that it had reached the point that if they were shooting a Western, they'd probably cast him as the lawyer from the East.

There were a few offers from Broadway, but we had started a family in California and neither of us wanted to move. There was always television, but Ronnie was reluctant to sign up for a series because he didn't want to get typecast. Along with many other Hollywood actors in the early 1950s, he believed that too much television exposure could ruin your chances of getting good film roles. Why would people pay to see you on the screen when they could see you at home for free?

This was a difficult period for Ronnie and for us. He was, as you might expect, pretty low. One evening, when he returned from a meeting that had evidently been covered by the press, he told me he had overheard somebody say, "Well, at last Ronald Reagan is having his picture taken." He was crushed, and when he told me about it, I could have cried for him. I remember going over and putting my arms around him. How humiliating for a man to hear that!

Near the end of that year, Taft Schreiber, one of the agents at MCA, the agency that represented Ronnie, asked if he would be interested in being part of a nightclub act in Las Vegas. Ronnie hated the idea, but the money was good and we were broke, so he agreed to consider it. At first they wanted him to appear over Christmas, but we just couldn't see ourselves spending Christmas in Las Vegas, no matter how much we needed the money. Then Ronnie was asked to MC a show with a stripper, and he turned that down, too.

Finally, the agency put together a deal that had Ronnie appearing for two weeks with the Continentals, a well-known male singing group. Ronnie would open the show with a comic monologue, and would then appear with the four Continentals in several of their skits. Despite his misgivings, he agreed to give it a try.

Ronnie could have gone to Las Vegas alone, but if ever there was a time my husband needed me, it was then. We were coming off a terrible year, we had our first child, and Ronnie was about to try something altogether new. Neither of us could tell how it would go. It almost killed me, but I left three-month-old Patti at home with our housekeeper.

Ronnie and I are not exactly Las Vegas types, and when we arrived at the Last Frontier Hotel, we had enough books in our suitcase to stock a small library. When the owner brought us to our suite, he was astonished. "I've had a lot of entertainers at this hotel," he said. "But I've never seen anyone bring *books* to Las Vegas."

When Ronnie wasn't performing, we spent our time reading in the suite or by the pool. We weren't even tempted to gamble; we were there to make money, not lose it. And we had both heard too many stories about Hollywood entertainers who were paid fabulous amounts of money in Las Vegas and promptly gambled it all away between shows. We held out until the final night, when we risked the grand total of twenty dollars at the blackjack table—and lost it all.

Fortunately, Ronnie's act was a great hit. I should know—I attended every performance. The show was sold out every night, and people were standing in line to get in. Before the two weeks were over, offers had come in from nightclubs in Chicago, Miami, and New York. But two weeks in Las Vegas was enough to tell us what we already knew: The nightclub life was not for us.

A few weeks later, Taft Schreiber told Ronnie that General Electric wanted to sponsor a weekly dramatic program on television on Sunday nights. They needed a host who would introduce each of the shows, and who would also go on the road as a "corporate ambassador" for the company, visiting G.E. plants and offices all over America.

Again, Ronnie had doubts, but it was better than Las Vegas. And of course, as it turned out, Ronnie was a big success. And he *loved* the job. He introduced each episode of *General Electric Theater*, and signed off at the end with that familiar line, "Here at General Electric, progress is our most important product."

Ronnie's contract also called for him to star in four programs a year, and occasionally I appeared with him. These were live shows, which meant there was no time to change clothes between scenes. And so I'd be wearing three different dresses in the first scene, and I'd peel them off, one by one, while the camera lingered on some other character—or on the furniture.

The only bad part of Ronnie's job at G.E. was that he had to travel so much. The first time he left, he was gone for two months, so I took Patti with me to Chicago, where we stayed with my parents. That was far too long a separation for all of us, and Ronnie arranged a new travel schedule, which would never have him away longer than two weeks at a stretch. Even so, during the eight years he worked for General Electric Ronnie spent a total of almost two years on the road.

By 1956, two years into Ronnie's new job, we were able to build a new, larger house on San Onofre Drive, not far from where we had been living. Ronnie designed it with the architect Bill Stephenson, and it was Ronnie's idea to have the den, the living room, and the dining room all flow together in a way that made the house look much larger than it actually was. When the people at General Electric learned of our plans, they decided to turn our house into a showcase for the latest electrical appliances. They provided us with so many refrigerators, ovens, and fancy lights—not to mention a built-in garbage disposal—that they had to build a special panel on the side of the house for all the wiring and the switches. When we had company, Ronnie used to say that we had a direct link to the Hoover Dam. I wasn't wild about having my home turned into a corporate showcase, but this was Ronnie's first steady job in years, so it was a trade-off I was more than happy to make.

If you believe, as Ronnie does, that everything in life happens for a purpose, then there was certainly a hidden purpose in Ronnie's job with General Electric. Although he wasn't running for any political office, essentially he spent eight years campaigning—going out and talking to people, listening to their problems, and developing his own ideas about how to solve them.

It was during this period that Ronnie gradually changed his political views. He had grown up in a Democratic household, and was (and still is) a great fan of Franklin Roosevelt. During the 1948 race he had campaigned in behalf of Harry Truman for president and Hubert Humphrey for the Senate. Two years later, Helen Gahagan Douglas had decided not to ask for Ronnie's help in her Senate race against Richard Nixon because Ronnie was considered too liberal. Around the same time, Ronnie was part of a group of men who tried to convince General Eisenhower to run for president—on the Democratic ticket.

Meanwhile, Ronnie's brother, who was a conservative Republican, was always trying to convince him that the Democrats were all wrong. Moon (Neil's nickname) and Ronnie had terrible arguments, and every time Moon and Bess came over to our house, the two brothers would get into a loud shouting match while Bess and I tried to get them off the subject. It's hard to imagine now, knowing Ronnie's personality, not to mention his political views, but it really did happen.

But as he traveled across the country for General Electric, Ronnie started seeing things differently. He became increasingly concerned about government interference in the free enterprise system—and also in the lives of individuals. One day he came home from a speaking trip and told me he was starting to realize that the Democrats he had campaigned for in election years were responsible for the very things he was speaking out against between elections.

In 1962, when Richard Nixon was running against Pat Brown for governor of California, Ronnie wanted to campaign for Nixon, and he asked Nixon whether he should do so as a Democrat or a Republican.

"You'd be more effective as a Democrat," Nixon said.

A few weeks later, Ronnie was out speaking for Nixon when a woman in the second row raised her hand and said, "Mr. Reagan, are you *still* a Democrat?"

"Yes, ma'am, I am," said Ronnie.

"Well," she said, "I'm a deputy registrar and I'd like to change that."

Whereupon, to the delight of the audience, she came up on stage and registered Ronnie as a Republican. He had been planning to change parties for quite a while, and this seemed as good a time as any.

By now *General Electric Theater* had come to an end. It had been enormously popular in its time, and even today members of my generation remember it as one of the best shows on television. It went off the air in 1962, after NBC moved *Bonanza* from Saturday night to Sunday. *Bonanza* was a big-budget one-hour show in color, and the competition was simply too much. (Ironically, *Bonanza* was also a program Ronnie loved to watch.)

But Ronnie's career in television wasn't over. Thanks to his brother, who was a vice president at McCann Erickson, the advertising agency, Ronnie spent the next two years introducing *Death Valley Days,* a series of Western stories sponsored by the Borax Company.

Then, during the 1964 presidential campaign, Ronnie made a speech for Barry Goldwater that would soon change our lives.

Holmes Tuttle, a successful Ford dealer in Los Angeles, had organized a fund-raising dinner for Goldwater at the Ambassador Hotel and he had asked Ronnie to speak. Ronnie's speech went over so well that Tuttle came up to him afterward and said, "We've got to get that speech on television."

Holmes raised the money, and Ronnie's speech for Goldwater was scheduled to be shown across the country on October 27, exactly a week before the election. On the twenty-fifth, Barry called Ronnie at home to say his advisers wanted him to cancel the broadcast.

"Have you read the speech?" Ronnie asked.

"No," said Barry, "but they tell me you've got something in there about Social Security."

"That's true," said Ronnie. "I said that any individual paying into Social Security should have a right to declare who his beneficiary should be."

"I can't argue with that," Goldwater said.

According to Ronnie's brother, who was with Goldwater in Cleveland, Goldwater asked to see a tape of Ronnie's speech. When it was over, he looked at his staff and said, "Now what the hell was wrong with that?" And so they went ahead, and the speech was shown on national television.

Ronnie's speech, which he wrote himself, included the same themes he had spoken about during his years with General Electric: the dangers of big government, the loss of individual liberty, and the erosion of traditional morality. It ended on a dramatic note, with these words:

"You and I have a rendezvous with destiny. We can preserve for our children this, the last best hope of man on earth, or we can sentence them to take the first step into a thousand years of darkness.

If we fail, at least let our children, and our children's children, say of us we justified our brief moment here. We did all that could be done."

At three o'clock in the morning, Barry's representative in Washington woke us up with a phone call. "I just thought you'd like to know," he said, "that the switchboard back here is still lighting up with all the calls coming in."

Although Goldwater lost to Lyndon Johnson in the election, Ronnie's speech brought in more money than had *ever* been raised for a candidate—a total of eight million dollars. Almost immediately, Holmes Tuttle put together a committee to support Ronnie for governor of California.

Ronnie thought they were crazy. "Oh, no," he said. "You don't run for governor on the basis of a single speech. Besides, I'm not interested in going into politics. You find a candidate and I promise to campaign for him, the way I've always done."

But they knew Ronnie could win, and they kept after him, and pretty soon I just knew that he'd eventually say yes. By the end of 1964 Ronnie was receiving dozens of letters every day urging him to run for governor in 1966. Some of the people who wrote to him were Democrats, and they said that if Ronnie ran, they would switch parties in order to support him.

For about two weeks we talked about it constantly—during dinner, after dinner, and late at night, in bed. After the Goldwater defeat, with the Republican party in shambles, Ronnie felt he could play a role in helping to put it back together.

But I hung back. I had no clear idea of what a political life would be like, and I wasn't all that eager to find out.

After a lot of stewing on our part, Ronnie finally said, "I'm willing to consider it. Let me do some traveling around the state and make some speeches, and we'll see if there's really any support out there."

A few weeks later we went to a reception for Ronnie at one of the big hotels in San Francisco, where so many people wanted to meet him that they were lined up through the lobby and around the block, waiting to get in.

This was my introduction to politics, and when I woke up the next morning I couldn't move my neck. We called a doctor, who explained that when people are nervous, they tend to raise their shoulders—which I had apparently done for four hours. That, plus standing in an unnatural position with my arm extended, shaking hands, had sent me into a spasm. When I came home, a friend put me in touch with a Swedish woman, who put me in hot packs, massaged my neck, and used traction. Ever since, I've kept my shoulders down in a receiving line.

Ronnie did run, of course, and in the Republican primary he defeated George Christopher, a former mayor of San Francisco, by a wide margin. It was during that race that Gaylord Parkinson, the state Republican chairman, issued the famous Eleventh Commandment, which Ronnie has followed ever since: "Thou shalt not speak ill of thy fellow Republican."

But there was no such commandment in force for the general election. Governor Pat Brown was running for his third term, and he never took Ronnie seriously as an opponent. During the campaign, his people made a terrible commercial which showed the governor telling a group of black children, "I'm running against an actor. And you know it was an actor who shot Lincoln, don't you?"

Neither Ronnie nor I ever saw that commercial. We heard about it from Carl Greenberg of the _Los Angeles Times_ as Ronnie was leaving a speaking engagement, and I still remember how shocked we were when Carl described it. "No, it can't be," Ronnie said. "He couldn't have said _that_." But he did, although I'm sure he later regretted it.

When Governor Brown attacked Ronnie for his lack of political experience, Ronnie readily admitted that he wasn't a professional politician. "The man who currently has the job has more experience than anybody," he said. "That's why I'm running!"

Another of Ronnie's popular lines from that campaign had to do with the governor's generosity with public funds. "Keeping up with Governor Brown's promises," Ronnie said, "is like trying to read _Playboy_ magazine while your wife turns the pages."

But _this_ wife wanted no part of campaigning. I was shy in those days, and terrified that I'd have to give a speech. I have often been asked why I felt that way, given all the years I had spent in theater and in film. But to me the difference is enormous. When I was acting, I wasn't being myself—I was playing a role that had been created for me. But giving a political speech is completely different. You can't hide behind a made-up character, and I was far too private a person to enjoy playing myself.

I remember telling Stu Spencer, Ronnie's campaign manager, "I'd like to help my husband, but I won't give speeches or anything like that."

"Fine," he said, "but if you're introduced to an audience, you could stand up and take a bow, couldn't you?"

I allowed as to how I could manage that.

A few weeks later, Ronnie's advisers came to me and said, "Nancy, California is a big state. Your husband can't possibly get to every little town. We've already got him running around to so many places that the poor guy is exhausted. Could you help? It would be wonderful if you could visit some of these places and do a little Q-and-A with the people."

They certainly knew where my soft spot was! I'd do anything to help Ronnie, and so Q-and-A it was. This was a big step from simply standing up and taking a bow, but I was surprised that in fact I came to enjoy it. It was more informal and more natural than giving a speech, and I liked the give and take with the audience. It was also informative. From their questions, I soon learned what was on people's minds, and I could go back to Ronnie and tell him what I'd heard. I also felt that audiences had a better picture of me as a person in such a setting.

I began to pick up some tips about campaigning. I learned, for instance, that you should never say the name of the town you think you're in, because when you visit six towns in one day, there's always a chance that you're going to make a mistake somewhere. So instead of saying, "I'm glad to be in Fillmore," it was always safer to say, "It's nice to be here."

California is a big state, but even so, Ronnie and I managed to sleep at home most nights during the campaign. Still, the traveling does wear you down. And the food! After far too many political

dinners and banquets where they served chicken and beef, I started
to wonder why nobody ever thought of serving Mexican or Chinese
food for a change.

Ronnie won the election in a landslide, defeating Pat Brown by
almost a million votes. On election night, we had been out having
dinner with friends, and we heard the results on a car radio on the
way to Ronnie's campaign headquarters at the Century Plaza Hotel.
I had always thought you waited up all night listening to the returns,
and although this may sound silly, I felt let down. After so much
hard work, Ronnie's early and overwhelming victory seemed almost
an anticlimax.

Ever since 1967, people have speculated as to why Ronnie was
sworn in as governor at the unusual hour of one minute past midnight. No, it had nothing to do with astrology! During the election
year, Governor Brown had left many judicial vacancies unfilled, and
as soon as the election was over, he began appointing eight or ten
new judges a day. Ronnie was so frustrated that he asked: "What's
the earliest I can be sworn in?"

The answer was 12:01 on the morning of January 3. We arranged
to have a quiet ceremony, which would be followed two days later
by a large public inauguration.

I assumed that the swearing-in on January 3 would consist of a
brief informal ceremony in front of family and friends in the dimly
lit capitol, and then home to bed. Friends of ours, the Jorgensens and
the Wilsons, gave a dinner at the Firehouse, a great local restaurant,
and from there we went on to the capitol. Imagine my shock when
we walked in and saw a bank of television cameras, bright lights, a
choir, and people jammed into every corner! I guess everyone took
it for granted that we knew what to expect, and so nobody had
warned us.

The first speaker was Robert Finch, the lieutenant governor. He
was followed by Senator George Murphy. George had been Ronnie's predecessor as president of the Screen Actors Guild and had
been elected to the Senate in 1964. Like Ronnie, he was a former
Democrat. Both men spoke from notes, and I suddenly realized that

Ronnie would also be expected to speak. My Lord, I thought, what's he going to do? He hasn't prepared anything!

Because the hour was so late, and because it had been so long since a Republican had been elected, it was a dramatic and emotional moment. When it was Ronnie's turn to speak, I was hoping to heaven that he would think of something to say. And of course he did. He looked out at the crowd and then turned to George and said, "Well, Murph, here we are again on the Late, Late Show." The whole room erupted in laughter and the tension was broken. Then Ronnie gave a short, impromptu, and moving speech about his hopes and his plans. I was tremendously proud of him.

Now that Ronnie was governor, we had to move to Sacramento. A few weeks earlier, I had been taken through the governor's mansion by Mrs. Brown. When it came time to leave, the press asked me how I liked it. "I love old houses," I replied. I held back from adding, "But I hate unsafe, dilapidated old houses!"—which this one certainly was.

I remember lying in bed that night with Ronnie, back in Los Angeles. When he asked me how I liked the mansion, I said, "Oh, fine." But as soon as he turned out the light I started to cry. I'm sure I made Ronnie feel awful, but that house was so depressing that I just couldn't stand the thought of living there.

The so-called mansion, built in 1877, had been declared a fire hazard years before we moved in. It was a tinderbox, its wooden frame eaten through by dry rot. Mrs. Brown had been very clear about that, and had also told me that she and her husband had tried to get approval for a new mansion during their years in Sacramento. But their plan was for a kind of mini White House, and it turned out to be so expensive that the legislature turned it down.

Mrs. Brown had warned me that the house was noisy, but I didn't understand how bad it was until we moved in. The mansion was downtown, on a busy street that carried traffic from San Francisco to Reno, and the big trucks rolled by all through the night. They stopped for a red light outside our house, and even at four in the morning you'd hear the shifting of gears. When we had people for dinner, there were times when the traffic was so loud we'd have to stop talking. There were no grounds around the mansion. There was a motel across the street and gas stations on the other two corners, and the house backed up on the American Legion Hall.

For the first couple of months I lived in Pacific Palisades during the week and commuted to Sacramento on weekends, because I didn't want to take Ron out of school in the middle of a semester. (By this time Patti was going to school in Arizona.) But I hated leaving Ronnie alone in such a depressing house. The place reminded me of a funeral parlor. When we moved in, there were purple velvet drapes in each room—so old that when we took them down, they practically crumbled in our hands.

After dinner Ronnie would go right up to the bedroom, because there was no other place to read or watch television. The house was drafty, and we weren't allowed to use any of the fireplaces because they weren't safe.

The safety problem came to a head one Friday afternoon when the fire alarms went off. By then we were all living there, and I ran into Ron's room, grabbed him by the hand, and we tore down the stairs. It turned out to be a false alarm, but I couldn't help but wonder what had made the alarm go off. I still don't know.

There were no fire escapes in the mansion. There was a rope in our bedroom, which you could throw out the window and shinny down. Doesn't that sound like fun?

I went to the fire chief and asked, "What should I tell my son in case there's a real fire? We can't even open the windows because they were painted shut years ago."

He replied, "Well, Mrs. Reagan, it's very simple. Just tell him to take a drawer out the dresser, hold it in front of him, run across the room, break the window, and climb out!"

Terrific, I thought. How am I going to explain *that* to an eight-year-old without scaring him half to death?

When Ronnie came home that night, I said, "Guess what, we're moving. We can't live here anymore. I won't raise a child in a house that's not safe."

Ronnie supported me, but his advisers were outraged.

"It can't be done!" they said.

"Political suicide!"

"You'll get crucified!"

"It'll ruin the governor!"

I didn't like to go against my husband's staff, but I held firm. "I can't help it," I told them. "I can't fulfill my duties as the wife of the governor, and my responsibilities as a mother. Something has to give. Besides, I really think the people of California will understand."

And they did—especially the mothers. There were a few objections in the press, but I didn't receive more than four or five critical postcards. And I was vindicated a few years later, when the mansion was turned into a museum and the Sacramento fire marshal refused to allow visitors to go upstairs. We could *sleep* there, but visitors couldn't go up!

In April of 1967 we moved into an English-style country house in the suburbs. Although the governor's family is supposed to receive free housing, we paid the rent ourselves. Later, when the owners decided to sell, a group of our friends bought the house and we continued renting it from them.

Although we came to love that house, it was far from ideal. It was too small to entertain the legislators, for example, so we held an annual party for them in the summer—outdoors. We would bring in entertainers like Jack Benny, Danny Thomas, and Red Skelton, and I'd always send a note to our neighbors to explain that things would be a little noisy that night. At the first of these parties, I noticed all the neighborhood kids leaning over the fence to hear Jack Benny. I invited them in, and it became an annual routine— the kids would sit around the pool and watch the show.

The first time Ronnie came home to our new house, he said he knew we had done the right thing when he saw all the bicycles out on the lawn. Here, Ron could have a normal life. There was a big backyard where he built a treehouse, and he and his friends would sometimes sleep out there on warm nights. Back in the mansion there had been no grounds where Ron could play, and one of my saddest memories of that period was of looking out the window and seeing him throwing a football with a policeman in the driveway.

I hated that old mansion so much that during Ronnie's second term as governor I became involved in building a new governor's mansion for our successor. We found a fine property in the suburbs overlooking the American River, with lovely old trees and a beautiful view. The land had been donated to the state, so there was no cost to the taxpayer. All the legislature had to do was approve funds to build the house, which they did. And I began to collect furniture—shades of things to come.

Ironically, the governor after Ronnie was Jerry Brown, a bachelor (and Pat Brown's son), who decided not to live in the new mansion. He took two apartments, put them together, and slept on the floor.

We furnished the house we had moved to with items from our ranch in Lake Malibu, which we had sold after Ronnie was elected, and some new things I bought. I also took up a collection of donated items, and I was able to beg and scrounge some nice furniture from people who were breaking up old houses.

I certainly wasn't prepared to be attacked for my efforts by Jesse Unruh, the Speaker of the California legislature, who was running against Ronnie in 1970. When he accused me of collecting these items for my personal use, I got so mad that I decided to hold my first press conference. I answered all questions about the donated furniture, the house we were living in, the rent we were paying—anything anyone wanted to ask. This must have done the trick, because Jesse never brought it up again. As for the donated furniture, it was all stored for future use, and I've often wondered what became of it.

Once the housing problem was out of the way, the press started asking what my next project would be. Back in Los Angeles I had been a member of the Colleagues, a group which works for unwed mothers and their children. But when I came to Sacramento, I didn't have one particular project in mind. Eventually, however, I found one.

I had always been interested in hospitals, partly, I suppose, because of my father's work, and as the governor's wife I visited all kinds—for children, for the elderly, for the mentally retarded, and for veterans. One day, at Pacific State Hospital, I was introduced to the Foster Grandparents Program. This project, started by Sargent Shriver, made it possible for older people to befriend mentally retarded and institutionalized children. What excited me most about this program was that both sides benefited. Older people, who often feel lonely, unneeded, and unloved, have so much to give—especially to children, who need more love and attention than any institution can provide. When you bring these two groups together, each one provides what the other one needs, and everyone is better off.

The "grandparents," who work with the children five half-days a week, often come to feel that their lives have been given new meaning. Suddenly there's a reason to get up in the morning, and a purpose to their lives. They also tend to be patient and tolerant, and aware of the little changes and developments in the children. Naturally, the children respond well to this extra love and attention, and the difference it makes in their lives is remarkable.

I couldn't wait to tell Ronnie about this new program, which at the time was small and poorly funded. With his help, I was able to expand it to all state hospitals. It was then picked up by ACTION, the volunteer-service agency, which provided further funding. The Foster Grandparents Program eventually spread into other states too, and it now includes not only the retarded but also deaf children and youthful offenders. It's really a marvelous program, and I hope it will be expanded further.

I also spent a lot of time in veterans' hospitals, visiting American soldiers who had been wounded in Vietnam. If you ever start feeling sorry for yourself, try visiting hospitals. I'd talk with these men, and before I'd leave I'd ask if they wanted me to call their mothers or their wives. I'd take down the names and numbers and when I returned home I'd start making the calls, which always seemed to follow the same script—something like this:

"Hello, Mrs. Johnson?"

"Yes?"

"This is Nancy Reagan."

"Oh, come on."

"No, it really is. I saw your son in the hospital today and he sends his love."

Eventually they would realize that it really *was* me, and they'd start to cry. Then *I'd* start to cry. Then we'd both cry!

I soon became involved in the issue of prisoners of war, and I corresponded and talked on the phone with many of the mothers, wives, and children of these men. The women I came to know were just amazing. In many cases they didn't even know whether their husbands and sons were dead or alive. But they never gave up hope.

When the POWs started coming home, Ronnie, Ron, and I watched on television with tears streaming down our faces. "I can't stand it," I said. "I've got to get my arms around those boys. We've got to do something for them."

Ronnie and I gave four dinners for the returning POWs from California—two at our home in Sacramento for those from the northern part of the state, and two more in Los Angeles for those from the south. I felt it was important to hold these dinners in the warmth of a home, rather than in a hotel ballroom, and I told the former prisoners to bring along anyone they wanted—wife, mother, sister, girlfriend.

The first dinner in Sacramento was an unforgettable experience for Ronnie and me. The men had been home only a few days, and emotions were running high. The first men to come back were those who had been imprisoned the longest, and our neighbors lined up on both sides of the street to greet them. As they came into the house, I gave each one of them a hug. When Commander Charles Southwick presented me with the tin spoon he had eaten with during his seven years of captivity, I was in tears again.

During those dinners they told us stories that were so harrowing that we wondered how anyone could have survived such tortures. I could only think, Lord, I hope that if I had been in their position, I'd have had the strength to withstand it all.

The men also described some of the mental games they had played to keep from losing their sanity, and the systems they had devised to communicate with one another by tapping on the cell walls. We actually saw two men who had never met before suddenly throw their arms around each other. They had become friends during their years of captivity, when they lived in adjoining cells and communicated by tapping on the walls in code. Each one knew all about the other's wife, children, everything—just from the tapping.

At each of the dinners, one of the men got up to propose a toast to Ronnie, to thank him for what he had done by standing up for them and supporting them. And then Ronnie would get up and say, "No, we're here to thank *you*, for all you've done for us." Later, Ronnie and I attended all of their reunions. And I still have every letter a POW sent me, and every little memento—that tin spoon, a pair of lieutenant's bars, and even a package of Vietnamese cigarettes. Ronnie accomplished a great deal during his eight years as governor of California, and in my own way, I suppose I did too. But for me, the return of the POWs marked the high point of Ronnie's administration.

When Ronnie had decided to run for governor, I knew that our lives would be very different. But I couldn't imagine how different until we actually moved to Sacramento. For the first time we had to deal with a press corps that wasn't always friendly, and with political opponents who were constantly on the offensive.

One afternoon, shortly after the inauguration, I flew from Sacramento to San Diego during a big budget fight that Ronnie was having with the legislature. Sitting directly behind me, three men were having a heated discussion about Ronnie's attempt to cut state spending, which they opposed.

I was new as a political wife. I had been through a campaign, so I knew that not everybody in California agreed with Ronnie's positions. But never before had I been in a situation where, just a few inches away, people were ripping him apart. As these men talked on, I could feel myself growing more and more angry.

Finally, I just couldn't take it anymore. I pushed the button to lower the back of my seat until I was practically leaning into them. Then I turned around and said, "That's my husband you're talking about! You don't know what you're saying. He's going on television tonight, and if you watch him you'll learn the real story of the budget."

Those poor men! They probably wished they'd taken some other flight. The security officer traveling with me sank lower and lower in his seat, and I noticed he never went on another trip with me. But when we got off the plane, the people across the aisle said, "Good for you! It's wonderful to hear a wife stand up for her husband."

When your husband is in public office, you can't always speak freely and give your side of the story. So whenever a negative article about Ronnie came out, I got into the habit of taking a bath, where I would hold imaginary conversations with the reporter or the politician who had written or said something terrible. I was sensational during these encounters—I could always think of just the right thing to say. And of course, with nobody to answer back, I always came out the winner. I finished those baths feeling great. I stopped holding these imaginary conversations before we moved to Washington, and it's a good thing, too. Otherwise, I would have spent eight solid years in the tub!

Another new problem we had to deal with—and another harbinger of things to come—was death threats. In 1968, after the assassination of Robert Kennedy, the federal government had sent Secret Service details to protect several prominent governors, including Nelson Rockefeller in New York and Ronnie in California. A few weeks later, we were told that a woman in the East had called the police to say that her husband had left home with a gun after telling her he was going to kill the president of the United States and the governor of California. The FBI tracked him down and arrested him in Lake Tahoe.

I don't know how many threats came in during our years in Sacramento, and I never wanted to know. But at one point I heard over the car radio that there was a threat that I would be beheaded and my head sent to Ronnie unless he released a certain prisoner. Ronnie had been told about this but had decided not to tell me. He was upset to learn that I knew about it—but believe me, not half as upset as I was!

During our first year in Sacramento, Ronnie and I were in bed one night when we heard a loud bang. "That sounds like a gun shot," Ronnie said, whereupon I immediately ran out on the balcony to see what had happened—not a smart thing to do. Just then, a Secret Service agent came running upstairs with a shotgun. "Everybody downstairs!" he said. "Turn off all the lights and stay away from the windows."

One of the agents had spotted two men trying to light a Molotov cocktail beneath our bedroom window. He fired a shot at the men, but they escaped in a car. The next morning, the agents found the firebomb. Usually these things are Coke bottles filled with gasoline, but this one was a magnum-size champagne bottle. Only in California! It doesn't take much to imagine what would have been left of us if that bottle had come sailing through our bedroom window.

There are times when holding public office forces you to confront the fundamental issues of life and death. Early in Ronnie's term, a man named Aaron Mitchell was scheduled to be executed in San Quentin for murdering a policeman during a robbery. Ronnie has a soft spot for individuals in trouble, but he also supports the death penalty. After examining the case, he couldn't find any valid reason to pardon Aaron Mitchell.

The execution was set for ten in the morning. The night before, a group of protesters held an all-night silent vigil outside our house. I remember Ron, who was only eight, watching this strange and eerie scene through the window and wondering what it all meant. We tried to explain why Ronnie had made his decision, and why some people didn't agree with it. The protesters wanted to have church bells ring at the hour of the execution so everyone could pray for the man's soul. I had no objection to that, but I thought, Wouldn't it be nice if the bells could also ring when somebody is murdered, so we could also pray for that person's soul.

It was shortly after this that Ronnie received a letter from an elderly man in San Francisco who ran a little mom-and-pop store with his wife. He had been robbed a few days after the execution of Aaron Mitchell, which had been widely covered in the press. When one of the robbers tried to stab him, he had shouted out in desperation, "If you kill me you'll get the gas chamber!" When his assailant heard that, he hesitated for a moment and then ran off. It isn't always that simple, but this letter did reinforce our feeling that the death penalty really is a deterrent to crime.

This book isn't the place to discuss the political achievements of Ronnie's two administrations in Sacramento. But I was struck by how much Ronnie had taken to politics—partly, I'm sure, because he could make a difference in people's lives, even in little ways. When an eighty-year-old man wrote to say that he was getting married but didn't have a suit to wear, Ronnie sent him one of his own. When a soldier from Sacramento who was fighting in Vietnam sent Ronnie a money order and asked him to arrange for flowers to be sent to his wife on their anniversary, Ronnie delivered them personally to the astonished woman. When two sisters wrote to say that their retarded brother wanted a rocking chair, Ronnie sent them his own.

One day Ronnie received a letter from a kindergarten teacher who wrote that she had been preparing her class for a trip that would take them to the governor's mansion. "Does anyone know the name of our governor?" she asked.

Nobody did. "Come on, children," she said. "I'm sure you know his name. It's Ronald—"

At which point the entire class shouted in unison: "McDonald!"

One of Ronnie's biggest regrets during these years was that he was frequently at odds with college students. Back when he was running for governor, he had been welcomed on campus because he was running as an outsider. But as soon as he was elected, they saw him as part of the establishment.

Ronnie's first term happened to coincide with the big student protests of the late 1960s. I once accompanied him to a speech in Santa Barbara, where we were greeted by hundreds of young protesters. Some of them, including a number of professors, were barefoot and barechested and had obscenities written across their chests and their backs. They were gathered outside the hall, and when Ronnie started to speak they shouted the most obscene things I had ever heard. I just couldn't believe it! The organizers had to close the windows so Ronnie could be heard, but even then he had to shout above the noise. I remember thinking the world had gone mad.

Ronnie continued trying to keep up a dialogue. Once, at a meeting with students at the University of California, a student got up to say that it was impossible for people of Ronnie's generation to understand the next generation of young people. "You grew up in a different world," the student said. "Today we have television, jet planes, space travel, nuclear energy, computers . . ."

When he paused for breath, Ronnie said, "You're right. It's true that we didn't have those things when we were young. We *invented* them."

I remember the last hour I spent in our house in Sacramento, on the last day of Ronnie's second term. For weeks I had been packing and supervising the move. This piece of furniture went to the state, that one to our new ranch in Santa Barbara, and the rest back to our home in Pacific Palisades. It was so hectic that I hadn't had time to dwell on the fact that we were leaving.

Suddenly, I found myself sitting alone in the house. Except for our bed, all the furniture was gone. The sun was setting, and as I waited for Ronnie to pick me up so we could go to one last reception, I sat on the bed and looked out into the garden, which was so lovely, with all of the camellias in bloom. We'd come to love that old house.

As it grew darker outside, and I sat alone in that empty room, I thought, So this is how it ends. Our eight years of politics are over. True, some of Ronnie's advisers were talking about Ronnie's running for president in 1976, but I didn't really expect that to happen. As we left Sacramento that night, I honestly believed we were leaving politics forever.

9

Our Children

No mother finds it easy to write about difficulties with her children. But our children, and our relationships with them, became such an issue while Ronnie was president that I can't ignore the subject. I love our children, and I didn't want to talk about them while we were living in the White House. But yes, we had our problems. Every family has problems, and we were no exception.

I say every family, but in fact we are really two families, not one. I'm willing to take my lumps for what I did, but as I'll explain, I wasn't responsible for everything that happened.

What I wanted most in all the world was to be a good wife and mother. As things turned out, I guess I've been more successful at the first than at the second.

There are four Reagan children, and in order of birth they are Maureen, Michael, Patti, and Ron. Maureen and Michael are the children of Ronnie's first marriage, to Jane Wyman. Maureen was born in 1941, and Michael was born and adopted in 1946. After Ronnie and Jane separated in 1949, Jane had custody of the children. Ronnie—and when I came along, Ronnie and I—tried to be there for Maureen and Michael, but in fact we had little to say about their daily lives.

Patti was born in 1952, headstrong from the start. Ron came in 1958, and over the years I have probably been closest to him.

Each of the four Reagan children is completely different from the others. Apparently, all of them have felt at one time or another that Ronnie and I were so devoted to each other that there wasn't room for them in our affections, and that they were somehow left out. That was never our intention, and if they sometimes felt that way, I am truly sorry.

Maureen and Ron have both told me that they have sometimes felt their father was a little remote from them. When I mentioned this to Ronnie, he was surprised; he didn't *feel* distant. But now that we have left the White House, all these misunderstandings are easier to work out.

During Ronnie's presidency, our family and its problems were written about constantly. Ronnie had run for office on a platform of traditional family values, which both of us believe in and try to practice. But I always felt hurt when people said we were hypocrites because our own family sometimes fell short of those values. It's true that we weren't always able to live up to the principles we believed in, but that doesn't mean we don't believe in them.

I also think that our relationships with our children weren't as bad as they were portrayed. For example, it was often said that Ronnie and I had little contact with them while we were living in the White House. But while it's true that we didn't see each other as often as we would have liked, we also didn't notify the press each time one of us sent a letter, a card, or a gift, or picked up the phone.

Before Ronnie and I came to the White House, the American public had grown accustomed to having the president's children living there. Before us, there were the Carter kids, and before them, the Fords, the Nixons, the Johnsons, and the Kennedys. But when Ronnie was elected, our children were already grown and married; they had their own lives and careers. Except for Ron, who spent four years in New York, they were settled in California. In other words, our "children" weren't children at all. They were independent adults who lived three thousand miles away, and Michael had children of his own.

Like our own parents, Ronnie and I have always believed that when children get to be a certain age, you should let them live their own lives. As they become adults, it's up to them to determine how much closeness there should be. This wasn't always easy for us, and there were times when I wished they would call more often. But for better or worse, we wanted to give them their independence.

That's not to say that Ronnie and I were ideal parents, or that our children were angels. Ronnie's work was always demanding, and we faced the difficulties of a blended family without much communication between us and Jane Wyman. In addition, each of the children has a strong and independent personality. But we did the best we could, and we never stopped trying.

One of the disadvantages of living in the White House is that your family problems often end up on the front page. When that happens, even a minor misunderstanding can take on a life of its own. A dispute or a harsh word that might easily be resolved or forgiven in private gets blown out of all proportion when you're facing an audience of two hundred and forty million people.

My problems in 1984 with Michael are a good example of how the limelight can complicate family life. There had been some tension between us, and in November of that year, just before Ronnie and I left the White House to fly to the ranch for Thanksgiving, I was interviewed by the *Washington Times*. As usual, there were pointed questions about how the various members of our family were getting along—and especially about Michael and me.

"Are you going to see Michael?"

"Are you in touch with Michael?"

"Has Michael called you?"

"Will Michael and his family be joining you for Thanksgiving dinner at the ranch?"

Question after question. Finally, frustrated and at the end of my rope, I said, "No, there is an estrangement right now. We are sorry about it, and we hope it can be resolved, but we don't believe in discussing family matters in public."

That was true. There really *was* an estrangement, and I really *didn't* want to discuss it. But I should have known better than to use an inflammatory word like "estrangement" in an interview. I was feeling the pressure, and the following month, when I saw Michael, I apologized.

But by then the damage had been done. When the interview appeared, Michael and his wife, Colleen, were in Nebraska spending the holiday with Colleen's parents. Not surprisingly, my "estrangement" comment was repeated on the television news, and when Michael heard it he called Ronnie, hurt and outraged. Ronnie tried to calm him down, but Michael was furious. "I wish I had never been adopted by you," he said—and hung up.

The press didn't know about this, but they soon appeared at Colleen's parents' home, hoping Michael would respond to my comment. He didn't disappoint them. Nancy, he explained, was obviously trying to cover up for the fact that she hadn't yet seen his daughter, Ashley, who had been born about a year before.

Now it was my turn to get angry. But this exchange had already gone on too long, and I didn't want to extend it further. A month later, when Ronnie and I were in Los Angeles, Michael and Colleen came to our hotel to see us. We had a good, honest talk and were able to clear up some of our misunderstandings. But it would be a long time before Michael and I finally straightened everything out, because you can never fully take back a public remark.

Nor can you undo mistakes you've made along the way in raising your children—and I made my share. When Michael came to live with us (which I'll come to shortly), I didn't know how to handle a rebellious teenager. With Patti, I now think, we were too lenient. Maureen and I drifted apart for a number of years. Ron and I had a somewhat smoother time, although even with Ron there were bumps along the way.

It has been a difficult marriage as far as the children are concerned.

I became a parent the day I married Ronnie, and I learned what many other women know, that it's not easy to marry a man who already has children. You want them to like you, and so does your husband, but that usually doesn't happen overnight, and it may not happen ever. They may resent you—at least initially—and they're understandably jealous because you're taking away a piece of their father. It takes time before you can develop a relationship.

About a year before we were married, Ronnie introduced me to Maureen and Michael. Maureen was ten, and she and I hit it off right away. She used to visit me in my apartment with her Victrola and her records, and we'd listen to music together. She'd even help me clean the place, and although I never told her, I think she trailed in more dust than we cleaned up. But mostly we were together on Saturdays and Sundays, when Ronnie and I took the kids out to his new ranch in Lake Malibu.

During those car rides in Ronnie's beat-up old red station wagon, Ronnie used to entertain us with wonderful stories. Maureen, who has the sharpest memory of anybody I know, still remembers some of her father's tall tales about his "past lives." In one of her favorites, Ronnie told the kids how he used to be a cold germ who loved to infect innocent people with coughs, sneezes, and runny noses. One day, the little cold germ decides to take a nap in a strange, green substance, which turns out to be penicillin. End of germ. When Ronnie wasn't telling stories, he would pretend to listen in on people's telephone conversations as he drove by their telephone poles. He would then act out the little dialogues he had supposedly overheard.

As soon as I joined these car rides, Maureen and I started singing together. Ronnie had taught her the words to some college drinking songs, and to "La Marseillaise." (That couldn't have been easy.) I have always loved Broadway musicals, and I taught Maureen the duet "I Hear Singing," from *Call Me Madam*. We sang that song so often that Michael, who was five, began to groan whenever he heard it, while Ronnie would honk the horn and yell "Enough!" until we gave up. Years later, when somebody sang "I Hear Singing" at "In Performance at the White House," Maureen and I flashed each other big smiles across the room.

A few months before Ronnie and I were married, Maureen gave me an enormous vote of confidence. Ronnie used to ride a black thoroughbred mare named Tar Baby, which appeared with him in several of his movies. He bred Tar Baby to a gray stallion named Gypsy Minstrel, and the result was a beautiful spotted filly. Maureen loved that little horse from the moment it was born, and it was her suggestion to call it Nancy D. I knew enough to be flattered. I think Maureen liked me better when I was her friend Nancy Davis than she did when I became her stepmother, Mrs. Ronald Reagan.

. . .

Ronnie's divorce was difficult, and it had a great impact not only on Ronnie but on me—and certainly on the children.

Jane Wyman sent Maureen and Michael to Chadwick, a boarding school in Palos Verdes, about an hour from Los Angeles. Michael was only five and a half when he started at Chadwick, and I found that appalling. Ronnie did too, to the point where he thought seriously about filing for custody. But he gave up that idea when he was advised that it would mean an ugly court battle, with enormous publicity, in which he would have to show that Jane was an unfit mother. All of this would have been terrible for the children, and it was also unlikely to succeed, as it was almost unheard-of in those days for custody to be given to the father. Even so, I believe that Ronnie always felt guilty that he didn't step in and try to get the kids to live with us.

Now that I'm older and more experienced in life, I think there's probably more I could have done to help Maureen and Michael when they were young. If I had been more confident in myself as a mother, I think I would have. It's too bad that the most important job we have in life—parenting—is the one we have no training for.

And looking back now, I can see that the fact that I was never on close terms with Jane didn't help matters; we just didn't have the kind of relationship where I could pick up the phone and talk to her about the kids. And all of us were in unfamiliar territory. Ronnie had never expected to be divorced, and despite all the talk about the high divorce rate in Hollywood, we didn't know any other families with small children in which a divorce had occurred. It wasn't like today, when joint custody and blended families are so common. We didn't really know how to act, and it was tough on all of us.

But Maureen and Michael suffered the most. First they were hit with the divorce, which came without any warning. Then they had to get used to a new stepmother, me. But at least they *knew* me; when Jane Wyman remarried in the fall of 1952, a few months after Ronnie and I were married, the children met Fred Karger, their new stepfather, only the day before the wedding.

And then, just three weeks after their mother's wedding, Michael and Maureen suddenly found themselves with a half sister when Patti was born.

While Maureen and I got along well before Ronnie and I were married, our relationship started to deteriorate after I became Mrs. Reagan. Maureen was now eleven, and she surely must have resented me; as a young girl would see it, I had "taken away" her father. Neither of us can remember a specific incident or an argument, but we just saw each other less. Although Maureen kept in touch with her father, her relationship with me blew hot and cold.

When Patti was born in 1952, Maureen came by to visit. At the time, her class had just been shown a film about cesarean childbirth, and I have a distinct memory of lying in bed, talking to Maureen, who said, "Oh, is *that* what they did to you?" She was very concerned and sweet.

Then there was a long stretch when we rarely saw each other. Maureen was sent to a Catholic high school in Tarrytown, New York, and then, briefly, to college in Virginia. She dropped out of school when she turned eighteen, and moved to Washington, where she went to work in a real estate company and got married. Ronnie and I went back East for the wedding, and that was a close time for us with Maureen—perhaps because we were the only family there. It was in Washington that Maureen became interested in politics, and became a Republican. (She likes to tease Ronnie by telling him that she was a Republican before he was, which is true.)

Maureen and I drifted apart during these years, and somehow it became easier for us not to talk. Now, in hindsight, I wish I had made more of an effort, but Maureen always seemed to be on her way somewhere, taking charge of her life, and we never really connected. With Ronnie it was different. No matter how long Maureen was away, they stayed in touch and were always able to pick up where they'd left off.

In 1982, Maureen decided to run for the United States Senate. Privately, both Ronnie and I thought it might have been wiser—and that she would have had a better chance—if her first campaign had been on a smaller scale than a statewide Senate race. But when Maureen makes up her mind to do something, she does it. She entered the California primary as the only woman among eight Republican candidates, including Barry Goldwater, Jr., Pete McCloskey, Pete Wilson, and the incumbent, S. I. Hayakawa.

The press had a field day when the president of the United States did not endorse his daughter in the primary. But Maureen didn't ask for Ronnie's endorsement, and she didn't expect it, either. She was well aware that ever since her father was elected governor of California in 1966, he has never endorsed *any* candidate in the primaries. Instead, he has always worked to unify the party for the general election.

In 1981, before Maureen had made a final decision, Ronnie was asked by a reporter if his daughter really intended to run. "I hope not," he replied.

Ronnie wasn't sure Maureen was fully prepared for a life in politics, and he knew how tough campaigns can be. But that's not how the comment came across. Here again, family members were communicating through the media, and here again, feelings were hurt. Ronnie recognized immediately that his comment might be misinterpreted, and he called Maureen to apologize, and to explain what he'd really meant. She accepted his apology, but she was still embarrassed and hurt.

What upset Maureen even more was that her uncle Neil, Ronnie's brother, took a couple of shots at her in the campaign. "Just because her father is the president of the United States," he said, "is no reason for her to get very busy and ambitious." Then Neil made a radio commercial in which he said, "We Reagans urge you to support Pete Wilson."

This infuriated Maureen, and I can't blame her. Although Ronnie remained neutral, the Wilson campaign continued to use that misleading commercial, with Neil insisting that "we Reagans" referred only to himself and his wife. As a result, relations between Maureen and Neil have been frosty ever since. (Pete Wilson won the primary and the election, and was reelected in 1988.)

It wasn't until the White House years that Maureen and I really got to know each other again and gradually became close. One of the brightest spots in my life was when Maureen started calling me Mom. It didn't happen until Ronnie's second term, and neither of us has ever mentioned it, but I see it as a real hurdle that we overcame, and a reminder that it's never too late for family members to reconcile their differences and become friends.

Although Maureen was living in California with her husband, Dennis Revell, she made frequent visits to Washington in connection with her position as cochair of the Republican National Committee. Pretty soon she was there almost all the time, living with us and sleeping in the Lincoln Bedroom, which she loved. These visits solidified her relationship both with her father and with me.

Near the end of Ronnie's first term, Maureen became concerned that Ronnie's support among women wasn't strong enough. She decided to do something about it, and she started speaking to women's groups all across the country about the Reagan administration. I supported her in this project, at which she was remarkably effective. Ronnie's support among women increased dramatically, and during the 1984 race he received well over 50 percent of the female vote.

Although Maureen has worked extremely hard to campaign for her father, they don't agree on everything. Maureen has always been a strong supporter of the Equal Rights Amendment, which Ronnie opposes because he believes the Constitution takes care of the matter. And I doubt that they are in full agreement about abortion. But Maureen has never been bashful about expressing her opinions.

Maureen moved back to California when Ronnie's second term was over, and as this book goes to press, she has been filling in for Larry King on his television interview show. In my opinion, she's a natural talk-show host. Years ago she interviewed my father when he published his autobiography, and I remember his coming back and telling me that of all the interviewers he had met, Maureen had asked the best questions.

Unfortunately, Maureen isn't always diplomatic. She can be volatile, and occasionally she is intimidating, coming on too strong. Over the years these traits have made her some enemies.

One of those enemies was Donald Regan, and Maureen and I often commiserated during the period when not just the two of us but practically everybody in Washington thought he should leave—everybody except Ronnie. When Regan finally left, I was particularly upset at some of the press reports, which made it seem as if I, and I alone, were responsible. "I'm very unhappy about these articles," I told Maureen. "I don't want people to be afraid of me."

She said: "The people who know you aren't afraid of you, and those who don't know you *should* be. The best thing in the world is for people to be a little afraid of you. You can get a lot more done that way."

Well, perhaps. But I had never seen myself in those terms.

When Maureen first told me she was writing a book called *First Father, First Daughter,* I thought, Great, just what we need—*another* book by one of the Reagan children about how hard it is when your father becomes president!

Fortunately, I was wrong. Maureen's book is frank and interesting, and in it she provides details and insights about Ronnie that even I hadn't known.

My earliest memories of Michael are of rubbing his back during those car rides to and from the ranch. How he loved those back rubs! I felt sorry for that little boy. He was only three when his parents separated, and he didn't really understand what it all meant. He reminded me of a lost puppy who needed a lot of love and affection.

Mike was four when he learned that he was adopted. When he was old enough to understand what that really meant, he found it enormously upsetting. Although he never talked about it, we now know that he was constantly worried that he might have been born out of wedlock and was therefore illegitimate—and in his own mind, somehow worthless.

For this reason and others, Mike had a difficult time growing up and finding his own identity. No matter what he accomplished—and he eventually became a world-champion boat racer—he always carried the burden of being called "the *adopted* son of Ronald Reagan." I can understand how that must have felt, because I have always hated being referred to as the "*step*daughter" of Loyal Davis. To this day, I can't stand that word "step."

After Chadwick, Michael's mother sent him to St. John's Military Academy, a Catholic boys' boarding school in downtown Los Angeles. He hated it and used to refer to it as St. John's Miniature Alcatraz. He often spent weekends with us, and on Sunday afternoons we'd drive him back to school. He would cry when it was time to go back, and my heart broke for him.

Michael went through a turbulent adolescence, and when he was fourteen his relationship with his mother had deteriorated to such an extent that a psychiatrist recommended that he would be better off moving in with us. Suddenly I had a third child in the house, a teenager whom I barely knew. It soon became obvious that he needed a lot of attention—including a trip to the dentist, who discovered about ten cavities. He also needed clothes, and lots of care.

But I was flying blind with Michael, and I had no idea what was really going on with him. We tried to have a successful blended family, but it's hard when you haven't known each other all along, and when you haven't been in charge during the formative years.

Michael and I had such rough times during that period that there were days when I could have killed him. Teenagers can be difficult in any case, but Mike was especially troubled and rebellious. I was convinced he didn't like me, and I didn't know how to bridge the gap between us. I also had my hands full with Patti, who was seven, and Ron, who was just a baby. Michael later admitted that he was jealous of the attention I gave to little Ron.

Once, when Ronnie was away on a speaking trip, Mike asked if I could find out the name of his birth mother. He was sixteen at the time, and I thought his request was a fair one which deserved an answer. In those days, Ronnie and I had the same business manager as Jane Wyman, so I called and asked him to find out.

When I heard from him, I told Mike that the name of his biological mother was Irene Flaugher, and that he had been named John L. Flaugher at birth. His father had been a military man who went overseas, leaving his mother pregnant—and unmarried.

I was told that Jane was not pleased that I had answered Michael's question. But he was obviously troubled by having been adopted, and I thought he had the right to know the truth about his own background. It seemed like a natural thing to want to know, and I hoped this would give him some peace of mind.

But the fact that Michael's biological parents hadn't been married only confirmed his worst fear—that he was illegitimate. Moreover, he was convinced that his birth mother had given him away because she didn't love him. But Michael never talked about these things, and I learned them only much later, when I read his book.

By this time my own parents were living in Phoenix, and my father helped us get Michael enrolled in a boarding school in Arizona, where he flourished. Mother looked out for him, and when Michael graduated, she presented him with a gold signet ring. When Mother died in 1987, Michael wore that ring to her funeral. It was, he said later, the first time in his life that he had cried for a family member other than himself.

A year or two after the "estrangement" incident, I read a report in *Newsweek* that Michael was writing a book about his father—a kind of *Daddy Dearest*. I couldn't imagine what he could possibly say against Ronnie, but Patti's book had just come out—an unpleasant, critical "novel" about a girl whose father becomes president—and now, apparently, Michael was writing a book of his own.

When I called Mike to ask him about it, he said, "I've been asked to do a book about Dad for lots of money."

"Of course," I replied. "I could get lots of money for walking naked up and down Pennsylvania Avenue. It's a question of taste."

This was the last I heard about Michael's book until April 12, 1987, when Michael, Colleen, and their children, Cameron and Ashley, drove up to the ranch to celebrate Ashley's fourth birthday. Michael seemed anxious and upset, and although he didn't say anything, I could sense that he wanted some time alone with Ronnie and me. After lunch, I suggested that Colleen take the children for a walk around the pond. As soon as Mike was alone with us, he burst into tears.

"What is it?" I asked.

But Mike couldn't speak. He was trembling and gasping for breath and was obviously in great pain. I hugged him and started rubbing his back, the way I used to when he was little.

Then Mike poured out the terrible secret he had been keeping inside all these years. At the age of eight, he had been sexually molested by a camp counselor, who had also taken nude pictures of him. Poor Mike had spent his whole life racked with guilt and in constant fear that these pictures would someday surface in a way that might embarrass him and, especially, his father. Except for Colleen, he had never told anyone. And he had told her only a few weeks earlier.

Ronnie and I had absolutely no idea that anything like this had ever happened. I don't know if we would have picked it up if Michael had been living with us—I'd like to think so—but I can't be sure. I knew Michael had problems, but *this*? I never dreamed of it.

When he finally calmed down, Mike explained that he had given up the idea of writing a negative book about his father. He had been seeing a therapist, and he now understood that the problems in his life were not Ronnie's fault. He was still going ahead with the book, but it was now a different book—one that might be helpful to other victims of sexual abuse.

Michael now refers to that visit to the ranch as the first day of the rest of his life. I can understand why, and I can imagine how hard it must have been for him to share this terrible secret.

The following month, I wrote in my diary: "Mike and Cameron called to thank us for Cameron's birthday present. Mike told me more about the book. I hope it's the right thing for him. He ended by saying 'I love you,' which he had never said before. I'm urging him to call Mermie to re-establish that relationship. I'm so happy that hers and mine became strong a couple of years ago, and I hope that ours with Mike will, too."

I rarely lose an opportunity to worry, and even after Michael's visit to the ranch I was nervous about the book he was writing. When he sent us an advance copy in March 1988, I stayed up half the night reading it. I hadn't known what to expect, but I was tremendously relieved when I saw that it was a candid and soul-searching account of his life, in which Mike was at least as hard on himself as he was on the rest of the family.

I was pleased to see that Michael remembered those back rubs in the car when he was five, and I was touched to learn that he had been hoping that Ronnie and I would get married because he thought he could move in with us instead of living at school. He explained how unhappy he felt as a child, caught between Jane and me, neither of whom was his "real" mom. And he described his constant fear that those nude pictures would somehow surface during one of Ronnie's political campaigns and bring shame upon his father and the entire family.

It was wonderful to see how Mike had grown and changed, and how he was now able to take responsibility for his own life. Ironically, this book, which started off as one more source of friction between us, actually helped us develop a better relationship.

I wish we had been able to see Michael and Colleen's children more often, but we lived so far away, and we weren't in California that often. And sometimes when we were, Michael's family was away. Maybe we could have seen Cameron and Ashley more than we did, and I can understand how Mike sometimes resented the long periods between visits. But for eight long years, our time wasn't really our own.

A few days before we moved out of the White House, Michael started a new job as the host of an early-morning talk show for a radio station in San Diego. The first caller had a familiar voice. "Good morning, Mike," he said. "This is your old man. I'm a little far away to hear the show, but wanted to congratulate you on your first day and wish you well." Ronnie's call came as a complete surprise to Mike, and I know he appreciated it. And it's interesting that Maureen and Michael have both been active in broadcasting, because long before Ronnie became an actor, he made his living as a radio announcer.

I can't close this section about Michael without mentioning a story that I find very moving. During the course of writing his autobiography, Mike decided to search for his birth mother. When Jane did not respond to his request for information, he wrote to Ronnie, who put him in touch with the appropriate person on Governor George Deukmejian's staff. Soon Michael received a detailed reply from the California Department of Social Services, from which he learned, to his great joy, that his birth mother *had* wanted to keep him, but that this would have been impossible in her hometown.

Michael also learned for the first time that his birth mother had said she wouldn't give him up for adoption unless she met the woman who was going to take him. Later she told the social worker that she had recognized Jane Wyman, but she apparently never mentioned this to anyone else.

In the fall of 1987, Mike was in Canada when he received a startling piece of news. A woman who had been friendly with his first wife had recently met a man named Barry, who claimed to be Michael Reagan's half brother. Barry's mother had died in 1985, and on her deathbed she had told Barry that seven years before he was born, she had given birth to another son, who was adopted by Ronald Reagan and Jane Wyman.

Barry was incredulous—until he remembered that his mother used to keep scrapbooks on the Reagan family. He had always assumed that his mother had a crush on Ronald Reagan, but when he went back to look at the clippings, he realized that Michael Reagan was in every one.

Before long, Barry and Michael met. As Michael tells it, Barry was as excited as he was to find his long-lost brother. And Mike was thrilled to learn that he had other living relatives, and that, according to Barry, he bore a striking resemblance to one of his uncles in Florida. Later, we invited Barry to the White House, and I thought I could see a resemblance to Mike.

It all sounds like a soap opera, except that it actually happened. It was wonderful that Mike finally learned the true story of his origins, and discovered that another human being in this world was directly related to him. And that his birth mother had continued to love him and to think about him throughout her life. He had finally found his roots, and it helped him find peace.

Ever since Mike told me this story, I have been impressed by the way Irene Flaugher handled the situation. When Ronnie became governor, and then president, she kept silent. It was only when she was dying that she told her other son about Mike, because she thought he should know. I give that woman a lot of credit and think that Mike has every reason to be proud of her.

I've had my ups and downs with all four children, but my relationship with Patti has been one of the most painful and disappointing aspects of my life. I wish it weren't true, and I still hope it will change, but so far, at least, it hasn't been a happy story. Somehow, no matter what I do, we seem to square off. And it's been this way from the start.

When Patti turned out to be a girl, I thought Ronnie might be disappointed. "Not at all," he said. "The wonderful thing about having a girl is that you get to see your wife as a little girl, growing up." It was a very sweet thing to say, but things didn't quite turn out that way.

I was a nervous mother, and Patti was a difficult baby from the start. She demanded constant attention—and as I look back on it, I think we gave in to her too often. When we put her down at night, she would scream for hours—at least it *seemed* like hours. The doctor said to let her cry it out, and that if we kept going to her, she would cry all the more. But it was hard to stay away, especially during her many tantrums. When guests came for dinner, the noises coming from Patti's room were so terrible that I was afraid they'd think somebody was in there beating her up!

There were also problems with eating. Sometimes after she had been fed she would lean over in her high chair and throw up. That was *lots* of fun, as you can imagine.

Once, when Patti was around two, I was feeding her string beans. She held them in her mouth but simply refused to swallow them. I tried everything I could think of, but nothing worked. Finally I called the pediatrician. "Don't give in," he said. "Leave the room and get busy with something else, and go back to her later." An hour and a half passed, and by now it was past her nap time, but Patti was *still* sitting there with those damn beans in her mouth.

When I came in, she looked up at me with a mischievous smile on her face and said, "What I got in my mouth, Mommy!"

When I called the doctor again, he said, "Reach into her mouth and take out the beans."

This was a kid with a mind of her own. She was defiant, even angry, from the beginning, and with Ronnie away so often, I was the disciplinarian. I wish I had been better at it, but I did the best I could.

In 1958, when I was pregnant with Ron, Patti was excited. She loved to feel the baby growing in my stomach, and she wanted to come to the hospital to see him when he was born. At that time, however, hospitals didn't allow young children to visit, and Ronnie explained that they were afraid kids would carry in germs. But once Ron was born, it soon became obvious that Patti resented the new baby—as most six-year-olds would have.

As Patti grew older, it was clear that she had many talents. She taught herself to play guitar and piano. She made beaded flowers, which she sold to stores. She taught herself to type, and she wrote poetry, which she sent to William F. Buckley, Jr., for his comments. She loved to act, and she was always putting on plays and dressing up in costumes. After Ron was born, Patti would give him a part in her plays, but Ron's parts usually consisted of just standing there while Patti took center stage. During one performance, when Ron was old enough to realize what was going on, he finally got fed up and walked off.

I always encouraged Patti and praised her for her accomplishments, but much of the time she just didn't want to have anything to do with me. When I drove the car pool to school, she sat as far away from me as possible. When we were out together, she walked behind me instead of with me. I just didn't know what to do.

And yet I still have the notes that Patti would slide underneath my door, telling me how much she loved me, and that she hadn't wanted to hurt my feelings.

I now believe that Patti's anger toward me stems from her unresolved feelings about her father. I also believe that Ronnie and I were too indulgent with her; we gave in too often, and paid her too much attention. She demanded it, and we gave it. For six years she was the only one. We didn't plan it that way, but I had two miscarriages before Ron was born, and I was so happy to have a child that I was probably too protective and tried too hard with her. When Ronnie and I went out, and Patti would stand at the window and cry, we always came back to reassure her. Then, wherever we went, we called Patti when we got there. One night we forgot, and later, when we called, the housekeeper told us that Patti had been hysterical for hours. Looking back, I wish we'd helped her become more independent.

Patti attended the John Thomas Dye School in Bel Air, and then, when she was thirteen, she went to the Orme School in Arizona. Orme was a wonderful school, and Patti had already been there for a summer at camp, and for tutoring in math. (Like me, she was weak in math and science.) On most weekends, she stayed with my parents in Phoenix. Orme was located on a working ranch, and Patti loved to ride. Her psychiatrist had suggested that it might be good for her to have something of her own to take care of, and so we gave her a horse.

I wish she had used more of her talents and brains in school, but I guess she had other things on her mind. When she was fourteen, she tried to run off with the school's dishwasher! Because her stepbrother, Michael, was twenty-one, Patti asked him to drive to Arizona and sign her out of school. Michael told our business manager, who called me at home. Patti has never forgiven Michael for betraying her.

Although Ronnie and I often discussed Patti, he usually thought that whatever problem she was experiencing was "only a phase." I often wished he would be more assertive with Patti, and he now regrets that he wasn't.

I remember one time when he got mad at Patti, after she got mad at him. She wanted to live in a coed dorm in college, and Ronnie wouldn't even consider it. Patti was furious. "I can't believe *you're* saying this," she told him. I guess she expected that I would be the one to object—which I did!

After dropping out of college only a year before graduation, Patti left our home and went to live with Bernie Leadon, a guitarist with the Eagles, a popular rock group. Both Ronnie and I were very much opposed to this. You have to remember that we come from a different generation, and the idea of living together without being married was foreign to us.

During Patti's years with Bernie, we had virtually no contact. It wasn't because she was living with a rock musician, although the Eagles were not exactly a mother's dream. And when I finally met Bernie, I found him very likable. It was that they were living together, which we just couldn't accept.

One afternoon I was talking to a friend on the phone, and from the bedroom window I saw Patti's red Toyota come zooming into the driveway. At this point we hadn't seen each other in a couple of years, but she had a serious personal problem and wanted my advice. I was sorry she was upset, but I was also moved that she had come to me for help. We talked for hours, and when she finally left the house that night to go back to Bernie, Ronnie and I stood in the driveway and watched her pull away. Naturally, I was in tears.

It was shortly after that incident that Patti moved back home. This time, everything was different between us. For the first time ever, we were close. We went shopping together, we talked for hours—it was wonderful. Suddenly I had a daughter! This was the way I always thought mothers and daughters should be, and for the months that it lasted, I was incredibly happy.

When Patti decided she wanted to be an actress, I helped her get into the Screen Actors Guild, just as my mother had helped me. She soon found a part in a summer stock production of *Vanities* in Michigan, and she asked Ronnie and me not to fly out to see her perform. I understood; if we had been there, the attention would have been on us, instead of where it should have been—on her. In fact, I think that's been part of our problem with Patti all along. She would like the limelight to be on her, but that's hard when your father is so famous.

Patti was always drawn to acting, and she has never hidden her disappointment that her father gave it up and went into politics. The night Ronnie was elected governor, the first person we called was

Patti, who was in Arizona. There was a tumultuous celebration going on in our suite at the Century Plaza Hotel in Los Angeles, which was all the more exciting because Ronnie was winning by a bigger margin than anybody had expected. In the midst of it all, Ronnie and I slipped into the bedroom to call our daughter.

When we told Patti the good news, she burst into tears and said, "How could you do this to me?"

Granted, she was only fourteen, but I have never forgotten that moment. I didn't understand why Patti couldn't be happy for her father, even if she did hate politics. And I felt so badly for Ronnie. Patti and her generation have always defended the right of each person to do his or her own thing. Shouldn't that same right also apply to parents? Didn't Patti's father have the right to do *his* own thing, even if it wasn't what she would have chosen?

For a while during Ronnie's presidency, Patti was active in the antinuclear movement. Here, I believe, she was used by people with their own political agenda. People can disagree on the best way to prevent a nuclear war, but I have always resented the implication from the peace movement that Ronnie and other conservatives who believe in peace through strength were somehow in favor of war.

During Ronnie's first term, Patti asked him to meet with Dr. Helen Caldicott, the prominent antinuclear activist. The meeting lasted an hour and a half. To carve out that amount of time from the president's schedule wasn't easy, but Ronnie did it for Patti. It was supposed to be a private meeting, with neither one talking to the press afterward. But when Dr. Caldicott went public after the meeting and complained about Ronnie's views, he was furious.

Given our recent history, I was delighted when Patti asked for my advice and help in planning her wedding to Paul Grilley, her yoga teacher, in the summer of 1984. We were in the middle of Ronnie's reelection campaign, but a wedding is a wedding, and there was no way that Ronnie and I were going to miss this one.

They had originally planned to be married in an evening ceremony in a hotel, but when I heard that, I said to Patti, "I can't see you and Paul doing that. You two just don't strike me as indoors, nighttime people. You both love the outdoors. Have you considered the Hotel Bel-Air, where you used to go to dancing school? Maybe you could get married outside in the garden."

Which is what they did. To my surprise, Patti wanted a traditional wedding, with a gown, train, and veil, bridesmaids, a wedding cake, and all the trimmings. (I don't know if her intention was to make *me* happy, but she certainly did.) Patti made her own arrangements for the dress, but I provided "something old"—my maternal grandmother's bracelet—and "something blue"—a garter belt. "Something new" was her wedding dress, and "something borrowed" was her girlfriend's ring.

It was a beautiful wedding, and Patti looked absolutely radiant. When she walked down the aisle with Ronnie, carrying a bouquet of stephanotis, I had an enormous lump in my throat. It just didn't seem possible that this was the same little baby that the nurse had brought to my arms thirty-two years ago in the hospital. Despite the struggles we've had over the years, your child is still your child. I love Patti, and I thought she was a beautiful bride.

Later, when it came time to cut the cake, Ronnie and I went up on the stage with the new bride and groom. Ronnie told a story of how when Patti was a baby, she used to grab hold of his little finger. Before he was finished, mother and daughter were both in tears.

I had hoped that Patti's wedding would signal a new, happier stage in our relationship, but that was not to be. She came to Ronnie's second inauguration in 1985, but just for the day. When they took the family photograph, she was hiding in the back, and Ronnie kept saying, "Step forward, Patti, so we can see you." But she wouldn't do it. And Paul didn't come at all, which hurt me. He said he had to work, but it seemed to me that if you explained that you were taking a couple of days off because your father-in-law was being sworn in as president of the United States, most people would understand.

The following year we heard that Patti was writing a book, although she had never mentioned this to us. She sent us a copy when it was published in 1986, and I read it with sorrow and anger. It was a thinly disguised, self-pitying autobiographical novel about a young woman with left-wing politics whose conservative father becomes the president.

When Ronnie was asked about the book, he replied, correctly, that it was fiction. He did not add, as I was tempted to, that it was deeply hurtful to both of us.

A few weeks after sending us her book, Patti called her brother Ron to say that she couldn't understand why she hadn't heard from us. Ron was incredulous. "What did you expect?" he said. "You've trashed us all in a terrible book. You made Mom and Dad into cartoon characters! Did you expect them to call you and tell you it's great?"

Patti hung up on him, and they haven't spoken since.

The book was bad enough, but then came the author's tour. On March 4, 1986, I began the day by watching Patti on *Good Morning America*, followed by Patti on *Donahue*. Believe me, this wasn't exactly how I had hoped to spend our wedding anniversary! After the book was published, Patti was bumped from a couple of talk shows. Because Merv Griffin and Joan Rivers are friends of mine, some people assumed I had a hand in that. I didn't. But Merv may have done it out of loyalty, and Joan, who was hosting the *Tonight* show at the time, is very attached to her own daughter, and I suspect she just didn't care for what Patti had done to me in her book.

Ronnie and I said very little publicly about it, and Ron was always careful when he was asked about it. "It's always difficult to talk about someone in your family," he said on *Good Morning America*, "but I think Patti's book was wrong, and in bad taste." In another interview, he said, "I think someday she'll regret it."

I hope he's right.

Now, I recognize that it can be difficult to be the child of well-known people, which was something I learned long before Ronnie went into politics. I'll never forget the day that Ronnie and I took Patti and Ron to Disneyland—just the four of us. We had all been looking forward to it, but our visit was a complete disaster. Having seen us in the movies and on television, so many people wanted to talk to us, and ask for autographs, that we never made it onto any of the rides. Finally, we just gave up and went home. The kids were bitterly disappointed, and I felt terrible for them and for us. We had looked forward to enjoying this occasion with our children, but it just wasn't to be.

The following week we arranged for some friends to take our children to Disneyland, but I always felt cheated that it had to be this way, and I'm sure Patti and Ron did, too.

To some extent, then, I empathize with Patti. It *is* difficult to be the daughter of celebrities. It *is* hard to work out your identity while the whole country is watching. It *is* awkward when your father becomes governor, and then president—especially when he stands for positions which you oppose.

But you can't spend your life dwelling on these problems. I get impatient when I hear people complain that their parents are well known and successful, and therefore they have all these terrible problems. There's another side to it: My parents are well known and successful, and how fortunate I am! There are real advantages to having prominent parents. Ronnie and I were in a wonderful position to help our kids because of the people we knew, just as Mother was able to make things easier for me because of her many friends and connections. There are always pluses and minuses in life, and somehow you have to learn to concentrate on the positive—otherwise you'll be engulfed by the negative.

When Patti decided she wanted to be an actress, our friend Jimmy Cagney offered to help her, but Patti wasn't interested. As far as I know, Jimmy had never made such an offer to anybody, and it could have been a wonderful opportunity for her. But she probably saw Jimmy as too old-fashioned—not to mention that he was a friend of the family, which for her was the kiss of death. But when I think how much she could have learned from that man!

I also regret that Patti didn't take advantage of the opportunities that were open to her as the president's daughter. She could have gone on trips with us, she could have met Gorbachev, and witnessed any number of historic events. I realize that she doesn't like politics, but you don't have to like politics to take an interest in historic events. Such opportunities are open to very few people in the world, and they are not available forever.

My worst time with Patti came in 1987, when Mother died. Patti had called me a few days earlier, shortly after my cancer operation, and we had had a brief conversation on the telephone—the first one in a long, long time. But when my mother died there was no visit, no call, no wire, no flowers, no letter—nothing. My mother deserved a lot better than that, and so, for that matter, did Patti's mother.

Yes, I made mistakes with Patti, and with all the children. But one of the things I learned from the drug program is that parents are not always responsible for their children's problems. When your child has a difficult time, it's only natural to blame yourself and think, What did I do wrong? But some children are just born a certain way, and there's very little you can do about it.

And yet I remain optimistic. There is still time for us to improve our relationship, and now that our public years are over, I'm hoping Patti and I will be able to reach some kind of understanding.

I also hope Patti doesn't turn out to be an "if only" child. I've known people who, years after their parents had died, were still saying, "If only I had told my mother that I loved her," or "If only I had made peace with my father." What a terrible burden that must be to carry.

One of the great blessings of my life is that I've never felt that way. I had occasional moments of tension with my parents, but they both knew that I loved them, and I always knew that they loved me.

I hope and pray that before my own life is over, Patti and I will be able to put the past behind us and arrive at that same point. Nothing would make me happier than to work that out.

As a baby, Ron had such a cheerful disposition that his father used to call him Happy Jack. Like many second children, he was considerably easier than his older sister. But in fairness to Patti, I was also much more relaxed as a mother with Ron. I had been there before, and I wasn't nearly as nervous. With Patti, I had always been terrified of making a mistake.

In some ways, however, Ron had a harder time than Patti, because he had to make so many adjustments. Patti was already in high school in Arizona when Ronnie became governor, whereas Ron had to change schools and move with us to Sacramento at the age of eight. The day after the election, the kids in Ron's third-grade class were so excited that they picked him up and carried him around the room on their shoulders.

Although Ron was now the governor's son, I did everything I could to make his life as normal as possible. He bicycled around the neighborhood like every other kid. He went to school in a car pool just like his classmates. When it was our turn to drive, we used a regular car, and one of the policemen assigned to the house would take off his cap and his jacket, put on a sweater, and take the kids to school.

But it's impossible to have a completely normal life when your father is the governor. I remember going out to watch Ron play football on his sixth-grade team and hearing the boys on the other team saying, "There's Reagan. Let's hit him hard." They practically had to hold me back to keep me from going after those kids.

But Ron never complained. He has always had the inner resources to deal with things like that, and small setbacks have never gotten him down.

As first lady of California, I had a busy schedule and was often off visiting hospitals or attending meetings, luncheons, and other events. But I made a firm rule that no matter what was going on, I was home when Ron came home from school. The staff grumbled a little, but I refused to budge. I wanted to be there.

One afternoon, a young woman came to interview me. She asked if it was true that I was always home by four, and I told her it was. In the middle of our conversation, Ron came home, stuck his head in, said, "Hi, Mom," and went off to play. Whereupon the reporter said, "I don't understand. He didn't even come in here. What difference does it make if you're home?"

Well, I thought it was important for a child to come home from school and find his mother there. Even if they don't talk about anything right then, he knows she's there. I don't think the writer really understood the point, but I felt it strongly, and I still do.

When Ron was fifteen, he told Ronnie and me one night at the dinner table that he dared us to go on a backpacking adventure with him. We had sold the ranch when Ronnie became governor, and perhaps Ron needed some assurance that his parents still enjoyed the outdoor life—or that we could still handle it. He just wanted to go off on a trip alone with us, not realizing that this wasn't possible anymore.

Ronnie and I proposed a four-day horseback trip in the High Sierras. There would be no tents—just sleeping bags, horses to ride, and mules to carry the supplies. None of us had done anything like this before, but Ronnie was dying to try it. I was apprehensive, especially about riding through the mountains, because I have a fear of heights. But I wouldn't have missed this experience for anything.

It was a magnificent trip, with beautiful scenery, fresh mountain streams, and starlit nights. On the morning of our last day, we were riding along a narrow trail, with Ronnie in front and Ron bringing up the rear. I was tired and saddlesore and was looking forward to having a hot bath and sleeping in my own bed. Then Ron called out: "Mom, you're doing all right. I figured you'd only last about one day and then find an excuse to go home." When I heard that, *nothing* could have gotten me out of there.

It happened to be my birthday. When we stopped for lunch, Ron raised his tin cup and proposed a toast, and promised he would have the words engraved for me on that cup when we got home. I still have the cup, and I treasure it. The inscription reads: "To the World's Greatest Camper—Sport—and Mom."

Suddenly I felt fine. We rode down a steep, narrow trail into the valley of Yosemite National Park, but I felt no fear. When we reached the bottom, Ronnie turned around to ask if I was all right.

"Sure," I said. "Why not?"

"Turn around and look up."

Above me was a sheer three-thousand-foot cliff. I don't understand how I ever did it, but I'm sure that Ron's supportive words helped make it possible.

When it came time for Ron to start high school, we gave him a choice: He could go to school in Sacramento, but then he would have to leave in the middle when Ronnie's second term was up and we moved back to Los Angeles. The alternative was a boarding school in Los Angeles. Ronnie and I flew back to Los Angeles every Friday, so if he chose that option—which he did—he could be with us on weekends.

We enrolled him at the Webb School in Claremont, where he

slipped into some bad habits and found himself some less-than-terrific friends. When he broke one rule too many and left school one day without signing out, he was expelled. Needless to say, this came as quite a shock to us.

But that wasn't the end of Ron's rebellion. For several years he was romantically involved with a significantly older woman from a show business family who had a teenage daughter of her own. I was heartsick when I learned about it, because I believed she was robbing him of his wonderful teenage years. But there was nothing I could do about it. Their relationship ended while Ron was at Yale, when she dropped him.

Like Patti, Ron was a multitalented kid. He has always been good with words, and I thought he would become a writer. In high school, he was the only junior allowed to participate in the senior writing seminar, where he became motivated to write.

Which is why I was so surprised when he told us, out of the blue, that he had decided to become a dancer. Ronnie and I were spending Thanksgiving weekend with Bill and Pat Buckley in Connecticut, and Ron joined us from Yale, where he was a freshman. We were out for a walk when he turned to us and announced that he had decided to leave college to study ballet.

We urged him to at least finish his first semester at Yale. We had been so proud and excited when Yale had accepted him, and now, after only a few weeks, he wanted to leave. But Ron argued that he was eighteen, and that if he was going to be a dancer, it was already very late. He said he had always been interested in ballet, although I had never heard the word "ballet" cross his lips. And it was certainly a shock and a disappointment to have our son drop out of college during his first semester. (Ronnie and I have always regretted that none of our children graduated from college.)

But we also believe that you have to let your children find their own paths and live their own lives. We have tried to back our children in whatever they have chosen to do, and we could see that Ron was serious about ballet. Our friend Gene Kelly recommended the Stanley Holden Dance Center in Los Angeles, and Ron enrolled there and moved into his own apartment. And what a mess *that* was.

You had to fight your way through, as everything he had was piled up on the floor. Today his apartment is so clean you could eat off the floor; it's amazing what marriage can do for a man.

Ron did extremely well at Holden, in spite of the fact that he was much older than the other beginners. He also met Doria Palmieri, a lovely girl, whom he later married.

As I look back on that time, I think the press was surprised by our reaction to Ron's new career. They thought we would be embarrassed about Ron's decision to become a dancer, but we weren't. Some people expected us to distance ourselves from Ron, but that never entered our minds. We were surprised at his choice, but we were proud of his dedication and his talent. He worked hard, and it was a wonderful discipline.

Ron was accepted by the Joffrey Dance Company in New York, which was quite an achievement—especially for a late starter. He then moved to New York, where he joined the Joffrey II, the touring company. Although I was very proud of Ron, I had mixed feelings about New York. I knew how exciting the city could be, especially when you're young and artistic and your whole life is in front of you. But from a security standpoint it made me anxious that the president's son was living in Greenwich Village. I too had once lived in New York, but that was a different New York.

I was even more nervous when Ron dropped his Secret Service detail in 1982. It drove him crazy to have them there all the time, and one Sunday he came to the White House and discussed it in the solarium with Ronnie and me. "I'm sorry," he said, "but I just can't go through this anymore."

We tried to dissuade him, but he held firm. There was a great deal of concern about terrorism and possible kidnappings that year, and Ronnie explained to Ron that this was a risk he had to consider. There had been a death threat; he was the only one of our children to receive one. But Ron wanted to lead his own life, and we let him.

Shortly after Ron moved to Manhattan, Doria came to live with him. Although I didn't find this quite as shocking as I had in Patti's case a few years earlier, it still wasn't something I felt comfortable about—and I suspect Doria's mother felt the same way. Frankly, I didn't particularly like Doria then. I guess I was thinking back to Ron's other relationship, and because Doria, too, was older, I was afraid this one would come to the same disastrous end and Ron would wind up being hurt.

After Ronnie was elected president, I began to think about Ron and Doria and the sleeping arrangements when the whole family would be staying at Blair House in the days before the inauguration. When they decided to get married, I was relieved because it helped solve this immediate problem—although there were personal problems that wouldn't be resolved until later.

Ron and Doria went down to the federal courthouse to take out a marriage license, but when Ron learned there was a forty-eight-hour waiting period before they could actually marry, he realized that when they came back, there would be a media mob scene. He explained the problem to the judge, who understood, and they got married on the spot and then called us. Although Doria and I didn't start out on the best of terms, I grew to love her as time went on, and I hope she feels the same way.

They're very happy together, in spite of the periodic stories that they're planning to get divorced, or that I don't like Doria. In fact, I've saved a couple of letters she wrote me, saying how much she loves me and how much she's learned from me. A mother-in-law can't ask for more than that.

In 1984 Ron decided that he didn't want to continue in the ballet. Although he was doing well and had recently been accepted into the main company of the Joffrey, he had started dancing far too late to ever become one of the greats. He had proved to himself that he could do it, and now he was free to pursue other interests. There were more practical reasons, too. As he wrote in *Newsweek*, "I left because I want to make a home with my wife and to one day have a child. The finances of ballet and the prospect of touring for months on end made these goals distantly attainable at best."

Although Ron and Doria would now be three thousand miles away from Washington, I breathed a sigh of relief when they left New York and moved back to Los Angeles. Ron wanted to be a writer, and he started doing articles for *Playboy,* including one on the 1984 Democratic convention, one on the Soviet Union, and a third on the Geneva summit. Maureen, who believes *Playboy* is demeaning to women, did not let this go unnoticed. "Listen," she teased him, "do you have any idea how embarrassing it was for me to buy that magazine at a newsstand, just so I could read your article?"

During the past few years, Ron has been working for ABC's *Good Morning America,* and I watch the show every morning in the hope that I'll see him. He has taken on a variety of assignments, including several I wish I hadn't seen—like the time he went white-water rafting, or the time he jumped out of an airplane. But this is what he wants to do, and he obviously has a knack for it. He comes up with most of the ideas himself and does his own writing.

I guess I had better accept the fact that my son likes dangerous assignments. When Ron was nine, we sent him to summer camp for the first time, to a place in Colorado. I remember waiting nervously for his first letter. Finally a postcard arrived, with all of two sentences:

Dear Mom and Dad:
   Today we took rubber rafts down the Colorado River. Mine turned over and I almost drowned.
                                                                Love, Ron

He hasn't changed very much.

One thing I have always admired about Ron is that he handles his father's fame with a nice light touch. "You will have to deal with the press," he wrote in the *Washington Post,* describing what it's like when your father is president. "You have no choice. Lower-order types will rummage through your trash looking for that telltale God-knows-what. The more decent sorts will flatter you onto their talk shows, where you'll have an opportunity to embarrass your parents. If you have a sense of humor, it's kind of fun."

Fortunately, Ron has a wonderful sense of humor. In 1986 he made a commercial for American Express, part of the "Do You

Know Me?" series. As the commercial opens, we see Ron in the first-class section of a plane, being served an ice-cream sundae. "Do you know me?" he begins. "Every time I appear on a talk show, people ask me about my father. Every time I give an interview, people ask me about my father. Every time I pull out the American Express card, people *treat* me like my father. Come to think of it, that's not so bad!"

Then a credit card with Ron's name flashes across the screen. As the commercial ends, we see Ron standing in a phone booth at the airport. "Hello, Dad?" he says. Then he closes the door to carry on the conversation in private.

That commercial showed a lot about Ron, who has always been willing to acknowledge that there are real advantages to being the president's son. Most of all, it showed that, like his father, Ron Reagan can laugh at himself.

He really is a lot like his father—more than he knows. He is single-minded when it comes to accomplishing his goals, and he has a great sense of humor. He loves to read, and has a tremendous warmth, which I think comes across on television. He's also completely unpretentious. "I'm the least ambitious person you ever met," he once said. "All I want is to be insanely happy."

Like Ronnie, Ron is friendly but hard to get to know. Most people can only get so far with him in terms of intimacy. He and Doria are a self-contained unit, and they don't need a lot of other people around—which is what people say about Ronnie and me.

One thing that bothers Ronnie is that Ron doesn't go to church. It means a lot to Ronnie to attend church every Sunday, and since we left the White House he hasn't missed a single one, even when I was sick and couldn't go with him. But Ron has a broad view of religion, and his own faith is individualistic and private. It bothers him that his father doesn't understand that he is religious in his own way.

Ron and I don't always agree either. When he challenges me on issues, he makes me stretch, and that's one reason I enjoy being around him. His views on a number of important issues are different from his father's, although he has never said this in public, which I respect.

On the question of abortion, for example, he is decidedly pro-choice, and he wants me to be, too. I'm not exactly sure where I come down on that one, because I can't get past the feeling that abortion means taking a life. But in cases of incest, rape, or the mother's well-being, I accept it.

Like his father, Ron has always been there for me. In 1981, as I mentioned, when he heard that Ronnie had been shot, he chartered a plane from Nebraska in order to get to Washington as soon as possible. And when my mother died, Ron came to Phoenix immediately to be with me. When I've been down, he has tried to comfort me.

Ron and I had some rough moments while he was growing up, but we've now reached the point where, in addition to being mother and son, we're also friends. I consider Maureen a friend too, and I think Michael and I have also reached that point. A reconciliation with Patti, before I'm old, would be a dream come true.

10

❦❦❦

A Glorious Defeat
(The 1976 Campaign)

OF Ronnie's five campaigns for public office, the one I remember most vividly is the only one he lost. That was in 1976, when he challenged President Gerald Ford for the Republican nomination.

That campaign was so exciting, so dramatic, and so *emotional*—especially at the convention—that in my mind it almost overshadows Ronnie's four victories.

The morning after Ronnie's first victory, when he was elected governor in 1966, the press was already asking whether he was planning to run for president as a favorite-son candidate in 1968. I guess that's the first time I remember thinking that the White House might be a possibility.

Ronnie wasn't interested, but eventually the Republican party leaders in California persuaded him to change his mind, to prevent a bitter split in the state delegation between the supporters of Nelson Rockefeller and those who favored Richard Nixon. Before long, conservative Republicans across the country were talking about Ronnie as a possible candidate, and the discussion continued throughout the Nixon years.

It's often said that I was the one who pushed Ronnie into politics—that he was reluctant to seek office, but that I was ambitious enough for both of us. I suspect this myth got started because Ronnie really *was* reluctant. This is unusual in a politician, and so I suppose some people have have concluded that if *he* wasn't ambitious, *she* must have been.

But in fact I was more ambivalent than Ronnie. After eight years in Sacramento, I was dying to return to Los Angeles and a normal, private life.

Ronnie had already decided to go out on what he calls the mashed-potatoes circuit; he would travel around the country giving speeches. Mike Deaver and Peter Hannaford from Ronnie's staff in Sacramento opened a small public-relations firm in Los Angeles, and they scheduled Ronnie's bookings and arranged for him to do a syndicated newspaper column and a series of radio commentaries. For Ronnie, this was the perfect job: He could earn a good living by doing what he enjoyed—communicating his beliefs about the direction in which the country ought to move. And best of all, his schedule left him time to enjoy our new ranch near Santa Barbara.

The 1974 midterm elections, which were held only three months after President Nixon resigned, had been a disaster for the Republicans. In Ronnie, the party saw a fresh face, a popular and nationally known figure with no ties to Washington and a reputation for integrity. The conservative wing of the party was dying for him to challenge President Ford. Over and over, Ronnie heard the same message: "You *must* run. You owe it to the people who believe in you, who care about the same things you do."

Looking back, I realize it was inevitable that Ronnie would run. And certainly it was inevitable that I would go along with whatever he decided. I've always believed that if Ronnie feels strongly about something, I'd be foolish to go against him.

When Ronnie and his advisers first started talking about the 1976 campaign, they all assumed a wide-open race, and that Ronnie's most likely opponents would be Charles Percy, John Connally, and Nelson Rockefeller. Even after Watergate, almost nobody imagined that Richard Nixon would be forced to resign—or that Gerald Ford would be a candidate, much less the incumbent president.

Ronnie hated the idea of challenging a sitting president from his own party. He also realized that it would be enormously difficult. Everywhere Ford went, he brought with him the excitement of the presidency, including *Air Force One*, the podium with the presidential seal, and the band playing "Hail to the Chief." His press conferences received major coverage. He also controlled the party structure, so any Republican challenger would be battling the establishment in every state.

Still, Ronnie thought Ford was vulnerable. He was the only American president not elected by the people, or even nominated by his own party. Ronnie believed that under the circumstances, Republicans deserved a chance to choose, and given that choice, that a majority would vote for Reagan over Ford.

Ronnie's advisers and supporters began meeting in 1974 to discuss the possibility of a presidential run in 1976. I knew most of these men, but there was a new face—a thirty-four-year-old Washington lawyer with prematurely gray hair named John Sears. Sears had helped the Nixon campaign in 1968, and many people considered him a genius at political strategy. He also had excellent contacts with the Washington press corps, which would be very important if Ronnie entered the race.

John Sears was urbane and articulate, and he knew as much about politics as anyone I had ever met. I loved having lunch with him because he was bright, knowledgeable, and fascinating to listen to. John was not a dyed-in-the-wool conservative, and some of Ronnie's supporters didn't trust him. His mission was to bring home a winner, and he would do everything possible to make that happen.

John wasn't an easy man to know, and he was sometimes difficult to work with. Some people thought he had a private disdain for Ronnie, and there were times—especially later, in the 1980 campaign—when that seemed to be true. He was inscrutable and rarely showed emotion. "John doesn't look you in the eye," Ronnie once said. "He looks you in the tie. Why won't he look at me?"

"Ford is vulnerable," John would say. "The only thing he has going for him is that he's the incumbent. He's a weak leader with no national support. If we can beat him in the first two or three primaries, he's dead."

But with the New Hampshire primary only a few months away, Ronnie still hadn't decided whether to enter the race.

This was frustrating for his friends and supporters, who were dying for him to declare. But whenever Ronnie is faced with a major decision he moves deliberately. I had found that out for myself more than twenty years earlier, when it took him forever to consider running for another office—the husband of Nancy Davis. When he finally decided to enter *that* campaign, he won in a landslide. (Then again, he was unopposed!)

Finally, Ronnie decided to run. I asked the children to come to our house on Halloween so we could tell them ourselves. Maureen arrived first. Mike and Colleen had to drive in from Orange County and were held up in traffic. Patti was estranged from us during this period and didn't come. Ron was still living at home, at seventeen. Ronnie had been given an oversized pair of blue jeans as a joke, and while we waited for Mike and Colleen, I was stuffing them with pillows for Ron to wear to a Halloween party later that evening.

When everybody was there, we moved into the living room. Ronnie said, "Whenever I check into a hotel, the bellhop asks, 'Why don't you run for president?' The next morning, when I leave, the chambermaids come up to me and say the same thing. When I walk through the airports, people are always stopping me and saying, 'Please, we *need* you to run.'

"It won't be easy, but the grassroots support is there. I've been speaking out on the issues for quite a while now, and it's time to put myself on the line. In three weeks I'm going to announce that I'm entering the race. Otherwise, I'd feel like the guy who always sat on the bench and never got into the game."

Maureen, Mike, and Colleen were all supportive, but I think Ron was disappointed because there hadn't been more discussion of this decision in advance. He just sat there silently. Looking back on it, I think he was probably right—that we should have found more time to talk about this as a family.

Once the campaign began, Ron became very active in it. Seniors at his high school were allowed to spend their final semester working on a special project, and Ronnie's campaign was his. He helped with the luggage and worked on the sound system. When it came time to test the microphones, instead of "Testing, one, two, three," Ron would use his father's line about the Panama Canal: "We bought it, we paid for it, it's ours, and we're going to keep it!" It always made me smile to hear him repeating his father's lines.

On November 19 Ronnie and I flew to Washington, where he was going to announce his candidacy the next morning. As soon as we checked into the Madison Hotel, Ronnie placed a courtesy call to President Ford to let him know. Ford's tone was very cold. He told Ronnie that his candidacy would be "divisive," and that he was wrong to do it.

Ronnie explained that he had already made up his mind and assured Ford that he would not attack him personally. But it was a very short conversation.

John Sears had recommended that Ronnie make his announcement at the National Press Club. We were weak in Washington, where the national press corps often portrayed Ronnie as a right-wing extremist. Even after eight years as governor of California, Ronnie was still seen as a kind of novelty—"former actor Ronald Reagan." After the announcement, James Reston wrote in the *New York Times* that it was "astonishing . . . that this amusing but frivolous Reagan fantasy is taken so seriously by the media and particularly by the President. It makes a lot of news, but it doesn't make much sense."

Well, it certainly made sense to Republicans. Two weeks after Ronnie entered the race, a Gallup Poll showed that he was already the front-runner.

When Ronnie and I walked into the National Press Club that morning, Nancy Reynolds, my chief assistant and friend from our Sacramento years, was so excited that she picked me up and swung me around. Then, in a huge, cavernous room, facing more microphones and cameras than I had ever seen in my life, Ronnie read a short statement and answered questions for over an hour. This was my first exposure to the Washington press corps, and I remember thinking, Boy, these guys are *tough*.

Ronnie didn't mention Ford by name—a practice he has always followed in campaigns. But he charged that government in Washington had become a "buddy system," and that the nation needed leaders who were independent of Congress, the federal bureaucracy, lobbyists, big business, and big labor. "We need a government that is confident not of what *it* can do," he said, "but of what the people can do."

Later that day we flew to Miami to begin campaigning in the early-primary states. The first stop was an airport rally. As Ronnie was speaking, a voice in the crowd called out, "Hey, Dutch." We knew it was someone from Iowa, where Ronnie had worked as a sports announcer and was known as Dutch Reagan.

"Hi, there," Ronnie called back. "I'll come down to see you when I'm done."

When Ronnie finished speaking, one of the Secret Service agents said, "When you leave the platform, turn to your left." Instead, Ronnie veered right, to look for his friend. I was following behind when I heard Tommy Thomas, our chairman in Florida, yell, "What the hell do you think you're doing?"

Tommy plunged into the crowd, and I watched in shock as he and two other men tried to wrestle a dark-haired young man to the ground. The man was holding a gun, and it took all three of them to get him down. As it turned out, the gun was a toy, but it certainly looked real to me.

Before I knew it, the Secret Service had pushed me into the nearest building. I was scared, and when Ronnie came in, I blew up. "Now, listen," I said, "from now on, if the Secret Service tells you to turn to the left, turn left! Do what they tell you to do!" I was trembling, and Ronnie had to calm me down. If he was frightened, he didn't show it.

A few months later we had another close call. We had just left Ohio, and on the flight back to Los Angeles, Ronnie was sitting on the right side of the plane, next to the window. As usual, he was working on a speech. Martin Anderson was beside him, and I was across the aisle. I had just dozed off when I heard Ronnie gasping. When I looked up, there was my husband, standing beside me with his hand on his throat. His face was red and he couldn't talk.

"Heart attack!" somebody yelled. "Give him oxygen." Mike Deaver immediately got up and grabbed Ronnie from behind. Wrapping his arms across Ronnie's ribs, he gave a sudden pull. When nothing happened, Mike did it again—whereupon a bunch of peanuts flew out of Ronnie's mouth. Then Ronnie straightened up and began to breathe normally.

Mike told me later that he and Ronnie had once practiced the

Heimlich maneuver, just in case this problem ever arose. I learned
later that Ronnie had been tossing peanuts into the air and catching
them in his mouth. Believe me, he never tried *that* again!

In 1988, during our final year in the White House, I watched the
television news reports of the primary and election campaigns. And
I asked myself in amazement: Where did I ever get the strength to
go through all that? It's so exhausting! You move from town to
town, and the days and nights become a blur as one place melts into
another. It's an endless series of hotels and motels, buses and cars.
You rarely get a chance to wash your face. You fall into bed at
midnight, and the next day you're up at dawn to do it all over again.

But there also can be a wonderful spirit of camaraderie in a
campaign; everyone is working together and traveling toward the
same goal. It reminded me of being on location for a movie. You
become an extended family, and you make deep, lasting friendships.
Your whole life becomes those people and that plane you're all on.

Still, there were times when I had to be the tough guy because
of Ronnie's schedule. Ronnie was a vigorous campaigner—some of
the reporters who wondered about the "age factor" had trouble
keeping up with him—but I didn't think it was wise to overdo it,
to keep him going from early morning until late at night, day after
day.

But the campaign staff always wants the candidate to make "just
one more appearance," and the local chairman has "one more little
thing" that you've just *got* to do before you leave town.

And so sometimes I simply had to say "Enough. That's it. We
can't do any more." Even then, I felt that the staff was there to look
after Ronald Reagan the candidate, but I was there to look after
Ronald Reagan the man.

One memory of that campaign that stays with me was the time
Ronnie and I were riding in a parade, standing in an open convert-
ible. It was a cold spring day, and it was raining, but in spite of the
weather, we spent the afternoon waving to the crowds who were
lined up to see us. I was so busy waving that it took time before I
realized that every time I lifted my arm, the rain ran down my sleeve

and down the front of my dress. I was freezing. Then, when we finally returned to the hotel, cold, wet and exhausted, the heat had been turned off for the night. It was very cold. We begged them to turn the heat back on, and they finally did—for an exorbitant price.

I no longer remember what city this happened in, but I remember thinking: The people in this hotel are obviously not Republicans.

Although I often traveled with Ronnie, there were so many places to visit and so little time that I continued the practice of doing some campaigning on my own, especially in smaller communities that Ronnie just couldn't get to. Usually I was accompanied only by Nancy Reynolds and Barney Barnett, our old friend from Sacramento days. Whenever possible, I stuck to my old format of questions and answers.

Nancy and I spent a lot of time in Texas, Alabama, and North Carolina, where we visited an endless stream of hospitals, women's groups, colleges, and nursing homes. I was interviewed in hallways, lobbies, motel rooms, cars—just about everywhere except the ladies' room. What was fun was seeing the country and meeting the people, and I was always gratified to see how many supporters Ronnie had, especially in out-of-the-way places.

I'd get up in the morning and I'd go all day and well into the night. There was rarely time to change clothes or take a bath. If I was lucky I could powder my nose and run a comb through my hair once in a while, but that was about it. I learned to wear knit dresses, which would last all day without looking wrinkled.

Unless your husband is the incumbent president, there's nothing luxurious about campaigning. I remember seeing Mrs. Ford at a political dinner during the race. She looked so fresh and lovely that I thought, It must be wonderful to have *Air Force One*, where you can change your clothes and wash your face during the day.

I liked campaigning, but I hated the flying. Small towns usually meant small airplanes, and I have enough trouble with big ones. We were coming in to Aniada, Alabama, one night when the pilot turned to me and said, "This is just a tiny airport. They don't even have a tower. I don't want to alarm you, but there are no lights on the runway." When he saw the expression on my face, he added,

"But I'm sure I could get a few people to come out with their trucks and turn on their lights!"

We landed by trucklight, but by then I was a nervous wreck. I couldn't believe we were actually doing this. My only request had been that the plane have more than one engine—and two pilots.

Another time we had to fly into Banner Elk, North Carolina, where the "airport" consisted of a tiny grass runway in the mountains. It's a good thing I didn't know about *that* in advance. As we began our descent, Nancy Reynolds suddenly shoved a newspaper article into my hands—and the plane dropped down to the runway like a stone. She was hoping to distract me, but the feeling in my stomach gave it all away.

I don't know who decided that the presidential primaries should begin in New Hampshire in the winter, but he certainly wasn't from California. I was used to Chicago winters from my childhood, but New Hampshire was something else again.

On the other hand, the people there always asked the best questions—even if they did like to ask them while you were standing outdoors. They're accustomed to old-fashioned door-to-door campaigns, with a handful of neighbors meeting with the candidate in somebody's living room—the kind of politics that is quickly dying out in the age of television. We stumped that state thoroughly, riding our drafty campaign bus into just about every little town on the map.

Two days before the vote, the chairman of Ronnie's New Hampshire campaign urged Ronnie's advisers to take him out of the state so the campaign workers could spend their time working on getting a big turnout, instead of focusing on the candidate. With Ronnie ahead in the polls, it seemed like a sensible plan.

But what we didn't know was that Ronnie's lead had been slipping, and the race was now virtually tied. John Sears had this information, but for reasons I'll never understand, he didn't tell Ronnie or anybody else. And my husband, who is very trusting, never imagined that anything was being kept from him.

And so, foolishly, we spent the last two days campaigning in

Illinois and didn't return to New Hampshire until the night before the vote.

During the flight back, Sears asked Dick Wirthlin to brief Ronnie. When Ronnie heard that Ford had closed the gap in New Hampshire, he just stared out the window. Below us were the lights of Manchester: We were preparing to land. "Well, Dick," Ronnie said, "I hope some good people down there will light a few candles for me."

When we woke up the next morning, the weather was unusually mild. I thought that was a good sign—until somebody explained that Ronnie's supporters were so passionate that they would turn out in *any* weather, while Ford's support was softer. "We could have used a really big snowstorm," I was told.

The early returns showed that Ronnie had a slight lead, and as late as midnight he was still ahead. It looked as if Ronnie had won, but then the tide began to turn. When all the ballots were counted, Ford had won by 1,317 votes.

Coming that close to defeating an incumbent president was a real achievement, but the press had expected Ronnie to win. As a result, Ford's narrow victory was seen as a major achievement.

Momentum is everything in politics, and our loss in New Hampshire was a terrible blow to Ronnie's prospects in other states. It was even more painful when we learned that a majority of the voters had actually picked Ronnie! Because of a quirk in the New Hampshire law, three extra, unauthorized candidates ran as pro-Reagan delegates. But voters were instructed to choose no more than eighteen candidates, so anyone who simply checked off every pro-Reagan name had his ballot disqualified. Ronnie's advisers believed that between 5 and 10 percent of the voters made this error; their votes would have been more than enough to give us New Hampshire. There were also fifteen hundred Democrats who wrote in Ronnie's name, but their ballots didn't count either.

If Ronnie had won in New Hampshire, he probably would have won at least two other early primaries as well. And then President Ford might well have dropped out of the race—just as John Sears had planned.

But now Ford had the momentum, and he went on to win in Florida, Massachusetts, Vermont, and Illinois. In a three-week period, Ronald Reagan, who had never lost an election in his life, was defeated five times in a row.

Election days are always Tuesdays, and it got so bad that John Sears said, "I used to hate Mondays. Now I hate Wednesdays!"

By the time we got to North Carolina for the primary on March 23, Ronnie's prospects looked so bleak that the press had only one question: "When are you going to get out of the race?"

But Ronnie had no intention of quitting. He hadn't entered the race casually, and he wasn't going to leave until he had done everything he could.

Ronnie doesn't get angry very often, but after five consecutive defeats he took off the gloves. Instead of using his standard speech, he threw away his notes and spoke from the heart. And rather than ignoring the advantages of Ford's incumbency, he began pointing them out. "I understand Mr. Ford has arrived in the state," he said. "If he comes here with the same list of goodies he brought to Florida, the band won't know whether to play 'Hail to the Chief' or 'Santa Claus Is Coming to Town'!"

When you lose five primaries in a row, people aren't very eager to send you money. By this time our campaign was broke, and it got to the point where nobody would provide *anything*—hotel rooms, advertising, rental cars—unless we paid in advance. When we could no longer afford our chartered jet, we switched over to a little yellow prop plane, which became known as the Flying Banana. When we touched down, Mike Deaver would come down the aisle with two big buckets of Kentucky Fried Chicken.

By now Ronnie was under increasing pressure to drop out of the race. We didn't have much support from party officials and officeholders to begin with, but now the situation had deteriorated.

In February, eleven of the twelve former chairmen of the Republican National Committee had endorsed President Ford. (The only one who didn't was George Bush, but as director of the CIA, he wasn't allowed to.)

On March 17, the National Republican Conference of Mayors called on Ronnie to withdraw.

The following day, the *Los Angeles Times* wrote, "For Reagan, the real question ought not to be *whether* to bow out, but *when.*"

On March 20, seven Republican governors issued a statement calling on Ronnie to quit.

In the entire Republican party, Ronnie had only one major supporter—Senator Paul Laxalt of Nevada.

The biggest blow of all came when Barry Goldwater endorsed Gerald Ford. My parents, who were now living in Phoenix, had been friendly with the Goldwaters for years, and Mother was so furious that she called Barry and told him in no uncertain terms—and undoubtedly using some *very* colorful language—that he had been to their house for the last time.

Eventually, Mother and Barry made their peace. She could be hot-tempered, especially if she believed that a member of her family had been wronged, but eventually she let bygones be bygones. My father was different. He gave Barry the silent treatment, and I don't think he ever forgave him.

I was very hurt, because I had known Barry and his family for years. Ronnie and I had been at the 1964 convention to support him, and during that campaign Ronnie had raised a lot of money with his television speech. Now, twelve years later, Ronnie was still speaking out for those same principles. But where was Barry?

Ronnie was disappointed, too, but he chose to believe that Barry was supporting Gerald Ford out of loyalty to the president. Some people wondered if Barry had come to resent Ronnie's leadership of the conservative movement. I don't know about that, but if that's true, then I have some empathy for Barry. It must be very difficult to start a political movement and then watch somebody else take it over and make it more successful.

Still, I think Barry owed my husband a lot more than he gave him in 1976.

On the day of the North Carolina vote, Ronnie's campaign staff had an emergency meeting in a hotel room in Wisconsin, where John Sears came up with a bold proposal. "Governor," he said, "we don't have enough money to continue this campaign in the normal way. But I've been in touch with Jimmy Lyon down in Texas, and he's willing to lend us a hundred thousand dollars to put you on national television with that speech you've been giving about Ford and Kissinger being weak on defense. At the end, you'd make an appeal for funds. Now this is a gamble, and I can't guarantee that it will work. We would have to leave Wisconsin tonight and go back to Los Angeles. But I don't see any other way to raise the money we need."

What John was proposing was enormously risky, but nobody had a better plan. Finally Ronnie said, "Do it. Borrow the money. I'm taking this campaign right through to Kansas City, even if we lose every damn primary along the way."

That evening, Ronnie was speaking to a group called Ducks Unlimited, an organization of duck hunters in La Crosse, Wisconsin. When the first results from North Carolina started trickling in, Nancy Reynolds and I were sitting outside the hall in the back of a car, leaning forward and straining to catch every syllable coming from the tiny car radio. Ford was far ahead in the polls, but with 5 percent of the vote counted, Ronnie had jumped to a ten-point lead! Although it was still too early to tell what would happen, we cheered and hugged each other.

When we came inside, Frank Reynolds, who was covering Ronnie's campaign for ABC, told us that 15 percent of the vote was now in and that Ronnie's lead was holding. As soon as Ronnie's speech was over, we rushed up to tell him the good news.

The press sensed a real breakthrough in North Carolina and they started clamoring for a statement. But Ronnie refused to say a word. He still remembered New Hampshire, which had looked like a sure thing.

Later that night, as we took off for California, we still didn't know what the results in North Carolina would be. But the pilots received regular updates on the radio, and I remember Marty Anderson sitting with his calculator, trying to show Ronnie that the numbers looked promising. Although the lead was holding, Ronnie wouldn't believe it until we had a final count. Finally, with most of the precincts in, Marty showed him that even if every remaining vote went for Ford, Ronnie would still win. When Ronnie heard that, he broke into a smile and walked back to talk to the press. We celebrated with champagne and vanilla ice cream.

It was a long time coming, but we finally had our first presidential primary victory!

A week later, when Ronnie's speech was aired on NBC, we raised almost a million and a half dollars—more than enough to keep us going. The Sears gamble had worked.

Suddenly the momentum had shifted. In Texas, Ronnie won every county and all ninety-six delegates. On May 4, he won in Georgia, Alabama, and Indiana. The following night, Walter Cronkite uttered those magic words: "Ronald Reagan as of tonight looms as a serious threat."

Now it was a real contest—and better late than never.

Although it was by no means a dirty campaign—nothing to compare with the Bush-Dukakis race in 1988—there was an unpleasant incident just before the California primary. In response to a reporter's hypothetical question, Ronnie said he could imagine a situation where the United States might join in sending U.N. peace-keeping troops to Rhodesia, if Rhodesia requested it.

Stuart Spencer, who had been with us in Ronnie's two gubernatorial races but who now worked for the Ford campaign, quickly produced a television commercial for Ford which ended with these words: "When you vote Tuesday, remember: *Governor* Reagan couldn't start a war. *President* Reagan could."

It was quite a while before I could forgive Stu for that one.

But the people of California knew Ronnie, and the ad backfired. On election day, Ronnie won California by a two-to-one margin.

When all the primaries were over, an unofficial count showed that Ford was going into the convention with 1,093 delegates, while Ronnie had 1,030. Neither man had enough delegates to clinch the nomination, but the magic number was 1,130, so Ford was awfully close.

Now President Ford took full advantage of his office. He brought dozens of uncommitted delegates to the White House for lunches, cocktails, meetings, and dinners. He invited an entire state delegation to have lunch with him. In July, he invited Clarke Reed, the chairman of the Mississippi delegation, to a state dinner for Queen Elizabeth. (The Mississippi delegation was the largest uncommitted group attending the convention.) Over the July 4 weekend, he invited seven uncommitted delegates to watch the tall ships sail into New York Harbor from the flight deck of an aircraft carrier.

To this day, I have never known the White House to be used by either party the way it was in this campaign. I was furious. The White House stands for something more important than partisan politics and uncommitted delegates—or at least it should.

In July, a month before the convention, the press was starting to say among themselves that Ford had the nomination sewn up. If this perception became public, it would quickly become self-fulfilling.

And so with nothing left to lose, John Sears tried his second major gamble of the campaign: He persuaded Ronnie to announce his choice of a running mate several weeks before the convention. Not that it took much convincing. For years, Ronnie had felt strongly that it was a bad idea to have the nominee select his running mate in a last-minute high-pressure late-night meeting at the convention.

John hoped that Ronnie's early choice of a running mate would signal that the race still wasn't over. The man he recommended was Senator Richard Schweiker of Pennsylvania. Although Schweiker was known as a liberal, he had supported Barry Goldwater in 1964. Like Ronnie, he was in favor of a strong defense, school prayer, tax incentives, and the death penalty, and he was opposed to gun control and federally funded abortions. John believed that a Reagan-Schweiker ticket would be hard to beat in November, and I believe he was right.

But when Ronnie announced that he had chosen Schweiker, conservative Republicans were furious. They saw Schweiker as too liberal, as another Rockefeller, and they felt that in choosing him, Ronnie had betrayed the cause. Never mind that Kennedy had picked Johnson in 1960 to unify the Democrats. Never mind that two conservatives on the same ticket had no chance of winning. As always, some of Ronnie's supporters insisted on putting ideological purity ahead of victory.

John hoped that Ronnie's choice of Schweiker would pressure Ford into announcing *his* choice for vice president. Rockefeller had already been dropped from the Ford ticket, and John believed that no matter whom Ford selected, the choice would hurt him. If Ford picked a moderate, he would lose delegates in the South; a conservative would hurt him in the North.

When Ford refused to announce his running mate, Sears tried to force the issue by calling for *all* presidential candidates to name their vice-presidential choices before the nomination. By forcing a floor vote on this question, John wanted to show that some of Ford's support was soft. If our side could somehow win the vote on Rule 16-C, the uncommitted delegates might realize that a Ford victory was not inevitable.

And so the climactic night of the convention came twenty-four hours before the nomination, when the delegates voted on John's proposal. Emotions were running high, and I'll never forget how angry I felt when I saw Nelson Rockefeller walking up and down the convention floor twisting arms for Ford. I even saw him grab a Reagan placard from a Utah delegate and break it. I couldn't believe I was watching the vice president of the United States.

We made a good try, but we just didn't have the votes to change the rule. That was when we knew for certain that the race was over.

The next evening, before the nominations were made, our family had a quiet dinner together in our suite at the Alameda Plaza Hotel. Then we all gathered in the living room, where Ronnie explained what we already knew—that our long, emotional struggle was about to end in defeat. "I'm sorry that you all have to see this," he said.

We were all in tears, but Ronnie tried to lift our spirits. "You know what I regret the most?" he said. "I had really looked forward to sitting down at the table with Brezhnev to negotiate on arms control. He would tell me all the things that our side would have to give up. And then, when he was finished, I was planning to stand up, walk around the table, and whisper one little word in his ear: *Nyet.*"

I proposed a toast in honor of my husband. "Honey," I said, fighting back the tears, "in all the years we've been married, you have never done anything to disappoint me. And I've never been prouder of you than I am now."

By tradition, the candidates don't appear at the convention until the nominee has been chosen. On the first three nights, Ronnie had stayed in the hotel with several of his advisers while the rest of the family went down to the arena. The Republican National Committee had assigned us to a skybox at the far end of the hall, more than two hundred feet from the stage, with a thick glass panel separating us from the delegates. It was very comfortable, with plush seats, a buffet, a bar, and a private bathroom. But it was also remote. We were tucked away so far from the action that we couldn't really feel part of the people or the excitement.

The Fords had a similar skybox at the other end, but Betty Ford was also given a box right down on the convention floor. Maureen was convinced that this was done deliberately, to give the Fords an advantage, and she may have been right. In any event, she worked out a swap with several alternates from the Colorado delegation; they were thrilled to take our places in the box, and we were happy to take their seats, which were much closer to the convention.

The press made a big fuss over Betty Ford and me, and there were several stories about "the battle of the wives," or as *Time* magazine put it, "the contest of the queens." These reports centered on such "issues" as what each of us was wearing, and who came into the convention hall first. In its way, it wasn't all that different from what happened ten years later with Raisa Gorbachev, when, on a much larger scale, the media paid so much attention to the two of us, and to our feuds, both real and imaginary.

Every time Betty or I entered the convention hall, our husbands' supporters would put on a demonstration. On the second night, during an ovation for me, the band struck up "Tie a Yellow Ribbon Round the Old Oak Tree" and Betty started dancing with Tony Orlando, who was visiting the Ford box. The crowd went wild. Some of our people saw this as a deliberate attempt to upstage me, but I never thought that was her intention.

The night before, I was in our hotel suite when Ron called me to say, "Mom, Betty Ford just showed up and we all think you should get over here."

"But Ron," I said, "I'm already undressed. I was told that we weren't supposed to appear until tomorrow."

Ron persisted, so I got dressed and went over. I didn't really need to be there, but when everybody around you is caught up in a competition, it's hard to stay on the sidelines.

The "battle of the wives" at the 1976 convention created a lot of friction that shouldn't have been there. It made both of us feel self-conscious, and it took years to get over. As far as our relationship went—and that wasn't very far—it was hampered by the jealousies and the tensions of our staffs. Things were repeated to me about Betty Ford (and I'm sure to her about me) that weren't necessarily true. And I didn't appreciate it when Betty was quoted in *Time* magazine as saying that "when Nancy met Ronnie, that was it as far as her own life was concerned. She just fell apart at the seams."

The two of us were different people who came from different worlds. When she was interviewed on *60 Minutes*, Betty had come out strongly in favor of abortion and had implied that marijuana was no more dangerous than beer or cigarettes. Whenever I was asked about Betty Ford's views during the campaign, I tried to avoid the subject by saying I didn't think she should have been asked the questions she was.

Gerald Ford won the nomination at twelve-thirty in the morning, as Ronnie and I and Lyn Nofziger watched the proceedings in our hotel. When it was all over, Lyn went into the bathroom and cried. Then he poured himself a glass of gin. Finally he picked up the phone and called Bob Nieson, the head of the California delegation, to ask that California make it unanimous for Ford.

When the delegates refused, Lyn rushed to the convention floor and begged them to do it for the sake of party unity. He found Bill Wilson and Alfred Bloomingdale, and both men had tears in their eyes. Bill told him, "Lyn, I came here to vote for Ronald Reagan, and that's who I'm going to vote for."

When John Rhodes, the chairman of the convention, saw what was happening, he suddenly banged his gavel and announced that the convention had just made it unanimous for Gerald Ford. In the heat of the moment I thought this was outrageous. But in retrospect, it was probably a wise move.

John Sears had already worked out an arrangement with Dick Cheney, the White House chief of staff, that whichever candidate won the nomination would visit the other man in his hotel for a brief symbolic meeting of reconciliation. Because there was talk of a Ford-Reagan ticket, Ronnie asked John to make sure Ford would not raise this issue during their meeting. Ronnie still wasn't interested in being vice president, but he also didn't want to be in the position of having to turn down the president.

It was one-thirty in the morning when President Ford came to our suite, along with Dick Cheney, several aides, and Ford's Secret Service detail. The two candidates then met privately in the living room. Ford kept his word and did not ask Ronnie to be on the ticket. (I know that because Ron and Maureen were listening on the other side of the door. As I said, feelings run high during a campaign!)

Ford had brought along a list of vice-presidential prospects, and he mentioned six names: Howard Baker, Elliot Richardson, John Connally, William Simon, William Ruckelshaus, and Robert Dole. Ronnie told Ford that he thought especially highly of Bob Dole.

We didn't get much sleep that night. At seven-fifteen the next morning, Michael Deaver knocked on our bedroom door. "Governor," he said to Ronnie, "Holmes, Justin, and Bill Smith are here to see you. They think you should accept the vice presidency." (Holmes Tuttle, Justin Dart, and William French Smith were all longtime supporters and friends of Ronnie's.)

No such offer had been made, of course, but many Republicans believed that only a Ford-Reagan ticket could win in November. And many of Ronnie's supporters felt that half a loaf was better than none.

"No," said Ronnie. "We've been through all that. Please tell them I'm not interested."

"Governor," said Mike, "you'll have to tell them yourself. They're your friends, not mine."

Ronnie climbed out of bed, got dressed, and invited the three men into the living room. Once more, he explained that he simply didn't want to be vice president.

Just then the phone rang; Ronnie picked it up, listened, and said, "Terrific. I think you made the right choice."

When he put down the phone he said, "Fellows, that was Jerry Ford. He's just picked Bob Dole."

Dole had been selected in one of those high-pressure middle-of-the-night meetings that Ronnie had hoped to avoid. Justin Dart had been there, and he told us later that when somebody brought up Ronnie's name, Ford had said, "Absolutely not. I don't want anything to do with that son of a bitch."

On the final night of the convention, we all returned for Ford's acceptance speech. Ron and Maureen got there first, and when they arrived in our box, they found that all the Reagan stickers and banners had been torn down. They immediately started putting them back up.

This was Ronnie's first and only appearance at the convention, and the demonstration he set off was simply astonishing. It was the largest, loudest ovation I had ever heard. *Ever.* The place just went wild! People were screaming "We want Reagan." The band was playing "God Bless America," although you could hardly hear it. Down on the stage, John Rhodes was trying in vain to restore order. In the Florida delegation, Ronnie's supporters held up a sign: RON, WE ALMOST MADE IT.

Every few minutes, Ronnie would stand up and motion to the people to sit down. But each time he stood, the crowd would break into shouts of "Speech! Speech!" As the ovation continued, Frank Reynolds came into the box to interview Ronnie. "What do you think about this, Governor? Are you going to speak?"

"No, Frank," Ronnie replied. "This is someone else's night, not mine."

But the commotion just wouldn't stop. At one point, Ronnie got up to try to thank his supporters. I remember hearing Frank Reynolds say, "My Lord, he's trying to speak!" But there was no way Ronnie could address that huge crowd without a microphone.

Then, instead of trying to interview us, Frank said, "This may not be the best of journalistic derring-do, but I'm going to leave now and let the Reagans enjoy this moment." Before he left, Frank put his arm around me and I hugged him. He was a dear man, and I had grown very fond of him.

Eventually, order was restored and Gerald Ford began his acceptance speech. While Ford was speaking, Bryce Harlow, an elder statesman of the party, was conferring with Ronnie's top advisers to see whether Ronnie would agree to address the convention if Ford invited him down. Mike Deaver checked with Ronnie, who said yes. But nobody in our box expected that Ford would actually do such a thing, now that this long and difficult campaign was over.

As Ford finished his remarks, a big bunch of balloons was released. Then Ford looked up toward our box and said, "Governor Reagan, come on down—and bring Nancy with you!"

Ronnie couldn't quite believe it. "Does that mean I've been asked?" he said.

"Yes," said Mike. "You better get moving!"

A moment later the Secret Service led us through a labyrinth of back halls, stairwells, tunnels, and corridors as we made our way to the stage. We were running, as it was quite a distance away. And the whole time Ronnie was asking me, "What am I going to say? I don't know what to say!"

"Don't worry," I replied. "You'll think of something!"

When we finally reached the stage, the convention exploded all over again. They shouted *"Viva! Olé!"* again and again. The Fords were already on the stage, along with the Doles and the Rockefellers. Ronnie moved toward the microphone and I stood nearby. The stage was so crowded that I ended up standing over a grate that blew cool air up my skirt. It was hot in that arena, and the air felt good. But the whole time we were there, I had to press my skirt down so it wouldn't fly up. It's a good thing I was wearing a knit dress instead of silk! Funny, the things you remember.

As Ronnie began to speak, the delegates remained on their feet and continued standing until he was finished—the first time this had ever been known to happen. What was even more astonishing was that the immense Kemper Arena had become utterly still. I never knew that so many people could be so quiet, and I've never seen anything like it, before or since.

It was a glorious moment, but I was terrified for Ronnie. Here he was, facing the entire Republican convention—not to mention a television audience of fifty million people. He had had no idea this was coming and had nothing prepared. I prayed he would think of something.

And of course he did. As he began speaking, I remember wondering, Where did *this* come from? A minute ago he didn't know what to say!

"I had an assignment the other day," he began. "Somebody asked me to write a letter for a time capsule that is going to be opened in Los Angeles a hundred years from now, on our Tricentennial.

"It sounded like an easy assignment. They suggested I write about the problems and issues of the day. And I set out to do so, riding down the coast in an automobile, looking at the blue Pacific out on one side and the Santa Ynez Mountains on the other. And I couldn't help but wonder if it was going to be as beautiful a hundred years from now as it was on that summer day.

"And then I tried to write—let your own mind turn to that task. You're going to write for people a hundred years from now who know all about us. We know nothing about them. We don't know what kind of world they'll be living in.

"And suddenly I thought to myself, If I write of problems they'll be domestic problems, of which the president spoke here tonight, the challenges confronting us, erosion of freedom that has taken place under Democratic rule in this country, the invasion of private rights, the controls and restrictions on the vitality of the great free economy that we enjoy. These are the challenges that we must meet.

"And then again there is the challenge of which he spoke, that we live in a world in which the great powers have posed and aimed at each other horrible missiles of destruction that can, in a matter of minutes, arrive in each other's country and destroy virtually the civilized world we live in.

"And suddenly it dawned on me. Those who would read this letter a hundred years from now will know whether those missiles were fired. They will know whether we met our challenge. Whether they have the freedoms that we have known up until now will depend on what we do here.

"Will they look back with appreciation and say, 'Thank God for those people in 1976 who headed off that loss of freedom, who kept our world from nuclear destruction'?

"And if we fail, they probably won't get to read the letter at all because it spoke of individual freedom and they won't be allowed to talk of that or read of it.

"This is our challenge. And this is why, here in this hall tonight, better than we've ever done before, we have got to quit talking to each other and about each other, and go out and communicate to the world that we may be fewer in number than we've ever been, but we carry the message they've been waiting for. We must go forth from here united, determined that what a great general said a few years ago is true: 'There is no substitute for victory.' "

When Ronnie was finished, the hall erupted in cheers. We left the stage with the sound of applause and with "California, Here I Come" ringing in our ears.

The next morning, before we left Kansas City, Ronnie held two final meetings. The first was with the California delegation. "The cause goes on," he told them. "It's just one battle in a long war and it will go on as long as we all live. Nancy and I, we aren't going to go back and sit in our rocking chairs and say that's all for us."

I wasn't at that meeting, but I'm told that Ronnie finished by quoting from an old English ballad he had learned in school years ago:

> I will lay me down and bleed a while.
> Though I am wounded, I am not slain.
> I shall rise and fight again.

I joined him for the second meeting, where he thanked all the young people and the volunteers who had worked so hard for him. "Don't get cynical," he told them. "Don't get cynical because look at yourselves and what you were willing to do, and recognize that there are millions and millions of Americans out there that want what you want, that want it to be as we do, who want it to be a shining city on a hill."

I remember that scene so well. I looked out on that sea of young faces, and so many of them were crying. I put my head down and tried to turn away so the cameras wouldn't see that I too was in tears.

Lyn Nofziger came up and gave me his handkerchief. "Would you like to say a few words?" he asked.

"I'd like to, Lyn," I said. "But I can't. I just can't."

Later that morning, on the way to the airport, we passed a hand-painted sign that said GOODBYE REPUBLICANS. YOU PICKED THE WRONG MAN.

It took years for the scars of 1976 to heal between the Fords and the Reagans. I can imagine how the Fords must have felt, to have Jerry win the nomination and then to have the delegates make it clear that Ronnie was their emotional favorite. There was so much more applause for Ronnie that it must have been discouraging for Ford. I know it would have bothered me.

Later, some of the Ford people complained that Ronnie didn't do enough during the fall campaign to help the president defeat Jimmy Carter. But he did everything he could to support the Republican ticket. When the convention was over, Mike Deaver had asked the Ford campaign to submit their schedule requests as soon as possible. Ronnie had been swamped by speaking requests from Republican candidates for Congress, including a few who had helped him in his campaign. (He also received requests from candidates who had opposed him, and in many cases he spoke for them, too.)

Deaver had been afraid the Ford people would come to Ronnie at the last minute, and then he would be unable to help them—which was exactly what happened. Ronnie campaigned for the Republican ticket in twenty-five states, but when the Ford campaign made a few late requests near the end, Ronnie just couldn't accept them without canceling previously scheduled appearances, which he has never been willing to do.

You can't work that hard and that long without being frustrated, and Ronnie and I were both deeply disappointed that he didn't win the nomination in 1976. But we were so moved by the outpouring of love from the delegates that it was impossible to be bitter. Besides, Ronnie has always believed what his mother taught him—that whatever happens, happens for a purpose. As he saw it, he lost the nomination in 1976 because God had other plans for him.

Four years later, we would learn what they were.

11

❧❦❧

Victory! 1980

RONNIE won the 1980 election because he was able to expand on the base of enthusiasm he'd built up during the 1976 campaign and the convention. And this time, as soon as the campaign ran into trouble, he got as angry as I've ever known him to be, and took control before too much damage had been done.

John Sears was again our campaign director. But he made a big mistake right at the start: He kept Ronnie out of the Iowa caucuses, where the campaign began in January. When the seven Republican candidates (Ronnie, John Connally, Howard Baker, George Bush, John Anderson, Philip Crane, and Robert Dole) were invited to participate in a nationally televised debate in Des Moines, John decided that Ronnie shouldn't be there.

His plan was to keep Ronnie above the fray. Ronnie was the acknowledged front-runner, and John didn't want him to seem like just another candidate scrambling for votes.

But when Ronnie failed to appear at the debate on January 5, all six of his opponents attacked him for not being there. Many Iowans obviously felt that Ronnie was taking them for granted, because his support in the polls dropped from 50 percent to around 25 percent. He made a few brief appearances in the state, but they didn't amount to much more than dropping in at the airport. George Bush was able to claim that he had spent more days in Iowa than Ronnie had spent hours.

Maybe John Sears hadn't really understood that before Ronnie moved to Hollywood, he had been a radio sports announcer in Iowa, where Dutch Reagan was the radio voice of the Chicago Cubs. Maybe he thought nobody would remember a broadcaster who had left Iowa more than forty years earlier. But even in 1980, after all that time, some Iowans still regarded Ronnie as the hometown boy. There was plenty of good will to build on, if only John had taken advantage of it.

When the returns came in from Iowa, Ronnie and I were back in California. We were watching a preview of the new film *Kramer vs. Kramer* at the home of our friends Hal and Martha Wallis, when Dick Wirthlin called with the shocking news that Ronnie had been defeated by George Bush, 33 percent to 30 percent. Although Bush's margin of victory was only 2,200 votes, here, as in the New Hampshire primary of 1976, Ronnie had been expected to win. When he didn't, our campaign was suddenly in deep trouble.

New Hampshire was next, and if we didn't win there, the whole race might be over.

After the Iowa defeat, Ronnie decided he'd better take over the campaign. "We're going to change our tactics," he told John. "We're going to take that bus into every village and town in the state. We're going to *live* in New Hampshire until election day. Last time, you took me out of there too early. This time, we're staying until it's over."

After Iowa, New Hampshire would not be easy. I remember George Bush getting off the plane in New Hampshire and bragging that he had the "Big Mo"—momentum. It was true: Bush had scored a big upset in Iowa, and now his New Hampshire campaign had a glow about it. Two weeks before election day, Dick Wirthlin's poll showed that Bush was ahead of Ronnie by nine points.

Ronnie campaigned harder in New Hampshire than he had ever campaigned in his life. The press could barely keep up with him. From the crack of dawn until late at night, Ronnie kept meeting the people. He talked about the economy, about abortion, about gun control, the Soviets, the Equal Rights Amendment. Ronnie is very competitive and runs best when he's behind, and I have never seen him work harder than he did that month.

Although he was in fine spirits, there were big problems just below the surface of the campaign. At the center of the conflict were John Sears and his two lieutenants, Jim Lake and Charlie Black. I don't know what made John change in the years between 1976 and 1980, but I thought he had become arrogant and aloof. Maybe he just didn't like that Ronnie took over, but whatever the reason, he seemed to resent anyone else in the campaign who was close to the candidate.

Before we even arrived in New Hampshire, John had eliminated his main rivals from the team, including Lyn Nofziger, Martin Anderson, and Michael Deaver. Mike had quit in a dramatic show-down with John at our house in Pacific Palisades, on the Sunday after Thanksgiving. John and Mike had been fighting for weeks, and Ronnie had called a meeting to see if they could work out their differences. But John wasn't interested in reconciliation. He went through a whole list of complaints against Mike and claimed that Mike's PR firm was overcharging Ronnie. John announced that he, Lake, and Black would quit the campaign unless Deaver was out.

I didn't envy Ronnie's predicament. Mike Deaver was an old, trusted friend and adviser, and it was difficult to imagine Ronnie continuing in politics without him. But John Sears was the wonder boy of 1976, and at the time he seemed like the best man to lead us to victory in 1980.

"Honey," I told Ronnie, "it looks as if you've got to make a choice."

"No, Governor," said Mike. "You don't have to, because I'm leaving."

And with that, Mike walked out of the room.

Ronnie went after Mike and tried to get him to change his mind, but Mike was too angry at the things John had said. When Ronnie returned, equally angry, he said, "The biggest man here has just left the room."

Ronnie made a big mistake when he let Mike go, and I think he realized it at the time. I've never known Ronnie to carry a grudge, but after that day I think he resented John Sears. The chemistry between the two of them wasn't good to begin with, and now it was worse. Ronnie prefers a relaxed environment, but John was anxious and tense, especially after the Iowa defeat. In New Hampshire, he avoided the other members of the campaign staff and spent most of his time alone in his room or talking with Jim and Charlie. Sometimes he would simply disappear for a couple of days, and we had no idea where he was.

Instead of the unified campaign staff that we had in 1976, we now had a team with low morale that was split between Ronnie's people and John's. Every night when we returned to the hotel, Ronnie would get ready for bed, but I would go from one room to another, meeting in corridors and corners with John and the others, trying everything I could think of to bring people together and smooth things over. When I finally got to bed, Ronnie would ask me where I had been, and I would make up various excuses. For as long as possible, I delayed telling him how much tension there was; I wanted to protect him from these undercurrents so he could concentrate on campaigning. For a while I succeeded. But I soon realized that we were merely putting a Band-Aid over a serious problem.

One night, about a week before the end of the New Hampshire campaign, Ronnie and John really went at it. It was about two in the morning, after another long day of campaigning, and John started talking against Ed Meese for allegedly leaking stories to the press. He also claimed he had overheard Ed (through a bathroom wall!) telling somebody on the phone that he, John, would soon have to leave the campaign.

Ronnie rarely loses his temper, but he certainly was angry that night. "You got Deaver," he told John, "but, by God, you're not going to get Ed Meese! You guys have forced me to the wall." I was sure he was going to hit John, so I took his arm and said, "It's late, and I think we should all get some sleep."

It was impossible to work under these conditions. I didn't think Ronnie could take many more days of campaigning all day and then staying up until two or three in the morning, dealing with problems among the staff—and frankly, I couldn't either. Finally, with my encouragement, Ronnie decided that Sears and his two deputies would have to go. There was no way to avoid it.

It was Ronnie's idea to let them go on the day of the New Hampshire primary, before the returns were in. In case we lost, he didn't want John to think that was the reason he was fired. And if we won, he didn't want John to think he was ungrateful.

On February 26, John, Jim, and Charlie had lunch with a few reporters and then came to our third-floor suite in the Manchester Holiday Inn for a brief meeting. Ronnie explained that he appreciated all they had done for the campaign, but that he needed to make some changes. Then he handed each of them a statement saying that Sears had decided to return to his law practice, and that Black and Lake were leaving with him. Ronnie thought this was the least embarrassing way to do it.

This time there were no raised voices. I guess John already knew this moment was inevitable.

During the meeting, John's expression never changed. When it was over, I went with him into another room. "I'm sorry this happened," I said, "but I hope we can still be friends." To the end, John and I had remained on good terms. At least I hope so.

I don't recall what he said, but I haven't seen him since that day, except on television, where he sometimes provides political commentary. I've often wondered what he thought during those eight years of Ronnie's presidency. John Sears was one of the brightest and most talented men I have ever known, but in 1980 he just couldn't work as part of our team.

I was also sorry to see Charlie and Jim leave. Later, after Ronnie became president, Jim's son worked for us as an advance man.

Once Sears left, it wasn't long before Deaver, Nofziger, and Anderson all came back into the campaign.

Our new campaign director, William Casey, had been chairman of the Securities and Exchange Commission. His immediate priority was to raise money for us, and to cut expenses. We were just about broke after the loss in Iowa, and John had spent money rather freely during the early weeks of the campaign. Casey quickly reduced the staff in both our Los Angeles and Washington offices by nearly half.

Despite what people have said, Ronnie was never the rich man's candidate. If he had been, we wouldn't have been so short of money in both 1976 and 1980. The Republican candidate with the support of big business was not Ronald Reagan but John Connally. When Connally dropped out, the corporate givers went for Bush. Most of Ronnie's support came from small businessmen and entrepreneurs.

The key moment of the New Hampshire campaign came on the Saturday night before election day, just before a scheduled debate between Ronnie and George Bush in the town of Nashua. I've always thought of it as the night Ronnie got furious in public, and I was so glad he did!

The debate, which was held in a high-school gymnasium, was originally sponsored by the *Nashua Telegraph*. But the paper had to withdraw its financial support at the last moment when Robert Dole, one of the five candidates who hadn't been invited, complained to the Federal Elections Commission that this constituted an illegal corporate contribution to the Reagan and Bush campaigns. Our people offered to split the cost with the Bush camp, but the Bush people refused. Finally, we said we'd pay for the whole thing. Although the newspaper was no longer underwriting the debate, both sides agreed that they would continue to run it.

The other Republican candidates were angry about being excluded, and Ronnie thought they had a good case. But the executives of the newspaper, which seemed to be supporting George Bush, still preferred a two-man debate. So did the Bush camp. After his victory in Iowa, George Bush was the only Republican with a good chance to beat Ronnie in New Hampshire. If he could face Ronnie alone, it would further enhance his position.

A few minutes before the debate was scheduled to begin, we still didn't know exactly who was going to participate. I was with Ronnie and all the other candidates except Bush, as we stood in a small classroom in the school basement and tried to work out a compromise with the Bush team. They wanted a two-man debate, and they wouldn't budge.

Ronnie wanted to walk out if the other candidates were not allowed to participate, but his advisers saw this debate as his best chance to eliminate Bush as a serious rival, and they prevailed on him to stay. The last thing they wanted was for Ronnie to leave now and have it appear that he was afraid to debate Bush.

As we were discussing our options, a messenger from the *Telegraph* came to the classroom where we had gathered. "Mr. Bush is already on the stage," he said. "If Mr. Reagan does not appear within five minutes, the debate will be canceled and Mr. Bush will be declared the winner."

Finally, with time running out and nobody knowing what to do, I said, "Why don't you *all* just go out?"

That seemed to suit everybody. Ronnie led the way and the others followed—John Anderson, Bob Dole, Phil Crane, and Howard Baker. (John Connally was campaigning in South Carolina.) Ronnie took his seat at one end of the stage, across from Bush, and the other four candidates stood behind him as a loud roar of recognition went up from the crowd. I sat in the audience with Ronnie's staff and supporters. Although the whole place was in chaos, George Bush just sat there and looked straight ahead as if no one else were there and none of this were really happening. Later, one of the New Hampshire newspapers wrote that George looked like a small boy who had been dropped off at the wrong birthday party.

Jon Breen, the editor of the *Telegraph,* tried to get the audience to settle down. Then Ronnie spoke up and said he thought all the candidates should be allowed to participate.

"Mr. Reagan is out of order," said Breen. "Turn off his microphone."

Ronnie just looked at him, with an incredulous expression on his face. He couldn't believe what he'd heard.

"Turn off Mr. Reagan's microphone," Breen repeated.

That did it. Ronnie banged his fist on the table and said, "I *paid* for this microphone, Mr. Green!"

Ronnie was so mad that he got the man's name wrong.

But there was no mistaking the emotion in his voice. And with that, everybody started yelling, including me. Suddenly I was on my feet, shouting, "You tell him, honey, you tell him!" A moment later I caught myself and thought, Oh Lord, I hope the cameras weren't on me.

But the cameras were on my husband. When the audience finally calmed down, Ronnie explained why he thought the other candidates on the stage should be given a chance to speak.

Not everybody in that gymnasium was a Reagan supporter, but you could see that most of them agreed with Ronnie. "Bring some chairs," people shouted. But the organizers of the debate and the Bush people would not allow it, and the four other candidates angrily left the stage.

I remember very little of the actual debate, but by then it was anticlimactic. Although it was televised only locally, the network crews had been there, and over the next few days the clip of Ronnie getting angry was shown again and again, not only in New Hampshire, but all over the country. With those seven words, "I *paid* for this microphone, Mr. Green!" Ronnie took control of his own campaign. Later, the news media called this the turning point of the entire race, and I think that's true.

After what had happened in 1976, Ronnie wouldn't even consider leaving New Hampshire before the primary. Although the polls now showed him well ahead, and Dick Wirthlin called from California two days before the vote to predict that Ronnie would win by seventeen points, we stayed until the very end. On election day, Ronnie won with 51 percent of the vote. George Bush was a distant second, twenty-seven points behind. Howard Baker finished third.

From New Hampshire we flew to Vermont, where Ronnie won the primary a week later. Then, on March 8, Ronnie finished first in South Carolina, which led John Connally to withdraw. Three days later, Ronnie won Alabama, Florida, and Georgia. One by one, all of Ronnie's opponents dropped out, except for John Anderson, who decided to run as an independent. Throughout the primaries, George Bush provided the only real opposition, but it was never close. In the thirty-three races where both men were on the ballot, Ronnie finished first in twenty-nine. Bush eventually withdrew, and Ronnie coasted into the convention in Detroit, where the only topic of suspense was whom Ronnie would choose as his running mate.

I couldn't believe it, but most of Ronnie's advisers wanted him to pick Gerald Ford. They saw Reagan-Ford as a "dream ticket" which would unite the Republican party and would prove unbeatable in November. The polls supported this judgment, and Ronnie liked it too. During the convention, he and Ford had several meetings to discuss how it might work.

I thought the whole idea was ridiculous. I didn't see how a former president—*any* president—could come back to the White House in the number-two spot. It would be awkward for both men, and impractical, and I couldn't understand why that wasn't obvious to everybody. "It can't be done," I told Ronnie. "It would be a dual presidency. It just won't work."

But he didn't see it that way. So much for my famous "influence" over Ronald Reagan.

When Ronnie's advisers asked me to call Betty Ford, to see what she had to say about the idea, I went along for my husband's sake. But I was relieved to find that Betty felt pretty much as I did. "No," she said, "as much as we'd like to help, I don't think it's a good idea." I didn't press the point. She also made it clear that now that the Fords were back in private life, she wasn't eager to return to politics.

But our husbands continued to pursue the idea, and so did their staffs. On the third day of the convention, Ford met with Ronnie and told him he would want a voice in the selection of the Cabinet, and that he preferred Henry Kissinger as secretary of State and Alan Greenspan as secretary of the Treasury. Ronnie listened but didn't commit himself.

A few hours later, Ronnie and I were in our suite at the Detroit Plaza, watching the *CBS Evening News,* when Ford suddenly came on for a live interview with Walter Cronkite. The rumors had been flying around all day about the "dream ticket," and about an arrangement that would give Ford, as vice president, enhanced powers and responsibilities. There had even been talk that Ford would be a "deputy president."

So far, neither man had said a word to the press. But as Ronnie and I watched in astonishment, .Ford laid out his conditions on national television. "I would not go to Washington and be a figurehead vice president," he said. "I have to have special assurances. I have to go there with the belief that I will play a meaningful role across the board in the basic and the crucial and the important decisions that have to be made."

When Cronkite asked if he had in mind a kind of "copresidency," Ford didn't argue with that term. "The point you raise is a very legitimate one," he said.

As far as Ronnie was concerned, that did it. Later that evening, he and Ford had a brief final meeting in our suite. But the Ford option was now over.

I'm not exactly sure what I would have done if Gerald Ford hadn't taken himself out of the race. (To this day, I don't know whether he did so intentionally.) But I think I would have done almost anything to prevent Ronnie from picking a former president as his running mate.

The delegates, however, were infatuated with the idea. They must have assumed Ford would never have said these things publicly unless Ronnie had already agreed to them. Shortly after the Cronkite interview, the networks started talking of a Reagan-Ford ticket as though it had already been decided. On CBS, Dan Rather even announced that Reagan and Ford were preparing to make a joint appearance before the convention later that evening.

As soon as Ford left our suite, Ronnie called George Bush to offer him a place on the ticket. By this time, George and Barbara Bush had already gone to bed. Like everyone else, they had assumed from the news reports that Ronnie and Ford had it all arranged. But when Ronnie called, George was up like a shot.

Later, George told us that shortly before Ronnie called, he and Barbara had been sitting around talking about what they were going to do with the rest of their lives. Politics is a funny business, and for all the planning and the meetings, you can never predict what's going to happen. In a way, George Bush became the forty-first president of the United States because the thirty-eighth president had said too much during a television interview eight years earlier!

At the time, I didn't like George Bush. The bitter campaigns of Iowa and New Hampshire were still fresh in my memory, and George's use of the phrase "voodoo economics" to describe Ronnie's proposed tax cuts still rankled. That's why I've always hated primaries—you're forced to go on the attack against candidates from your own party.

I soon came to realize, however, that George was a good choice. He was experienced in government and he knew his way around Washington. He had served in Congress. He had been ambassador to the United Nations. He had been director of the CIA. More recently, he had stayed in the race the longest, and had run energetically in the primaries. He was a fine campaigner, and both geographically and philosophically, he broadened the ticket.

He also turned out to be a good vice president.

Still, I think Ronnie would have preferred Paul Laxalt. That night, as he went out on the platform to announce his choice, he said to Paul, "Why the hell do you have to live in Nevada?" Geographically, a Reagan-Laxalt ticket just didn't make sense.

The following night, Ronnie returned to the convention hall to give his acceptance speech. Referring to the Carter years, he asked, "Can anyone look at the record of this administration and say, 'Well done'? Can anyone compare the state of our economy when the Carter administration took office with where we are today and say, 'Keep up the good work'? Can anyone look at our reduced standing in the world today and say, 'Let's have four more years of this'?"

Ronnie ended on a note of inspiration, and when he was finished, the crowd was completely still. Then he looked out on the convention floor and surprised everyone—including me—by saying, "I'll confess that I've been a little afraid to suggest what I'm going to suggest, what I'm going to say. I'm more afraid not to. Can we begin our crusade joined together in a moment of silent prayer?"

The entire convention rose up and bowed their heads. After a few seconds, Ronnie looked out on that great hall and said, "God bless America."

Now that Ronnie was the nominee, we had to start all over and run a national campaign against an incumbent president. Although Jimmy Carter was not especially popular, in the 1976 race against Gerald Ford he had shown himself to be a very competitive campaigner. Ronnie expected a mean and tough race, and that's what we got.

Although Ronnie would have liked to maintain our campaign headquarters in California, once we got past the primaries that was no longer practical. In addition to the enormous amount of additional travel, the three-hour time difference was a problem when we tried to keep in touch with key people on the East Coast.

And so, shortly after the convention, we rented a country house known as Wexford in the Virginia hunt-country, near Middleburg, about an hour from Washington and only thirty minutes from Dulles Airport. Wexford had been built by the Kennedys during the early 1960s and was named after the Kennedys' ancestral county in Ireland. Mrs. Kennedy had designed it as a weekend retreat when she and her husband lived in the White House, but by the time it was finished they were able to spend only one weekend there before the assassination. A few years later, Wexford was bought by Bill Clements, the former governor of Texas, who made it available to us. It was the perfect place to come home to and relax.

I loved Wexford, especially the stone patio in the back where you looked out over the wonderful green rolling hills. Although we were there only on weekends, it helped me survive the rigorous schedule of the campaign. I had never been in the Virginia countryside before, but I fell in love with those wooden fences and stone walls. For me, Wexford was the happiest part of the 1980 campaign.

Senator John Warner was one of our neighbors, and at the time he was married to Elizabeth Taylor, an old friend of mine from Metro. Elizabeth was nursing a bad back, but John used to come over, and the three of us would ride by and wave to her. There wasn't much free time during the campaign, and even at Wexford, most of the days were taken up with meetings, phone calls, and planning. There were always people coming for lunch or dinner, and I did a lot of hostessing and serving coffee. Even so, it was a relaxed and happy place, and I just loved being out in those wide-open spaces, away from the crowds, the cities, and the noise.

. . .

As in 1976, I did a fair amount of campaigning on my own in 1980, traveling to some of the smaller cities and towns that Ronnie couldn't reach. Typically, I'd fly out with Ronnie on *LeaderShip '80*, our campaign plane, to some large center like Chicago, and while he campaigned in the city, I would take a smaller plane to another part of the state. Peter McCoy from our staff was with me, along with a pair of Secret Service agents, and, occasionally, a reporter.

Many of the hotels we stayed in were so honored to have Ronald Reagan's wife as a guest that they painted our rooms just before we arrived. I appreciated the gesture, but have you ever slept in a freshly painted room? The smell is overpowering, and in many hotel rooms you can't open a window. I'd arrive exhausted, wanting only to sleep and breathe some fresh air, and what I'd get would be paint fumes strong enough to knock me out.

I shook a lot of hands during that campaign, and the best advice I can give to anyone in that situation is that you should never, ever, wear a ring on your right hand. There's always going to be some little lady—for some reason it's never a big strong man—who will grab your hand in such a way that she presses the ring right up against a nerve. The pain is excruciating, so it's a mistake you don't make more than once.

During a presidential race you spend a lot of time in the air, and there was a wonderful feeling of camaraderie on that campaign plane. Every time we took off, the PA system would play a tape of Willie Nelson singing "On the Road Again." Then I would roll an orange down the aisle. That was my little ritual, and it quickly became a game with the press. I would try to get the orange to the end of the plane without having it carom off under the seats. When I finally got the knack of it, the press started setting up little roadblocks to make it more challenging.

Once we were in the air, I would walk back and pass out chocolates to the press. People were always giving us boxes of candy, and since Ronnie and I don't eat candy (I prefer cookies, while Ronnie sticks to jelly beans), I would give them away. It was all done in good fun, and it never entered my mind that anyone would think I was forcing it on them. When one of the reporters wrote a column

saying that unless you ate your candy, you wouldn't get an interview with Ronnie, I was so hurt and embarrassed that I never
wanted to go down that aisle again. But with Stu Spencer's encouragement, I did—with a sign around my neck that said: TAKE ONE OR
ELSE!

We had a lot of laughs on that plane. The pilot kept a rubber
chicken in the cockpit, and as soon as we landed he would stick it
on the windshield. Then he would radio the tower to report that we
had evidently hit something on the way down. As the plane taxied
to the gate, the man on the runway would be moving his arms
slower and slower as he stared at this unidentified object on the
windshield.

You're *always* working on those flights—talking strategy, working on speeches, doing interviews, and making plans. It's a very
intense and close experience, and when it's over there's a terrible
letdown, even if you win.

The first few weeks of the 1980 campaign had been dreadful, but
the spirit was a lot better in the fall—especially when Stu Spencer
joined our team after the convention. Stu had been the key man in
Ronnie's two gubernatorial campaigns, but in 1976, as I've already
described, he had gone with Gerald Ford. In the summer of 1980,
when Mike Deaver called and asked him to join us, Stu had only one
question: "Does Nancy want me?" He knew I had been upset about
his role with the Ford campaign, but I was more hurt and disappointed than angry. I've always been very fond of Stu, and it was
great to have him back.

Years earlier, during Ronnie's first gubernatorial campaign, Stu
had come to our house for a meeting. After an hour or so, I suddenly
felt overwhelmed by all of the political talk, and I went into the
bedroom and lay down. Stu came in looking for me, and said,
"Nancy, what's wrong?"

"I don't know," I answered. "It's just too much. It's a whole new
world and I'm not sure I'm ready for it."

"You can do it," he said. "But I don't want to kid you. This is
just the beginning. It's going to get much worse."

I wasn't happy to hear that, but I could see that Stu cared. He may
be gruff on the outside, but underneath he's a very sensitive man.

He's also a real character—short, rumpled, and tough-talking. He always gives you a straight answer. Stu has the greatest political instincts of anybody I've ever met, but he doesn't get carried away with his own importance, the way John Sears sometimes did. He never acts as if he were the candidate, and he never tries to force his opinions. And unlike most people in a presidential campaign, who hope to be offered a position in the administration, Stu Spencer never wanted anything for himself.

One of Stu's first observations was that Ronnie was spending too much time talking to the press. That was fine when he was governor of California, but now, in a national race, every syllable a candidate uttered was weighed and examined, and Ronnie's friendly and casual style occasionally got him into trouble. Like the time in September when Ronnie mistakenly referred to Tuscumbia, Alabama, where President Carter had opened his campaign, as the birthplace of the Ku Klux Klan.

Or the time that Ronnie charged that Carter had led the country into a depression.

"That shows how little he knows," Carter said. "This is a recession."

At least Ronnie had a good comeback: "They say I can't use the word 'depression.' Well, if the president wants a definition, I'll give him one. A recession is when your neighbor loses his job. A depression is when you lose *your* job. And recovery will be when Jimmy Carter loses *his.*"

The stress of a political campaign can be unbelievable, and sometimes you get tired and say things that just come out wrong. It happened to me in February 1980. Ronnie's plane was stuck in New Hampshire during a snowstorm, so I filled in for him with a speech in Chicago. A telephone hookup had been arranged, and Ronnie called me so he could say hello to the crowd. When he mentioned that he was looking out at all the beautiful white snow, I replied, "And I'm looking out at all these beautiful white faces."

As soon as the words left my mouth, I thought, Oh my God, I didn't mean it *that* way. I quickly corrected myself, but it was too late. The press took it as a racial remark, which is certainly not what

I had intended. It soon blew over, but I took a lot of heat for a couple of days.

It's incredibly easy to make this kind of mistake during a campaign. You get tired and numb, and reporters keep after you. If they persist long enough with the same question, you're liable to blurt out anything, just to get them off your back.

The wrong spontaneous remark can be deadly, but as we learned during the final week of the campaign, the right one can help you enormously. It occurred during Ronnie's one and only debate with Jimmy Carter, which turned out to be as important in the general election as the Nashua debate had been in the primaries.

Not all of Ronnie's advisers were convinced that he should debate Carter, and I too had reservations. Although Ronnie was in favor of a debate, it wasn't until he saw Carter at the annual Alfred E. Smith Dinner in New York, where both candidates appeared together for the first time in the campaign, that he knew for sure that he wanted to go head-to-head with the president. That night, the contrast between the two men was remarkable: Ronnie gave a short, light, self-deprecating speech, while Carter delivered a boastful foreign policy address that was completely off the mark.

The dinner is not supposed to be political, and Carter's advisers should have known that. The president had also refused to come downstairs during the meal. Instead, he remained in his hotel room until it was time for him to speak. Everybody in the hall knew he was upstairs, and that certainly didn't win him any votes.

The next morning, in a meeting in our suite at the Waldorf-Astoria, Ronnie said, "I can beat that guy!"

The debate took place in Cleveland on October 28, just a few days before the election. Throughout the evening, Carter consistently misrepresented Ronnie's position on the issues. As the debate was ending, Carter charged that Ronnie had begun his political career by campaigning against Medicare. That was true, but Carter neglected to say that at the time, Ronnie was supporting an alternative health-care plan sponsored by the American Medical Association.

When it was Ronnie's turn to respond, he smiled at Carter with a look of mock exasperation, shook his head, and said, "There you go again." For millions of viewers, that phrase said it all. Carter may have been well informed, but there was something grim and moralistic about him that made people feel bad. "There you go again" quickly entered the language, and a few weeks after the election, when Ronnie used it again in a White House press conference, he brought the house down.

Earlier in the debate, Carter had tried to portray Ronnie as a warmonger. He said Ronnie had a "belligerent attitude," and a "long-standing inclination" toward the use of military power. Then Carter mentioned that he had recently asked his daughter, Amy, who was twelve at the time, what the most important issue was, and that she had answered, "Nuclear weaponry and the control of nuclear arms."

Many people in the studio audience laughed at that remark, because it didn't seem very likely that a twelve-year-old would be all that interested in "nuclear weaponry." Carter took a lot of heat in the media for bringing Amy into the discussion, and some of Ronnie's supporters started carrying ASK AMY signs at his campaign rallies.

But it was Ronnie's final statement in the debate that really sealed Jimmy Carter's fate. This was vintage Ronnie—clear, personal, and empathetic:

"Are you better off than you were four years ago? Is it easier for you to go and buy things in the stores than it was four years ago? Is there more or less employment in the country than there was four years ago? Is America as respected throughout the world as it was? Do you feel that our security is safe, that we're as strong as we were four years ago?

"If your answer to all of these questions is yes, why I think your choice is very obvious as to who you'll vote for. If you don't agree, if you don't think that this course that we've been on for the last four years is what you would like to see us follow for the next four, then I could suggest another choice that you have."

In the final days of the campaign, Carter stepped up his attacks and again tried to suggest that Ronnie was a warmonger. Back in September, Carter had said that the upcoming election would decide "whether we have peace or war." This remark had infuriated Ronnie, who called Carter's statement "unforgivable." But as the campaign drew to a close he responded, characteristically, with humor. "I'm sorry I'm late," he told one rally after the debate, "but I was busy starting a war."

Back in March, Ronnie had been campaigning in Brooklyn, where a group of hecklers started yelling that he wanted to start a war. "No," he answered them, "I don't want to do that. But if I did, I'd start it right here with you guys!"

There was heckling throughout the campaign, but Ronnie always handled it with a light touch. The final appearance of the 1980 race was in San Diego, where Ronnie was repeatedly interrupted by a heckler who kept shouting throughout his speech. Finally Ronnie looked at the man and said, "Ah, shut up." When the cheering died down, he added, "My mother always told me I should never say that, but I've been dying to do it throughout the whole campaign." The crowd loved it, and I'm sure that anyone who has ever gone through a long political campaign knew exactly how Ronnie felt.

From San Diego we returned to Los Angeles, and the night before the election we went to bed not in some freshly painted hotel room but in our own bed in Pacific Palisades. Heaven—sheer heaven. The next morning we went to vote in the same house where we had voted for the past twenty-five years. The women put out jars of jelly beans for Ronnie, and we were greeted by hordes of photographers and reporters. As we left, Ronnie joked with the press that he had voted for me.

"And what about your wife?" somebody called out. "Who did she vote for?"

"Oh," he replied, "Nancy voted for some has-been actor."

It's quite a feeling to see your husband's name at the top of the ballot. Voting for Ronnie as governor was a little strange, but for president—even after all our work, I found it almost unbelievable.

Ever since Ronnie's first campaign in 1966, election day has always seemed like the longest day of the year. You feel it will never end, and you look for ways to pass the time. When Ronnie first ran for governor, we invited some of the press back to our house for coffee and sweet rolls. Then, after lunch, Ronnie went off to play golf with Holmes Tuttle and a couple of other men. He did the same thing four years later.

This time he went out to get a haircut, but we both spent most of the day at home, catching up with odds and ends as the telephone kept ringing. I wanted to rest, because we were both exhausted from the long campaign. And as usual, I expected we'd be in for a long night as we waited for the votes to come in. We planned to spend part of the evening at the home of our friends Earle and Marion Jorgensen, and to watch the election returns with the same friends who had been with us on Ronnie's two previous election nights. In 1966, and again in 1970, we had gone there to watch the early returns before going on to Ronnie's campaign headquarters at the Century Plaza Hotel, and we planned to follow the same routine tonight. It had become a superstition: Marion would always ask the same people, have the same help, and serve the same food—chicken curry.

A few minutes after five, I took a bath and Ronnie went into the shower. We had the television on very loud in our bedroom so we could hear the news. Suddenly, I heard John Chancellor say that Ronnie was going to win in a landslide victory.

I leaped out of the tub, threw a towel around me, and started banging on the shower door. Ronnie got out, grabbed a towel, and we ran over to the television set. And there we stood, dripping wet, wearing nothing but our towels, as we heard that Ronnie had just been elected!

Then the telephone started to ring. It was President Carter, calling to concede, and to congratulate Ronnie on his victory.

I was thrilled, and stunned. We hadn't even gone to the Jorgensens' yet!

"Congratulations, honey," I said, as I hugged the fortieth president of the United States.

12

On to Washington

AFTER the election, I was excited about moving to Washington. Still, it was harder than I expected to pack up our house in California and leave it for the last time. For twenty-seven busy years, 1669 San Onofre Drive, Pacific Palisades, had been our home. When Ronnie and I had first moved in, he had drawn a little heart with our initials in it in the wet cement on the patio off our bedroom. It was still there, of course, and to me it symbolized the many good times we'd had in that house.

Although we were moving to the White House, I knew I would miss *this* house, with all its memories, and the magnificent view. From the deck, you could look out over the Pacific, and then turn and see the city, and turn again and see the mountains. One night shortly after we moved in, Ronnie and I were sitting outside after dinner. Below us, the city lights were sparkling like fallen stars. Ronnie reached over and took my hand. "You see," he said, "I've given you all these jewels." I felt as if he truly had.

The house meant far more to me than jewels ever could. We had been happy there. Our children had grown up there. And I had always expected that this was where Ronnie and I would live out our lives together. But everything was different now, and once we left, we would not be coming back.

It was a matter of security. Ronnie and I now had Secret Service protection, and they would be with us even after we left Washington. After the election, the Secret Service had set up headquarters in an enormous trailer at the end of our driveway. It wasn't an ideal arrangement, to put it mildly. There was no room left for anyone else to park, and it became increasingly awkward all around. When Ronnie's term was over, we would need another house, which would provide all the Secret Service requirements without infringing on our privacy and the privacy of our neighbors.

Ron and Patti were already living on their own, but even so, our leaving the family house was traumatic for them, too. Ron called me from New York and begged me not to sell the house. "You can't," he said. "It's our home." Patti called from Santa Monica and started to cry. "It just won't be the same without having you up there on the hill," she said.

Packing up a house is an enormous task for anyone, but it's particularly hard for me, because I'm a saver who hates to throw anything away. I save my clothes, and I still have every letter that Ronnie and the children ever wrote me. And zillions of photographs. And old movie scripts, and baskets, which I love. I can't begin to list the things I had squirreled away over the years, telling myself, You never know when you might want this.

Since the election, I had been sorting through our belongings, trying to decide what should go into storage, what should be shipped to Washington. I had no idea what the residential floors of the White House were like, and I wasn't even sure how many rooms there were in the family quarters, or how they were furnished.

The first time I was in the White House was in 1967. Lyndon Johnson was president, and Ronnie and I were invited to the annual governors' dinner. I saw only two or three of the public rooms that night, but even so, I was awed by the majesty and dignity of the place.

Right after dinner, the president took off in his helicopter. True to his reputation, he wanted all the guests to gather on the lawn to watch him depart. I had a terrible cold that day, and Mrs. Johnson found me and made sure I was standing well back, out of the draft. Earlier in the day I had stayed in the hotel with a sore throat and had missed a tree-planting ceremony for the governors' wives. But there was no way on earth I was going to miss that dinner.

It was hard to believe, but now I was going to be the hostess for the governors' dinner. Other women would be coming to the White House, some of them just as nervous as I had been that night, and now it would be up to me to make them feel at home.

It's traditional for the outgoing first lady to give her successor a tour of the residence, and a few weeks after the election, Mrs. Carter invited me to come for coffee and a look around. The first thing that struck me about the White House was how cold it was. The country was still suffering from the energy crisis, and President Carter had ordered that the White House thermostats be turned down. (Later I was told that Miss Lillian, the president's mother, had found the place so cold that she decided to move out.)

Mrs. Carter met me in the Diplomatic Room and took me to the Yellow Oval Room on the second floor in the residence, where she told me about her efforts to obtain fine American paintings for the White House collection. But the chill in her manner matched the chill in the room. I was disappointed, but I also understood. It's bad enough to lose an election, but it must be awful to be voted out of office so decisively. In recent years, the wives of defeated presidential candidates have suffered terribly—much more so than their husbands. And it must be painful to have to show the residence to the wife of the man who defeated your husband.

And as I eventually learned for myself, the White House is not an easy place to leave. Ronnie and I departed under the best of circumstances, but even so, it was a wrenching experience.

Finally Mrs. Carter turned to me and said, "I guess you'd like to see some things."

Oh my, yes! She led me out to the West Hall, which is at one end of the Center Hall, which runs the length of the White House. Most presidential families have used the West Hall as a sitting room, as we did, but that day it struck me as cold and bare.

"Where would you like to start?" she asked.

"Well," I said, "I know there are two connecting rooms that can be separate bedrooms or, if you sleep together, a master bedroom and a study. I'd like to see those rooms to get some idea of what they're like. I'm trying to decide what furniture to bring."

"Well," she said reluctantly, "things are so messed up these days. We're packing, you know. I'll open the door of the study and you can look in."

They *were* packing, but I also had the feeling that Mrs. Carter just couldn't bring herself to actually take me into these, their most private, rooms. We looked in the doorway, and then she said, "I have some things to take care of. My secretary will show you the rest." So on that visit I never really saw the rooms we'd use as our bedroom and study.

Eight years later, when I took Barbara Bush around after George had won the 1988 election, I showed her *everything*—every closet, every detail, from the laundry room on the third floor and the closets where the tablecloths are kept to the beauty parlor that Pat Nixon had installed. Barbara had been to the residence many times, but she hadn't seen every nook and hideaway. As we walked through, I couldn't help but think, Boy, it sure would have been nice if I had been shown some of this back in 1980!

On that first visit, my overall feeling was of surprise that the residence looked so dreary and uninviting. It just didn't look the way the president's house should look. It wasn't a place we'd be proud to bring people—our personal friends or our country's friends. Frankly, the White House was run-down and a bit shabby. When my son, Ron, arrived for the inauguration, he said, "Mom, this place is a mess. It looks low rent."

I have always felt that the White House should be magnificent, and I made up my mind that as soon as we moved in I would fix it up.

Somehow, a rumor got started—where do these stories come from?—that I wanted to renovate the White House *before* the inauguration, and that I had asked the Carters to move out early, so I could get started. I *never* asked the Carters to move out, and I wouldn't even think of it. According to another report, I intended to knock down a wall in the Lincoln Bedroom—the Lincoln Bedroom! I would never dream of doing that, either.

At the time, I had no idea that stories like these would be typical of the press coverage of me during our first year in the White House.

On the morning of January 14, six days before the inauguration, Ronnie and I left the house in Pacific Palisades for the last time. As I walked out, I thought it had never looked so beautiful. Patti had come to say goodbye, and we hugged each other. We'd had our differences over the years, and she blamed me for the fact that Ronnie had run for president, which she had been dead set against. She couldn't have been more wrong. But for now, at least, all that was put aside.

Our neighbors had gathered at the bottom of our driveway to see us off, and people lined both sides of the street, waving tiny American flags, all the way to Sunset Boulevard. When the limousine turned onto Sunset, led by a convoy of police cars and motorcycles, people started honking their horns and flashing their lights. I hadn't expected this, and I'm afraid it made our leaving an even more emotional experience.

But soon we were at the airport, where I had my first glimpse of *Air Force One,* all shining blue and white, with the words "United States of America" on each side, the American flag on the tail, and the presidential seal on both sides of the plane's nose.

One of the pilots welcomed us aboard, and the stewards showed us around. It was a wonderful surprise to find that the president and first lady have a little two-room suite with a private bathroom. I also discovered that you can order virtually any food you like on *Air Force One,* as the kitchen staff can cook up practically anything. (For security reasons, food is bought randomly, and never from the same place twice in a row.)

During our flight to Washington, Ronnie read reports and attended to paperwork, while I kept busy writing letters to friends back home, on *Air Force One* letterhead. Look at me, I'm riding on *Air Force One!*

After landing at Andrews Air Force Base, we were driven directly to Blair House, at 1651 Pennsylvania Avenue, right across from the White House. Blair House, which consists of four small

41. *At the White House, after Ronnie became president. He asked all of the former presidents to go to Sadat's funeral. I don't think there's ever been a time when there have been so many living former presidents.*

42. *The private swearing-in, in 1985, at the White House on Sunday. The next day, Monday, we planned to have the public ceremony outdoors, but it was so cold that the doctors said we'd have to move it inside.*

43 *The 1985 public swearing-in ceremony.*

44. *Trying to comfort the families of the Challenger's crew. There seemed to be so many of these sad times.*

45. *Going to Camp David with Lucky, who would immediately get on the plane and sit in Ronnie's seat. I told him when he started to wave to the crowds we were in trouble. The time had come for him to go to the ranch with the other dogs. By then, he was so big I could have ridden him to the helicopter.*

46. *Ronnie loves to doodle and I think he's very good. His inscription obviously made me very happy, and it was signed with our usual "I.T.W.W.W." (I love you more than anything "in the whole wide world").*

47. *Father and son in the Oval Office.*

48. *I don't remember what Queen Elizabeth said in her toast, but obviously it broke Ronnie up.*

49. *Toasting Prince Charles at the Winston Churchill dinner in Texas, where I represented Ronnie.*

50. *I went alone to the Vatican to talk with the pope about the drug problem. Imagine holding hands with the pope!*

52. Opposite page above: *It was unusual for guests to come to Camp David. We really used it as a retreat. But Margaret Thatcher was a close friend. And Ronnie loved driving the golf cart—maybe because the golf cart at Camp David and the jeep at the ranch were the only vehicles he got a chance to drive.*

54. Opposite page below: *With Princess Grace for Prince Charles's wedding in London. We had been at MGM together, and she gave up her career after about the same amount of time as I did, and for the same reason—to be a wife and mother.*

51. *I got dressed up that day for Nakasone. Usually at Camp David I was in blue jeans.*

53. *Dancing with Mikhail Baryshnikov at Ford's Theater was one of my biggest thrills, and we became good friends. I was praying I wouldn't step on his feet!*

55. The things a first lady is asked to do! Here I am christening a ship. How do you like my perfect coiffure?

56. We had Ashley up to the ranch for her birthday. After the cake, Mike told us of the experiences at the day camp that had so greatly affected his life.

57. *At the state dinner for Duarte. Obviously, my mind is not on the proceedings. The next day I went into the hospital for cancer surgery.*

58. Center: *My brother, Dick, Dr. John Hutton, Ronnie, Paula (one of the nurses), with me in the recovery room.*

59. Bottom: *Ronnie bringing me cookies and cards, some of them quite large!*

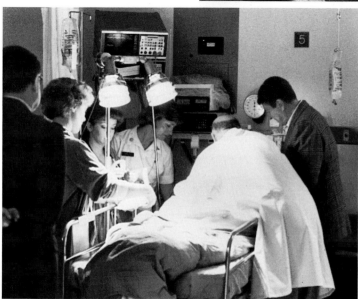

60. Left: *Ronnie, my strong right arm—in this case, left—taking me for a walk in the hospital, the day after surgery.*

61. Right: *Rex Scouten (head usher at the White House) and I had become friends, and I was so happy to see his face, and thrilled to be home.*

62. *I tried to thank everybody for the warm homecoming, but my voice cracked and I didn't get very far.*

63. *One of my first public appearances after the surgery. By mistake, Ronnie raised my arm too high and I whispered to him, "You're hurting me!" And so he kissed me.*

64. *My darling mother, whom I loved dearly, wearing her red mittens. I saw her as often as I could—not often enough—and I called her every night, even toward the end.*

65. *Doria, Ron, and me, with Ronnie, after he had given the eulogy for my mother.*

66. *Gromyko, when he said to me, "Whisper peace in your husband's ear every night," and I said, "I will, and I'll also whisper it in your ear."*

67. *In Geneva at the Soviet mission to the U.N., where I'd gone for tea. Raisa is dressed in a shirt and skirt, for reasons I didn't understand until later— this was the only picture publicized in Russia, and any other outfit would have been considered too frivolous.*

68. *Our dinner for the Gorbachevs in Geneva—Ronnie and Gorbachev toasting each other.*

69. *In Geneva, where Ron had been sent on assignment for* Playboy. *Boy, was I glad to see him.*

70. *After the signing of the INF Treaty in Washington in 1987. I've often wondered what Raisa was thinking as she looked at me.*

71. *Gorbachev and me toasting, at the dinner they gave for us at the Soviet embassy in Washington.*

72. *Seeing the Gorbachevs off from Washington. Obviously it was raining, but to them that meant good luck.*

73. *Raisa when she came to tea for the first time in Geneva in 1985. She had finally found a chair she liked, having moved twice.*

74. *In Russia, when Ronnie talked Gorbachev into looking at his watch, to tease Raisa and me for being late.*

75. *An unforgettable evening at the Bolshoi Theater with the Gorbachevs, with the flags of both nations on either side. The Russians played our national anthem beautifully.*

76. *In Russia, the ladies who waited for me gave me lilacs and hugged me when I left.*

77. *Leaving Moscow—in the Kremlin with the Gorbachevs.*

78. *Riding at Camp David with Doria and Ron.*

79. *One of my favorite pictures of the man I know so well.*

80. *Happy to be back at the ranch.*

81. *I think Ronnie left the presidency with such dignity. Here he is, getting on board Air Force One on January 20, 1989, to fly to California, saying goodbye and saluting.*

82. *With Aaron Shikler, who painted the official portraits of us that will hang in the White House.*

83. *Our last day, and each of us filled with our own private thoughts and memories.*

houses joined together, is the president's official guest house for foreign leaders, and the president-elect generally stays there during the week before the inauguration.

"Blair House *really* needs fixing up," I wrote in my diary. Well, what an understatement *that* turned out to be! Although Blair House is a beautiful and large house with fifteen bedrooms, it was badly in need of renovation—and I mean *badly*. In 1982, a chandelier above the bed in the head of state's room broke loose from the ceiling and plunged to the floor. Thank God nobody was sleeping in that bed at the time!

It took six years and almost ten million dollars to renovate Blair House, and during that period we had no place to house foreign visitors. I always found that embarrassing—here we were, the United States of America, and we had to put state visitors up in hotels. But Blair House just wasn't safe.

The next morning the Secret Service arrived to fit us with bullet-proof protective coats. They were heavy, cut like trench coats, and we were supposed to wear them whenever the Secret Service told us to. I knew in the back of my mind that this kind of thing might be necessary, but I preferred not to think about it.

Then Ronnie and I walked across Lafayette Park to the Hay-Adams Hotel for a quiet lunch. The Secret Service was with us, of course, but by now we were used to them. People seemed startled when we entered the dining room, and then, spontaneously, everybody stood and applauded. It was such a nice gesture, and it made us feel so welcome. Little did I realize that this was the last time in all of our Washington years that Ronnie and I would just walk out the door and down the street like ordinary people. The enormous changes in our lives had yet to sink in.

While Ronnie was busy with meetings, I started trying to assemble a staff. I had hired housekeepers, babysitters, and gardeners before, but putting together a professional staff was a new experience for me. In Sacramento, I had had one secretary, in addition to Nancy Reynolds, who dealt with the press. But now there were all sorts of positions to fill—chief of staff, social secretary, press secretary, and many more.

This was new territory for me, and I found it difficult and confus-

Nancy Reagan

ing. Hundreds of people had applied for about twenty jobs, and I spent hours reading résumés and conducting interviews. But I didn't really know what questions to ask, or how to decide which applicants were most suitable for jobs I myself didn't yet understand. Some of the people I hired turned out to be terrific, and a few worked for me throughout both of Ronnie's terms. Two or three others were gone within the year.

One highly recommended member of my staff, who was supposed to be experienced in the ways of Washington, arranged a White House reception for big donors to Ronnie's campaign. We always had a buffet for those occasions. But after Ronnie and I came down, we learned that there had not been enough food and that the guests had been sent home early—which isn't exactly how you treat your biggest campaign donors.

Letitia Baldrige was indispensable during this period. She had been Jacqueline Kennedy's chief of staff and social secretary, and had later helped Lady Bird Johnson, Pat Nixon, and Rosalynn Carter. "Make sure you get along with the chief usher at the White House," she told me. "He runs the place. Next to your husband, he'll be the most important man in your life."

I had already met Rex Scouten, and Tish was right: He did become the second most important man in my life. Despite his title, which makes him sound like the head man at a movie theater, the chief usher is in charge of almost everything at the White House: budget, personnel, entertainment, maintenance, and much, much more. Rex had been at the White House since 1949, when he was in the Secret Service, and had been made chief usher in 1969. He helped me in countless ways, especially in steering me through landmines and traps along the way, and we became such good friends that I named our dog after him.

Tish also warned me about the huge volume of mail I would be receiving as first lady—something like five hundred letters and invitations *a day*. "Get somebody who's really smart about answering letters," she said. "And never have them go out over your name."

"Why not?" I asked. "I always sign my own mail."

"Let me tell you," she said. "When I worked for the Kennedys, one of the local priests invited the president and the first lady to attend the opening of his art show. Mistakes do happen, and some-how, a volunteer in the social office sent him a letter that said, 'Dear Father. The President and Mrs. Kennedy have asked me to congrat-ulate you on the birth of your son.'

"The priest was livid, and he made a huge fuss. Nancy, can you imagine what would have happened if Mrs. Kennedy herself had signed that letter? Remember, any letter with your signature could end up on the front page."

The final days before the inauguration were a dizzying kaleidoscope of events. I remember going to a luncheon given by our California friends. I also remember sitting on some steps outdoors, watching a fireworks display. The fireworks were spectacular, but it was terribly cold, and I was huddled in a blanket next to a portable heater, wondering if I was going to freeze to death right there, without ever seeing Ronnie sworn in. And I remember dancing with Walter Cronkite at a party and finding, to my delight, that he was one of the world's great dancers.

Then our family started arriving, streaming in from all over the country.

My parents flew in from Phoenix. Neither of them was well, and I worried that the trip might be too much for them. But they wouldn't have missed it for the world.

My brother, Dick, and his wife, Patricia, and their children drove in from Philadelphia.

Ron and Doria, newly married, came down on the shuttle from New York.

Patti arrived from California with a lovely red chiffon evening dress for the inaugural ball. But I could see that she really wasn't comfortable at the White House, and she didn't stay long.

Maureen and her fiancé, Dennis, flew in from California, as did the rest of the California contingent: Michael, his wife, Colleen, and their little boy, Cameron; Ronnie's brother, Moon, and his wife, Bess; Anne Allman, our housekeeper, and Barney Barnett, who had been with us since Sacramento, with his wife; and lots of other friends.

The night before the inauguration we all went to the inaugural gala at the Capital Center in Landover, Maryland, a gigantic sports arena. It was a great evening, with performances by Frank Sinatra, Ethel Merman, Bob Hope, Rich Little, and Donny Osmond, among others, with Johnny Carson as the master of ceremonies.

The most touching moment of the evening came when our old friend Jimmy Stewart appeared on stage with General Omar Bradley, the nation's only living five-star general, who was confined to a wheelchair. They stopped in front of Ronnie, and both Jimmy and the general saluted the president-elect. Ronnie immediately stood and returned the salute. It was the first time I had ever seen him do that, but from then on it became standard practice.

When Jimmy wheeled General Bradley back off the stage, Ronnie leaned over to me and whispered, "I think it's finally sunk in."

When the program was over, Ronnie insisted on thanking the performers. I was especially moved by what he said that night, because he was true to his roots and so proud, as always, of his former profession:

"I'm going to say something that I've dreamed of saying to an audience like this sometime, in the presence of these wonderful people. If it is true that when the curtain goes up on eternity, all men must approach the gates bearing in their arms that which they have given to life, the people of show business will march in the procession carrying in their arms the pure pearl of tears, the gold of laughter, and the diamonds of stardust they spill on what otherwise might have been a rather dreary world. And when at last all reach the final stage, I'm sure the keeper will say, 'Let my children in.'"

At Blair House the next morning I woke up earlier than usual. Inauguration day was jammed with activities, but there was also the excitement of trying to get everybody ready in time. We had a full house, and my parents needed extra help to prepare for the busy day ahead.

Traditionally, the president-elect has worn a morning suit for the swearing-in. President Kennedy, who was famous for going bareheaded even in the coldest weather, chose to wear a top hat. Lyndon Johnson, under the circumstances of his swearing-in, wore a business suit. Nixon wore a club coat with striped pants, whereas Carter, who wanted a less elaborate presidency, wore a business suit. Ronnie wore a club coat, striped pants, and a gray vest, but without the top hat. I wore a red dress and coat by Adolfo.

The day began at nine-thirty with a brief service at St. John's Episcopal Church, around the corner from Blair House. St. John's, which is known as the president's church, is a small, beautiful building. We sat in George Washington's pew, and I couldn't help but feel history closing in on us that morning. There was only room for our family and a few close friends to join us, along with George and Barbara Bush and their children.

After church, most of our party went on to the Capitol to get seated for the swearing-in. Ronnie and I went back to Blair House to wait for Senator Mark Hatfield, chairman of the Joint Congressional Committee on Inaugural Ceremonies, who would escort us to the White House for the traditional coffee with the outgoing president and first lady.

We entered the White House through the North Portico and walked directly to the Blue Room with the Carters and the Mondales. President Carter had been up all night working on the Iran hostage situation—and it showed. His face was pale and he looked exhausted. It was impossible not to feel for him. Rosalynn was visibly uncomfortable and unhappy. She said hello, but aside from that we barely spoke to each other.

The hostages had been freed, but they hadn't yet left Iran. And now it was becoming clear that the Iranians must be waiting until Carter was out of office before releasing them. Ronnie thought this was inexcusable. "If they're released during the swearing-in," he told Mike Deaver, "even if it's during my speech, I want you to pass me a note. Interrupt me, because I want to announce it."

Traditionally, the outgoing and incoming presidents ride together from the White House to the Capitol, and so do their wives. Then, after the swearing-in and the inaugural parade, the new president and first lady return to the White House—this time not as guests but as residents.

And so Rosalynn and I rode to the Capitol together, along with

John Rhodes, the House minority leader. Thank God John was with us, because he kept up a steady stream of conversation in a very awkward situation. Rosalynn just looked out the window and didn't say a word. I didn't know *what* to say, so I kept quiet, too. Fortunately, it's a short ride.

Ever since Andrew Jackson's inauguration in 1829, the swearing-in ceremony had been held on the steps of the East Front of the Capitol. This time, Mark Hatfield had suggested that we move it to the West Front, with its breathtaking view of the Mall, the Washington Monument, and the Lincoln Memorial. Ronnie loved the idea. From the East Front all you saw were government buildings, and Ronnie preferred to take the oath as he looked out westward toward the rest of the country. As soon as we got there, I could see it was the right decision.

When I reached my seat, I turned to make sure that my parents and our children were there. All our friends were in place, and nobody looked too cold. Although the sky was overcast, the weather was remarkably mild. At fifty-six degrees, this was one of the warmest inauguration days in history.

While the Marine Corps Band played "Yankee Doodle" and "The Battle Hymn of the Republic," the official guests marched in to take their seats. Majority Leader Howard Baker led his fellow senators, and I smiled when I noticed that Howard had brought along his camera. Then came George Bush, President Carter, Vice President Mondale, and the justices of the Supreme Court. Everybody was there except Ronnie, who was waiting in a special room in the Capitol along with John Rhodes and Mark Hatfield.

Just before Ronnie appeared, I looked around and caught the eye of my friend Betsy Bloomingdale. She started to cry, and naturally I did too. *Stop it,* I told myself. *The television cameras are watching you.* But I'll never forget Bets's face at that moment, and I'm sure she'll never forget mine. I know we were both thinking the same thought—that from now on it would never be the same again.

We quickly turned away from each other, and I tried to focus on the view, the enormous crowd, and the overwhelming meaning of this event. The Capitol was covered with flags and red-and-white bunting, and today it looked more beautiful than ever.

I was terribly proud and excited, but it all felt unreal. Could it really be that Ronald Reagan, *my husband*, was about to become the fortieth president of the United States? How did this ever happen? It was like a dream: You're going through something momentous, but it hasn't really sunk in that it's actually happening.

At 11:39, while the trumpets played "Jubilant," Ronnie arrived on the podium. George Bush was sworn in first. Barbara held a Bible that had been given to them by Billy Graham, as Justice Potter Stewart administered the oath.

Then it was Ronnie's turn. I stood beside him, holding the Reagan family Bible. It had belonged to Ronnie's mother, and inside she had listed the births and deaths in her family, the Wilsons. It was old and crumbling and taped together, and it seemed just right for the occasion.

On the inside front cover, Nelle had written these words: "A thought for today: You can be too big for God to use, but you cannot be too small."

Just before noon, Chief Justice Warren Burger administered the oath, and Ronnie repeated the words after him. At that moment I found it difficult to concentrate on the history of it all. But as I stood there with my husband, holding Nelle's Bible in my hand, I thought, *My Lord, here I am standing here, doing what I've seen other women do in photographs and on television. And it's me. And it's us. And it's really happening.*

Then, suddenly, it was over. The president kissed me, and a booming twenty-one-gun salute rang out in honor of the new president. The first man to shake Ronnie's hand was Jimmy Carter, who was now a private citizen again. Then Ronnie walked to the podium to begin his inaugural address. What happened next—well, you'll never believe me, so I'll quote from the coverage in *Time*:

> As he raised his head to look out at the crowd, a strange and wonderful thing happened. The dark cloudy sky over his head began to part slightly, within seconds there was a gaping hole in the gray overcast, and a brilliant, golden shaft of wintery sun burst through the clouds and bathed the inaugural stand and the watching crowd. As Reagan spoke a slight breeze ruffled his hair and the warm golden light beamed down on him.

Later, a few minutes after he finished speaking, as if on cue from some master lighter backstage, the hole in the clouds shrank, the sky darkened, and Washington grew gray and cold once again.

What was even more amazing was that the same kind of thing had happened in Sacramento during Ronnie's first inauguration as governor. It had been a cold, drizzly, and overcast day, but when Ronnie got up to speak, the sun came out.

When it happened again this time, I was overcome with joy. Maybe this is an omen, I thought. Maybe it was meant to be.

Ronnie started his inaugural address, which he had written himself, by thanking President Carter for a smooth transition. He called for a war against inflation, which, he said, "distorts our economic decisions, penalizes thrift, and crushes the struggling young and the fixed-income elderly alike."

He stated again, as he had in so many campaign speeches, that "government is not the solution to our problem; government *is* the problem." Then, as he loves to do, Ronnie talked about an inspiring example of individual initiative and heroism. He had recently received a letter about Martin A. Treptow, a little-known American hero who fought and died in World War I. Private Treptow was killed on a courier mission in France, but his diary survived. "America must win this war," he had written. "Therefore, I will work. I will sacrifice. I will endure. I will fight cheerfully and do my utmost, as if the issue of the whole struggle depended on me alone."

Soon Ronnie was finished, and the band played "Hail to the Chief."

We moved inside the Capitol for lunch. The children told Ronnie how proud they were, and an enormous crush of well-wishers tried to shake his hand and offer their congratulations.

By this time, President Carter was already on his way to Andrews Air Force Base for the flight back to Georgia, and Walter Mondale was with him. I read later that when the phone rang in their car with news that the hostages had finally left the airport in Tehran, Carter and Mondale looked at each other and cried. I'd had my differences with the Carters, but they certainly deserved better than that.

At the luncheon with the congressional leaders in the beautiful

Statuary Hall, I sat between Senator Hatfield and Speaker Tip O'Neill. My mother sat on the other side of Tip. My strongest memory of that lunch is of watching Mother and Tip swapping stories as if they had been friends all their lives. There were California roses on each table, and all the ladies received a souvenir—a small silver-plated box filled with jelly beans.

Toward the end of the lunch, Ronnie made the announcement that everybody had been waiting for: "With thanks to Almighty God, I have been given a tag line, the get-off line everyone wants at the end of a toast or speech. Some thirty minutes ago, the planes bearing our prisoners left Iranian airspace and are free of Iran."

Before we left the Capitol, Ronnie paid a brief visit to the Speaker's office. Tip asked him to autograph a pile of special inaugural programs, and as he signed them, Ronnie joked that this little favor would cost Tip a few votes in the House. There was also a fair amount of baseball talk that afternoon. In the years to come there would be many political battles between these two men, but there was a warmth and a personal chemistry between them that day that never faded.

Then we were off to the inaugural parade, which marches down Pennsylvania Avenue from the Capitol to the White House. As a special treat for Ronnie, one of the bands had come from the high school in Ronnie's hometown of Dixon, Illinois, and he seemed to get a little misty-eyed as they marched proudly by. The final float in the parade held the entire Mormon Tabernacle Choir, which stopped in front of us to sing "The Battle Hymn of the Republic," which Ronnie and I both love.

The parade was great, but my mind was somewhere else. That night we were supposed to appear at ten different inaugural balls, and I wondered what had become of my gown, shoes, and purse. We had left our bags at Blair House that morning—all that now seemed like days ago—and everyone had assured me that all our possessions would be moved into the White House during the luncheon and the parade. Immediately after the swearing-in, our housekeeper, Anne Allman, and Ted Graber, our decorator, had hurried back to Blair House to supervise the move.

But as a world-class worrier, I kept wondering how on earth the

White House staff could move one family in and the other family out in a matter of hours without losing *something* important in the process. Naturally, I was sure that this "something" would be my gown. I know this may seem a silly concern at such a moment, but I think most women will understand.

Nobody can imagine what it's like to walk into the White House after the inaugural parade, when, for the first time, you're coming *home* as the new president and first lady. You feel awed. You think about all the families who have lived here before. It's very humbling.

I remember thinking: When we left here this morning, Ronnie wasn't president. Now he is. And from now on, whatever happens, we're going to be part of history. Whatever we do will be recorded, debated, and remembered.

We went upstairs to the residence, and there was my gown. And our furniture from California was in place in the West Hall, which made me feel that this strange and wonderful new place really was our home. The wonderful and efficient White House staff, with help from Anne and Ted, had taken care of everything, and I still don't understand how they did it so quickly.

I had hoped to spend a few minutes resting, but I was concerned about my parents, and the house was new to us, and there were all kinds of details to take care of. Toward evening, the rest of the family came over from Blair House to share a glass of champagne and to pose for a portrait before we fanned out to the inaugural balls. When they left, we noticed flashes of light outside, and Ronnie and I stepped out onto the Truman Balcony to see what it was.

"It looks like they're welcoming you with fireworks," I said.

"Do you really think so?" he asked. He just couldn't imagine that all of this was for him.

When they hear the words "inaugural ball," most people think of a grand ballroom with a huge dance floor and a lot of people dancing and enjoying themselves. I know I did. But the reality is very different: Crowds of people are jammed together, shoulder to shoulder, just standing there; there's no way you can dance, and it's so noisy that you can't even hear the orchestra.

When you have forty-three thousand guests attending ten events, something is bound to go wrong. Some ticket-holders never even got in, and when Ronnie's brother, Neil, showed up at one of the balls with his wife, he had a terrible time getting past security. "You've *got* to let me in," he said. "I'm the president's brother."

"Sure, fella," replied the agent. "You're the fourth guy who's tried that today!"

Somehow, we went to all ten inaugural balls in just under four hours. At each one, Ronnie spoke about the returning hostages, which always produced a strong reaction from the crowd. But mostly it was a night of celebration. At the last of the balls, Ronnie said, "I'd like to dance with my lady." The floor was so crowded that we danced on the stage as the Tommy Dorsey Orchestra played "You'll Never Know."

We got back to the White House very late that night, happy, and totally exhausted. It had been an incredibly long and full day—the church service in the morning, coffee with the Carters at the White House, the swearing-in, the inaugural address, the luncheon, the release of the hostages, the parade, moving into our new home, followed by ten balls. As I closed my eyes that night, I remember thinking, My Lord, here we are, sleeping in the White House. And here *I* am, sleeping with the president of the United States.

It's only now, after Ronnie and I have returned to Los Angeles, that I fully appreciate how truly wonderful it was to live in the White House. Believe me, it doesn't take long to grow accustomed to all the services that are provided, the many things that are taken care of for you that you would normally do for yourself. Whatever you wanted, there it was.

If we needed a plumber, we'd call the usher's office and he'd be there in five minutes. If I needed a package wrapped, somebody took care of it. There was a wonderful man named Johnny Muffler who would come around and wind all the clocks and set them. He had been there for years, and he'd fix anything you needed. And then there were the butlers, who were always trying to make sure I was getting enough to eat, and who, I found out much later, would report to the doctors as to how well I was doing!

Sometimes it's hard to appreciate what you've got until it's gone. Early in 1989, just a few days after we returned to Los Angeles, I was waiting at home one morning for the electrician. He simply didn't show up. This is, of course, a perfectly normal occurrence, but after eight years in the White House, I was spoiled.

Every evening, while I took a bath, one of the maids would come by and remove my clothes for laundering or dry cleaning. The bed would always be turned down. Five minutes after Ronnie came home and hung up his suit, it would disappear from the closet to be pressed, cleaned, or brushed. No wonder Ron used to call the White House an eight-star hotel.

When you live at the White House, the world is yours. When I wanted to call somebody, I would just pick up the phone and an operator would be there to help me reach that person. They would track him down *anywhere*—unless I specifically said that if he wasn't at home or in the office, they shouldn't bother. A couple of weeks after we moved in, Ronnie put in a call to somebody—I don't remember who—and then almost fainted when he learned that the man was in Japan, where it was three o'clock in the morning!

We grew very fond of the White House operators, but during Ronnie's first term, one of the people I called the most was Michael Deaver, who worked right in our building.

Of all the advisers who have worked for my husband over the years, I was closest of all to Mike, who was my link to the West Wing. Mike's title was deputy chief of staff, and along with Jim Baker and Ed Meese, he formed what was known as the troika— Ronnie's three-man team of senior advisers during his first term as president.

Ronnie and I go way back with Mike, who served as Ronnie's deputy executive secretary during the Sacramento years. From the very start, the three of us hit it off. By the time he came into the White House, he really knew Ronnie and understood when to approach him, and how. Mike was never afraid to bring Ronnie the bad news, or to tell him when he thought he was wrong. Because we were so close, and because he served Ronnie so well, I was heartbroken when Mike left the White House in 1985 to go into business on his own. But even then, we spoke often on the telephone.

It has sometimes been implied that Mike Deaver was more than Ronnie's trusted aide—that while Ronnie was a great communicator, Michael Deaver was running the show behind the scenes. I am second to nobody in my admiration for all that Mike accomplished, but as he'd be the first to acknowledge, he was more interested in public relations than in policy. Ronnie made the decisions, and Mike, along with Ed Meese and Jim Baker, helped implement them.

His greatest skill was in arranging what were known as good visuals—televised events or scenes that would leave a powerful symbolic image in people's minds. One that I'll always remember came during the fortieth anniversary of D-Day, June 6, 1984. Mike arranged to have Ronnie go to Pointe du Hoc, Normandy, an isolated cliff overlooking the sea, where he made a speech with a group of D-Day veterans gathered around him.

In early 1986, a few months after he left the White House, Mike's picture appeared on the cover of *Time*. In the photograph, he was sitting in the back of a chauffeur-driven car, talking on a cellular phone, with the Capitol dome in the background. The caption read: "Who's This Man Calling?" And in smaller type: "Influence Peddling in Washington."

Mike quickly became the symbol of government officials who convert their access into a salable commodity. He did what hundreds of people had done, but he did it too conspicuously and too quickly. When I saw his picture on *Time*, I called and said, "Mike, you've made a big mistake and I think you're going to regret it." Unfortunately, I was right.

Later, Mike was accused of lying to Congress and to a federal grand jury considering allegations that he had violated the Ethics in Government Act, which places severe restrictions on lobbying by former senior government officials. When his legal troubles began, I was told by the White House counsel that I couldn't call him, so I was reduced to sending messages of support through Richard Helms, our mutual friend, to let Mike know I was thinking of him.

When it was all over, and Mike was convicted, I called him again, but our relationship hasn't been the same since.

Somewhere along the line in Washington Mike Deaver went off track and caught a bad case of Potomac fever. He had suddenly become a national figure, a genius of public relations, and when something like that happens, it can be hard to keep your perspective. Mike was also frustrated by his relatively low government salary in a town where some of the people he was meeting were earning many times as much in the private sector.

But even after he left the White House he remained one of my closest friends. Suddenly, in late 1986, I had trouble reaching him on the phone. I kept calling his house every day, and Carolyn, Mike's wife, kept giving me evasive answers. Finally she said, "Nancy, I can't say where he is; he made me promise not to. But I'm going to be seeing him later and I'll ask him if I can tell you."

I immediately assumed that Mike had suffered a nervous breakdown. Then Mike called me and said, "I'm sorry I haven't been in touch. I'm an alcoholic, and you're the first person I've told. I'm staying at an addiction center in Maryland."

"Oh, Mike, is that all?" I said. "I was afraid you'd had a breakdown! Alcoholism is a disease that can be cured. You can handle it."

I must have said the right thing, because Mike told me later that my comment had encouraged him.

A year or so later, William Safire, who has never been my biggest fan, wrote in a column, "Was the First Lady so involved with her crusade against drug addiction that she failed to notice that her closest confidant was a drunk?" That was a heartless and dumb remark. Alcoholism can be hard to detect, and Mike kept his secret so well that nobody in the White House even suspected he had a drinking problem. Ronnie, Ed Meese, and Jim Baker were with him every day, but they never saw him take a drink or act strange. Some alcoholics never act drunk.

Ed Meese had also been with us in Sacramento, where he was chief of staff during Ronnie's second term. But Ed and I were never close. He was by far the most ideological member of the troika, a jump-off-the-cliff-with-the-flag-flying conservative. Some people are so rigid in their beliefs that they'd rather lose than win a partial victory, and I always felt that Meese was one of them.

It also made me squirm that he kept getting into trouble in his financial life. He made a series of mistakes which embarrassed the presidency, and some men in his situation would have stepped down. Eventually he did, but in my opinion he waited far too long and weakened both the Justice Department and the presidency.

I think Ed had been hurt that he wasn't made chief of staff in 1980, but he wouldn't have been good in that job. Among other things, he wasn't well organized. He was famous for his bulging briefcase; if you wanted a document to disappear, you'd give it to Ed. And he made a serious mistake in August of 1981, when American Navy jets shot down two Libyan fighter planes off the coast of Libya, and Ed waited five and a half hours before calling Ronnie to wake him up and tell him about it.

But there was one major thing in Ed's favor: He was very loyal to Ronnie.

Of the three members of Ronnie's troika, I knew Jim Baker least of all. He managed George Bush's 1980 campaign against Ronnie, and when George became vice president, Baker came along. It was Mike Deaver's idea to make him White House chief of staff, because Jim was well connected in Washington. Ronnie had been leaning toward Ed Meese, but Mike prevailed.

I thought Jim Baker did a fine job. He knew a lot about politics and had many good contacts in Congress. He was more inclined than Ronnie to compromise and make deals, but he was loyal, and he was certainly effective in helping get Ronnie's programs through Congress. He also cultivated the press assiduously—perhaps too much, because he leaked constantly.

Although Jim did a lot for Ronnie, I always felt that his main interest was Jim Baker. He was an ambitious man, and when he was worn out after four years as chief of staff, he made it clear to Ronnie that he wanted to be secretary of State. Ronnie stuck with George Shultz, but when Bush became president, Jim got his wish. I wouldn't be surprised to see him run for higher office in the future.

The troika worked out well, but I can't say the same for Al Haig,

Ronnie's first secretary of State. As far as I'm concerned, Haig represented Ronnie's biggest mistake in the first term.

He was too power-hungry. He saw himself as the only person in the administration who should be making decisions on foreign policy. When Ronnie was shot, Haig alarmed Ronnie's aides and much of the country with his famous statement "As of now, I am in control here." At the time, I was too busy worrying about Ronnie to pay attention to Haig, but I always thought that comment was revealing.

Haig was obsessed with matters of status—with exactly where he stood on a receiving line, or where he was seated on a plane or helicopter. If he didn't think his seat was important enough, he'd let you know. He had a prickly personality and was always complaining that he was being slighted.

He also struck me as eager for military action. In the first month of Ronnie's administration, he apparently implied to Tip O'Neill that he wanted to invade Nicaragua. Tip, and many others in Washington, assumed that Haig spoke for Ronnie. But in reality, Haig alarmed Ronnie and his top advisers with his belligerent rhetoric. Once, talking about Cuba in a meeting of the National Security Council, he turned to Ronnie and said, "You just give me the word and I'll turn that f—— island into a parking lot."

If Ronnie had given him the green light, Haig would have bombed everybody and everything.

Haig threatened to resign any number of times, and finally, in June 1982, Ronnie accepted his resignation. In this case I didn't have to say anything to my husband; Ronnie just didn't care for him, and we were both relieved when Haig finally left.

Bill Clark, who came in in 1981 as deputy secretary of State, was another bad choice, in my opinion. I didn't think he was qualified for the job—or for his subsequent position as national security adviser. I wasn't the only one who felt that way; he embarrassed himself in front of the Senate Foreign Relations Committee when he couldn't name the prime minister of Zimbabwe.

Clark had been in Ronnie's administration in Sacramento, but even then I had never really gotten along with him. He struck me as a user—especially when he traveled around the country claiming he represented Ronnie, which usually wasn't true. I spoke to Ronnie about him, but Ronnie liked him, so he stayed around longer than I would have liked.

One man Ronnie and I both respected and admired was George Shultz, who came in to replace Haig in 1982 and remained as secretary of State throughout the rest of Ronnie's presidency. George reminded me of a big teddy bear, but underneath that soft exterior was a tough negotiator with enormous energy. I still don't know how he made all those trips. He would arrive back in Washington from a long trip and would fly off again the next day for another mission, accompanied by his wife, Obie.

I trusted George completely; if he said it was raining, I didn't have to look out the window. I believe that Eduard Shevardnadze, his Soviet counterpart, also trusted him; one reason that Ronnie and Gorbachev were able to accomplish so much is that Shultz and Shevardnadze worked so well together.

George loves to dance, so when Ginger Rogers came to a state dinner, I seated them together and asked one of the White House photographers to take as many pictures as she could of George and Ginger dancing. A few days later, I sent George a whole pile of photographs—enough to paper his entire office.

It soon became a joke: Whenever we had a dinner, I would seat George next to a glamor girl, until Obie finally came up to me and said, "Well, Nancy, what are you going to do for *me*?"

13

How We Lived

PEOPLE often ask me what it was like to live in the White House, and what routines we followed there. Our day normally began at seven-thirty, when a White House operator called on the telephone on my side of the bed and said, "Good morning, it's seven-thirty." Sometimes I was still sleeping, but Ronnie was usually awake. I would push a button by the side of the bed, which rang a buzzer in the second-floor kitchen, and a minute later a White House butler would come into our room, pull open the curtains, and bring us the morning papers, which we read in bed.

Ronnie would start with the *Washington Post,* followed by the *New York Times,* and as for that persistent rumor that he turned first to the comics—it's true. Might as well begin the day on a light note. Later, at the office, he'd look through the *Wall Street Journal.* I usually began with *U.S.A. Today* and the *Washington Times* while waiting for Ronnie to finish the *Post* and the *New York Times.* Sometimes the butler would also bring the *New York Post* and the *Daily News,* and on Monday mornings they'd bring us *Time, Newsweek,* and *U.S. News,* all hot off the press.

While we read the papers, the television would be tuned to *Good Morning America,* in case Ron was on. All the morning news shows were taped by the White House, and if there was anything Ronnie's staff thought he should see, they'd show it to him at the office. The same was true with the print media: We both received a daily packet of press clips so we wouldn't miss an important story.

By the time the papers arrived we'd be sharing the bed with Rex, our brown-and-white King Charles spaniel, who was given to us by Bill and Pat Buckley. Rex slept just across the hall from our bedroom, in a basket in the kitchen. A few minutes later another butler would come in with the breakfast tray and lay it on the bed. The butlers worked in shifts, so it wasn't the same man every morning. But everybody who served us was from the White House staff. Apparently, we were one of the very few presidential families to arrive without any personal servants.

Breakfast was always the same: orange or grapefruit juice, cold bran cereal with milk (and sometimes cut fruit), and decaffeinated coffee. Ronnie would also have bran toast with honey, and once a week we'd each have an egg.

About a month after we came to the White House, I was surprised when the usher's office sent up a bill for our food. Nobody had told us that the president and his wife are charged for every meal, as well as for such incidentals as dry cleaning, toothpaste, and other toiletries. We paid for our guests' meals, too, unless they came on official business. Fortunately, state dinners were paid for by the State Department. I suspect people think everything is paid for by the White House, but that's not true.

At around eight forty-five, Ronnie would lean over the bed, kiss me goodbye, and leave for the office. On his way out, he took Rex back to the kitchen so that Dale Haney, one of the White House gardeners, could take him out for his morning walk. Then Ronnie went downstairs in the elevator, where he was met by Jim Kuhn, his personal assistant, and a Secret Service agent, who walked with him across the colonnade along the Rose Garden, and into the West Wing. He would pass the doctor's office, and John Hutton was always in the hallway to say hello. (Sometimes, on his way home, Ronnie would stop in for his allergy shot.) His first appointment of the morning was usually a nine o'clock meeting with his chief of staff and the vice president.

I almost never saw Ronnie during the day, and never for lunch. Sometimes he ate alone in the Oval Office study (which had been Mike Deaver's office during the first term), where a typical lunch consisted of a bowl of soup followed by half a grapefruit. Staying at the office, he could get more work done and continue to make calls. Every Thursday, Ronnie had lunch with George Bush.

When Ronnie left for work, I went into my dressing room, a soft, romantic room just behind the bedroom. I loved that room, with its peach-colored carpet and the peach-and-white floral draperies and upholstery. In there I had hung a wonderful nineteenth-century painting of a woman with her dog, a scene so peaceful it sometimes made me feel that I was born in the wrong century.

Outside the window was a magnolia tree that had been planted by Andrew Jackson. You could see the Rose Garden from that window, and if Ronnie was participating in an outdoor ceremony, I'd often perch up on the radiator and watch. Sometimes he'd wave to me, and the photographers would turn around and take my picture, too.

In addition to Pat Nixon's small beauty parlor, the first lady also has her own bathroom, a small one by today's standards. On the side of the washbasin I kept an inspirational text that a friend had sent me years ago, and I looked at it often during our years in the White House. It's called "One Night I Had a Dream," and the author is unknown:

> I dreamed I was walking along the beach with the Lord, and across the sky flashed scenes from my life. For each scene, I noticed two sets of footprints in the sand; one belonged to me, and the other to the Lord. When the last scene of my life flashed before us, I looked back at the footprints in the sand. I noticed that many times along the path of my life there was only one set of footprints. I also noticed that it happened at the very lowest and the saddest times of my life.
>
> I questioned the Lord about it. "Lord, you said that once I decided to follow You, You would walk with me all the way. But I've noticed that during the most troublesome times of my life, there is only one set of footprints. I don't understand why, in times when I needed You most, You would leave."
>
> The Lord replied, "My precious child, I would never leave you during your times of trial and suffering. When you see only one set of footprints, it was then that I carried you."

I love that reading, and I've sent copies to many of my friends as they were going through difficult periods in their lives.

. . .

My first stop of the day was down the hall in the exercise room, which had been an empty bedroom until we converted it after the shooting. Amy Carter used to sleep here, and before that, Tricia Nixon, Luci Johnson, and Caroline Kennedy. Now it served as a mini gym, with a treadmill, and a central unit with different stations for various exercises. I used to watch Cable News Network as I went through my morning routine.

Depending on my schedule, I might spend the rest of the morning working in my office, which was next to the exercise room and was once Lynda Bird Johnson's bedroom. I had a private line in my office, and my visitors were always amused by how often it rang with wrong numbers. Between these two rooms were closets, where I kept my clothes.

When I didn't go out to lunch, I usually had a light meal alone in the West Hall. Or, in nice weather, I sometimes ate on the Truman Balcony. In either case I sat by the phone, because by lunchtime in Washington I could start calling friends in California. To warm up the West Hall, I had moved in our two red floral-print couches from California, along with some lamps and tables, and two little needlepoint chairs that Colleen Moore had made for Patti and Ron. As Patti's godmother, Colleen had made her a chair showing a girl standing next to a grandfather clock. There was a mouse at the bottom of the clock (as in the nursery rhyme), and the hands of the clock showed 1:58, the exact time of Patti's birth. Six years later, when Ron was born, Colleen said, "His sister has one, so I'm going to make one for him, too." Ron's chair shows a little boy with his dog, sitting on a fence at a ranch. I'm sentimentally attached to these little chairs, because they remind me not only of my children but also of my mother and her friend Colleen.

The private living quarters are on the second and third floors of the original White House (that is, the original building, minus the West Wing, which was built in 1902, and the East Wing, which was completed in 1942). They're much smaller than you would expect. Ronnie and I certainly didn't need more room for ourselves, but there were times when extra bedrooms would have been useful, such as the two inaugurations, Christmas, and right after the shooting.

Although the White House is a state home, its scale is nothing like that of Buckingham Palace or Windsor Castle.

Mostly it was just Ronnie and I, with frequent visits from Maureen. Like the Carters and the Fords, Ronnie and I slept in what is sometimes called the First Lady's Bedroom, and I loved its beautiful airy shape and high ceilings. To warm it up, I covered the walls with wallpaper in an eighteenth-century Chinese print, with hand-painted yellow, green, and blue birds. The carpet was salmon-colored.

Maureen generally stayed down the hall in the Lincoln Bedroom, partly because Dennis, her husband, is very tall, and the bed in Lincoln's room is the longest one in the White House. Lincoln never actually slept in that room, although he did hold Cabinet meetings there. He slept in the same room we did.

But apparently his presence remains. Neither Ronnie nor I ever saw the legendary ghost of Lincoln, but one night Dennis woke up and saw a shadowy figure by the fireplace. Maureen just laughed at him when he told her about it—until *she* woke up one night and saw a man who seemed to be wearing a red coat. At first she thought it was Ronnie in his red bathrobe, but when she looked again she noticed that the figure was transparent! Maureen says he was staring out the window and then turned around to look at her before he vanished.

When Ronnie heard these stories, he just laughed them off. "If you see him again," he told Maureen, "why don't you send him down the hall? I've got a few questions I'd like to ask him."

But even Ronnie had second thoughts one night when Rex started barking and running toward the Lincoln Bedroom. Nobody was sleeping there at the time, but Rex wouldn't stop. Ronnie went in, looked around, and saw nothing, but Rex absolutely refused to enter that room.

I was in the Lincoln Bedroom one afternoon, and when I leaned over to straighten one of the pictures, the maid, who had come in to dust, said, "Oh, he's been here again." And when I asked one of the butlers if he had ever seen Lincoln's ghost, he told me that once, from the kitchen, he had heard the piano playing in the hall. When he walked out to see who was there, the music suddenly stopped.

Most of the White House staff seemed to believe in Lincoln's ghost, and they told stories of Eisenhower and Churchill both seeing him. Who's to say? But if he is there, I wish I could have seen him before we left.

Off the Lincoln Bedroom is the Lincoln Sitting Room, which Lincoln used as his office. The furniture there dates from Lincoln's period, and the room includes a number of historical artifacts, including a signed holograph of the Gettysburg Address, and a dance card from Lincoln's inaugural ball.

President Nixon used this room as his study and spent many hours here. When Ronnie and I first moved in, I noticed a dark, smoky pattern on the walls and ceiling of the Lincoln Sitting Room. Then I remembered a famous story: Nixon used to come in here, turn the air conditioner up high, and then light a fire in the corner fireplace. This was one of the rooms I did over. I painted over the smoke stains, slipcovered the couch, and collected more Lincoln memorabilia.

Across the hall from the Lincoln Suite is the Queens Bedroom, so named because five different queens have stayed there: Queen Elizabeth (now the Queen Mother), Queen Wilhelmina and Queen Juliana of the Netherlands, Queen Frederika of Greece, and Queen Elizabeth II. Winston Churchill used to sleep in this room when he came to see President Roosevelt during World War II. More recently, the Queens Bedroom was used by my brother, Dick, and his wife.

The Queens Bedroom is decorated in shades of rose and white and furnished with antiques from the federal period. But what most visitors remember is the queens bathroom, where the toilet is disguised as an elegant wicker chair. (The same is true in the Lincoln bathroom.)

On a typical day, Ronnie came back to the residence in the late afternoon and went right into his study—a room that is often called the President's Bedroom, from the days when the president and first lady had separate rooms. Ronnie's study was one of my favorite

places, partly because the carpeting, upholstery, and drapes were a
rich red. Practically every surface was covered with photographs of
family, friends, and members of the British royal family—Queen
Elizabeth and Prince Philip, the Queen Mother, Prince Charles,
Princess Diana, Princess Anne and Mark Phillips, Princess Alexan-
dra and Angus Ogilvy, and Princess Margaret. Our relationship
with the British royal family began when Ronnie and I met Charles
in Palm Springs when Ronnie was governor, and it continued when
I attended Charles's wedding in 1981.

At around six o'clock Ronnie did his exercises, followed by a
shower in the president's bathroom, where Lyndon Johnson had
installed a telephone, a very elaborate shower, bright lights, and
enough electrical power to run a small country.

About once a month we hosted a state dinner, which began with
cocktails with the visiting party in the Yellow Oval Room, just
down the Center Hall from our bedroom. Betty Ford used to call
this the "leg room," because there were so many table and chair legs
for the maids to dust. It's a lovely room, with a beautiful view of the
Washington Monument and the Jefferson Memorial. When we first
moved in I found it cold, with too many chairs and bare surfaces,
but over time, and with the addition of two sofas from storage, two
or three coffee tables, porcelain figurines, and other *objets,* the room
seemed more inviting and became a favorite of mine. I also used the
Yellow Oval Room to entertain the wives of visiting heads of state,
or for tea with a friend. Ronnie used it occasionally—like the time
in 1984 when he met with the congressional leaders to inform them
of the rescue operation in Grenada. We also used this room for
cocktails and coffee when we had guests for dinner in the private
quarters.

We didn't have much occasion to go to the third floor, which
consists mostly of five guest bedroom suites. But we had fun decorating the billiard room, which was a great place to hang family
pictures and mementos—movie posters, a photograph of Ronnie
playing in his high-school band, a *Peanuts* cartoon that Charlie
Shultz had dedicated to me when Ronnie was governor, our wedding certificate, pictures of us at the ranch, a gag poster of *Gone With
the Wind,* starring Ronald Reagan and Margaret Thatcher, and my

special favorite—a picture of two hogs, who appear to be kissing, over the slogan "Hogs Are Beautiful."

Down the hall and up a ramp was the solarium. You get a lot of privacy there, which is why the teenage children in several administrations have used this room for courting. (The Johnsons even put in a soda fountain, but it's no longer there.) My niece Anne and her future husband, Jon, became engaged there one Christmas Eve and the next morning came bursting into our bedroom to tell us. This is the sunniest room in the White House, and it's where Ronnie spent much of his time recuperating after the shooting. Sometimes I would have lunch there with a friend, and on the few weekends when we weren't at Camp David, Ronnie and I would have lunch and spend time there.

If we were having company, or if Maureen was joining us, we had dinner in the family dining room. It's hard to believe, but until the Kennedys came to the White House, there was no dining room on the second floor of the residence, and no kitchen, either. And so, for example, the Eisenhowers often ate at a card table in the West Hall, with meals brought up in the service elevator from the main kitchen on the ground floor.

There *is* a family dining room one level down, on the state floor, but that's a public area, with security guards, visitors, and not much privacy. President and Mrs. Hoover used to go down there every night for dinner, dressed in formal clothes. I can't imagine anything more awful, but that was another era. When we arrived, the old family dining room was being used as a butler's pantry for state dinners. It's a pretty room, so I fixed it up with furniture and paintings, and Ronnie used it for luncheons for visiting heads of state. With the fire going, it provided a less formal atmosphere than the large State Dining Room.

To create the new family dining room on the second floor, Mrs. Kennedy had converted one of the bedrooms, and had the adjoining bathroom made into a small kitchen; the work was done so quickly that the original bathtub remained there for close to ten years. She decorated the dining room with historic wallpaper from an old house in Maryland, which depicted scenes from the Revolutionary War. Betty Ford had this taken down because she felt it looked too

violent for a dining room, but Mrs. Carter put it back up. I agreed
with Mrs. Kennedy and Mrs. Carter; I thought it added a nice
historical feel to the room, and I was grateful to Mrs. Kennedy for
finding it.

When it was just the two of us for dinner, we usually ate in
Ronnie's study, sitting at tray tables as we watched the evening
news. We watched all three networks, one after another, on the
White House taping system. (Yes, we had to sit through the com-
mercials, too.) We watched ABC first, followed by NBC, and then
CBS, which happened to be our order of preference.

Dinner was usually meat loaf, veal, chopped steak, or lamb chops,
although we also had chicken or fish. Or, if Ronnie was lucky,
macaroni and cheese. Just about the only food we don't agree on is
liver. Ronnie hates it, so whenever I had liver, he would usually kid
around and make a face. I'd kid him back and say, "Come on, honey,
it's good for you." But he never gave in.

Dinner was served by two butlers and always included dessert. I
tried not to let them serve a rich, gooey dessert every night, although
Ronnie would have liked that. Roland, the pastry chef, was excep-
tionally skilled, and on special occasions—Mother's Day, our anniversary, a birthday—he'd bake a cake with a message on it.

Some people have the impression that the president and first lady
are wining and dining every night. Not us. But for eight years, we
always attended the annual dinners that a president is expected to
go to (although not all of them do), such as those given by the
Gridiron, the White House Press Corps, and the White House
Photographers, the Ford's Theater Benefit, and many more, as well
as many fund-raisers, receptions, and Christmas parties. And sometimes we were invited to friends' houses.

But when we could grab an evening alone, we did so gladly. So
much of your life is on display that to be alone and relaxed was a
luxury we looked forward to. Besides, we like being alone. When
we had no plans, we could talk, read, and do some work after
dinner—Ronnie in his study, I in my office. We rarely watched
television in the evening, although on Sunday we usually saw *60
Minutes*, followed by *Murder, She Wrote*, with Angela Lansbury.

Most nights we were in bed by ten. When I pushed the button twice, it was a signal to the usher's office that we were turning in for the night. They would turn off all the lights and hold all calls, except for emergencies. We both love to read in bed. Ronnie would usually fall asleep around eleven, and I'd continue reading for another hour or so.

As much as Ronnie and I loved the White House, we found it very difficult to live in a place where you couldn't ever go out for a walk. We're both outdoor types, and it didn't take long before we started feeling cooped up.

Thank God for Camp David! I never expected that we would use it practically every weekend, but it became a regular and welcome part of our routine.

As most people know, Camp David is a rustic presidential retreat in Catoctin Mountain Park, seventy miles north of the White House. Franklin Roosevelt was the first president to use it, and he referred to it as Shangri-la. Eisenhower changed the name to Camp David in honor of his grandson.

It was impressed on us from the beginning that Camp David was the president's most private retreat, and that every president who has used it has gone to great lengths to keep it that way. So did we. We really guarded the privacy of the place. Prime Minister Nakasone of Japan once joined us there for lunch, and Mrs. Thatcher came twice, and we had a visit from President Lopez Portillo of Mexico, but except for family—mostly Ron and Doria, when they lived in New York, and my brother, Dick, and his family, from Philadelphia—that was about it. Even Ronnie's closest advisers were rarely there.

The only people who came with us regularly were John Hutton, the White House doctor; Jim Kuhn, Ronnie's personal assistant; Mark Weinberg, Ronnie's deputy press secretary; and the military aide who carries the "football"—a briefcase containing special codes in case of a nuclear war. Jim and John used to bring their families, and for me, part of the charm of Camp David was being with Jim's young children and John's daughter.

Most Fridays we would leave the White House around three.

Usually we went to Camp David by helicopter, which took about twenty-five minutes. In bad weather we drove, which added an extra hour or so to the trip.

I was never crazy about the helicopter, although as helicopters go, ours was large, and the ride was fairly smooth. I'm sure one image that people will always remember of the Reagan years is of Ronnie and me leaving the South Lawn of the White House for Camp David. Sam Donaldson would be shouting something to Ronnie, who could rarely hear him over the noise of the helicopter's engine. I would be walking behind Ronnie, led by one of the dogs—either Lucky, until he became too big to live at the White House, or Rex. Lucky is a black Bouvier sheepdog who was given to me as a small puppy in 1986 by the March of Dimes poster girl; I named her Lucky after Mother. She was just a little bundle of fur when I got her, but she grew to be the size of a pony. When she became too big for the White House, we took her to live at the ranch, with the other four dogs. She's in heaven.

Both dogs loved to ride in the helicopter; they knew we were headed for Camp David, where they had room to run around. During the flight, they would sit peacefully and look out the window. Lucky usually sat on Ronnie's lap.

When we drove to Camp David, we left the White House quietly, without the press. We'd just get into the car and drive off—almost like ordinary people. I loved passing through the pretty towns along the way, which always reminded me of Galesburg, Illinois, where my grandparents (Loyal's parents) lived. As we passed by the houses and the shops, I found myself wondering about the lives of the people who lived there. What were they thinking about? What would they be doing this evening? That's always been a favorite game of mine. Invariably a handful of people stood along the road and waved to us, which gave me a neighborly feeling.

When we arrived, whether by car or by helicopter, the camp commander would be there to greet us. A marine stands by the flagpole, and the moment the president arrives at Camp David, the presidential flag goes up. The moment he leaves, it comes down.

I had a tremendous feeling of release when we got to Camp

David. It was so important to us, in keeping our perspective on things, to be able to be there alone, to have quiet time together to think and reflect and get our thoughts in order.

By the time we arrived it was usually too late in the afternoon to go riding, and there were always phone messages for Ronnie. When you're president, there no such thing as a vacation. No matter where you go, there are always briefing books to study, papers to read, intelligence reports to review, speeches to work on, decisions to be made. You might be off in the mountains, but you're still president, and the world doesn't stop turning.

All the buildings in Camp David are named after trees, and we stayed in Aspen Lodge, which has a combined living-dining room, a bedroom suite, a guest room, and a kitchen, which we enlarged, to the delight of Eddie Serrano and his staff, who cooked for us. (Eddie, the president's valet, came on all our trips.) There was also a study in Aspen, but Ronnie preferred to work in the living room and used the study only when he had to take a phone call on the secure line—most often from the national security adviser, or from George Shultz.

Behind the living room was a picture window with a wonderful view across the valley. On our very first visit to Camp David, we looked out and saw eight deer staring in at us. "Look," Ronnie said, "we have a welcoming committee."

Although the White House has a movie theater, we rarely used it. But at Camp David we watched movies every Friday and Saturday night in our cabin, together with John Hutton and his wife, Jim Kuhn (or his wife, Carole, depending on who was babysitting that night), Mark Weinberg, Eddie Serrano, the helicopter pilot, the camp commander, and the Secret Service agents. Ronnie and I sat together on the couch, and everybody else settled into his or her personal chair. Eddie made popcorn in the kitchen, and Mark brought along peanut brittle. (We had to stop serving popcorn after Ronnie's cancer operation, and instead of peanut brittle, Mark started bringing chocolates.)

John's wife and I were generally the only women there, and the men loved Westerns, so we ran a lot of those. We saw a number of current films, but Ronnie and I both love golden oldies—the pictures from our day, such as *North by Northwest*, with Cary Grant and Eva Marie Saint; *The African Queen*, with Bogart and Hepburn; *Separate Tables*, with Rita Hayworth and Burt Lancaster; and *Yankee Doodle Dandy*, with James Cagney. Ronnie enjoys John Wayne pictures and I love Fred Astaire, so we must have seen just about all their pictures.

Before long, even the younger members of the audience started asking for more golden oldies. These pictures were made before they were born, but they appreciated them—especially when Ronnie would tell behind-the-scenes stories about the actors and the studios, which he generally did when the movie was over. We even screened some of our own pictures when we were asked to, including *King's Row*, *Bedtime for Bonzo*, *The Winning Team*, *Cattle Queen of Montana*, and *Knute Rockne, All American*, all starring Ronald Reagan, and *Night into Morning*, with Nancy Davis, and *Hellcats of the Navy*, which Ronnie and I made together in 1957.

On Saturday morning we'd read the newspapers, and Ronnie would work and go over his radio script. Then we'd walk up to Laurel, the main building, where Ronnie would do his weekly radio broadcast. We'd get there a few minutes early, pulled along by Rex, and Jim's kids would be waiting for us—and especially for Rex, whom they loved. Ronnie would do the broadcast from a conference room, with a radio crew supplied by one of the networks on a rotating basis. I was always in the room with him, along with Jim, Mark, a military aide, and a Secret Service agent. The broadcast began at 12:06 and lasted for five minutes.

From there we walked over to the gym, which had been built for the men stationed at Camp David. After my operation in 1987, John Hutton gave me a series of special therapeutic exercises to do, and I kept up with them while Ronnie lifted weights and used the treadmill. Then it was back to Aspen for lunch.

In good weather, we rode after lunch. I would ride behind Ronnie rather than beside him because our horses didn't like each other; if my horse got too close, Ronnie's horse would try to kick him. But even when we ride together at the ranch, we don't talk much. One thing I hate is riding with someone who keeps up a steady stream of conversation. You're there to relax, to look at the trees and the sky, to think. At Camp David, sometimes we'd see deer, which would suddenly jump right in front of us, frightening the horses.

I knew almost nothing about riding when I first met Ronnie, but I soon realized that if I wanted to marry this man, I'd have to trade in my tennis racket for a saddle. I still remember the first time he helped me up on a horse at his ranch. "It's easy," he assured me. "You just show him who's boss."

Well, that horse was enormous, and I remember thinking that this was the silliest thing I'd ever heard. At least my horse and I had one thing in common: We both knew who was *really* the boss.

I'm still not the world's most enthusiastic rider, and I don't ride nearly as well as Ronnie does. I'm still slightly afraid that my horse will jump. I don't enjoy riding fast, and Ron kids me about the time he and Doria were with us, and I called ahead to Ronnie, "Honey, Doria thinks we're going too fast." I'll use *any* excuse to slow us down.

When we first came to Camp David, we found that all the riding trails had been paved over by Richard Nixon so he and his guests could go around in golf carts. Ronnie and I had them restored. At first we confined ourselves to the grounds of Camp David, but soon Ronnie started pushing to go farther, beyond the fence, and eventually the Secret Service relented. It made for a pretty ride, but I don't think the security people were ever too crazy about it.

We always rode by the remains of an old stone house that had been owned by a woman named Bessie Darling. Bessie had a lover, a doctor, who was terribly jealous, and who thought she was cheating on him. One night he rode to her house, along the same trails that Ronnie and I were riding. He was sure he was going to find her with another man, and he brought along his shotgun.

Now Bessie had a maid, a young girl, who slept in front of Bessie's door, and when she saw the doctor, she tried to keep him out of Bessie's room. The doctor pushed his way in; Bessie was alone. When she saw him with his gun, she got out of bed and reached for her own gun—whereupon her lover killed her. When they found Bessie's gun, the safety catch was still on.

Bessie's maid is still alive, which is how the story is known. Every time I rode down that trail I thought about Bessie and the doctor, and how he had seen these same trees on that fateful night. What was he thinking? There I go, playing that game again.

In rainy weather and in the winter we wouldn't ride at all. While Ronnie worked, I was happy to curl up in front of the fire with a good book. Aside from the gym and the outdoor pool, we didn't use the other facilities very much. But Camp David does have a two-lane bowling alley, an archery range, two clay tennis courts, and, thanks to President Eisenhower, a putting green in front of Aspen. I tried skeet shooting once, but once was enough. Too loud!

Saturday night was another movie. On Sunday morning we watched the television news and interview shows, especially *This Week with David Brinkley*, which is one of my favorites. I often wished that Camp David had a chapel, because after the shooting, the increased security measures made it virtually impossible for us to go to church without causing an enormous disruption. If it was known in advance that we were coming, everybody had to go through a metal detector, which just didn't seem right. But if we showed up unexpectedly, the congregants were so busy watching us that they didn't pay attention to the service. That didn't seem right either, so we rarely went to church during our years in Washington.

Ronnie and I are religious in our own way, and it bothered me when people said Ronnie was a hypocrite because despite everything he said, we never went to church. Until we moved to Washington we always went to church, and now we do again.

But Camp David is secure and private, and the setting is awe-inspiring, so before we returned to California we started to help raise funds to build a simple wooden chapel there. We left before it was completed, but it's good to know that just about the only thing Camp David lacked will be in place one day. It will be nice for the men stationed there, and for the president, whoever he is.

For me, one of the best parts about Camp David was that there wasn't a whisper of controversy about the renovations I made there. Because the entire place is off-limits to the press, nobody ever knew what I did. Not that I changed all that much. The furniture was drab, so I had some of it slipcovered and painted. I dressed up the dining room in Laurel with some new tablecloths, painted the walls white, and found some great old army, navy, and marine posters to hang. And when I saw how narrow the windows were in the cabins, I had them enlarged so you could enjoy the magnificent view.

We left after lunch on Sunday, and that was always a painful moment. In the fall, Ronnie would bring back a large plastic sack of acorns to feed to the squirrels outside the Oval Office. They came right up to the window and looked at him, as if to say, "Well, what are you going to do for us?"

We usually arrived at the White House around three. Ronnie would have a pile of work waiting for him in his study, and I'd have papers and messages in my office, so we'd spend the rest of the afternoon working. But coming back was always a slight letdown, and even now, when Ronnie looks at pictures from Camp David, he feels a pang.

If the White House had been in Los Angeles, we would have spent most weekends at our ranch near Santa Barbara. As it was, we got there three or four times a year. We had sold the Lake Malibu ranch after Ronnie was elected governor, and bought this one, which we named Rancho del Cielo, shortly before we left Sacramento.

Ronnie is so happy there! He loves to be outside, building fences, cutting down trees and brush, and chopping wood for the two fireplaces, which are our only source of heat. The ranch is on top of a mountain, and when you get up there, the rest of the world disappears. Here, as at Camp David, we were usually alone, except for the Secret Service, the White House physician, and the military aide.

Although the ranch is fairly big—688 acres—the few visitors who do come up are always surprised by the small size of our adobe house, which was built more than a hundred years ago. Everyone expects that the ranch house will be large and elaborate, but it's very modest. George and Barbara Bush once came to the ranch on their way home from a foreign trip, and I remember Barbara saying, "You know, Nancy, this house gives me a whole different picture of you." A lot has been written about my supposed love of big houses, but visitors to the ranch see a tiny two-bedroom house, with Mexican rugs, wicker chairs, and newspapers piled on a pool table. On the front door there's a sign that reads:

ON THIS SITE

IN 1897

NOTHING HAPPENED

When we first bought the ranch, the house was even smaller. It had a million problems, but we loved it. Our bedroom was originally so narrow that I couldn't make the bed without kneeling *on* the bed. We knocked out walls, laid new tile floors, painted the house, converted the screened porch into a family room, and made a rock patio in front.

And I do mean *we*—with the help of Barney Barnett and Dennis LeBlanc. Dennis is originally from Sacramento, and he worked in several of Ronnie's campaigns. Barney was a member of the California Highway Patrol; he was Ronnie's driver during the governor years and has been with us ever since. He and Ronnie are almost like brothers; they were even born on the same day. Whenever we go to the ranch, Barney comes too. Ronnie is especially proud of the roof, which he and Barney put up together, using a plastic imitation mission tile that looks just like the real thing.

Few things give Ronnie as much pride and satisfaction as the work he does at the ranch. When we go up there, he just can't wait to start in on another project. And there's always work to be done on a ranch. While Ronnie is working outdoors, I catch up on mail, read, talk on the phone, or just putter around.

During the presidential years, there were many times when the real world intruded on the serenity of the ranch. I remember the night in 1983 when Ronnie received a call that a Korean jumbo jet was missing en route from Alaska to Seoul. Early the next morning the phone rang again, and I heard Ronnie say, "My God, have they gone mad? What the hell are they thinking of?" The Russians had shot down KAL 007 with an air-to-air missile, killing all the passengers.

Ronnie's advisers urged him to fly back to Washington, which he did, although the ranch contained all the communications equipment that a president could ever need. (So did Camp David.)

At the ranch, you could forget the world for a few hours, but every day a government car would drive up the mountain road with a big envelope of mail, security documents, and newspapers. And even when Ronnie went into the woods, he would be followed by the Secret Service, the doctor, and a military aide with a portable telephone, just in case.

Like Camp David, the ranch was off-limits to the press. Every time we were there, a large contingent of reporters would camp out at the Biltmore Hotel in Santa Barbara, where their information was limited to occasional press briefings which went something like this: "The weather is warm and sunny. The president attended to routine paperwork this morning and is now getting ready to go horseback riding with Mrs. Reagan. After lunch with Mrs. Reagan, the president will chop wood and clear brush on the ranch property."

Although there was usually nothing to report, the press rarely complained about coming to Santa Barbara—especially those who remembered what Plains, Georgia, was like. Every summer we gave a barbecue for them in town, and at the last one, in 1988, Ronnie got up after dinner and said, "As soon as I'm out of office, I'm going to start working for a constitutional amendment . . ." Everyone assumed he was about to refer to the two-term limit for presidents, which Ronnie opposes, but he finished the sentence by saying ". . . to make every president spend his vacation in Santa Barbara."

This was greeted by cheers. When Jerry O'Leary of the *Washington Times* (and president of the White House Correspondents Association) got up to thank Ronnie, he said, "The press is supposed to be impartial as far as the candidates go. But we do measure them a little bit by their vacation spots." He went over some of the past presidents, and when he got to Carter, he said, "With President Carter you couldn't stay in Plains, Georgia, because there was no place to stay. So we all stayed in Americus, Georgia, where the big excitement of the week was watching them spray their vegetables."

In March 1983 we invited Queen Elizabeth and Prince Philip to visit the ranch. Although their visit to California coincided with a terrible rainstorm, and the weather was so bad that they weren't even sure they could leave the ship, the queen was a wonderful sport and refused to cancel their plans. The road to the ranch was so muddy that she and Philip ended by driving up the mountain in a Land Rover through a fog that was so thick you couldn't see a thing. We had told them about the ranch during our visit to Windsor Castle, and the queen was dying to go riding with Ronnie. That plan, of course, went right out the window. But despite the weather, the queen had a wonderful attitude: "Don't be silly," she said when I tried to apologize. "This is an *adventure.*"

She was wonderful, and she really endeared herself to me by the spirit she showed that day. I ended up leaving the ranch with them and continuing our visit on the royal yacht *Britannia.* I spent that evening with the queen, sitting on a sofa in the large living room, talking about our children like old friends.

I sailed with them to San Francisco, where somebody suggested that we should all go out to dinner at Trader Vic's. I remember saying to Philip, "Oh, Trader Vic's, that's a wonderful Polynesian place where you really feel like you're on a Pacific island." What I hadn't realized was that we would be seated not in the main restaurant but in a private dining room that looked just like any other private dining room. When we walked in, Philip looked at me as though I had five heads.

Later in the week, the queen and Prince Philip gave Ronnie and me an anniversary dinner on board the *Britannia.* What more could a girl ask? Ronnie got up and said, "I know I promised Nancy a lot of things thirty-one years ago, but I never promised her *this.*"

It was an unforgettable evening—to be on the queen's private yacht, celebrating our anniversary. A few friends were with us, including Mike and Caroline Deaver and Lucky Roosevelt. The chef made us a special cake, and the crew presented us with an enormous greeting card. After dinner, Mike played the piano and I sang "Our Love Is Here to Stay." The queen and Prince Philip even gave us an anniversary present, an engraved silver box.

We still have that box, but we had to buy it from the United States government. Yes, we had to buy our own anniversary gift! The rule is that any gift you receive from a foreign official becomes government property if it's valued at over $180 (the figure changes slightly from year to year). That's the law, and it doesn't matter how personal the gift is—even if it's engraved with your name or initials. Ronnie and I wanted to have some mementos of those eight years of our lives, so before leaving the White House, we bought several of the gifts we had received.

We were allowed to keep gifts from our personal friends, but Ronnie had to declare each one he received. In other words, even if somebody has given the president a birthday gift every Christmas for twenty years, when you're in the White House that gift—and its estimated value—becomes public knowledge. That's one thing I won't miss about the White House—together with the fact that our tax returns were published in the newspapers every April. I hated that.

During eight years in Washington, I almost never carried money —except when I went out for a manicure. During that whole period, I didn't once set foot in a supermarket or almost any other kind of store, with the exception of a card shop at Seventeenth Street and K, where I used to buy birthday cards.

When you live in the White House, it's very hard to do *anything* on the outside. During the middle of Ronnie's second term, I started looking at houses so we would have someplace to live when the time came to leave Washington. I found a nice three-bedroom house in the Bel-Air section of Los Angeles, but I just couldn't see making such a big decision without showing the house to Ronnie.

On the other hand, I didn't want to go there with the usual retinue of more than a dozen vehicles, including a van full of armed Secret Service agents. One afternoon, when we were in Los Angeles, I persuaded Ronnie to lie down on the floor of the car so we could leave the hotel and he could go to see the house without letting the press know about it, and without inconveniencing the neighbors. After all that trouble, it's a good thing he liked it!

I was proud of myself for finally doing something that the press didn't report. We kept that secret for about two years—and by Washington standards, that's almost forever.

14

Landslide (1984–85)

HAD it been up to me, Ronald Reagan might well have been a one-term president.

In 1983, I tried to persuade him not to run again. After eight years in Sacramento and four more in Washington, not to mention the many long months of campaigning in 1976 and in 1980, we hadn't been settled at home in a long, long time. I yearned for more family time, and more privacy. I missed my friends and my family, and I missed California. Ronnie had already accomplished so much that maybe it was time to pull down the curtain.

I was also concerned about his safety. True, there had been no incidents since 1981, but why press your luck?

Ronnie, however, was determined to run again. There were still things he wanted to do. He also thought it had been too long since an American president had served two full terms in office.

In the end, it was just a matter of convincing me.

For a while we talked about it every night, until it became more and more obvious that this was something Ronnie just had to do. Finally I said, "If you feel that strongly, go ahead. You know I'm not crazy about it, but okay."

I had to laugh when I read in the papers that President Reagan was reluctant to run for reelection, but Nancy had pushed him into it.

Looking back, I'm glad I lost that argument—especially in view of what Ronnie was able to achieve with the Soviets in his second term. But it has to be said that, politically, his second term was a lot tougher than the first one.

Ronnie announced his decision on January 29, 1984, in a broadcast from the Oval Office. I went over there with Mermie and Dennis. Because the announcement was going to be carried live on the networks, Ronnie began with a run-through so the television crew could time his remarks.

Ronnie hadn't told anybody except the children and me what his plans were, and until the last moment there was some speculation that he might announce his retirement. "It's been nearly three years since I first spoke to you from this room," he began. "Tonight I'm here for a different reason. I've come to a difficult personal decision as to whether or not I should seek reelection. . . ."

Maureen told me later that when Ronnie said this, she wondered for a moment whether he had changed his mind. He kept up the suspense until finally he announced that, yes, he was running again. When they heard that, the crew broke into applause.

"Come on, honey," I called out. "Aren't you going to time the speech you're *really* going to give?"

There was a stunned silence until people realized I was joking. I guess my reservations were showing through.

The wires and calls that came in later that evening ran ten to one in favor of Ronnie's decision to run again.

That night, I wrote in my diary: "I think it's going to be a tough, personal, close campaign. Mondale is supposed to be an in-fighter. . . . Ronnie is so popular that they might be desperate. I'll be glad when the next nine months are over."

I was mostly right. It *was* a tough and personal campaign, and I *was* glad when it was over. In the end, however, it was anything but close.

The 1984 campaign was easier than those in 1976 and 1980, when Ronnie was trying to unseat an incumbent president. It was also a much shorter campaign, because Ronnie had no opposition in the primaries. But campaigns are never pleasant, and this one was no exception.

For me, the most nerve-racking moments of the campaign were the two debates between Ronnie and Walter Mondale.

I'm against debates. They're long, often boring, and the incumbent is at a disadvantage. The candidate who has never held the office can just attack, without having to defend his own record. And when it comes to foreign policy, the incumbent knows information that, for security reasons, he can't use.

With one exception, which I'll come to in a moment, Ronnie has been a very successful debater. Many people think that he won the nomination in 1980 as a result of his debate with George Bush, and that his debate with Carter won him the presidency. In 1976, Ronnie's supporters wanted to arrange a debate with President Ford, and if they had, Ronnie might have won the nomination.

The first of the 1984 debates was held in Louisville, Kentucky, on October 7. In my view, it was the worst night of Ronnie's political career.

Right from the start, he was tense, muddled, and off-stride. He lacked authority. He stumbled. This was a Ronald Reagan I had never seen before. It was painful to watch. There was no way around it; that debate was a nightmare.

When it was over, I ran up on the stage, as did Joan Mondale. We all shook hands, but as we were leaving, Ronnie said to me, "I was terrible." I made some sort of comforting remark, but we both knew he was right.

Neither of us slept well that night. In part, it was because the hotel room was so stuffy, but we both knew that the real reason was that the debate had been a disaster.

Even Ronnie, the eternal optimist, was down in the dumps.

He told me he had felt "brutalized" during the rehearsals, and that his mind was so jammed with facts and figures that he hadn't been able to focus on what Mondale was saying. Ronnie has always been an inspiring leader who outlines broad themes and visions, but his staff had spent weeks cramming him full of details and statistics. Instead of letting Ronnie lead with his strengths, they tried to turn him into somebody he wasn't.

"What have you done to my husband?" I said to Mike Deaver angrily, back at the hotel. "Whatever it was, don't do it again!"

The press was highly critical. Even some of Ronnie's supporters became concerned when the *Wall Street Journal* ran a headline that said: IS OLDEST U.S. PRESIDENT NOW SHOWING HIS AGE? REAGAN DEBATE PERFORMANCE INVITES OPEN SPECULATION ON HIS ABILITY TO SERVE. For the first and only time in the campaign, it actually seemed possible that Ronnie could lose.

After the shock of that first debate, the second one, scheduled for October 21 in Kansas City, became even more important. This time the preparations were very different. "Let Ronnie be Ronnie," I told Mike, but he already knew that.

Mermie and Dennis flew out with us to Kansas City. I had also arranged for Ron and Doria to join us at the hotel, for additional moral support. Still, I don't think I have ever been more nervous than I was that evening. Everybody assured me that this time would be different, and that Ronnie would be his old self, but I was still very worried. I felt as if I had a basketball in my stomach, and my hands were like ice.

A few minutes into the debate, Henry Trewhitt of the *Baltimore Sun* asked Ronnie, indirectly, about the so-called age factor. "I will not make age an issue of this campaign," Ronnie replied. Then, after a pause, he added, "I am not going to exploit, for political purposes, my opponent's youth and inexperience."

The audience laughed, and I slowly began to unclench one of my fists.

I didn't know it at the time, but the election had just been decided.

With that one quip, Ronnie had disposed of the only issue that could have defeated him in November 1984. All the news shows picked up this remark, and people saw it over and over again.

I felt that a majority of the voters were willing to forgive Ronnie's performance in that first debate if he could reassure them that it had been nothing worse than an off night—which he did.

Walter Mondale and Geraldine Ferraro did not wear well on me. They kept hammering on Ronnie's "secret plan" to raise taxes after the election, and I resented that Ferraro criticized Ronnie's religious beliefs.

As I saw it, the Democrats turned nasty at their 1984 convention, and that set the tone for the rest of the campaign. The night of the acceptance speeches, Ted Kennedy introduced Mondale with a string of cheap shots at Ronnie, fired off in a shout. If Ronnie had to go the hospital for an X ray, Kennedy said, "all he has to do to call his helicopter is push a little button. I just hope it's the right button."

I knew the Democrats had a problem, but that remark was inexcusable. Ted Kennedy has written both of us nice notes, thanking us for having his mother to the White House, and for allowing the South Lawn to be used for the Special Olympics—which I gather even his brother Jack would not allow. Even now, after all these years in politics, it still strikes me as strange when somebody bashes you in public and then expects your private contacts to be friendly.

Ron covered the Democratic convention for *Playboy,* and after listening to speaker after speaker bash his father, he wrote that the Democrats wanted the country "to believe that Ronald Reagan plans to put the elderly and the handicapped to work barbecuing minority children on the South Lawn, while he and his fat-cat country-club cronies sit back, licking their fingers." Ron was exaggerating—but only a little.

As for Mondale's acceptance speech, I had never heard the word "family" mentioned so often. It sounded so much like one of Ronnie's speeches that when Mondale finished, Ronnie turned to me and said, "Didn't I write that?"

Except for the debates, you rarely find yourself in the same room as your opponent during a presidential campaign. But on September 15, all four candidates were scheduled to appear at the Italian-American Federation dinner in Washington. After we entered the holding room with the Bushes, we were told that Geraldine Ferraro had decided to bring her husband, although she had previously said that she wasn't going to. Then we were told that her dress hadn't arrived, and that Mondale refused to go into the hall without her.

The protocol is that the president is the last one to appear, so we had to wait. But Ronnie, who gets very edgy about keeping people waiting, said, "I'm afraid the audience will blame *me* for this. Let's forget about protocol and just go in." So we did.

Four minutes later, Mondale and Ferraro came into the room. She certainly got her dress quickly! I could have understood a half-hour delay, but this attempt to be the last ones to enter the room struck me as childish. They shook hands as they went by, but they never apologized.

During the dinner, Ferraro stood up and started testing the microphone and measuring the platform she would stand on. Later, I noticed that she and her husband were down on the floor, working the crowd. I thought it was inappropriate in a presidential campaign, to say the least.

When it was Ronnie's turn to speak, I noticed that Mondale didn't applaud—not even once. And all through Ronnie's speech, Ferraro talked to Joan Mondale. She didn't even give Ronnie the courtesy of *pretending* to listen to him.

Ronnie and Mondale were scheduled to meet again the following month, at the annual Al Smith dinner in New York. The day before, we got word that Mondale had backed out because he wanted to prepare for the second debate. I was sure the audience would read into it that Mondale just didn't want to be on the dais again with Ronnie—which is exactly what they thought.

Because of a freak accident, I almost missed election night.

We spent the final night of the campaign at the Red Lion Inn in Sacramento, where, for reasons I'll never understand, the bed in our suite was mounted on a platform. I woke up in the middle of the night feeling cold, and I climbed out of bed to look for a blanket. Naturally, I forgot about the platform. I fell off, slid across the floor, and banged my head against a chair.

It hurt, and then it began to swell. Ronnie was fast asleep, and I didn't think it was serious enough to wake him. In addition to being a sound sleeper, he's also hard of hearing, so he didn't know anything about it until the next morning.

I went into the bathroom and put some cold water on the lump that was now rising on my head. I managed to get a little more sleep, but all through the next day I was wobbly and off-balance, and my speech was slurred.

Our staff people wanted me to spend the day resting, but this was the final day of our last run for the presidency. That morning we went to the capitol, where Governor Deukmejian dedicated the Cabinet Room to Ronnie, and then we flew to San Diego for a rally. Then on to Los Angeles, and finally it was over—the end of campaigning forever. Talk about ending with a bang . . .

But there are parts of that day, and of election day, that I can't recall. I remember standing on the stage at the hotel and holding Doria's hand for support, but large chunks of that period are still a blank. I'm told that a doctor came to examine me, and that I had a small concussion, and that Ronnie was so concerned that he was going to call off his press conference, but I have no memory of these events, either.

The next night, as always, we went to the Jorgensens' to wait for the election results. We expected a victory, but we weren't prepared for a landslide: Ronnie won every state except Minnesota and the District of Columbia. And despite the presence of Geraldine Ferraro on the Democratic ticket, Ronnie won more than 55 percent of the female vote.

Ronnie's second inauguration was a lot less difficult than the first one. Unfortunately, the weather did not cooperate. It was such a cold day that the medical people urged us to cancel the parade and move everything indoors. Ronnie and I felt very bad for all the kids in the bands who had saved up their money to come to Washington for the great event, but everyone would have ended up with frostbite, and the poor kids in the band wouldn't have dared put a horn to their lips. It was hard to call it off, but we had to.

Like last time, the whole family was there for the inaugural. Patti came alone, because Paul said he had to work.

Ron and Doria got dressed for the photograph, but instead of going to the balls, they invited some friends in for a buffet in the Yellow Oval Room, and Doria cooked up a spaghetti dinner. They had gone through one round of inaugural balls and knew what they were like, so I couldn't blame them for staying home. As in 1981, the balls were jammed with people, everyone very enthusiastic.

Because January 20 fell on a Sunday, there had to be two swearing-ins—a private one on Sunday, and then a public one on Monday. The private ceremony took place in the White House, at the bottom of the Grand Staircase, witnessed by a total of eighty-four people, mostly family and Cabinet officials. Ronnie and I stood on the first landing of the Grand Staircase, and there was such an intimacy to the ceremony that I wondered if this was what the inaugurations were like in the early 1800s.

A few days later, I learned that while we were at church on the day of the private swearing-in, a man had sneaked into the White House with the Marine Corps Band. Rex Scouten, who used to be in the Secret Service, thought this fellow looked a little strange and stopped him outside the Blue Room.

All I could think was: What if he had been carrying a gun? I prayed that this wasn't a bad omen for the next four years.

Ronnie's second term got off to a bumpy start, and for several weeks in the spring, just about the only topic of conversation in Washington was his plan to visit the Bitburg cemetery on his forthcoming trip to Germany. There was a feeling in the air that the administration was drifting, and I now realize that a lot of that had to do with staff changes in the West Wing, which I'll discuss later.

The next big event came in July.

It was supposed to be a routine medical procedure. On July 12, 1985, a Friday, Ronnie was scheduled to have a small benign polyp removed from his colon. The doctors had discovered it in March. The plan was to have him stay overnight at Bethesda Naval Hospital, and from there we would continue up to Camp David on Saturday.

On Thursday, Ronnie started his preparation diet, which consisted of liquids for lunch and dinner. On Friday he had apple juice for breakfast, and then began drinking Go Lightly, a special formula that cleans out your system. It's awful stuff, and he had to drink a glass of it every ten minutes until it was gone.

Removing the polyp was a relatively minor procedure which we had been through before. While it was being taken care of, I sat in the waiting room and talked with Larry Speakes. Ronnie was alert and fine afterwards, and making jokes as usual.

But I noticed that the doctors weren't laughing. I also had the feeling they were looking at me a little funny—especially John Hutton, who seemed to be avoiding my eyes.

The doctors suggested that Ronnie lie down, and that I come with them into the other room. Then one of them pulled up a chair and said, "We have some bad news for you."

I felt as if I had been hit by a ten-ton truck.

"Tell me everything," I said. And they did.

The doctors had found a large, suspicious mass, the size of a golf ball, on the lower right side of the colon where it goes into the intestines. Although they weren't sure it was malignant, they thought it probably was. At best, they told me, it was "precancerous." In any event, they would have to operate. The doctors were concerned about the surrounding areas, especially Ronnie's liver. If there was any evidence of cancer in the liver, we were in very big trouble.

It was all so sudden that I had trouble believing it.

John Hutton explained that we had three choices: We could continue up to Camp David, as we had planned, and then return to Bethesda on Sunday for an operation Monday morning. Or we could stay where we were and have it taken care of the following morning. Or, if absolutely necessary, we could wait ten days and schedule the operation after the state visit by President Li of China.

John and I both wanted it done immediately. "He's already here," I said, "and he's already done the bowel prep. He might as well stay."

All I cared about was getting the operation over with as quickly as possible. Now that we knew about the polyp, I couldn't stand the prospect of letting it stay inside Ronnie any longer than we had to.

But I wasn't sure how Ronnie would react to the prospect of major surgery the next day. I felt that my best approach was to play on his feelings about Go Lightly, which he absolutely hates. Otherwise, he might have wanted to go right on up to Camp David. It was obvious—to me, anyway—that this had to be taken care of right away. But I didn't want to get too specific with Ronnie, because it wasn't absolutely definite that he had cancer.

"I want to be the one to tell him," I said to the doctors. "And please, when we go in to see him, don't mention cancer. We don't know for sure that it *is* cancer, and there's no point in using that word unless we're positive."

When we walked into Ronnie's room, I sat down on the edge of the bed and put my arms around him. "Honey," I said, "the doctors have found a polyp that is too large to be removed the way the other ones were. The only way they can get it out is surgically. As long as we're here, why don't we do it tomorrow and get it over with? Because if we come back next week, you'll have to drink that Go Lightly all over again." Somehow, Ronnie was able to smile. "Does this mean I won't be getting dinner tonight, either?" he asked.

That broke the tension, and after the doctors explained the details of the operation, Ronnie said, "Let's get it done." Everything was put into motion for the next morning, and Larry Speakes went to inform the press.

If Ronnie guessed the truth, he didn't say so, to me or to anyone else.

Later, he got annoyed when people said he'd had cancer. "No," he would say, "I didn't have cancer. I had something inside of me that had cancer in it, and it was removed." That's Ronnie, my beloved optimist.

As soon as I left Ronnie's room, I leaned against the wall and started to cry. And once the tears started flowing, they just wouldn't stop. For the next two hours I was in and out of Ronnie's room, but every few minutes I'd make an excuse to leave. I didn't want him to see me in tears.

I wanted to spend the night at the hospital, but as at the time of the shooting four years earlier, I didn't want people to be alarmed. I stayed with Ronnie until six and then went back to the White House and started calling the family—Patti, Ron, Michael, and Ronnie's brother, Neil, who, strangely enough, had undergone the very same operation only a few days earlier. (Maureen was traveling in Africa.) I told everybody there was no need to come to Washington.

That night, the doctors did a CAT scan. There were electrical storms in the Washington area, and the power went out twice, so they didn't finish until midnight. When they finally called me at the White House, the news was good: There was nothing suspicious in his liver or his lungs.

Please, God, I prayed. Take care of this.

I wrote in my diary, echoing March 1981, "What would I ever do without him?"

That night, again echoing 1981, I slept on his side of the bed.

The next morning, the doctors came in again to explain the operation to both of us. They expected it to take three hours. I walked along with Ronnie, holding his hand as they wheeled him to the operating room. Naturally, I was more nervous than he. "After what they did to me yesterday," he said, "this should be a breeze."

Yesterday, at Ronnie's request, the small polyp had been removed without an anesthetic. He has a very high pain threshold.

The operation began at eleven o'clock that Saturday morning. Half an hour earlier, Ronnie had signed the papers authorizing George Bush to be acting president for the next eight hours. This was the first time the provisions of the Twenty-fifth Amendment had ever been put into effect. It had been passed in 1967, after Lyndon Johnson had been without a vice president during the fourteen months between Kennedy's death and the 1965 inauguration. Fred Fielding, the White House counsel, came in with the documents, which were then delivered to Speaker Tip O'Neill, and to Strom Thurmond, president pro tempore of the Senate.

The operation went well, more smoothly than expected. They removed the large polyp, which measured five centimeters, and two smaller polyps. They also took out close to two feet of Ronnie's large intestine. I hadn't expected that.

"It's almost certainly cancer," they told me. "But we won't know for sure until we do a biopsy."

A word here about the timing of Ronnie's operation: On Friday afternoon, as soon as Ronnie agreed to have the operation, I called Don Regan at the White House to tell him what had happened, as he had asked me to do. Because we didn't know for sure whether the polyp was malignant, and because cancer is not a word you toss around casually, I spoke carefully.

"I'm reading something into this," he said. "Am I on firm ground?"

"Yes, possibly," I replied.

I meant, of course, that Ronnie's condition was probably more serious than I was willing to say over the phone. But Don evidently took my comment to mean that the reason the surgery was scheduled for the next morning—or, as he wrote, was "delayed for a day and a half"—had something to do with astrology.

That's not true. There was no delay. Ronnie went in on Friday and had the operation the next morning. Astrology had nothing to do with it.

This was a painful period for me. From my diary:

July 13: Dick came in from Philadelphia to be with me. [My brother is a neurosurgeon.] A few minutes after seven P.M., he and I went into the recovery room to see Ronnie. He was fine, but groggy. He said he couldn't remember anything after I had kissed him in the operating room this morning.

There was a tube coming out of his nose to remove fluids and gases from his stomach, and another one going into his arm to give him antibiotics and a sugar solution.

A little later, Fred Fielding came in with Don Regan and Larry Speakes, and Ronnie signed a document in which he reclaimed the powers of the presidency.

Dick and I went back to the White House, where we had a chance to talk when the phone wasn't ringing. Maureen called from Nairobi, where it was the middle of the night, and I filled her in. Ronnie called around nine to say they had given him a sleeping pill. He sounds drowsy. I hope he sleeps.

July 14: Back to the hospital. Ronnie looks fine, but is in some pain. They say the first three days are always rough. Calls are pouring in, but I just can't talk to anyone. I hope they understand.

Left the hospital around 5:30. By the time I got back, my desk was filled with mail, messages, and flowers. So tired I can't eat.

July 15: Still not a good night for Ronnie, but the doctors say he's doing remarkably well. God, I hope so. He has to blow up those ping pong balls to keep his lungs clear, as he did when he was shot. Today I brought in photographs for the walls and put them around his room, just like in 1981. One of the pictures is of Ronnie riding his horse.

After lunch, two of the doctors—Dale Oller, head of surgery at Bethesda, and Steven Rosenberg, chief of surgery at the National Cancer Institute—came in to give me the pathology report. The tumor was malignant. Damn! But they swear they got it all.

From now on Ronnie will need more frequent checkups, including CAT scans and chest X rays.

But it was good to hear they had gotten it all. And good for people to know that you can have this problem and it doesn't have to be fatal.

Dr. Rosenberg said: "Prospects are for a full recovery and a normal life."

Together with the doctors, and Larry Speakes, I went to tell Ronnie the whole story. "I'm glad it's all out," he said. As far as he was concerned, he was now fine, and that was that.

Months ago, we had invited the Boston Pops to give a concert for the diplomatic corps on the South Lawn today, in celebration of the orchestra's one-hundredth anniversary. Ronnie was supposed to give the remarks, and he insisted that I go in his place. He told me this just after we got the news that the polyp was malignant!

As I was leaving the sitting room to return to the White House, John Hutton suddenly sprang up and put his arm around my waist.

"John, what is it?"

"You were about to faint," he said.

"No, I wasn't. My bag is heavy."

"No," he repeated. "You were about to faint. I'm worried about you."

John came back with me to the White House. Unbeknownst to

me, he told everybody to keep an eye on me, especially in this heat.

Back home, I changed my clothes and went out to the South Lawn to make a few remarks. It was very hot, and those poor people had been sitting out there for quite a while, so I spoke briefly, and we all came inside where it was cool. Then I had to greet four hundred and twenty-two diplomats in a receiving line, none of whom knew why Ronnie was in the hospital. I wanted to get through it as quickly as possible, and it was hard to concentrate. I never thought I'd get through it.

July 16: Ronnie had a good day. Last night he stayed up late and watched a movie on television with Bogart and Bacall. His walls look much better with all the pictures, and he even took a couple of brief walks around the room.

He is reading a biography of Calvin Coolidge. Ronnie has always believed Coolidge was underrated.

I brought him a Cabbage Patch doll in a nurse's outfit. The doll's name is Nancy, and she's sitting by his bed to remind him to take it easy. Or so I told him.

Joan Rivers sent two hundred and fifty balloons. I took them down to the children's ward, together with some of the flowers. They told me that one fifteen-year-old boy's blood pressure zoomed from 80 to 130 when I got to his bed. When I came back, I told Ronnie that he had better do the same or we were finished.

July 18: Arrived at the hospital today a little later than usual because, of all things, the driver lost his way. The poor man was so embarrassed. Ronnie was up. He had taken a shower and washed his hair. He was tired after that, but they're gradually getting him back on solid food.

We went to the window and waved to the press so they could take pictures. They were yelling questions to him, but he couldn't answer because his throat was still sore from the tube. I had to answer for him, but I don't think they understood why we were doing it that way, and I was afraid they thought I was taking over.

I'm so mad at the doctors who have nothing to do with this case, rushing to go on television with their diagnoses and explanations! I'm just furious about it, and so is Dick. We were brought up to believe that this was unethical.

Ronnie and I were watching the news the other night when a doctor came on and said, "He probably has about four years to live." I was furious, but Ronnie just said, "What do you think about that? Ridiculous!"

But I wondered if he wondered if there's something we hadn't told him. He probably wasn't thinking along those lines, but in that situation, I would have.

July 19: This morning they made it official—he goes home tomorrow. Whoopee! He'll do his [regular Saturday] radio broadcast from the hospital, and then we'll leave. I can't wait!

When I told Ronnie, he said, "Well, I guess you can start taking down the pictures." Then, after most of them were off the wall, he said, "Why don't you leave those three in front? It does look kind of bare in here."

And this from the man who said I was silly to put them up in the first place.

I left, then came back for dinner and to get things ready for tomorrow. Ronnie's worst moment came when they told him he could no longer eat popcorn. You would have thought his whole world had come to an end.

July 20: Arrived in time for Ronnie's radio broadcast, and I went in with him. After thanking the hospital personnel and the doctors, he decided to use his own experience as a warning for other people: "It's important to have a checkup if you think something isn't right. So if you're listening to this right now and it reminds you of something that you've been putting out of your mind, pick up the phone, call your doctor or local hospital and talk to somebody. Just tell them Dr. Reagan sent you."

Then Ronnie began to thank me for all I had done and what I meant to him. He said: "I'd like to indulge myself for a moment here. There's something I want to say, and I wanted to say it with

Nancy at my side, as she is right now, as she always has been. First ladies aren't elected and they don't receive a salary. They've mostly been private persons forced to live public lives. Abigail Adams helped invent America. Dolley Madison helped protect it. Eleanor Roosevelt was FDR's eyes and ears. Nancy Reagan is my everything.

"When I look back on these days, Nancy, I'll remember your radiance and your strength, your support, and your taking part in the business of this nation. I say for myself, but also on behalf of the nation, thank you, partner, thanks for everything.

"By the way, are you doing anything this evening?"

It's a good thing this was radio and not television, because I was sitting there with tears streaming down my face—of course.

We left the hospital at around noon, and all the Navy men in their whites were lined up. Ronnie tried to thank everybody, but it was hard because the band was playing "Anchors Aweigh," and it was a very emotional moment. I didn't even try to talk.

July 21: Today I couldn't get Ronnie to take a nap. I see I'm going to have quite a month.

July 22: Ronnie had a staff meeting here [in the residence] in the morning. George Opfer came to see me in the afternoon. We are trying to conspire to prevent Ronnie from riding at the ranch. It would be a big mistake, but Ronnie thinks he can do everything.

July 23: President Li came today. Even before Ronnie's operation, the Chinese had asked that the ceremonies be scaled back because of Li's health. So with Ronnie's operation, it couldn't have worked out better.

Only ten days after surgery, and Ronnie went through the arrival ceremony, and did it well. But my heart was in my mouth. It was so touching to see Ronnie helping Li up the steps to his chair. We did away with the receiving line after the arrival ceremony, and we cut down on moving around as much as we could.

Following the arrival ceremony, I had coffee with Madame Li

upstairs in the Yellow Oval Room. She is very nice, a doctor. I told
her I was wearing a red Chinese dress that they had given me when
we were in China. She replied that she had tried to bring me another
one, but they couldn't find the tailor who had my measurements.

When we joined the men, Li told me that he had a message for
me from Deng—that I should be sure to come back to China. [When
Ronnie and I were in China, Deng had playfully invited me to come
back—"without your husband."] I laughed and replied that I remembered the first invitation, and felt very flattered.

After the meeting, we saw them out the door and then came up
for lunch on the Truman Balcony. It was nice to get some fresh air.
Then a rest for Ronnie.

Tonight, at the state dinner, we didn't have the usual cocktail
hour upstairs in the Yellow Oval Room. And Li couldn't go down
the grand staircase, so we used the elevator. We also skipped the
receiving line, and in a way I missed it, because I couldn't say hello
to all our friends who were there. We shortened the dinner and had
coffee at the tables instead of in the Blue Room.

When Ronnie got up from the table to give his toast, everyone
at the dinner stood up and applauded him.

Li mentioned again at the table that the last thing Deng had told
him was to be sure to invite me back.

Liz Taylor was at the table, looking lovely.

After dinner, Li went home right away. He said to me, "I'll be
seeing you in Beijing."

Ronnie went upstairs [to our living quarters], which took a great
deal of coaxing on my part. He wanted to stay for the entertainment
and was hoping to go the whole route, but I put my foot down.
Madame Li and I went into the East Room for the entertainment,
which consisted of Grace Bumbry and another singer doing songs
from *Porgy and Bess*. Grace even sang a song in Chinese to Madame
Li. When the entertainment was over, I got up to make a few
remarks to fill in for Ronnie.

George Shultz and I started the dancing. Only then did I finally
get to see some of my friends. It was a very different dinner, but
filled with warmth.

July 24: I tried to sleep late, but didn't do too well. Had lunch at Meg Greenfield's with Kay Graham, who had written me a very sweet letter about Ronnie. She has invited me to come and stay with her on Martha's Vineyard, so I'll be going for two days. Getting away from Washington and being near the water should be good for me.

News came today that Rock Hudson had lung cancer in Paris, so we called. But now there seems to be some question. [Later, of course, we learned that it was AIDS. He had been to a White House dinner and had been at my table. I remember sitting across from him and thinking, Gee, he's thin. I asked if he had been dieting, and he said he had been hard at work on a new picture and had lost weight.]

July 25: I flew to Columbus, Ohio, a pretty town, to the Denison campus, where they had young kids taking part in an antidrug program called youth-to-youth.

Had an interview in the plane on the way back that I had committed to months ago. Another one tomorrow. I wish I didn't have to do them. Enough has been said about Ronnie's operation.

Ronnie went to the office today for a Cabinet meeting.

July 26: Ronnie had meetings in the morning, and we left for Camp David around one. It was raining, which was frustrating because the doctor had told us that Ronnie could walk in the shallow end of the pool and start to get his toning back.

July 27: We had a restless night. Calls came for Ronnie from Bud McFarlane and Bill Casey on the secure line. I don't know what they were about.

Weather improved, so Ronnie put on bathing trunks and walked around the shallow end of the pool as the doctor had suggested.

July 29: I met with the doctors about Ronnie's diet, which we can loosen up a little now. This week—the third one—is especially important in his recovery, but the damned budget is making it really tough.

July 30: Busy day. Meeting with Bob Tuttle, then a meeting with Don Regan and Bill Hinkle about the Geneva summit in November. Talked about where we'd be staying, what the plan was for the meetings with Ronnie and Gorbachev, and what I was supposed to be doing.

Early dinner because I filled in for Ronnie at the Boy Scouts Jamboree in Virginia. It was like flying over a small city when I looked down and saw a hundred thousand scouts. Of course, I had never talked to that many people before. It's a funny feeling because it takes your voice so long to reach everyone that it bounces back at you and throws off your timing.

August 1: The press is making a big fuss about a pimplelike thing that was removed from Ronnie's nose. At first we thought it was an irritation from the tape that held the tube to his nose after the surgery, but Dr. [Burton] Smith wanted it biopsied.

August 2: Early start for Camp David. Press still asking questions about Ronnie's nose. They did the biopsy and it was basal cell carcinoma [skin cancer]—from the sun, the kind that thousands of people get, including me.

I never thought that Ronnie's skin cancer had anything to do with the other cancer, but I was afraid the press would make that connection. So I told Larry Speakes to say it was a pimple, but that didn't wash. I shouldn't have done that to Larry, because it damaged his credibility with the press.

August 5: Ronnie had a mini press conference with six reporters in the Oval Office. They asked about his nose, and he explained, but they continued to ask questions even though they all admitted it was nothing serious and very common.

Sometimes you wonder if they *want* you to be sick.

August 6: Ronnie stayed at the office until three, when I finally forced him to come home and lie down.

August 7: I tried to keep the day clear for packing and cleaning off my desk. Gail [Burt, my social secretary] and I had to finish planning two dinners. Had to schedule a press party for Santa Barbara. Rex Scouten had things that had to be settled.

August 8: I left for Boston to visit a college where kids from all over are meeting. They have formed anti-peer-pressure groups, which is important. They put on a skit and we had a rap session, and then I spoke. Great group of kids.

Then I took off for Martha's Vineyard. Short flight, but everyone was nervous on the plane because it needs a five-thousand-foot runway, and the Vineyard's is 5,400. Not much leeway.

Kay was there to meet me and we went directly to her lovely old white house. Changed quickly into slacks and went out for a walk. The air is so good and the ocean smells terrific. [For me, the ocean is a real tranquilizer. If something's bothering me, just seeing the ocean makes me feel better.]

Quiet dinner—just the house guests, the Deavers, Meg Green-field, Warren Buffett. Mike Wallace came too, he has a house nearby. He told funny stories about Mother in Chicago, which was nice for me because Kay and Meg had a chance to learn about her. It was fun and the evening went by quickly.

August 9: My room is so pretty, with a lovely view of the water. Kay took me to South Beach, which is beautiful. She knows that I love to walk on the beach. This one stretches for miles, and was practically deserted. Rick Smith from *Newsweek* joined us, and we walked. It was heaven and I could have stayed all day, but we had to go back for a luncheon that Kay was giving.

She entertains beautifully and the food is so good. We ate out on the porch. The Cronkites were there. Ruth Gordon and Garson Kanin. Beverly Sills and her husband. Margaret Jay [whose former husband had been the British ambassador to Washington]. Kay's son and his girl. Ardie Deutsch with Mr. Gordon. Other people, too.

After lunch, Mike [Wallace] came by to take me for a walk on another beach. They all knew my weakness.

Then back to Kay's to get ready for a dinner party. Lally Wey-mouth [Kay's daughter] had arrived that afternoon. Jackie Onassis, Maurice Tempelsman, Cyrus Vance, Bob McNamara, Edward Bennett Williams, Peter Sharp, Anne Buchwald, Bill Styron, Jennifer Phillips and husband, Mike Wallace, Henry Grunewald and Louise Melhado plus Kay's houseguests.

Jackie and I were at the same table, and I invited her to the White House to see the changes. She said she prefers not to return to Washington, but if she changes her mind she'll let me know.

August 10: I left at noon and Meg flew back with me. It was a letdown to eat that tuna salad on the plane after the food at Kay's house.

Ronnie was waiting for me. He has started to do some mild arm and leg exercises, which pleases him.

August 11: Left for California, and got to the ranch around two. It was so foggy we weren't sure we could land, but it cleared in time. The ranch looked great, and we could see that the new man has really been working.

August 12: Walked in the afternoon.

August 13: Hard to keep Ronnie down. Walked in the morning and again in the afternoon. But I played policeman the whole time. Don't do this! Don't do that!

When this is over I'm going to need a vacation.

15

◈◇◈

A Terrible Month

"I GUESS it's my turn." Those were my first words when they told me I probably had cancer in October 1987. Then, just a few days after the operation, I was faced with a second ordeal, from which I still haven't recovered.

Once again, my diary seems to convey, better than I can, now, just what those weeks were like. What follows is essentially what I wrote at that time, with a few explanations and additions.

October 5, 1987: Today I went out to Bethesda with [White House physician] John Hutton for my annual mammogram. John had never come with me before for a mammogram. Perhaps he sensed something.

There was a darling nurse who did it. When she was finished, she said, "Wait, we'd like to do a couple of X rays over again." I felt my stomach start to tighten.

When she completed the additional tests, John came in and asked her to leave the room. Then my stomach *really* tightened. I knew something was wrong.

"We think we've seen something," John told me. "We think it's a tumor in the left breast. We'll need a biopsy. There's an outside chance it isn't malignant, but it probably is."

I have cancer.

Cancer. There's something about the sound of that word which makes your heart stop.

It can't be. I feel fine. There must be some mistake! This is the last thing in the world I ever expected.

"Please call Ollie Beahrs," I said. "I want him to be involved." [Dr. Oliver Beahrs, a specialist in cancer, had been a student of my father's, and he's been close to our family ever since.]

It was very quiet on the drive back to the White House, and John and I barely spoke. He came up with me in the elevator, and when we got to the West Hall, he said, "You're taking this awfully well."

"No," I replied. "I feel as if I've been kicked in the stomach."

"I know," he said, as his eyes filled with tears.

Then I turned away and went into the bedroom to lie down.

Later on, Ronnie came in. John had gone to the Oval Office to give him the news. John told me later that when he told Ronnie, Ronnie had an expression on his face that he'd never forget. "I think the president has always believed that nothing would ever happen to you," John said.

October 6: I have to keep up my schedule, so when the crown prince and princess of Japan arrived, she and I could have coffee together. We had met them in Tokyo, where I sat next to their son at dinner. He told me that night that he had just returned from America and that the best thing about our country was Brooke Shields. (I had expected him to say the Statue of Liberty!) I told his mother that I was sorry he hadn't come along on this trip, because I could have invited Brooke Shields to join us for dinner.

When Ronnie came home to dress before the dinner, we didn't have much time to talk. And I think we both knew that if we started to talk, we would get upset. We had to get through this dinner, so there was no point in doing that. We comforted each other without really talking about it.

Went down to the doctor's office [on the first floor of the White House] for a meeting with Ollie Beahrs, who had come in from the Mayo Clinic. I was so happy to see him, and so relieved that he was there. He had been with us during Ronnie's cancer operation, and I knew he'd level with me. [I'm no good if anybody, even in the kindest way, doesn't level with me.]

Ollie had seen the X rays, and he examined me. We decided that I would go into the [Bethesda Naval] hospital on the 16th and that I would have an operation the next morning. I had a busy schedule coming up, and if it didn't make any difference, I wanted to keep it. Ollie said that was fine, that there was no danger.

He explained that there were two ways to excise the tumor. I could have a lumpectomy, which involved removing only the tumor itself and a small amount of tissue. But you can't be sure whether or not the cancer is all out. Or I could have a radical mastectomy, which means removing the entire breast.

I chose the mastectomy. A lumpectomy seemed too inconclusive, and I know, given my nature, that I'd be worried to death. It will be hard enough to go through the ten days of waiting, and I know I can't spend months, or years, wondering. Besides, a lumpectomy entails weeks of radiation on an almost daily basis. In my job, there is no way I can do that.

[At the time of my operation, there were some people, including doctors, who thought I had taken too drastic a step in choosing the mastectomy. The director of the Breast Cancer Advisory Center was quoted in the *New York Times* as saying that my decision had "set us back ten years."

I resented these statements, and I still do. This is a very personal decision, one that each woman must make for herself. This was my choice, and I don't believe I should have been criticized for it. For some women, it would have been wrong, but for me it was right. Perhaps, if I had been twenty years old and unmarried, I would have made a different decision. But I've already had my children and I have a wonderful, understanding husband. For me, a mastectomy seemed the sensible thing to do, and the best way to get it all over with.

I wish that people would understand that I was making this decision only for myself. I would never presume to make it for other women. The only thing I would presume to tell other women is that every woman over forty—and perhaps even earlier—should have a yearly mammogram. Right now, more than 60 percent of women over forty have *never* had one.]

I almost certainly have breast cancer, but this can't be confirmed until the operation. Meanwhile, I don't want anybody to know about it—not even the children. There's no point in making anybody else go through these ten days of waiting and worrying.

I made an exception for Doria [Ron's wife]—partly because she called to say that her mother had cancer, and that she needed help getting her into a hospital. A weird coincidence. Ron is away in Russia, on assignment for ABC television. I called my brother, and Dick made arrangements for Doria's mother.

October 7: Not much sleep. Left for Chicago to receive an award at the Ronald McDonald Children's Charity Foundation Dinner. On the plane, I told Elaine and Jane [Elaine Crispen, my press secretary, and Jane Erkenbeck, my personal assistant]. I would have preferred not to tell anyone, but they did my scheduling, and they had to know, and I knew I could trust them. We were sitting at my usual table on the plane, and they were completely shocked. Elaine grabbed hold of my hand and said, "Oh, no!" We all started to cry, and then we all put on our dark glasses. Jane said, "We can't sit here crying, because people will start to wonder." [The stewards, the Secret Service, the advance team, and members of the press were on the plane with us.]

We decided to announce it on the 15th, the day before I go into the hospital.

Stayed at the Drake. Great view of the lake that brings up so many memories. We drove by our old apartment building and it was so nostalgic to see the lake view again, the same one I used to look at every day when I came home from school. I hope my children have memories like mine—happy memories, that now take on deeper meanings. I can close my eyes and see a girl named Nancy Davis, walking along the lake to school, or roller-skating down Michigan Avenue.

And now, here I am with cancer, and nobody knows. I ache for my parents' advice, and their comfort. I miss them terribly. [My father had died in 1982. My mother was still alive, but she no longer knew me.]

Everything went well at the dinner, where I was presented with a check for $100,000, a donation to the Nancy Reagan Drug Abuse Foundation. I couldn't sleep. Both Jane and Elaine cried when they said good night.

October 8: [Robert] Bork is coming in today to meet with Ronnie about his appointment to the Supreme Court.

I got back to the White House around two. Now Bork has decided to come tomorrow.

Rex [Scouten, the head usher at the White House] and Gary [Walters, his assistant] came to see me about the upkeep of the house. Work has to be done, especially on the first floor, where all the visitors walk through. And there isn't enough money.

Then a meeting with John Hutton, who gave me more details. I may need radiation—even after the mastectomy. God, I hope not.

John had called my brother and told him. Then Dick called after dinner and said he wanted to come here and be with me, which I very much appreciate. He's coming in from Philadelphia on Friday night, in time for dinner. He and Ronnie will go out to the hospital with me, and then they'll come back and spend the night at the White House. The next morning they'll fly out to the hospital again.

The waiting is killing me.

October 9: Gail Burt came for coffee at eleven. [Gail is a darling girl who until recently was my social secretary. Before that she had been working at the State Department and met Rick Burt. As is my wont as a born matchmaker, I had pushed them to get married. They did, and then he was appointed ambassador to Bonn. Poor girl—she was in tears because of having to move. They had just bought a house, and she didn't want to leave Washington.] Short visit because I had to attend a luncheon.

In the afternoon I met in the Red Room with a Japanese man who gave a large donation to the Drug Abuse Foundation.

Ronnie came upstairs [to the residence] to meet with Bork and his family. Bork said he wanted to stay in—not for himself, but out of principle. He has no illusions about his own prospects, but he thinks that dropping out would set a dangerous precedent. It should go to the Senate floor for a vote, because otherwise all future nominees to the Supreme Court would have to go through what is really a political campaign.

There was a huge group waiting to see us off as we left for Camp David, with signs about Bork, shouting, a lot of noise.

October 10: [Camp David] Woke up to gray skies that cleared in the afternoon. Ronnie did radio broadcast on Bork. We rode after lunch.

I kept thinking: A week from now I'll know if I've lost a breast or not. I'm frightened, and I pray I won't need radiation.

Doria called, and we had a nice talk. She asked me to reconsider my decision about not telling any of the other children. She said that her relationship with her family and especially her mother had become so much closer because of her mother's illness—and how grateful she was for that. How it changes your priorities. How you never really think that anything can happen to your parents. How they seem invincible, and you think they'll go on forever.

I said, "I know only too well." It has been five years since Bapa [my father] died, and I still think about him all the time.

She said: "I know Ron would want to know. It would be terrible for him to hear about it some other way. You've got to remember that he loves you, and that you mean so much to him."

I knew she was right. Yes, it *would* be awful for him to pick up the paper in Russia and read about it over there.

She hasn't heard from Ron in days, but I thought of a way she could tell him about me without having it end up in *Pravda* the next day. She could use my original name, and say, "Do you remember somebody named Anne Frances Robbins?" And if that didn't click, she could say, "You know, the daughter of Ken Robbins? He left his wife and she later married a doctor?"

Doria thinks this is a fine idea. She is very solicitous and caring about me, and it means a lot.

[When Doria finally spoke to Ron, she asked if he remembered Anne Robbins. He caught on right away, and said, "Sure, I know who you mean." Then she told him the news.]

We changed the day of my announcement from Thursday to Friday, because when I go to New Hampshire I don't want people to be staring at me. [I was planning to attend a meeting of the Foster Grandparents Program. I was hoping to start bringing together the Foster Grandparents Program with the drug program, so this was a meeting I didn't want to cancel.] Now, by the time Marlin [Fitzwater, Ronnie's press secretary] gets through briefing the press, I'll be on my way back from New Hampshire and out of the public eye.

It's probably my imagination, but my breast seems to hurt.

October 11: Restless night. Gray skies and rain, so we canceled the ride. Watched the [Sunday] morning talk shows.

Doria called to thank me for putting Dick in touch with her about her mother, and to say how grateful she was for his help.

October 12: Beautiful day. Had a good night's sleep so I felt better. Worked on my book [which eventually became *My Turn*]. Had my hair done for [old family friend] Charlie Wick's surprise seventieth-birthday party. All their kids were there, plus Sarah, Doug's baby, and they all gave darling toasts. Ronnie gave a nice toast. We left after dinner because Ronnie had to go to New Jersey the next day. And my mood was running out.

October 13: I awoke at three and that was it for the night. I kept thinking of all the things I had to do. They came up before breakfast and drew forty cc's of blood in case it's needed during the operation. Doctor told me that if I felt weak or tired later in the day I should drink some orange juice and lie down. I forgot all about it until I had been working for two hours, and Elaine said, "You look tired." I went to bed and slept for an hour and a half. Unheard of.

October 14: Final preparations for the state dinner for Duarte. [President José Napoleón Duarte of El Salvador. I have a picture of me that was taken at that dinner, and it's quite obvious that my mind was elsewhere.]

At the arrival ceremony in the morning, Duarte said, "I'm going to do something outside of protocol to show the American people

how much we love them, and how grateful we are to you." And
with that, he left the platform and walked down on the South Lawn
to the American flag and kissed it. It brought tears to everybody's
eyes.

They had their family with them, including their daughter Inez,
who had once been kidnapped. Pretty girl.

The dinner went well. Lionel Hampton entertained. He's eighty
years old, but wonderful. He played all the old, great songs.

Ralph Lauren was on the other side of me [Duarte, by protocol,
was on my right]. Ralph had had a brain tumor, although he's fine
now. He was telling me about it, and I was thinking, Boy, he's going to be awfully surprised when he reads about me in a couple of
days!

October 15: Elaine, Jack [Courtemanche, my chief of staff], and I
had a meeting with Marlin in the West Hall to tell him the news
and to decide what he should say tomorrow. Marlin was shocked.
We really *did* keep this secret for ten days. Amazing! They ought
to hire me over in the West Wing, because *everything* leaks over
there. They say that women talk too much, but it was the women
who kept the secret.

I asked Jane to call our kids tomorrow morning, while I'm in
New Hampshire, so they won't learn about it from the media.

Tried to go to bed early because this waiting is so awful.

October 16: Flew to New Hampshire early for the meeting. It was
a beautiful day with the leaves turning. I hadn't been in New Hampshire since the 1980 campaign.

When I came out a group of kids were waiting for hugs and
autographs. By this time Marlin had given his briefing and word had
reached a CBS reporter. Elaine saw him coming over to me, and
stopped him as we hurried to the car.

When I got back, Robin [Weir, my hairdresser] came to wash my
hair before I went to the hospital. He said he had received a call from
People magazine asking when he had last seen me, and about my
going to the hospital. He told them, "I don't know what you're

talking about. She's in New Hampshire." It was the first he had heard about it, and he was as surprised as everyone else.

Dick arrived at five. He, Ronnie, and I had an early dinner in the family dining room, quiet and quick, with all of us trying to talk about anything but where I was going. We left for the hospital at 6:45. There was a large crowd on the South Lawn. The press wished me luck. I just wished we would get there.

And then, there I was, walking into the same building, the same room [where Ronnie had been for his cancer surgery in 1985 and his prostate surgery in January]. God, how many times.

[I stayed in the presidential suite, which consists of a large bedroom, a sitting room, a conference room, two bedrooms in case you want somebody to stay over, two or three examining rooms, and a communications room.]

The doctors came and talked to Ronnie and Dick while I went downstairs for a chest X ray. When I got back, Ronnie and Dick left, and Dr. McIlrath, who was doing the surgery, examined me and explained everything. Again, they gave me the choice of what I wanted them to do, assuming they found a malignancy. Again, I opted for the mastectomy. I said, "Look, if you get in there and find out that's what it is, please don't wake me to have a conversation about it. Just do it. It shouldn't take you long, because there isn't much there to take off. Dolly Parton I'm not."

I was supposed to take a shower before bed, but just then they announced on TV that they were getting little Jessica McClure out of the well. So of course I stopped and sat in my robe at the end of the bed and watched them get her out. I couldn't get into the shower until I knew she was all right. When she was safe, I was so happy for her parents.

After shower, bed. Nothing to eat or drink after midnight. Not even water, which is hard for me. They gave me a sleeping pill, because otherwise I wouldn't have slept.

October 17: They woke me at 6:30. Ronnie and Dick were supposed to come out by helicopter, but there was a thick fog in Washington. Ronnie was getting upset and impatient. He finally said, "Just get me into a car and let's go. I want to be there before she goes into surgery."

Meanwhile, I was saying, "Just take me in. Let's get this over with." Ten days of waiting was enough.

The operation was scheduled for 7:30. Dr. Hutton came in to say that Ronnie and Dick were on the way. "But let's get you on the gurney." When they arrived, Ronnie and I had a quick chance to kiss and say goodbye.

They took me first to a room where they put a wire in my breast to be sure they had the exact location of the lesion. It looked worse than it was, but it sure wasn't pleasant. I knew what to expect because last night I saw it on the television news. I told Ronnie that for Christmas we could always exchange framed diagrams of our cancer operations.

And then up to the operating room. They put something in my vein to make me sleep. I remember asking, "How long will it take? Let's get going." Somebody answered, "It won't take long," and it didn't. I was out like a light.

Ronnie and Dick had breakfast while they waited. I found out later that when the pathology report showed the tumor was malignant, which had been expected, Ronnie wept. One of the nurses put her arms around him to comfort him.

[I have no memory of this, but they told me later that in the operating room I asked at least four times if they had removed my breast. I kept falling asleep before they could answer me, but finally I stayed awake long enough to hear them say, "Yes, we have."

I have no memory at all of the recovery room. Evidently the first thing I managed to say to Ronnie was "They took my breast," followed by "I feel so sorry for you." And he said it didn't make any difference.

He said, "Honey, I know you don't feel like dancing, so let's just hold hands."

When we got back to my hospital room, I remember trying to talk to Ronnie and Dick, and not being able to get the words out. They told me later that I had said, "Please don't let Bob Woodward in my room." Where did *that* come from? I must have been flashing back to William Casey.]

Ronnie stayed until Howard Baker called and said he had to return for a meeting at the White House regarding Iran and the Persian Gulf. An American-owned ship had been hit by one of their missiles. John Hutton came and explained why Ronnie had to leave.

Dick went back to Philadelphia. Ronnie met with Admiral William Crowe, Cap Weinberger, and Frank Carlucci, and it was decided that our ships would destroy an oil-drilling platform in the ocean that was being used as a radar base to track our shipping.

Cardinal O'Connor had a mass for me in New York. Stu Spencer went and lit a candle.

October 18: I slept until 8:30. Then the IV came out and I felt well enough to eat a full breakfast. Ronnie arrived around ten. When he left the White House, he told the press, "I've got a date with a girl in Bethesda."

The drains in my breast were still in, but I walked in the hall with Ronnie carrying the tubes for me. Everyone was amazed that I was walking only twenty-four hours after surgery. I remember my father telling me how important it was to get up as soon as possible after an operation, so you don't get bedridden—or too comfortable.

After lunch, Ronnie had to go back to fill in for me for the taping of "In Performance at the White House." Linda [Faulkner, my social secretary] had called Marvin Hamlisch when my surgery was announced to tell him that I wouldn't be able to do my usual part in the show, and that Ronnie would fill in. It was a tribute to Jerome Kern—romantic music that I would have loved. And when I watched it later on tape, Marvin said that he missed me, that he knew I loved this kind of music and was dedicating the program to me. So sweet of him, and typical. When they played "Don't Ever Leave Me," it just about did me in.

[Originally, Marvin came to do one "In Performance," but we quickly became good friends, and he ended up doing all of them. He even talked me into singing "Our Love Is Here to Stay," and from then on, he usually had me in on the performances.]

Then Ronnie went upstairs for a meeting about Iran with the congressional leadership and Colin Powell [the national security adviser]. Carlucci had left to join Shultz in Russia. Linda canceled the Cabinet dinners we were supposed to have on the 20th and 21st.

So many calls: Betty Ford, Happy Rockefeller, Margaret Thatcher, the Nixons, many more. Mary Jane Wick came out in the afternoon to see me, because they were leaving the next day for Europe. She said, "I couldn't leave before seeing your little face again." Doug and C.Z. [her sons] called.

I had called Marge [who was in charge of caring for my mother] at Mother's house to tell her before I went into the hospital, but have not felt up to calling back yet.

Good news! John Hutton released a statement that said, "Final laboratory analysis of tissue and lymph nodes removed during yesterday's surgery confirm there is no further malignancy or evidence of other disease. No further treatment is expected, other than normal routine examinations. Mrs. Reagan's prognosis for full recovery is excellent."

When the doctors came in to tell me, I was happy and relieved.

October 19: Elaine and Jane came for the first time, bringing letters, cards, telegrams. Doria called, crying. Her mother's cancer had invaded her liver. I called Dick again and he contacted her and they got things calmed down.

I walked around again dragging the suction machine. Feeling strong, but napping in the afternoons. I am moving my arm well and I feel quite proud of myself.

To top off everything, the stock market went down 500 points today. Nobody can figure out why. The economy is sound, interest rates are down, and the GNP is up. The market was due for a correction, but this is ridiculous.

Poor Ronnie. What a week for him! Me, Iran, and now the stock market.

Today the drains came out. Whoopee! Now I don't have to drag that thing around the hall with me. I had my first shower since the operation.

Bets [my friend Betsy Bloomingdale] came to see me. She brought me a pretty robe that I wore when Ronnie and I had our pictures taken leaning out the window.

Ronnie came for dinner. We talked about the operation and he said, "That's all right, honey. I've always been a leg man myself."

Many messages arriving from dozens of foreign heads of state. Very personal, not the standard formal messages you might expect. There was even a message from Mrs. [Daniel] Ortega. Flowers keep coming in. We gave them to children in the hospital, and we got some of the cutest thank-you notes.

I can't get over all the people I've heard from, even from people I don't know at all. Jane has been staying at the hospital the whole time. I don't know what I would do without her and Elaine.

Doria called to say that she and her mother felt better, and then I talked to her mother.

Then Jane stuck her head in and said, "Your daughter's on the phone."

"My daughter, Patti?"

"Yes."

I couldn't believe it. I hadn't talked to Patti in two years. She said that she and Paul were thinking of me, and asked me how I was feeling. Then right away she urged me to have reconstructive surgery. That seemed abrupt. I told her I really wasn't thinking about that, that I was just taking one day at a time. I was barely out of one operation, and certainly wasn't ready to go through more surgery right away.

It was a short and rather stiff conversation, although I was glad she called. But I couldn't help wondering if she talked about reconstructive surgery because she couldn't think of anything else to say. I longed to hear something more comforting about what I had just gone through.

October 20: I heard a couple of comments on television that I had made the wrong choice, that I should have had a lumpectomy. But that's a very personal decision. I chose what I thought was best for me.

The important thing is that every woman should have an annual mammogram. That's the message I want to get out. What they decide after that, if they find a problem, is up to each individual woman.

Ronnie had a late meeting at the White House with Alan Greenspan, Beryl Sprinkel, and Jim Baker on the stock market, which closed up 108 points. Dick came in this afternoon and stayed for dinner.

A press conference has been announced for Thursday, so Ronnie prepared in the afternoon.

October 21: Ronnie told the press on the way to the hospital that he was going to bring me home the next morning. Doria called to say that Ron had left a message on their machine to say that he was fogged in and couldn't leave Moscow. It was the worst fog in Russian history. Shultz is over there too, and they had to send a train to get him from Helsinki to Moscow.

Dr. Donald McIlrath, who did the surgery, went home. He said I was the best patient he'd ever had. I wanted to say he was the best doctor I'd ever had, but I'd never had this done before. But I'm sure he was anyway.

Market closed up 186 points. Crazy. George Will came out to see me in the morning. Just back from one speaking engagement and then on to another at noon. Nancy Reynolds came after lunch. All my dear old friends. They mean so much at a time like this.

October 22: Got up early to leave. It felt funny to get into real clothes. I put on a bra with padding in it. Ronnie arrived around ten. When we left the room, we saw that the nurses had put a sign on the wall, saying MRS. REAGAN, WE LOVE YOU.

Paula, one of the nurses, put her arms around me and cried, and said, "You're the best patient I've ever had, and that includes your husband."

All the doctors and nurses lined up to say goodbye.

Arrived back to a huge group on the South Lawn to welcome me, including Foster Grandparents, Just Say No kids, plus lots of others. The band played songs like "Ain't She Sweet," and I did a little dance and kicked up my feet. We went up on the balcony to say thank you and wave.

Ronnie had to go to a meeting on financial problems. I came upstairs to find huge bunches of flowers, and the butlers and the maids waiting for me. I was still swollen, and the bra was cutting into me and hurting me. I took it off and don't know when I'll put it back on.

Jane and I tried to get some work done before and after lunch. But I was too tired, so I took a nap.

Ronnie came home early because of his press conference. [As always, I watched it on television in the West Hall.] All they wanted to talk about was taxes. Would he raise taxes? He refused to get boxed in, saying that everything was on the table except Social Security, and he wasn't going to announce in advance what he expected to discuss. He did well.

October 23: Tried to sleep late this morning. So tired that I couldn't even get dressed until after lunch. We left for Camp David at 3:30.

Beautiful weather, with the leaves turning. Ran an old picture with John Wayne and Kate Hepburn.

They counted up all the letters, cards, and wires, and it came to something like thirty-six thousand! One of the most touching was a gift of two red carnations from Celia, one of the bag ladies who has established herself in Lafayette Park. Somebody called the flower shop and they told us who it was. That was all the money she had.

October 24: The doctors showed me some arm exercises to start, and said that I should walk with my arms swinging. So later [at Camp David] we took another walk. I think the Secret Service men in back of me must have thought I was crazy because I was swinging my arms back and forth so vigorously.

I still haven't shown Ronnie—me.

Even though he says it doesn't make any difference, and I believe him, I somehow can't bring myself to do it yet. I'll know when the time is right.

Ron called, just back from Russia. Finally got on a train to Helsinki and flew to Frankfurt and on to Los Angeles. He couldn't get to Washington. We had a long talk about the operation, and then about his trip. I told him I'd received the dearest letter from Doria, and how much it meant to me. It was full of love and concern, and I'll save it forever. I couldn't help wishing it had come from my own daughter.

October 25: Watched morning shows. Lots of speculation about Gorbachev and the date of the summit. [The Washington summit took place in early December.] Mermie was here when we got back, very solicitous of me.

Took a nap and some calls. Ronnie met with Shultz and Carlucci for a report on their meeting with Gorbachev.

October 26: More calls, flowers. Had my hair washed, which, as any woman knows, always makes you feel a little better.

I was supposed to have tea with Joan Rivers at four-thirty, and I thought I should lie down for half an hour. I was missing the naps I took in the hospital. Just as I lay down, the phone rang and it was Ron. A moment later, the bedroom door opened and in walked Ronnie.

What in the world was Ronnie doing home at four o'clock in the afternoon?

I said to Ron, "Hold on a minute. Daddy just came in and something must be wrong."

I looked at Ronnie's face and it was just stricken. I could see that something terrible had happened, and that he didn't know how to tell me. He sat down on the edge of the bed, and I kept saying to him, "What is it? Tell me. What's wrong? What is it?"

Finally he said, "Honey, Edie is now with Loyal."

I started to shout: "No, no!," crying at the same time.

Ronnie picked up the phone and told Ron that my mother was dead, and that he'd call him later.

Mother had died of a stroke. Tom Chauncey [an old family friend in Phoenix] had called Elaine [Crispen] to tell her. Elaine went to John Hutton, and John walked over to the Oval Office to tell Ronnie.

Ronnie had said, "My God, how will I tell her? On top of everything."

Just a few days ago Jane and I had made arrangements for me to go out and see Mother next month.

I kept saying, "Please, let me go to her. Please. Just let me go to her. And don't let them do anything to her. Don't do anything to the apartment. Just get me there."

Mother had asked to be cremated, but I wanted to see her one last time. Oh, my darling little mother! No longer there to go and see. [Toward the end there was no longer any communication, but at least I could touch her and kiss her.]

I feel so guilty that I wasn't there when it happened. Tom Chauncey was there and I wasn't.

Tom told me that her eyes had been closed most of the time. He was sitting with her, holding her hand. She opened her eyes and looked at him, and then closed them and died. It was peaceful, but oh, how I will miss her.

Everybody busy changing plans. Ronnie and I will fly out in the morning. Ye gods, everything at once. I'm just getting my head up from one thing and now I'm hit with another. So tired. Tried to pack. Don't know what to pack.

October 27: Left early for Phoenix. In a daze. Breakfast on the plane. Met with Jane, Elaine, and Jack regarding funeral arrangements and then tried to take a nap. John Hutton kept reminding me that this has been a double-whammy, and that he's concerned about my recovery.

I still can't believe Mother is dead.

When we landed in Phoenix, we went right to the mortuary where Mother was. She was in her red robe, gold beads, and her little red mittens. Whether it was summer or winter, in her last years she wore those mittens. I took them off. I just wanted to have them.

"I don't know if you should do that," Ronnie said.

And for one of the few times in our life together, I got mad at him, and shouted: "Do you want me to leave them there to be burned?"

Then I really went to pieces. It seemed as if she should open her eyes and talk to me. I kept telling her I loved her and thanked her for all she had done for me. Oh, how I hope she heard me! I hope she and Bapa are together now, like Ronnie said.

I couldn't bear to leave her, but Ronnie and John Hutton took my arm and said, "We've got to leave now." If they hadn't done that, I'd still be there.

We went to her apartment. Tom described again what had happened, and said it was peaceful. But she's gone. My little mother.

When you mentioned her name, the other person always smiled.

Tom is a big help. We are giving Mother's wheelchair and her walker to a home for elderly people. She would have liked that. I gave the girls [who took care of her] some clothes that they wanted.

Jane and Elaine called everyone. Barry Goldwater canceled plans in Washington to be here for the funeral.

Denominations never meant much to Mother. Although she was a Presbyterian, in Phoenix the Catholic church was closer, so she would go there. She was always a regular churchgoer. Funny, with her outrageous sense of humor and all, but she read the Bible every night. I have her Bible now, and there are passages marked in it. She had a deep, deep faith which really helped her through Bapa's death, and also through her own last days, I'm sure.

Those wonderful priests at the Catholic church would come over every Sunday to give her communion. They once wrote me to say that they thought she didn't really know what was happening, but they would be glad to keep it up if I wanted them to. I wrote back and said, "Please do, because I would like to think that she really does know what you are doing, and I know she cares."

So they kept on. And out of the blue, there was a Sunday when she recited the Twenty-third Psalm. Perfectly!

It was decided that the service would be at the Catholic church on Saturday at two. I would love to have someone talk about Mother. I wish it could be Ronnie, but I hate to press him—he has so much to do.

I talked to Ron. He's flying here tomorrow just to be with me. That means a lot to me.

By the time we left the apartment I was exhausted—emotionally and physically. Dinner at the hotel in front of the television. Ronnie had to fly back to Washington but he will return on Friday with Dick and his family.

The people who bought my parents' old house have offered to have everyone over after the service. It was very sweet of them, but emotionally, there is no way I can do that. It would bring back too many memories. It will be hard enough to go to the Boitches', who live next door to their old house. [They had very kindly asked people to come to their house after the service. Oddly enough, Cynthia Boitch had had a mastectomy years ago, and had turned to my father for advice and help during that time. It's amazing how many women told me afterward that they'd had a mastectomy, but that nobody knew about it.]

John came to examine me. Then I went to bed.

October 28: Didn't have a good night. I would wake up wondering where I was. Then, when I remembered, I would start crying. How I am going to miss Mother!

We all went over to the house at 9:30 and started working. The Goodwill people came for Mother's clothes, but I think they'll have to come back tomorrow. I gave her mink jacket to Marge, who had been there a long time. Went through the linens—so much stuff. I had no idea it would take this long.

Ron arrived around two, and I was so glad to see him. We had lunch out on the patio where Mother and I used to eat. She loved sitting there, watching the birds and the golfers. She'd send the girls out to collect the golf balls, and then she'd try to sell them to her friends when they came to visit.

After lunch we went back to work. Everybody was wonderful. Reminded me of the day we moved her into the apartment. Everybody was working—Elaine, Jane, Mary Ann, Anita, John Hutton, all down on our hands and knees.

There was a nice feeling about it. Somebody would send out for lunch and we would put it on the dining room table and all sit around and eat. I am trying to eat out on the patio as much as possible.

Back to the Biltmore with Ron. I wanted to walk around the hotel because I hadn't been there in so long. This is where we used to go on Easter vacations when I was in school, and where Ronnie and I spent our honeymoon.

But everything has changed. There used to be a drugstore here with a soda fountain, but no longer. I wanted to show Ron the cottage where Ronnie and I stayed during our honeymoon, but I couldn't find it anywhere. But there's a familiar smell to the Biltmore—a warm, welcoming smell, and it's still here.

They have built on some new wings. And they took down the diving board. Ronnie was a big diver, and I remember sitting there on our honeymoon and watching him dive from the high board. Everybody at the pool was watching my new husband, and I was so proud.

The hotel brought back so many memories, which make me sad. I told Ron how I used to come here when I was in school, and how you had to dress for dinner every night. I told him about Roy, who ran the stables, who used to tell me about the girls who got crushes on the cowboys who took the guests out riding. Roy had a way of solving that. He'd take the girls to see the rooms where the cowboys lived, and when they saw those unmade beds and all the clothes on the floor, most of them lost interest. It was hard to describe to Ron what this place had once been like.

Nobody bothered us as we walked around. They all knew why I was there, and they stayed back. Couldn't have been nicer.

Ted Graber came in, but before he got here, Ron and I had a good talk. It's not often there are just the two of us. Ted will be coming to Mother's tomorrow to help me with the furniture to go into storage in Los Angeles.

Letters of condolence from Kay Graham and Walter Cronkite, who were out here at a convention. Very sweet.

Mike Wallace called to see how I was doing. He said Meg Greenfield had asked him to write an op-ed piece on Mother for the [*Washington*] *Post*. He said he didn't know whether he could do justice to Mother as she really was.

[But he did. Mike wrote a beautiful tribute called "The Roles of Edie Davis." He closed with a brief description of my surgery, and ended with these words:

"Nancy survived and smiled, though, and went about her appointed rounds. Then came Edie Davis' death, and somehow it seemed to take Nancy Reagan's breath away. I can understand why."]

Ronnie called. I told him about wanting somebody to speak at the funeral, and he said, "Well, I didn't want to push myself on you, but I'd love to do it." I burst into tears. I know it would have meant a lot to Mother, who loved him so much.

Ron and I and Ted had dinner in the suite. We tried to watch Buckley's debate with the Republican candidates, but we were so tired and preoccupied that we didn't stay with it very long.

October 29: Ted and I went over to the apartment early to work. We picked things out to go to Los Angeles, things for Goodwill. Ron came and I gave him Mother's silver coffee set, and I picked out things for Dick and his children, and for Maureen and Mike. It was a long, tiring day.

Today Ronnie announced a new choice for the Supreme Court— Douglas Ginsberg.

Mother had once shown me two little boxes, one labeled for Ron, one for Patti, filled with mementos, to be given to them when she died. I gave Ron his.

As for Patti—she had said she couldn't come to the funeral, that she had travel plans that couldn't be changed. I sent her box to her.

There was a lovely editorial in today's Phoenix paper about Mother and all of her charity work.

I found a ring that Mother had with both of our initials on it, *E* and *N*. It's tiny, and she must have worn it on her little finger, because it's not a baby ring. I immediately put it on.

I had to leave before the movers were through, but I hope they did everything. I'll check tomorrow. Amazing, that there was so much to do in this little apartment.

Knowing how Mother felt, I want the church to be pretty, and I asked for white flowers all around. Nobody knows yet that Ronnie is going to speak.

Colleen Moore came in for the funeral and had dinner with Ron and me the night before. She's eighty-five, but you'd never know it. She and Mother were such a pair in Chicago. She told Ron how, when my father would leave for the hospital each morning, and her husband, Homer, would leave for the office, she and Mother would be on the phone with each other planning their day. What one didn't think of, the other did. They worked together on opening the gift shop at Passavant Hospital, and many other projects.

We had a wonderful talk, but I noticed that Colleen wasn't eating anything. When I asked about it, she said, "Well, when I eat, it gives me a stomachache. So I really don't eat very much."

[Colleen died of cancer a few months later, so I'm glad Ron got to know her a little. When she died, I was happy for Mother, knowing these two friends would be reunited.]

October 30: I wanted to sleep late, but couldn't. Had an early lunch with Ron at the hotel before he went to pick up Doria at the airport. She couldn't come with him yesterday because she had classes.

I watched Ronnie on television with Shevardnadze announce the summit meeting in Washington, from December 7 to December 9. It was good to get it pinned down, but I wish it could be a few weeks later, after I've had a chance to catch my breath and to grieve.

I went to the apartment to make sure everything was out. Marge was there cleaning, and it looked so strange.

I went out on the little patio and remembered all the happy and, as Mother used to say, peaceful times we had there. Eating lunch, or just holding hands. Very painful for me.

My mother loved to watch the birds, so we had put in a birdbath for her. I took it and I'm going to set it up in our new house. [It's there now, in the back, by the pool.]

As I left Mother's apartment for the last time, I tried not to look back.

I went to Sybil Harrington's [Sybil is an old friend of my family's]. I had called her and asked her if I could come by. Everything else had changed, and I wanted to be somewhere that was exactly the same. I also wanted to just sit and look out at green grass. Next door is the house that Brooke and Vincent Astor had at one point, and then Adele Astaire [Fred Astaire's sister] had it. Fred used to come out here to visit her.

Back to the hotel. Ronnie arrived with Dick and the family and everyone came over at six-thirty for dinner. Mail still pouring in—it just amazes me. People from my past, my mother's past, and heads of state. The mix is so surprising.

October 31: Not a good night. Rosie Grier called. [Rosie is an old friend who used to be close to Bobby Kennedy.] He was in Phoenix, so I asked him to come to the service. Oh, I hope it's nice for Mother. The White House sent lots of white flowers. And I asked for a nosegay from me to Mother to be on the altar.

Ron and Doria came after lunch, and Dick and his family, and Charlotte Ramage [my cousin, with whom I had lived as a little girl] and her family. Terrible weather in Los Angeles, so Mermie, Dennis, and Mike's plane was late, and they went straight to the church.

There were over two hundred people at the church, which is a real tribute to Mother, especially when you realize that she was ninety-one. But she had touched a lot of people's lives.

The church looked beautiful. There was a boys' choir and they sang beautifully and looked darling in their white robes. Mother would have liked that. And Nancy Joachim [a friend of Jane Erkenbeck] sang beautifully. Father Doran and Monsignor Donahue spoke, and read from Mother's Bible.

Father Doran said, "There is only one word to describe Edie Davis, and that's 'delightful.' When you came into a room and she was there, it was just delightful. She made everything that way."

Then he made us all laugh by telling how he had introduced Mother to the bishop of Phoenix. He said that Mother was very formal, and gave a little curtsy to the bishop. Then she turned to Father Doran and said, "Well, aren't you and I going to kiss? We always do that when the bishop isn't here!"

Then Ronnie spoke. As he began, Ron reached over and held my hand.

Ronnie talked about his friendship with Mother. He said, "Meeting her was like opening a bottle of champagne," and that she "gave wit and charm and kindliness throughout her life."

He spoke beautifully, and personally. He described how she seemed to know everybody in Chicago, and how he first realized this when he was in town on business one evening. He was supposed to meet my parents for dinner, but he was running late and couldn't find a cab. When the doorman of the hotel heard that he was going to see Edie Davis, he hailed a squad car. Both of the officers in the car knew Mother, too, so they drove Ronnie right to her door.

The service lasted forty-five minutes, which was just the right length for Mother. I think she would have liked the whole thing. I hope so.

Even the press were making remarks about Patti's not being here. No call, no card, no flowers—nothing. Elaine told them she didn't know where Patti was. She said, "This can only be another crack in an already broken heart. I don't mind saying it because I think Mrs. Reagan has gone through an awful lot and that had to be an additional hurt."

True.

After the service, we went into a holding room and suddenly I was aware that Ron and Doria weren't there. They had gone back into the church—Doria is Catholic—to light a candle for Mother. I was very touched, and followed them in and did the same.

Doria hugged me. She said she loved me and had learned so much from me.

Then to the Boitches' for the reception. So many of our friends from California and New York, and just about everybody Mother had known. Stu Spencer came in from Los Angeles. Also, my old friend Jean Wescott from Chicago with her daughter.

I was getting awfully tired so we came back to the hotel and had dinner in bed. It felt so good to lie down. There was a terrible storm in the middle of the night: hard rain, thunder, and lightning. I guess Mother is trying to get things organized up there!

November 1: Early start to get ready to fly back to Washington. I'm exhausted, but there's a mountain of mail and calls waiting for me. I don't know how I got through these past few days. I still haven't had a recuperation period, and I don't have as much movement and flexibility in my arm as I should. I've got to start taking care of myself—that's what everybody keeps telling me.

November 2: [Back at the White House] Slept late. Far more tired than I realized. Mail and flowers still pouring in. And Mother's things and messages—I can't seem to get out from under.

I called Mike Wallace to thank him for the piece he wrote on Mother. Also for the flowers he sent to the church.

After dinner I automatically reached for the phone to call Mother.

November 3: Slept late again. Trying to exercise my arm. Worked with Elaine on interview requests. Lots came in after the mastectomy, but before Mother's death. I really don't want to go around from network to network talking about the need for mammograms. Maybe one general PBS announcement will do it. They said the number of women going in for mammograms has skyrocketed, which is great.

In the afternoon, Ronnie went down for the Arts and Embassies reception, but I couldn't. Many of my friends were there and I would have loved to see them, but not now. No time to nap and I was tired. Dinner on trays.

November 5. Found out today that Raisa is coming with Gorbachev next month. Now we've got to figure out what to do with them.

Ronnie's nominee for the Supreme Court is accused of smoking marijuana in college, which he admitted. Ye gods, when will all this stop?

Meeting with Howard Baker, Ken Duberstein, and Tom Griscom on the Gorbachev visit. We plan to have a state dinner for the Gorbachevs, and people are already breaking down the door to get in. So much to do, so little time to do it. And me not feeling so hot.

All of this could not have happened at a worse time.

Left for Camp David. Much cooler now.

Ralph Lauren called. He was very sweet, and he said, "I wish you had told me. Maybe I could have been helpful to you."

We ran a darling movie with Lillian Gish and Bette Davis. Seeing Lillian brought back memories of when I lived in New York, and I'd often go over to her apartment for dinner.

November 7: Three weeks ago today I had the mastectomy. Still doesn't seem possible.

Douglas Ginsberg wants to have his name taken out of consideration. I think that's smart. I believe Ronnie wants to go with [Judge Anthony] Kennedy.

[At Camp David] I went up for the radio broadcast and on the way back I stopped at the gym with John Hutton to do my exercises. I had taken my weights with me.

November 8: Howard [Baker] called Ronnie about a story in the *Washington Post* that upset him. I said to him, "Howard, Ronnie's been putting up with this for years now, reading in the paper and seeing on television that he's over the hill, that he sleeps all the time, and so on. And if he can take it, so can you."

Howard said, "Well, you make a good point."

November 9: All the girls in the office are working so hard. So much mail has come in that they have been taking letters home to answer on weekends.

A woman from one of the shops in Washington came with the prosthesis and bras, and I took care of all that. She was a little self-conscious, but I accepted it and even joked about it. She told me that her business had increased after my mastectomy.

November 10: My "coming-out" party—a state dinner for President and Mrs. Herzog of Israel. They are both charming. He speaks with an Irish brogue—he's the son of a rabbi from Dublin.

At dinner, I had asked that Dr. Paul Marks, the head of the Sloan-Kettering Cancer Institute in New York, be seated next to me. I wanted to hear what he had to say about the mastectomy. He told me about the calls they had received from the different networks and television stations, asking for a doctor to go on television to discuss my surgery. He told everyone not to do it because it was unprofessional.

He also told me that there has been a sharp increase in the number of women coming in for mammograms, which certainly pleased me.

Dr. Marks said, "I'm going to tell you something. It's really none of my business, but you shouldn't even be at this dinner. It's too soon. It normally takes six weeks to recover from surgery, but you had a setback with the death of your mother. It's very emotional, mentally and physically, and you won't start to get your energy back for at least three months. I understand you're going to New York tomorrow for the Feltsman concert. I think that's crazy. [Vladimir Feltsman is a renowned pianist from Moscow who was a refusenik for years. Ron met him when he was over there, and Ronnie and I were helpful in getting him out of Russia. I had invited him to give his first concert at the White House, which he did, and I was looking forward to being at his New York debut.]

"The trouble is, you look well, so people assume you *are* well, but you're not. You haven't healed, and it's important that you concentrate on your exercises."

Everything he said was right, and I canceled my plans to go to the concert.

With the Gorbachevs coming next month, I have plenty to do.

16

❦❧

Showdown (Donald Regan and Iran-Contra)

IF, by some miracle, I could take back one decision in Ronnie's presidency, it would be his agreement in January 1985 that Jim Baker and Donald Regan should swap jobs.

It seemed like a good idea at the time—a little unusual, perhaps, but reasonable. Jim, who had served Ronnie well as chief of staff, was worn out, and Donald Regan was more than willing to come to the White House after four years as secretary of the Treasury. When Baker and Regan suggested the switch, there was no reason to expect that this new arrangement would lead to a political disaster.

I never knew Donald Regan before he came over as Ronnie's new chief of staff. I knew *of* him, of course. We had met socially, and I had heard that he was a bright man and a strong manager. During Ronnie's first term he had evidently done a good job at Treasury, where he had helped put through the administration's new economic program.

But during the second term, Don was not my favorite person in the White House. And he wasn't exactly cuckoo about me, either.

For the first few months, we got along fine. It wasn't until July 1985, when Ronnie had his cancer operation, that Don and I had our first run-in. Within forty-eight hours of the surgery, Don wanted to bring in George Bush and Bud McFarlane to meet with the president.

I thought that was much too soon—and so did the doctors. But Don thought it was more important for Ronnie to resume his schedule of appointments.

"Let's wait," I told Don. "Remember, he's just had major surgery. I know he's the president, but don't forget that he's also a patient like any other patient. If you push him too hard, he could have a relapse."

Before Ronnie was out of the hospital, Don and I had another disagreement. Don came out to Bethesda every day, and he wanted to make the trip by helicopter. That seemed wrong to me. I thought it was inappropriate for anyone other than the president to use the helicopter except in an emergency. The drive to the hospital took about forty-five minutes, and everybody else who came traveled by car. I must have had some inkling, even then, of what increasingly bothered me about Don Regan, which was that he often acted as if *he* were president.

His very first day on the job, Don said that he saw himself as the "chief operating officer" of the country. But he was hired to be chief of *staff*. He liked the word "chief," but he never really understood that his title also included the words "of staff." And he often acted as if his position had some independent government standing.

And so, for example, he was the first chief of staff ever to have regular Secret Service protection. And he evidently admired the patio outside Ronnie's office, because when he had his office renovated and enlarged, a beautiful flagstone patio was put in—which was noticeably larger than the president's. I was in the West Wing one day when Don spotted me and said, "I'd like you to see my new office." When he showed me the new patio, he said, "I didn't want any fuss, so I paid for all of this myself."

I learned later that the patio was paid for primarily by government funds.

As Ronnie returned to the White House and gradually resumed his normal schedule, Don and I started getting along better. But over the next few months he made several public statements that annoyed me.

On the subject of economic sanctions against South Africa, Don said that American women might not be eager to give up their diamonds, platinum, and gold. I thought that remark was insensitive and demeaning to women, and I resented it.

Then, just before the Geneva summit, he told the *Washington Post* that women were not "going to understand [missile] throw-weights or what is happening in Afghanistan or what is happening in human rights."

That sounded like a man who didn't think women had any brains. I don't usually agree with Eleanor Smeal from the National Organization for Women, but I could certainly understand when she said she was glad to learn that the president took Bonzo with him to Geneva.

It was bad enough that with these two comments Don Regan had offended more than half of the American people. But then, after the Reykjavik summit in October 1986, he went on to insult Ronnie and the whole administration. "Some of us," he told the *New York Times*, "are like a shovel brigade that follows a parade down Main Street."

I was furious when I read that. I didn't think the chief of staff should be making any public statements except to explain or clarify the president's position, but this one was incredible. If that's how Don saw his job, what kind of loyalty could Ronnie expect from him on other issues? And what kind of example was he setting for the rest of Ronnie's advisers?

But that was the problem: Don Regan didn't see himself as one of the president's advisers. He didn't consider himself to be part of the White House staff. He saw himself as a kind of deputy president.

I wasn't the only one who felt this way. By the time Ronnie returned from Reykjavik, I had been approached by a stream of high government officials and congressional leaders. Some came to see me in the White House and others phoned me, but all were concerned about Donald Regan. They told me he had poor relations with both Congress and the media. That he was restricting their access to the president. That he was explosive and difficult to deal with. That he was intimidating his subordinates in the office. And that good, experienced people were starting to leave the West Wing because they couldn't work with him.

Some of those people were calling me and saying, "We're scared of this guy. The tensions over here are incredible. Morale is low. Can't you *do* something?"

I gave the same answer to everybody: "What are you telling *me* for? You ought to be telling my husband!"

But almost nobody did. Maybe some were embarrassed to complain to the president about his chief of staff. Others were intimidated by the Oval Office. And still others found that under Donald Regan it was virtually impossible to see the president alone. It's difficult to talk to the president if you can't *get* to the president.

Even George Bush came to see me in the residence about Don. As he got off the elevator and we walked into the West Hall, he said, "I didn't want to say this on the phone, but I think Don should resign."

"I agree with you," I said, "and I wish you'd tell my husband. I can't be the only one who's saying this to him."

"Nancy," he said, "that's not my role."

"That's exactly your role," I replied.

But as far as I know, George Bush never spoke to Ronnie about Don Regan.

It was around this time that Donald Hodel, secretary of the Interior, told Maureen that he had called the White House to ask for a fifteen-minute meeting with Ronnie. But even *he* couldn't get in. Don Regan told him that the president didn't meet with anyone in the Cabinet individually except for the secretaries of State and Defense.

Then there was an incident with Kathy Osborne, Ronnie's personal secretary, that I found alarming. Apparently, she sent a certain document to Ronnie without first showing it to Don. When he heard about it, Don stormed out of his office and exploded: How dare she send that paper to the president? Didn't she know that everything went through him first? If she ever did this again, she'd be fired!

I couldn't believe it. He was threatening to fire Ronnie's personal secretary? Everybody knew that Kathy reported directly to Ronnie. She had been with him for four years in Sacramento, and seven more in Washington. Ronnie has always been very fond of her, and she works for him to this day. The fact that Don thought he could fire her struck me as a very bad sign.

By now it was clear to me that Donald Regan was in the wrong job. He may be a talented man, but this was the wrong place for him. First, a good chief of staff should remain in the shadows. He operates behind the scenes and should not be making statements to the media. Most good chiefs of staff are relatively anonymous.

Second, the chief of staff must have political skills. He works with Congress, and he serves as the president's ambassador to a wide segment of Washington—including the press. Don Regan knew a lot about business and finance, but he had little experience in politics.

Third, chief of staff is fundamentally a people job. But most of the people Don came in contact with couldn't get along with him. It's true that he got along with Ronnie, but Ronnie gets along with everybody.

But Ronnie wasn't hearing any of this because people were coming to me instead of to him. And the three men who *could* have told Ronnie what was going on were no longer in the White House. Jim Baker was over at Treasury. Ed Meese was running the Justice Department. And Michael Deaver had left government. Of the four people who had been closest to Ronnie during his first term, I was the only one left.

Although I believed for a long time that Donald Regan was in the wrong job, my "power" in getting him to leave has been greatly exaggerated. Believe me, if I really were the dragon lady that he described in his book, he would have been out the door many months earlier.

Later, when Don did leave, I took a lot of heat for protecting Ronnie, and for allegedly interfering in the affairs of state. But I had to get in there because nobody else would tell Ronnie what was going on.

Did I talk to Ronnie about Don Regan? Absolutely. Did I pass on what I was hearing from White House officials and congressional leaders? Of course.

But that doesn't mean Ronnie listened.

For a long time, he just didn't take these reports seriously. Eventually, I came to realize that there were, in effect, two Donald Regans: the one people were telling me about, and the one Ronnie saw every day. With Ronnie, Don was jovial, affable, and good-humored, the genial Irishman who always had a good story. Ronnie genuinely liked him, and they had a good rapport.

So when I tried to tell Ronnie what I was hearing, it was hard for him to believe. It was a side of Don he never saw, and he honestly couldn't see why anyone was complaining.

Then, in November 1986, a series of events occurred which turned a difficult situation into a full-blown crisis. Suddenly the Don Regan problem became subsumed into a much bigger problem—Iran-contra.

It began on November 3, when a Lebanese magazine reported that the United States had been supplying military spare parts to Iran, and that Robert McFarlane, the president's national security adviser, had visited Tehran to discuss the possible release of American hostages in Lebanon. Ten days later, Ronnie went on television to explain what he knew about all of this. When he was done, the polls showed that, for the first time during Ronnie's presidency, most Americans did not believe him.

As it turned out, people were right to be skeptical. Although Ronnie thought he was telling the truth, he was relying on information provided by Admiral John Poindexter, who had replaced Bud McFarlane as national security adviser. And that information was—to put it mildly—seriously incomplete.

On November 19, Ronnie held a press conference to try to clear things up. Here, too, he made several major errors. I'm still angry that Poindexter sent Ronnie out there without telling him everything.

By now, both the House and the Senate intelligence committees had announced that they would convene hearings on the arms sale to Iran.

I'll never forget the expression on Ronnie's face after Ed Meese came to him on the afternoon of November 24 with astonishing and alarming news: that although Iran had paid $30 million for American military equipment, less than half of that money had been accounted for. Oliver North had admitted diverting at least some of the profits to the Nicaraguan contras.

The news was so shattering that everything just stopped. Ronnie came into our bedroom looking pale and absolutely crushed. "Honey," he said, "I've got some bad news. Ed Meese just came in and told me that money from the sale of arms to Iran went to the contras."

Although I didn't really understand it yet, I could tell from his voice that this was very serious.

"First thing tomorrow," he said, "Ed and I are going right to the press about this so they won't think we're hiding anything."

If Ronnie was incredulous, I was furious. Later that evening I called Don Regan from my office to let him know how upset I was. I felt very strongly that Ronnie had been badly served, and I wanted Don to know. Maybe this was unfair of me, but to some extent I blamed him for what had happened. He was the chief of staff, and if he didn't know, I thought, he should have. A good chief of staff has sources everywhere. He should practically be able to smell what's going on.

Later, in his own defense, Don asked, "Does a bank president know whether a bank teller is fiddling around with the books?" Maybe not, but this was the same man who once bragged that not a sparrow could fly through the White House without his hearing it.

I'm not saying that Iran-contra was Don Regan's doing. But it did occur on his watch, and when it came out, he should have taken responsibility. I can't imagine that this problem would have developed during Ronnie's first term, when the "troika" of Baker, Meese, and Deaver was in charge. The West Wing was far more open then, and if anything devious had been going on in the White House basement, it would have come to light—and certainly to Ronnie's attention. But now all the power of the troika was concentrated in one man.

I must have dropped ten pounds over the next few months. I tried to eat, but I couldn't eat much. Every day when we turned on the television, we didn't know what we were going to hear. It was crazy—I was relying on the media for information about what was going on in our own house. In eight years in Sacramento and six more in Washington, we had never experienced anything like this. The entire government seemed to grind to a halt, and only Iran-contra mattered. Every day Ronnie was being accused of things I know he didn't do.

Ronnie was genuinely baffled. He kept expecting that everything would fall into place, that there was a rational explanation for all this. But he couldn't stop it, and he couldn't control it.

He did, however, make three important decisions during the early weeks of the crisis.

First, he established a three-man commission, headed by Senator John Tower, that would take an independent look at what had happened.

Second, Ronnie brought in David Abshire, our ambassador to NATO, to ensure that all of the ongoing investigations—the Tower Commission, the congressional investigations, and the independent counsel—received the right information. Whatever had happened, there would be no cover-up in Ronald Reagan's White House. Despite the inevitable comparisons, Iran-contra was not Watergate, and the Reagan White House was not the Nixon White House. By dealing with the problem openly, Ronnie may have saved his presidency.

Ronnie's third decision was that he wouldn't comment on the daily charges that were swirling around Washington until all the facts were in and the Tower Commission had issued its report. This took a great deal of restraint, but he didn't want to be in the position of responding today to information that might well be contradicted tomorrow. In other words, no more press conferences until he had some answers.

Ronnie was in an impossible bind: Holding a press conference would have created the risk of being contradicted by new information, but not holding one created a vacuum and gave some people the impression that Ronnie had something to hide.

It was terribly hard for both of us to sit through those long months and have him accused of making secret deals and being part of underhand arrangements. Ronnie has always had a reputation for integrity, and it went right to his soul to see his character being questioned every day. At the time, a large segment of the public assumed that Ronnie must have known everything, but as this book goes to press, some of the basic facts about Iran-contra are still in dispute.

It was a dark and hurtful time, and it lasted for months. Every time I opened a newspaper or turned on the television, there was the same drumbeat. My pals called me often with encouragement: Kay Graham, Meg Greenfield, George Will, Mike Wallace, and Dick Helms. "I've been through this sort of thing," Dick said, referring to the Watergate era, "and you just have to sit it out. I know how painful and difficult it is." I felt a great empathy from people during this period. They didn't always know exactly what to say to me, but they made it clear that they understood and sympathized.

On December 1, 1986, a *New York Times*–CBS poll showed that Ronnie's overall approval rating had dropped from 67 percent to 46 percent *in a single month.* No matter how often he said that he hadn't known about the diversion of funds, the same message kept coming back: *Oh yes, you did.*

With the presidency under siege, the Don Regan problem grew more serious. I was told that in one meeting, the entire Cabinet asked Don to resign. Congress couldn't deal with him, and both privately and publicly, members of the House and Senate were calling for his resignation. Even Senator Orrin Hatch, a conservative Republican from Utah, said that Don had to go.

In spite of what's been said or written, I did not mastermind a plot to get rid of Don Regan. There was no cabal. I wasn't in cahoots with anybody to bring about his downfall. I didn't have to be. By the end of 1986, half of Washington wanted him out.

On the evening of December 4, 1986, an unusual meeting took place in the White House residence. Michael Deaver, who shared my concern that Ronnie was being isolated, had quietly arranged for two visitors to come in to discuss the current situation with the president. One was William Rogers, who had been secretary of State during the Nixon administration. The other was Robert Strauss, a prominent Democrat and the former national chairman of the Democratic party. Mike hoped to expose Ronnie to fresh, frank advice from two respected outsiders—a Republican and a Democrat—who had been around Washington a long time, and who would level with Ronnie about the political crisis he now faced. I didn't normally attend meetings with Ronnie, but this was a special situation, and it was held in the residence, and I wanted very much to be there.

Bill Rogers didn't say much that evening. The gist of his message was that the Don Regan problem was manageable and that it would soon blow over.

Robert Strauss, on the other hand, had a great deal to say. "Mr. President," he began in his Texas drawl, "let me tell you about the first time I was up here in the residence. LBJ was in office, and a few of us came to see him about Vietnam. When my turn came to speak, I held back. I didn't tell the president what I really thought. Instead, I told him what I thought he wanted to hear.

"When I went home that night, I felt like a two-dollar whore. And I said to myself, If any president is ever foolish enough to invite me back, I hope I show more character. I came to see Carter on many occasions, and I always told him what I thought.

"Now, I have no quarrel with Don Regan," Strauss went on. "But you've got two serious problems right now, and he's not helping you with either one. First, you've got a political problem on the Hill, and Don Regan has no constituency and no allies there. Second, you've got a serious media problem, and Regan has no friends there, either. It makes no difference how earnest he is, or how much you like him, or how well the two of you get along. He's not the man you need. You're in a hell of a mess, Mr. President, and you need a chief of staff who can help get you out of it."

I had never heard anyone who wasn't in Ronnie's inner circle come in and talk to my husband as strongly as Bob Strauss did that evening. Later that night, I called Bob at home to thank him for having the courage to tell Ronnie what he truly believed, and what he thought Ronnie should do. Nobody else was doing that.

Unfortunately, Ronnie wasn't responsive to Bob's message. At one point during this period, I said to him, "I was right about Stockman. I was right about Bill Clark. Why won't you listen to me about Don Regan?"

But until the very end, Ronnie continued to believe that the problems with Don would work themselves out. So much for all that power and influence I'm supposed to have.

Then, as if we didn't have enough to deal with that month, William Casey collapsed in his office. As head of the CIA, Casey probably knew as much as anyone about the Iran-contra affair. But now his doctors discovered a serious brain tumor which required major surgery. Suddenly, one of the principal players in the whole drama was out of commission—possibly forever.

As I look back on that period, I find it amazing that almost nobody seems to have thought about the possible long-term effects of Bill Casey's illness, and how his condition might have affected his judgment in the months before it was discovered. Because my father was a neurosurgeon, I wondered about this at the time. But it wasn't until I read *Revolution,* a book about Ronnie's presidency by Martin Anderson, that I saw my own hunch confirmed by somebody else. As Anderson points out, lymphoma brain cancer, which Casey had, affects the left side of the brain—the side that controls judgment. Brain tumors grow slowly and insidiously, and as they expand, they can cause paranoia, suspicion, and distrust. Because they are rarely detected early, they can develop over a course of months, and sometimes as long as two years.

"Is it possible," wrote Anderson, "that Bill Casey's mind, his sense of judgment, his ability to discriminate, to reason, to think clearly was becoming increasingly impaired as the Iran-Contra affair unfolded? The answer is clearly yes, it is possible. If the symptoms began subtly, perhaps as much as two years before the tumor was detected, his brain would have started to feel the effects in early 1985. By the summer and fall of 1985, when the foundations for the general scheme of selling arms to Iran, paying ransom, and secretly diverting money to the Contras were laid in place, it is possible that

Casey's brain was feeling the ravages of cancer, suffering memory loss, making bad decisions."

I think Martin Anderson is right. With hindsight, I now see that Bill Casey gave us several warnings that we all missed. During 1986 his speech had become even more slurred than usual, to the point where it was very difficult for Ronnie to understand what he was saying. (Casey was always difficult to understand; I often wondered whether this was partly intentional. "I *never* understood him," Bob Dole once told me.) He had also become irascible and explosive, more difficult than usual to deal with. Then, in November, a month before the tumor was discovered, he wrote a letter to Ronnie recommending that Ronnie replace George Shultz with Jeane Kirkpatrick because George wasn't loyal enough!

I believe that Bill Casey was deeply involved in the Iran-contra affair during a period when he wasn't thinking clearly, and that he was making decisions he wouldn't have made if he had been a well man. When he testified, just before going into the hospital, he wasn't telling the whole story. I think his judgment was impaired, and that he had been doing things for a long time that nobody knew about.

Both Ronnie and I tried to get through to Sophia Casey to offer our sympathy. I reached Sophia once, but they were not taking calls—even from old friends like Charles and Mary Jane Wick. (Ronnie and I were not old friends of the Caseys, although it was said in the media that we were.) Sophia sounded optimistic on the phone, but knowing a little about neurosurgery, I had some idea of how serious this really was.

With Casey in the hospital, the CIA was left without a director. It seemed to me that this especially sensitive position ought to be filled as quickly as possible, especially during a government crisis. But Don, who had originally joined the administration at Casey's suggestion, thought it was cruel of me to want Casey fired before Christmas. That wasn't my intention, but I did feel that something had to be done.

I felt at the time that Don was more interested in protecting Bill Casey than in protecting Ronnie and the country, and in one of our phone calls I told him so.

Poor Bill Casey lingered in the hospital for months before he finally died, in May 1987. Whatever he knew about Iran-contra, he took with him to the grave.

Ronnie and I went to Casey's funeral on Long Island, which was a bizarre experience. I sat between Ronnie and Richard Nixon, and while we were waiting for the service to start—Casey's family and the bishop were half an hour late—Nixon mentioned that Eisenhower had hated going to funerals, so he, Nixon, attended quite a few. Eisenhower made an exception for John Foster Dulles, but that was about it.

The bishop was supposed to be an old friend of the family, so when he started to speak, I thought it would be about Bill Casey, the man. But instead he started talking about his disagreements with Casey over the contras. I couldn't believe what I was hearing. Jeane Kirkpatrick was supposed to give the eulogy, and all during the bishop's talk she had her notepad out, jotting down points she wanted to make.

She was marvelous. When she finished, the whole congregation applauded, even the priest. This was the first time I had ever heard applause in a church—and it seemed especially surprising at a funeral—but the congregation was obviously offended by what the bishop had done. Vernon Walters was so angry that he wrote the bishop a scorching letter with a copy to the Vatican.

In December, after Don Regan and I fought about Casey, our relationship went from bad to worse. Christmas, even in Washington, is normally a respite from politics and feuds, but that certainly wasn't true in 1986. Early in the Christmas season, a story had come out that Ronnie and I had fought about Don Regan, and that Ronnie had supposedly said to me, "Get off my goddamned back."

Now there *was* some tension between us over Donald Regan, but Ronnie and I just don't talk to each other that way.

But once a story gets into circulation, as I've said before in this book, it has a life of its own. Shortly after this report came out, I took the press through the White House to see the Christmas decorations. In the middle of our tour, Sam Donaldson called out, "Did you and your husband have a fight, and did he tell you to get off his back?"

"No," I said.

"Don't you ever fight?" he asked.

"We have disagreements, like everyone, but not what you're talking about," I replied.

Then Chris Wallace asked, "Do you think Don Regan should be fired?"

That was too much.

"Come on," I replied. "It's Christmas!"

That ended it—temporarily.

That same week, Ronnie and I attended the annual production of "Christmas in Washington." When it was over, and we came up on stage, a woman from the Shiloh Baptist Choir kissed me and said, "You hang in there. You'll be all right."

That meant a lot to me. But then, when I looked out into the audience, the first person I saw was Ben Bradlee, the editor of the *Washington Post.* My heart sank. This was the man who had recently called the Iran-contra affair "the most fun I've had since Watergate."

What a terrible thing to say! *Fun?* I'll never understand that remark. I had met Bradlee before and he seemed perfectly nice. But he was married to Sally Quinn, who had written a very negative article about me for the *Washington Post.* And I often wondered whether he resented my friendship with Kay Graham.

Early in January 1987, Ronnie went into the hospital for a prostate operation. After the surgery, Don and I fought (again) over Ronnie's recuperation period. Don was determined to schedule a press conference on Iran-contra. Ronnie was leaning against it because there was still too much we just didn't know. I was opposed to it on medical grounds, and so were the doctors. We all knew men who had undergone this particular operation and had tried to recover too soon, only to end up back in the hospital with a relapse.

The standard six-week recuperation period after an operation applies to *any* kind of major surgery. And this was a man in his late seventies, who had already been shot, who had undergone a cancer operation, and who was now under enormous political pressure.

A speech is hard enough, but the demands of getting ready for a press conference are massive. The doctors hadn't even wanted

Ronnie to deliver the State of the Union Address three weeks after his operation, but Ronnie was so determined to give that speech that he overruled everybody. Believe me, there were some nervous people in the audience that night, including the doctors and (you bet!) me.

In February, Don Regan announced that Ronnie would hold a press conference at the end of the month. I was furious, and on February 8 we had a heated argument about it on the telephone. When it was clear that I wasn't going to change his mind, I said, "Okay, have your damn press conference!"

"You bet I will!" he said. Whereupon Don Regan hung up on me.

He had hung up on me once before, after a similar argument following Ronnie's cancer surgery, but I hadn't mentioned it to Ronnie. It's quite a feeling. You're standing there holding a dead phone in your hand, and there's absolutely nothing you can do. It's infuriating. You want to shake the phone and say, "Talk to me!"

After several days, Don called me and said, "My wife said I shouldn't have hung up on you."

I said, "That's right, you shouldn't have. Don, don't ever do that to me again."

What I felt like saying was "Do you need your wife to tell you that you shouldn't hang up on people?"

That's when I finally told Ronnie.

Meanwhile, there were further developments on the Iran-contra front. On February 9, I was en route to a speaking engagement in Los Angeles when I heard that Bud McFarlane was in the hospital from an overdose of Valium. When I called Ronnie from the hotel, he told me that Bud had tried to commit suicide. The poor man was supposed to talk to the Tower Commission the following day.

Then, when I returned to Washington, Ronnie told me that the Tower Commission had decided to delay its report until February 26 because of new evidence about Oliver North. Among other things, North had said he spent several weekends with us at Camp David. But he was never at Camp David. He said he sometimes spent time alone with Ronnie in the Oval Office. But that never happened. And he apparently told the Iranians that President Reagan wanted them to win their war with Iraq. But Ronnie never said that. His position was always the same: No winner and no loser.

The Don Regan problem finally came to a head during the second half of February. Here again, I am quoting from my diary:

February 13: Today, at Camp David, I talked with Ronnie about Don Regan. For the first time I think he listened. I told him again how disappointed I was in the whole situation, and how morale had sunk very low in the office.

In bed that night, we talked a little more. Ronnie didn't know about Don's conversation with Mermie, so I'm going to have to tell him. He should know these things.

[When Maureen gave Don her views on how the administration could win the congressional vote on the contras, Don had exploded at her. "Goddamn it!" he said. "Who do you think you are? You've been trying to run the West Wing for too long, and you're a pain in the ass."]

February 16: Mermie talked to Ronnie and told him about her conversation with Don Regan. I think Ronnie finally understands that he has a real problem, and that something has to be done about it.

February 17: It broke tonight on the news that Don and I are not speaking because I want him to leave. It's true that we're not speaking, and it's true that I want him to leave. But that's not the reason we're not speaking.

February 18: Press asking lots of questions about Iran, and about Don and me. Today, for the first time, Ronnie left the door open on whether Don would go. When reporters asked him if Don would be staying on, Ronnie said, "Well, that's up to him. I have always said that when the people I've asked to come into government feel that they have to return to private life, that's their business and I will never try to talk them out of it."

That's a pretty broad hint, but I don't think Don will take it.

Ronnie and I had another conversation about the Don Regan situation. Even Rex [Scouten] came to see me about it. He can't work with him, either. Nobody can work with him, but everybody is afraid to tell Ronnie.

The Tower report comes in on the 26th and Don wants Ronnie to go on television on the 27th to make a speech. Ye gods! You can't prepare a good speech in twenty-four hours. Any fool would know that.

John Herrington [secretary of Energy] came to see Ronnie about Don, and I left them alone. Somehow Ronnie seems calmer about it, almost as though he has made a decision.

February 20: Before he left this morning, I asked Ronnie if this was going to continue much longer, and he said No. I hope that means what I think it means.

Richard Nixon called to say that if Ronnie wanted him to talk to Don about resigning, he would.

It came out on the news last night that Don had hung up on me, and that's why we haven't been speaking. Everyone wants him out.

People are being very sweet to me, but I feel like I'm going through a nightmare—a long, unending nightmare. And I can't even see any light at the end of the tunnel. I'm beginning to wonder if this is going to last until the end of Ronnie's presidency. God, I hope not.

My feud with Don was reported today as a front-page story in the *New York Times.* The article began: "Two of President Reagan's closest advisers, Nancy Reagan and Donald T. Regan, have apparently reached the point where they cannot stand each other."

Left for Camp David. Mike Wallace called, and I told him to please tell Chris [Wallace, his son] that I did *not* leak the story to the press about Don's hanging up on me. [On the *NBC Nightly News,* Chris Wallace had quoted "a source very close to Mrs. Reagan" to the effect that I had purposely leaked this story as a way of forcing Don to resign.] Mike called Chris and told him. Chris told Mike that he'd heard it from two sources, and he couldn't believe

I hadn't told these people, hoping they would tell the press. I told Mike that I don't work that way, which Mike already knew.

February 21: [At Camp David] Ronnie and I took a walk after lunch. Lots of calls, all regarding Don Regan. Ronnie is eager to go ahead with his speech on the 27th. I can understand his wanting to get out there after so long a period of not being able to say anything, but how can you prepare a good speech in twenty-four hours?

ABC announced tonight that Regan had ordered a cover-up on Ronnie's participation in the Iran affair. Boy! This is a rough town, and you have to be very strong to survive.

February 22: This is going to be an eventful week. I just hope that the Don thing will be settled tomorrow, and that Ronnie stands firm. We are coming to a climax.

I'm not looking forward to the [annual White House] governors' dinner tonight because the press will be swarming all over us. I almost wish Cuomo were going to be there to take some of the attention away. [At the time, there was a lot of speculation as to whether Mario Cuomo was going to run for president in 1988.]

February 23: Before the dinner, I couldn't believe it when I saw Don Regan coming down the receiving line. I think it showed arrogance, and I wouldn't have done that in his place. There are so many people at these dinners that many of the staff don't even bother with the receiving line because they want to save your hand.

During the dinner I sat next to the governor of Arkansas, a Democrat, very nice and likable. Sarah Vaughan entertained and for a few minutes I could forget. She said, "I know Mrs. Reagan likes Gershwin, so I'm going to sing some." And no one can sing it the way she does.

Lots of press. Ronnie refused to answer questions, saying he would have no comment until after the Tower report comes out.

Lots of phone calls regarding Don Regan. Sam Donaldson said I was masterminding his departure. I suspect that Don's people have been very busy talking to the press.

Ronnie told Mermie last night that he would be taking care of the Regan problem today. He told me this morning, and I haven't been able to think of anything else all day.

February 24: At the lunch for the governors' wives, Jack Courtemanche told me he was there when the Koehler nomination came up. [John Koehler was Ronnie's choice to replace Pat Buchanan as director of communications, until it came out that Koehler, who grew up in Germany, had briefly belonged to the Hitler Youth when he was ten years old.]

"I had nothing to do with that," Don said. "Blame it on the East Wing." [In other words, on Nancy Reagan.]

Jack said, "Don, are you sure that's the way you want this story to go out?"

And Don said, "You're goddamned right. That's the way I want it to go out, and that's the way it *will* go out."

That was uncalled for—and mean.

[Don said he preferred Stu Spencer for the job. Stu would have been a great choice, but knowing how he felt about Don, I knew he would never take the job. And Stu had always said that he would never live in Washington, although he'd be happy to come back and help us from time to time.]

All the press turned out for the lunch—Donaldson, Wallace, Plante, Thomas. Hardly a typical luncheon coverage.

After lunch, I came upstairs for a meeting with Ross Perot, who told me such amazing things that I couldn't believe them. [Perot was convinced that American MIAs were still in Vietnam, and he wanted to organize a rescue mission.] He had given the materials to Don, but they never reached Ronnie. I said he would have to tell Ronnie, so he's coming back tomorrow.

Ronnie came home at five. The deed is done, and Don is leaving next week. I can't believe it—and I won't, until it really happens.

[But it did happen. Ronnie pressed him, and Don agreed to leave the following week, on Monday, March 2. In fact, Don had written out a letter of resignation a few weeks earlier. He told Ronnie that he felt burned out, and wanted to spend some time in Florida. But he didn't want to leave until the Tower Commission's report came out because he thought if he left earlier, it would make him look guilty. And no matter what effect he was having on the presidency, Don Regan wanted to be vindicated. He was invariably more concerned with his own reputation than with Ronnie's.]

February 26: The Tower report came out today. I was on my way to a local elementary school to see a skit about drugs, and fifty members of the press showed up, as well as live TV. Of course it was because they were so interested in drugs!

On the way back in the car, I heard the last part of the press conference. Tower was asked about Ronnie's managerial style, and he replied, "Everyone has their own style, and this one had worked well for him for six years. What happened was an aberration. It is up to the staff to adapt to the president's style. They clearly let him down."

The report criticized Ronnie, but also came down heavily on Poindexter and North, as well as Shultz and Weinberger. The report blamed Don for the "chaos" and said: "More than almost any Chief of Staff in recent memory, he asserted control over the White House staff and sought to extend this control to the National Security Adviser. He was personally active in national security affairs, and attended almost all the relevant meetings regarding the Iran initiative. He, as much as anyone, should have insisted that an orderly process be observed."

Now we had to find a replacement for Don. Ronnie's first choice was Drew Lewis, the former secretary of Transportation and the president of Union Pacific. Lewis was not available, but he suggested our old friend Paul Laxalt.

A day or two later, Paul came to tell Ronnie that he knew his name had been mentioned for chief of staff, but that he was seriously considering running for president. He offered to help in any way he could, and he recommended Howard Baker.

Ronnie liked that idea. Although he and Howard did not always agree on the issues, they had worked together very effectively when Howard was majority leader during Ronnie's first term.

I myself thought Howard Baker was a wonderful choice. He was calm, easygoing, congenial, and self-effacing. He was politically astute. He had credibility with the media. And after serving three terms in the Senate, he had many friends on Capitol Hill. Howard was a complete change from what we had, and he gave us a chance to restore some morale to the office.

And because of his role in the Watergate hearings, Howard's arrival at the White House was seen as a major signal of confidence in the integrity of Ronnie's administration. Howard, after all, was the same senator who, back in 1974, had put principle ahead of party by asking that famous question: "What did the president know, and when did he know it?"

On February 26, Ronnie called Howard to see if he would take the job. Howard was on vacation in Florida, and Joy, his wife, told Ronnie that her husband had taken their grandchildren to the zoo.

"Terrific," Ronnie replied. "Wait until he sees the zoo I have in mind!"

Although Ronnie and Don had agreed that Don's departure wasn't supposed to be announced until Monday, March 2, when Howard Baker was scheduled to take over, somebody leaked it to CNN on Friday. Don heard about it from Frank Carlucci, and he immediately sent a curt letter of resignation to Ronnie. "Dear Mr. President," he wrote. "I hereby resign as Chief of Staff to the President of the United States."

CNN called Elaine, asking for a comment from me. I made an innocuous statement, telling her to say that I wished Don good luck and that I welcomed Howard Baker. Then CNN announced that I had given out a statement before Ronnie did! Elaine was furious that they had used her, and I sent Don a note explaining that they had twisted my remark to make it seem that I was trying to push him out. I gather that Don still believes that I leaked the news to the press. I did not. And I never received an answer to my note.

Despite everything that had happened between us, I was sorry that Don Regan left the White House in such a disagreeable way. But the relief was palpable, and the change from Don to Howard was applauded by both Democrats and Republicans. Morale soared in the White House, and people felt as if a great weight had been removed. A lot of calls came in supporting the move, including one from Margaret Thatcher. I even had calls from Democrats, and from members of the press, thanking me.

That night, for the first time in weeks, I slept well.

But while Don Regan was gone, the debate and the attention over his departure wouldn't go away. That same weekend, I addressed the American Camping Association, which was meeting in Washington. In my remarks, I said how much I loved my days at Camp Kechuwa in Michigami, Michigan, in spite of the fact that there were leeches in the lake. But we were taught how to get rid of leeches—you poured salt on them, and they fell off.

The next morning I read in the paper that my remark about leeches was obviously a reference to Don Regan. Believe me, that was the furthest thing from my mind. I was talking about how much I loved camp. Again, I wrote a note to Don. Again, no answer. Yes, we were feuding, but this was a question of courtesy. I also didn't hear from Don a few months later, during my cancer surgery, or when my mother died a few days after I left the hospital.

On Monday, March 2, William Safire wrote a scathing and cruel piece about me in the *New York Times*. By 1987 I had been attacked in the press many, many times, but Safire's article was unbelievable. FIRST LADY STAGES A COUP, read the headline. "At a time he most needs to appear strong," Safire began, "President Reagan is being weakened and made to appear wimpish and helpless by the political interference of his wife." Later in the article, Safire referred to my "extraordinary vindictiveness," called me "the power-hungry First Lady," and "an incipient Edith Wilson, unelected and unaccountable, presuming to control the actions and appointments of the executive branch."

This was the most vicious and unbelievable article about me I had ever read—and I had read quite a few. Ronnie was also upset by the column; he felt it was a terrible thing for a man to do to another man's wife.

Safire's column was so one-sided that two days later, the lead editorial in the *Times* took exception to what he had written. Although the editorial didn't mention Safire by name, it argued that "It's unrealistic and unreasonable . . . to suggest that the First Lady should not advise her husband. Spousal advice is part of any marital relationship—and so is the right of the partner to ignore that advice."

The editorial concluded by asking, "What advice is right for a First Lady—or anyone else—to give? Any advice a President wants."

Safire had gone so far that even Judy Mann, a columnist in the *Washington Post* and normally a critic of mine, was moved to defend me. Describing Safire's article as "vicious, below-the-belt commentary," she wrote:

> First Lady Nancy Reagan managed to do what nobody else was able to do—namely, rid the administration of someone who was literally crippling the presidency. White House Chief of Staff Donald Regan hung on and on in an unprecedented display of supreme arrogance, placing his own self-interest above that of President Reagan and, certainly, above the welfare of the country. Calls, pleas, messages through the media, and personal visits from Republican leaders could not move the president to replace him.
>
> The gentlemen who could exercise the greatest influence on the president couldn't do the job. Mrs. Reagan did the dirty work for them, and now they are out to get her.
>
> The Republican and conservative power brokers ought to be sending her bouquets of long-stemmed red roses. Instead, she's being depicted as a power-hungry dragon lady. . . .
>
> The President didn't look like a wimp. He had a wife who understood what had to be done and was willing to do the dirty work. That makes him a pretty lucky man.

But the criticism continued. A few days later, I watched the Saturday talk shows—*Agronsky & Company* and *The McLaughlin Group*—at Camp David, and they really tore me apart. She's a dragon lady, they said. She was entitled to her opinions about Don Regan, they said, but she shouldn't have made them public.

But I *didn't* make them public. I didn't speak to a single reporter about Don Regan. I spoke to Ronnie a number of times, but never to the press.

On March 20, Phil Donahue did a show about me, with Evans and Novak, the columnist William Raspberry, and a writer from Boston who seemed to hate both Ronnie and me. It was not pleasant. There was Phil, the great feminist, talking about the first lady and not even inviting a woman onto the panel.

But not all the reaction was negative. At a dinner for newly elected members of Congress, Barbara Mikulski, a Democratic senator from Maryland and a strong liberal, came up to thank me and to say that I had done what needed to be done with regard to Don Regan. A number of others said the same thing, which made me feel better, particularly after the Safire column.

On March 5, the day after Ronnie's speech on the Tower report, Ken Bode was on the *Today* show to discuss the speech with David Broder and Jack Kilpatrick. "I'd like to say something about Mrs. Reagan," said Bode. "I think she's getting a bum rap. Let's face it: what happened with Donald Regan was what everybody wanted to happen, and I think the people of the United States should give her their gratitude."

I almost fell off the bed! Sometimes help comes from the press when you least expect it.

The comments and the controversy continued for weeks. When Vic Damone came to the White House to rehearse an "In Performance" show on Rodgers and Hart, he took me aside and said, "I don't know how you feel about Lee Iacocca, but he was my house guest and when I told him I was coming here, he said, 'Tell the president that any time he wants me to come, I'll come. But I'll be damned if I was going to set foot in that place while that son of a bitch Regan was there.' "

It was that widespread.

17

❖❖❖

The Russians

ANYONE who followed Ronnie's summit meetings with Mikhail Gorbachev might have concluded that there were two sets of issues: relations between the two superpowers, and relations between the two wives. Every nuance of my encounters with Raisa Gorbachev was scrutinized. Every meeting between us was treated like a test of wills. Every time we appeared together, we were seen as contestants in some international pageant. When you think about it, the whole business was ridiculous.

Did it really matter what dress each wife was wearing, or what kind of earrings? Did it make any real difference whether Raisa and I became close friends? Obviously not. Only one thing matters in a summit: what the two leaders decide, and how well *they* get along.

Fortunately, Ronnie and Gorbachev got along remarkably well. As for the wives—well, Raisa and I did have some rough moments. We were thrust together although we had little in common, and had completely different outlooks on the world. Once it became clear that we weren't getting along, the media's curiosity only increased.

Ronnie hadn't intended to wait almost five years before he started meeting with his Soviet counterpart. But the Soviet leaders kept dying—Brezhnev, Andropov, Chernenko—until we began to wonder if anyone was going to stay around long enough so we could get something constructive started.

With the world so dangerous, I felt it was ridiculous for these two heavily armed superpowers to be sitting there and not talking to each other. I encouraged Ronnie to meet with Gorbachev as soon as possible, especially when I realized that some people in the administration did not favor any real talks. So yes, I did push Ronnie a little. But he would never have met Gorbachev if he hadn't wanted to.

In all, they met four times: Geneva in 1985, Reykjavik in 1986, Washington in 1987, and Moscow in 1988. I was with Ronnie for three of them, and each time, Raisa and I became a major story. In part, this was because the negotiations were closed to the press, which left thousands of reporters with very little to write about. So we were the best they could do. The truth is that Raisa and I were only a minor footnote to great events. But she did play a big role in my experience of the summits, and I guess I'm one of the ranking experts on the Russian first lady.

The first time we met was in Geneva, when I invited her to tea at the house where we were staying. I was surprised by her appearance: She was shorter than I expected, and her hair was more reddish than it appeared on television. (It became less red over the years.) But other than the pictures I had seen, I knew almost nothing about her.

That in itself was unusual. Normally, whenever I met my counterpart from another country, I prepared by reading about her. But Mikhail Gorbachev had suddenly come to power in 1985, and Raisa was a mystery. She had never given an interview. Nobody knew her age. It was thought that she had a daughter and two grandchildren, but nobody seemed sure. Practically the only thing that was known about her was that she had taught school, and had lectured on Marxist philosophy at Moscow State University.

As I tried to learn a little about Raisa Gorbachev, I wondered what would happen if she wanted to learn something about me. I imagined a huge truck pulling up in front of the Gorbachevs' apartment in Moscow, with stacks of books, articles, profiles, interviews. It would take her weeks to plough through it all.

That's one of the basic differences between our societies, and why communication between us was never easy. There isn't even a Russian word for "first lady." Until Gorbachev came to power, the wives of Soviet leaders were virtually unknown, both at home and abroad. Almost nobody knew that Yuri Andropov even had a wife until she appeared at his funeral.

I have already said that I was unprepared for life in the White House, but at least I had some experience with fame and flashbulbs. Raisa, however, made the leap from obscurity to international prominence overnight. But while she was becoming an object of great interest in the West, she was still unknown at home. Until the Geneva summit, I don't believe her name had ever been mentioned on Soviet television.

If I was nervous about my first meeting with Raisa Gorbachev— and I was—she was probably even more nervous about meeting me. I didn't know what I would talk about with her, but I soon discovered that I needn't have worried. From the moment we met, she talked and talked and *talked*—so much that I could barely get a word in, edgewise or otherwise. Perhaps it was insecurity on her part, but during about a dozen encounters in three different countries, my fundamental impression of Raisa Gorbachev was that she never stopped talking.

Or lecturing, to be more accurate. Sometimes the subject was the Soviet Union and the glories of the Communist system. Sometimes it was Soviet art. More often than not, it was Marxism and Leninism. Once or twice, she even lectured me on the failings of the American political system.

I wasn't prepared for this, and I didn't like it. I had assumed we would talk about personal matters: our husbands, our children, being in the limelight, or perhaps our hopes for the future. I was prepared to tell Raisa about our drug program, because the first ladies of many other countries had found it relevant to their own societies. But when I brought it up, she promptly dismissed the subject by assuring me that there was no drug problem in the Soviet Union. Oh, really?

When she came to tea in Geneva that first day, she struck me as a woman who expected to be deferred to. When she didn't like the chair she was seated in, she snapped her fingers to summon her

KGB guards, who promptly moved her to another chair. After sitting in the new spot for a couple of minutes, she decided she didn't like that one either, so she snapped her fingers and they moved her again.

I couldn't believe it. I had met first ladies, princesses, and queens, but I had never seen anybody act this way. I'm still not sure whether she wanted to make a point with me or was just trying out her new position. Or perhaps she was nervous or uncomfortable. Whatever the reason, nothing like this ever happened again.

That first tea in Geneva lasted slightly more than an hour. I offered Raisa a choice of coffee or decaffeinated almond tea, my personal favorite. She chose the tea and seemed to enjoy it. We sat in the drawing room in the late afternoon. There was a fire in the fireplace, but the conversation was dry, impersonal, and tedious. She was lecturing me about Communism, and I couldn't wait for her to stop.

The following day she invited me for tea at the Soviet mission to the U.N. She was dressed severely—in a black skirt, a white blouse, and a black tie. At the time I wondered about that outfit, which was so unlike anything she had worn before, and which didn't seem to be her style. Later I learned that this was the standard uniform for teachers in the Soviet Union, and that Raisa was wearing this outfit, which made her look like a prison matron, because they were taking the only photograph of her at the Geneva summit that would be shown back home.

For all my difficulties with Raisa, I knew she was under pressures that I couldn't even imagine, and I didn't envy her. When the Gorbachevs landed in Geneva, for example, I noticed that they got off the plane together. But when they returned to Moscow, he got off in front, without her, and she left discreetly through the rear exit. It would have driven me crazy to have to act one way at home and completely different abroad.

Still, her conversational style made me bristle. When I came to tea at the Soviet mission, the hall was decorated with children's paintings, and Raisa insisted that I look at each one while she described the meaning behind it. I felt condescended to, and I wanted to say, "Enough. You don't have to tell me what a missile is. I get the message!"

Tea was served at a long table. "Welcome," she said. "I wanted you to see what a typical Russian tea looks like." On the table was a lovely antique samovar, and next to it was a mouth-watering array of delicacies: blinis with caviar, cabbage rolls, blueberry pie, cookies, chocolates, honey and jam. I couldn't possibly try everything, and I finally had to give up. It was a beautiful spread, but if that was an ordinary housewife's tea, then I'm Catherine the Great.

The day before the summit began, Ronnie and I had a tour of Fleur d'Eau, the twenty-room nineteenth-century château overlooking Lake Leman, where the talks were going to take place. When we walked into the meeting room, Ronnie sat down in his chair, and I impulsively sat in Gorbachev's. Ronnie looked over at me and smiled. "My, Mr. General Secretary," he said. "You're much prettier than I expected."

About a hundred yards from the château was a beach house on the lake. Inside, we found a beautiful room with a fireplace, and a breathtaking view of the water. Ronnie was eager to meet with Gorbachev privately, without their advisers, and as soon as we walked into this room we knew it was the perfect spot. Here, by the warmth of the fire, they could take a few minutes to begin to know each other as human beings. There were people on our side—and presumably on the other side, too—who didn't think a private meeting was such a great idea, but I strongly encouraged Ronnie to follow his instincts. We both felt that it was important for these two men to begin building a personal relationship, and that this was far more likely to occur if they had a few minutes alone with just their translators.

The following afternoon, as planned, Ronnie suggested that he and Gorbachev take a break from the larger meeting on arms control and walk over to the beach house. Gorbachev was out of his seat before Ronnie had finished his sentence.

Their tête-à-tête in front of the fire had been scheduled to last fifteen minutes. After twenty-five minutes had gone by, Don Regan came up to Jim Kuhn, Ronnie's personal assistant, and asked him to break up the meeting because it was running over schedule.

I can't do that, Jim thought. The two most powerful men in the world are meeting together for the first time. *History* is being made here!

Ten minutes later, Regan said to Jim, "Haven't you broken up that meeting yet?"

Jim still didn't think it was a good idea, so he raised the question with Bud McFarlane, the national security adviser, who suggested he ask George Shultz.

So Jim went into the room where Shultz was meeting with Eduard Shevardnadze, his Soviet counterpart. "Mr. Secretary," he said, "here's the situation. The president's private meeting with Mr. Gorbachev was scheduled for fifteen minutes, and they've been together almost forty. Don thinks I should go in and break it up. Bud said I should check with you. What do you think?"

George was shocked by the question: "If you're stupid enough to go in and break up that meeting," he said, "then you don't deserve the job you have!"

The meeting between Ronnie and Gorbachev ran for an hour and twenty minutes. As they finished up, Ronnie invited Gorbachev to visit Washington. Gorbachev immediately agreed—provided that the summit after *that* would be in Moscow. When the two leaders returned to the meeting and reported that they had just made plans for two additional summits, their advisers just about fainted.

While the Gorbachevs stayed at the Soviet mission, Ronnie and I were at Maison de Saussure, a charming eighteenth-century château on Lake Geneva, which was the home of Prince Karim, Aga Khan, and his wife, the Begum Salina. The prince and his wife are friends of ours, and when they heard we were coming for the summit, they offered to move out and lend us their house for a few days. When we arrived, I found that Sally, who is a most thoughtful hostess, had emptied all of her drawers and closets, and had even restocked the bathroom cabinet.

On the first night of the summit, the Gorbachevs had us to dinner at the Soviet mission, which was the coldest, barest, and most impersonal building I had ever seen. We began with fruit juice instead of cocktails, because Gorbachev was cutting down on the consumption of vodka in the Soviet Union. We all sat at one long table, with the overhead light turned up full force. It wasn't exactly what I would call cozy. It was also my first taste of Russian food, which I didn't find very tasty.

The following night, the Gorbachevs came to dinner at Maison de Saussure. In addition to the four of us, there were eight other guests: George Shultz, Donald Regan, Bud McFarlane, and Arthur Hartman (our ambassador to Moscow) from our side, as well as Foreign Minister Eduard Shevardnadze, Ambassador Dobrynin, and two of Gorbachev's advisers. The house looked wonderful with the fireplaces lit and plenty of flowers all around, and I couldn't help but wonder if the Gorbachevs were aware of the difference.

Dinner, which was prepared by the house chef, consisted of soufflé of lobster, suprême of chicken Périgourdin, endive salad, mousse de fromage with avocado, and, for dessert, hot lemon soufflé with raspberry sauce. As always, we served California wines.

The previous night, when I met Gorbachev for the first time, I felt a certain coldness from him. At our dinner, however, he warmed up considerably. From then on, the more I saw him, the more I liked him. Whereas Raisa tends to be serious, almost solemn, and takes the lead even at the dinner table, her husband has a fine sense of humor and is not very formal. That night, he told me a little about where he had gone to school, and how he'd met Raisa, and how they didn't have much money when they got married.

He also asked Ronnie a number of questions about Hollywood and seemed genuinely interested in hearing about the great film studios of the 1940s. And he was particularly happy when the soufflé was served for dessert. "Oh, this is good," he said. "I *like* this. What do you call it?" He had, it seemed, never tasted a soufflé!

Even in Geneva, when Ronnie and Gorbachev were just starting to know each other, I noticed an unmistakable warmth between them. By the time the Gorbachevs came for dinner, the two men had already met for a second private talk. I knew they must have been getting along when Ronnie mentioned that he had told Gorbachev a joke he'd heard about *glasnost*. An old Russian woman comes to the Kremlin and demands to see the general secretary. When she reaches Gorbachev's office, she says, "We must have a more open society. Why, in America, anyone can go to the White House and walk up to President Reagan and say, 'I don't like the way you're running the country.' "

"My dear lady," replies Gorbachev. "You can do the very same thing right here in the Soviet Union. Anytime you like, you can come into my office and tell me that you don't like the way President Reagan is running his country!"

Most people might have been careful about telling such a joke to Gorbachev unless they knew him awfully well, but Ronnie uses humor whenever he can. It must have worked, because Gorbachev responded with a hearty laugh.

Our dinner was supposed to have been a largely social affair following the final meetings between the two sides. But apparently the talks had not gone as well as we had hoped. Our negotiators felt that the Soviets had gone back on promises they had already made, and George Shultz was furious. Dinner was pleasant enough, but when we adjourned to the library for coffee, George told Gorbachev how angry he was. Pointing to Georgi Korniyenko, the Soviet first deputy foreign minister, he said, "Mr. General Secretary, you and the president have agreed on several important points. But the reason we don't have an agreement yet is because *this* man is holding up progress."

Suddenly the entire room fell quiet. Raisa had been talking to me, but she immediately turned around to see what was going on. Gorbachev seemed very concerned about what George said, and in the end, the two negotiating teams stayed up all night to produce an agreement to continue talking and to speed up progress on arms control.

Ronnie's main objective for the Geneva summit had already been met: Above all, he had wanted to establish a personal working relationship with Gorbachev. Everything else would follow from that.

. . .

A year later, Ronnie and Gorbachev met in Reykjavik, Iceland. The idea for the meeting came from Foreign Minister Shevardnadze, who was in Washington for talks with George Shultz. He delivered a letter to Ronnie from Gorbachev, who wanted to meet with Ronnie as soon as possible to speed up talks on the intermediate-range nuclear missiles in Europe. This would be not a summit, but a preparatory meeting to set the stage for the real summit, which we'd already agreed would be held in Washington.

But at the time Ronnie was furious at the arrest of Nicholas Daniloff, the Moscow correspondent for *U.S. News & World Report*, who had been accused of spying. Without even opening the letter from Gorbachev, he really lit into Shevardnadze. (I wasn't there, but George Shultz, who was, told me later that he had never seen Ronnie so angry for so long.) *"Daniloff is not a spy,"* he said, *"and there won't be any meeting until he's free."*

Ten days later, as soon as Daniloff was released, a meeting between Ronnie and Gorbachev was scheduled for October 11 and 12 in Iceland. From the outset, this was a business meeting, and wives were not invited. But then, just a few days before it began, it was announced that Raisa would be coming. This put me in an awkward position: Should I go simply because she was going? No, I decided. Raisa's last-minute reversal struck me as a bit of one-upsmanship. I had a full schedule in Washington, as I'm sure she knew, and I didn't want to change it.

Besides, I thought it was important, as my son Ron put it, not to be jerked around. I felt that Raisa was testing me, to see if I would cave in and change my mind. But she had to know that schedules are made out long in advance, and I was determined not to give in. This was supposed to be a meeting, not a formal summit, and as far as I was concerned, that's the way it would stay.

Still, it felt strange to be among those saying goodbye to Ronnie on the White House lawn as he boarded the helicopter for Andrews Air Force Base. I hated to see him go off without me.

I followed the Iceland "summit" on television and saw more of Raisa than of Ronnie or Gorbachev. I saw her at a swimming pool with children—the first time I had seen her do anything with children. I also saw her at a school, where she handed out pins of

Lenin—which I thought was a bit much. Then, when an interviewer asked her why I wasn't there, she said, "Perhaps she has something else to do. Or maybe she is not feeling well." Oh, please!

The following afternoon, Ronnie and Gorbachev had their final meeting. I was watching on television, and when the two leaders came outside, I knew from Ronnie's expression that something had gone wrong. He looked angry, *very* angry. His face was pale and his teeth were clenched. I had seen that look before, but not often— and certainly not on television. You really have to push Ronnie very far to get that expression.

Gorbachev and Ronnie had made great progress in their talks. By the end of the meetings, they were on the verge of a historic agreement providing for the elimination of all strategic nuclear weapons by 1996. But there was a catch: Gorbachev suddenly insisted on a ten-year ban on the development and testing, outside the laboratory, of our Strategic Defense Initiative (commonly known as Star Wars).

Ronnie was enraged, because there had been no mention of this condition during the meetings. Gorbachev knew full well that Ronnie was irrevocably committed to SDI research as an insurance policy for our national security. Ronnie was perfectly willing to share our research with the Soviets, but he refused to abandon SDI, or to tie his own hands and the hands of future American presidents.

Later, Ronnie told me that when the session ended, Gorbachev said, "I don't know what more I could have done."

"I do," Ronnie replied. "You could have said yes."

That evening, Ronnie sent word from *Air Force One* that the plane would not be landing until eleven at night, and that I shouldn't bother coming out to Andrews to meet him. Fat chance! I couldn't wait to get there.

We didn't get to bed until very late that night, because Ronnie wanted to tell me everything, just as Gorbachev, presumably, had told Raisa. As I listened to his account of the meetings, I was furious at the Russians for not negotiating in good faith. I was also angry that Raisa had been there; her presence seemed frivolous, as mine would have been.

But I was proud of Ronnie for having the strength to reject a bad proposal. He would have received a great deal of praise for reaching a dramatic agreement with Gorbachev, and as I expected, he took a lot of heat for not signing it.

I now believe that Gorbachev was testing Ronnie at Reykjavik. By standing up to him, Ronnie paved the way for future summits and further progress toward peace. I think Gorbachev learned a lot about Ronnie at that meeting.

The Washington summit finally took place in December 1987. Raisa and I hadn't seen each other in two years, but nothing much had changed. Following the traditional arrival ceremony at the White House, the men went off for meetings in the West Wing while I entertained Raisa, Barbara Bush, Mrs. John F. Matlock (whose husband was our ambassador to Moscow), Mrs. Yuri Dubinin (whose husband was the Soviet ambassador to the United States), Obie (Mrs. George) Shultz, the translators, and one or two others for coffee in the Green Room—which is the normal procedure for state visits.

I had a fairly good idea of what to expect, but my guests were taken completely aback when Raisa proceeded to lecture us for the entire hour about the history of Russia, its political system, and how there were no homeless people in the Soviet Union. (When I mentioned that last item to Ronnie, he said, "Sure. If anybody over there is homeless, they throw him in a labor camp!")

Later, one of the guests came up to me and said, "That was the rudest thing I've ever seen." The others just shook their heads in amazement. I was glad that other people could see what I had been going through.

Raisa and I saw each other several times that week, but she never once mentioned my recent breast cancer surgery, or asked me how I was feeling. Nor did she offer condolences on the death of my mother. The Soviets know everything, so I can't believe she didn't know what I had gone through only a few weeks earlier. Maybe I was overly sensitive, but I don't think so.

The following day, Raisa returned for a private tour of the White House. It should have been a simple matter, but arranging it had been anything but. Three weeks earlier, after Raisa had told Ambassador Matlock that she was interested in seeing the White House, I had invited her to come on December 9 for tea and a private tour. Two weeks passed, and I still hadn't received a reply, although she had already accepted an invitation from Pamela Harriman, the prominent Democratic fund-raiser, which had been arranged by the Soviet ambassador.

I was offended. In the circle we moved in, you don't ignore an invitation from the head of state or his wife.

Finally, with time running out, I had to insist on an answer. Two days later, I was informed that Raisa *did* want to come, but that she couldn't be there for tea and a tour of the house at three o'clock, as I had suggested. But she could come for coffee at eleven-thirty. I agreed, although this plan would not allow me enough time to show her the residence. I found out later that she intended to join her husband at an afternoon meeting with American publishers and editors at the Soviet embassy.

Because we had only one hour, I was eager to get things moving. But that was difficult because Raisa kept stopping to talk to the press. When I put my hand on her arm, she pulled away. I finally had to say, "If we don't move along, we'll never have time for coffee."

When a reporter asked her whether she would enjoy living in the White House, Raisa replied, "It's an official house. I would say that, humanly speaking, a human being would like to live in a regular house. This is like a museum."

It wasn't a very polite answer, especially from somebody who hadn't even seen the private living quarters!

We ended up keeping Ronnie and Gorbachev waiting for fifteen minutes, but there was nothing I could do about it. When we arrived at the Diplomatic Entrance, our husbands were frowning and looking at their watches. But they didn't mean it; this mock show of impatience had been Ronnie's idea.

For me, the main event of the Washington summit was the state dinner for the Gorbachevs, which was my responsibility. State dinners are always grand occasions, but this one promised to be especially exciting, and everyone was clamoring for an invitation.

The Gorbachevs were understandably tired from their long trip. Because they had specifically requested an early evening, we made several changes in our routine to allow them to leave by ten o'clock, as they had asked. We canceled the private cocktail reception in the Yellow Oval Room. We served coffee at the tables instead of in the Blue Room. We even cut down on the time of the strolling violinists, who always came into the State Dining Room to play three or four numbers during dessert.

We had asked the renowned pianist Van Cliburn to provide the entertainment, and at our request, he held his program down to just a few minutes. Although he hadn't played in public for nine years, he agreed to make an exception for this unique occasion. (Cliburn has had a big following in the Soviet Union since 1958, when he won the Tchaikovsky Piano Competition in Moscow.) He was a great hit with our guests, who sang along with him as he played "Moscow Nights" for an encore.

After making all these changes to ensure an early evening, I was slightly annoyed when the Gorbachevs arrived late for the dinner. But the real holdup came in the receiving line. Maybe it's a cultural difference and she was merely trying to be polite, but Raisa tried to have a real conversation with practically every guest. "What is your name? How many children do you have?" She seemed very well briefed on who many of our guests were, and she obviously wanted them to know this. But the line was moving like molasses, and I thought I would go crazy. The same thing happened the next day at a State Department luncheon, where the receiving line took so long that the meal didn't begin until two-thirty.

Our Soviet guests had informed us in advance that they would not be wearing black tie, although all state dinners are formal affairs. Tuxedos just aren't worn in Soviet society, where they're seen as a symbol of bourgeois capitalism. This situation had come up before, with the Chinese and with President Sadat. The Americans wore black tie, and our guests came in business suits. Raisa wore a black brocade gown.

Dinner consisted of Columbia River salmon with lobster medallions, loin of veal with wild mushrooms, and zucchini boats filled with fresh vegetables. Dessert was honey ice cream with petits fours, and we served a champagne that was made especially for this dinner. The mix of guests was a little unusual, because aside from Raisa, Mrs. Shevardnadze, and Mrs. Dubinin, there were no women in the Soviet party. As a result, we ended up with a number of extra men.

As always, we invited a number of distinguished Americans from various fields. Joe DiMaggio was there, and Meadowlark Lemon, the basketball star, and Mary Lou Retton, the Olympic gymnast. (DiMaggio brought a baseball, and he asked Maureen to help him get both Ronnie and Gorbachev to autograph it. Now *that's* a collector's item!) Saul Bellow represented the world of letters. Other guests at the Gorbachev dinner included Armand Hammer, David Rockefeller, Billy Graham, Pearl Bailey, Jimmy Stewart, and Claudette Colbert.

Following protocol, Raisa sat next to Ronnie at his table, while Gorbachev sat with me. On the other side of Raisa we put Vernon Walters, our ambassador to the United Nations. He speaks Russian, and I knew he'd keep the conversation going. And maybe Ronnie would be spared a lecture!

Next to me I put Richard Perle, the brilliant and controversial assistant secretary of Defense. Richard has very strong views on the Soviet Union, and he isn't shy about expressing them. Gorbachev seems to enjoy a good give-and-take, and he likes it when people challenge him.

The other guests at our table were Richard Cheney (who was then a congressman and who sat next to Gorbachev), Nancy Mehta (the wife of Zubin Mehta), Jim Billington (the Librarian of Congress and a top Soviet scholar), Cynthia Helms (the wife of Richard Helms, the former head of the CIA), and Robert Strauss. (On either side of Gorbachev, and a few inches back from the table, sat the interpreters.) There wasn't much small talk that evening, although Gorbachev did mention that he had never heard the Russian anthem played better than it was by our Marine Corps Band during the arrival ceremony that morning.

Gorbachev had never met Richard Perle, but he certainly knew who he was. Moreover, he had recently seen a dramatic reconstruction of the Reykjavik meeting, which was produced in England by Granada Television. Perle, who is portly, had been played by a rather slim actor. "Oh, yes," teased Gorbachev when I introduced them. "When I saw you on television, you were a lot thinner."

I didn't hear all of their conversation, but at one point Perle asked Gorbachev flat-out: "What percentage of the Soviet GNP goes for defense?"

"That's a secret," replied Gorbachev, "and I won't answer it."

"Are you sure you know?" asked Perle.

"I know *everything,*" Gorbachev replied. "I'm head of the Defense Council, so you're dining with a military man."

"I think you're spending twenty percent, and probably more," said Perle. Gorbachev just looked at him without any expression.

"If you really want to save money," said Perle a little later, "we should arrange a reduction of conventional arms. That's where the real money is spent."

"That's true," said Gorbachev, "and we should do it. But there are other reasons for reducing nuclear weapons."

"Such as?"

"For one thing, there's always the danger of a war starting by accident."

"You're right," said Perle. "And that's why we want SDI."

"Okay," said Gorbachev, who seemed to be conceding the point. "But let's not talk about that tonight."

It was a lively and unusual conversation. Later, when Cynthia Helms told her husband that Gorbachev had briefly discussed decision-making in the Politburo, Dick Helms sighed and shook his head. "When I was intelligence chief," he said with a wry smile, "I would have *killed* for that kind of information."

Before he left Washington, Mikhail Gorbachev held an extended press conference, which Ronnie and I watched on television. His opening statement went on forever, and I kept waiting for the questions. Even the *Washington Post,* which was very hospitable to the Gorbachevs, called it an "interminable monologue."

When Gorbachev finally took questions, there was time for only three or four. And when he heard a question he didn't like, he simply said, "I'm not going to answer that." Gee, I thought, *that's* a way to handle the press!

Most of the networks gave up in the middle, but CNN showed the entire press conference. When Gorbachev was finally finished, Bernard Shaw of CNN said, "I'd like to say something about Nancy Reagan. She has had a very tough two months. She had breast cancer. Her mother died. Then she had to come back and face the summit, organize a state dinner, and take care of her husband. She did it all with grace and dignity and I think she deserves a lot of credit." I was very touched.

If someone had told me when Ronnie and I were first married that we would eventually travel to Moscow as president and first lady and would be the honored guests of the Soviet leadership, I would have suggested that he get his head examined. And yet, in May of 1988, that amazing prophecy came true.

It doesn't take much to make me nervous, but I was especially tense before going to Moscow. Although Ronnie and Gorbachev had built up a good and constructive relationship, I was terrified that I might say or do the wrong thing and find myself accidentally starting World War III. It's so easy to make a mistake when practically every word you utter is taken down by the press, especially when you're operating in an entirely different culture, with its own rules and customs—not to mention the language problem. In Washington, when Raisa had said that the White House was more of a museum than a home, I'm sure she hadn't intended to be rude; the comment just slipped out. Now the shoe would be on the other foot.

Although Jim Billington helped me study up on Soviet art and culture and taught me a few Russian phrases, I didn't really know what to expect on this trip—or even what to pack. The only thing I was sure of was that I wouldn't be needing a formal evening dress. I also decided to play it safe and not wear anything red. Although red is my favorite color, I thought that my wearing red in the Soviet Union might somehow be perceived as inappropriate or offensive. (I was wrong about that. At dinner at their dacha, Gorbachev assured me that red would have been perfectly acceptable.)

We arrived in Moscow on Sunday, May 25, after spending the

weekend in Helsinki to adjust to the time change. We didn't know how we would be received, so we were delighted to see all the people lining the streets as we came in from the airport. They seemed genuinely happy to see us, which pleased us enormously.

Following the arrival ceremony at the Kremlin, Ronnie and Gorbachev went off to a meeting while Raisa took me on a brief tour of the Kremlin. Here again, it didn't take long before the old tensions broke through. We were touring the fifteenth-century Assumption Cathedral, which had served as the coronation church for all the czars before the revolution. There was a powerful spiritual feeling in that church, and I asked Raisa a few questions about the icons, with their obvious religious significance. I was also curious to know whether religious services were ever held here—especially in 1988, which marked a thousand years of Christianity in the Soviet Union.

"*Nyet,*" she replied curtly. No services had been held there since the revolution, and the church was now a museum.

I had expected to see some of the other sights in the area, but as soon as we left the church we were ushered back into the Kremlin to wait for our husbands. I'm still not sure if my tour had been cut short because of my question, but I suspect it was. To me, the question was an obvious one, and I hadn't meant to be insulting. But that may have been how it was interpreted.

As we waited for the men to finish their meeting, Raisa and I tried valiantly to keep up a conversation. I was hoping that our husbands would be there soon, and I'm sure she felt the same way. Recalling the Washington summit, when our husbands had conspicuously looked at their watches when we were late, I suggested to Raisa that we might return the favor. She liked the idea, and when Ronnie and Gorbachev finally showed up, we all had a good laugh.

Two days later, Raisa and I had another encounter about religion. I had asked to see some of the famous icons at the Tretyakov Gallery, which has the finest collection of Russian art in the world. Raisa and I were supposed to meet there and tour it together. This time, she arrived a few minutes early. "Our guests are late," she told the press, "so I'll tell *you* about the gallery."

She then moved them upstairs and proceeded to hold a little press conference. I arrived at the gallery right on schedule to find that the plans had been changed. I went upstairs, and when Raisa saw me, she turned away from the press and started to escort me into the gallery. Just then, Bill Greenwood of ABC News called out, "Mrs. Reagan, Mrs. Gorbachev has been talking with us, and we all think you should have equal time. She said there was no religious significance to the icons."

"I don't know how you can neglect the religious implications," I replied. "I mean, they're there for everybody to see."

It wasn't exactly headline news, but the press was waiting for us to disagree about something, and this evidently did the trick. It seems so minor in retrospect, but at the time, the news media covered our little exchange in great detail.

Religion was very much on my mind during our visit. Every time Ronnie met with Gorbachev, he brought up the issue of religious freedom in general, and the rights of Jews in particular to leave the country. On several occasions Ronnie gave Gorbachev a list of people who, in our view, deserved to be allowed to leave. "Do what you can," Ronnie would say. "I'll never mention these names to the press, and I'll never take credit for it if you let them go." Many of these people were subsequently released.

During our visit to the Soviet Union, Ronnie spoke forcefully and often about human rights and religious freedom. He was criticized by the American press when he said that the problem lay in the Soviet bureaucracy, but his critics missed the point. Ronnie wanted to be as clear and as strong on this issue as he possibly could, but he also didn't want to embarrass our hosts. I still don't understand why so many commentators failed to understand this simple point.

Originally, we had planned to visit the apartment of Yuri and Tatyana Zieman, a Jewish couple in Moscow who had applied to emigrate in 1977. Yuri had been a computer specialist, but he lost his job when he applied for an exit visa, and he had been working as a plumber ever since. A few months before our trip he developed a mysterious brain ailment, and even the Soviet doctors told him that he should seek medical help abroad.

After it was announced that we would visit the Ziemans, their apartment building was painted and their street was repaved. But we canceled our plans when a Russian official called Ambassador Matlock to say that if we went to see them, they would never be allowed to leave. Was this a bluff? Nobody could say, but we didn't want to take any chances. No promises were made, but it was hinted that if we left the Ziemans alone, they would be allowed to leave the country. Two months later they were given their visas—but only after Ronnie called the Soviet ambassador and reminded him of the implied agreement.

We did see the Ziemans—not at their apartment, but at a reception we hosted for a hundred dissidents and refuseniks at Spaso House, the residence of the American ambassador. This was an event I'll never forget. It's one thing to read and hear about these brave individuals who risk beatings, exile, and long prison sentences in their fight for human rights, but to sit in the same room with them was a moving and unforgettable experience. I sat next to a man who has devoted his life to photographing old churches. "We're still trying," I told him. "Please don't give up." He has since emigrated to the United States.

Some of our guests had been threatened by the KGB and warned not to come, but they came anyway. Two of the refuseniks were in the midst of a hunger strike, while a third man, a Ukrainian dissident, had been released from a labor camp only a week earlier. Before we left Washington, I had told Vladimir Feltsman, the pianist and former refusenik, that I didn't want to make things even more difficult for the dissidents and refuseniks we hoped to see. "Don't worry about that," he assured me. "These people have nothing more to lose."

Three of our guests spoke, and then Ronnie got up and said: "I came here hoping to do what I could to give you strength. Yet I already know that it is you who have strengthened me, you who have given me a message to carry back. While we press for human rights through diplomatic channels, you press with your very lives, day in, day out, year after year, risking your jobs, your homes, your all. You have the prayers and support of the American people, indeed of people throughout the world."

Our Russian hosts were clearly unhappy about this meeting, and a few hours later, at the state dinner in the Kremlin, Gorbachev showed his anger when he said in his remarks that nations should get along "without interfering in domestic affairs." The Soviets may not have appreciated Ronnie's bold approach on this issue, but there's no question that they paid attention to his message. I don't think it's a coincidence that by the time Ronnie left office, there had been a major improvement in Soviet human rights. Much of the credit belongs to Mikhail Gorbachev, but it didn't hurt the cause of freedom for Ronnie to speak out as forcefully as he did on that visit.

The Soviet state dinner was held in the Kremlin's Hall of Facets, with its high ceilings and, yes, religious paintings. The tables were decorated with tall white tapers in silver candlesticks, so I found it surprising that the chandeliers were turned up full and the room was so brightly lit.

Soviet dinners go on much longer than ours, and include many more courses. I wasn't crazy about everything they served, but then, we hadn't come to Moscow for the food. And I was delighted to find that both the caviar and the ice cream were every bit as wonderful as I had been told. It's what came between the two that I had trouble with. (Ron had warned me about it: "Mom," he said, "don't be surprised if it looks like used food.")

During the dinner, Gorbachev turned to me and said, "You know, your husband and I have a certain . . ." and here he was obviously groping for the right word.

"Let me help you," I said. "Chemistry?"

"Yes, chemistry."

"I know you do. I'm very aware of it, and so is my husband."

"It's very rare," said Gorbachev.

"I know that, too," I replied.

Then Gorbachev made a remarkable statement: "I am familiar with your Constitution, but I wish your husband could stay on for another four years."

It was fascinating to hear this from Mikhail Gorbachev in the Kremlin. While it's possible that he was simply being polite, I believe he was sincere. After four meetings, he and Ronnie had developed a mutual respect and affection. Each of them understood and accepted that there were still major differences between them, that there were limits beyond which they should not press each other. But I also believe that each is profoundly grateful that the other was in power during those years, and that they were able to work together to reduce the threat of nuclear war.

The following night, Ronnie and I hosted a return dinner at Spaso House. Boy, *that* was a challenge. It took months to plan, and Linda Faulkner, my social secretary, did a heroic job. Every part of that dinner was brought over from Washington. The china and the silverware came from the State Department, and Linda rented and shipped over everything else, from tablecloths and flowers to sugar tongs, salt dishes, and ashtrays. It was by far the most complicated project I have ever been involved with.

Even the food was flown in from Washington, and prepared by the embassy chef. We hired Soviet waiters because Spaso House didn't have enough staff, and our people trained the serving staff in the American style of serving. As much as possible, we tried to organize this event as if it were a state dinner at the White House. And so, for example, there was an American host at each table, with an appropriate Soviet official to his right. Between them, but not actually at the table, sat a translator. Although wives are not generally invited to Soviet state dinners, we followed the American practice of inviting spouses. As in Washington, husbands and wives were seated at separate tables.

The guest list was far more complicated than usual, and the spelling of the names was enough to drive Linda crazy. The invitations were done in calligraphy and printed (in English) at the White House, and delivered personally by the embassy staff. The response cards were in Russian, and each guest was notified by telephone (also in Russian) that his invitation would soon be arriving.

While we wanted to bring together a diverse and interesting group, this was not the place to include refuseniks, dissidents, or anyone else whom the Soviet leadership might find embarrassing. (We did invite Sakharov, but he and Gorbachev had already met.) In their dinner for us at the Soviet embassy in Washington, the Gorbachevs had invited prominent Democrats such as Ted

Kennedy, Pamela Harriman, and Speaker Jim Wright. These were certainly appropriate choices, but how do you put together a politically diverse group in a one-party state without inviting dissidents? It wasn't easy, but we included a sprinkling of writers, journalists, filmmakers, actors, and musicians, much as we would have done at a White House dinner. Gary Kasparov, the chess champion, was invited, along with Andrew Lloyd Webber, the composer, who happened to be in Moscow on business. The menu consisted of lobster bisque, suprême of chicken with truffle sauce, carrot soufflé, salad, cheese, and frozen chocolate mousse with vanilla sauce.

As usual, I sat with Gorbachev, but this time our table included a cross section of Soviet writers and intellectuals. The talk was loud and boisterous, and the Russians at our table were eager to confront Gorbachev on any number of issues. I was surprised that nobody deferred to the chairman, but he seemed to be enjoying the exchange, just as he had at the state dinner in Washington. The discussion went so fast that the translators couldn't keep up, but when the dinner was over, Jim Billington filled me in on what it all meant.

One well-endowed woman at our table became so animated that I was afraid she was going to spill out of her low-cut dress. She was a writer who wanted Gorbachev to explain why a certain prominent historian had not been invited to the upcoming Communist party congress. This prompted a lively discussion on the topic, and a few days later it was announced that he would be attending the congress after all.

We had asked Dave Brubeck and his quartet to provide the entertainment, not only because the Russians love American jazz, but also because Brubeck is a great favorite in Moscow. I knew he was the right choice when the audience began applauding in the middle of the first song, the Duke Ellington standard, "Take the A Train." From start to finish, our dinner was a hit.

There were several other memorable moments during our visit to the Soviet Union, including my visit to a Moscow school. The children were darling—the girls in their brown dresses and white pinafores, and the boys in blue slacks and white shirts. Their eyes

were full of excitement, and they couldn't wait to ask me questions—in English—about their American counterparts:

What kind of uniforms do children wear in America?

What kind of games do American children like?

Do American children go on long camping trips like we do?

One of the boys led me into a special wing of the building which
commemorated the many graduates of this school who died during
World War II. Pointing to a piece of artillery, he said, "It's not usual
to see a gun in a school. But this is why it is here, because this is
a museum. We say that when a gun speaks, it's too late to talk. We
hope the gun will never be used again. You know, our country lost
twenty million people in the war."

I was deeply moved by his words, and very glad that we had made
this trip. I explained that American children didn't want war either,
and that I hoped both sides could move closer to peace. At that
moment it all seemed so simple. Kids are kids, and I couldn't help
but think that if it were up to the children, the world might be a
safer place. I made some remarks before leaving, and ended by
saying "I love you," which evidently made a big impression, because
some of the children came up and hugged me. Russian society tends
to be rather formal, and this was a rare and welcome example of
spontaneity.

A few minutes after leaving the school, I found myself in another
world entirely when I was driven out into the country to visit the
grave of Boris Pasternak. I have always been a great admirer of
Doctor Zhivago, which was first published in the West in 1956 but
did not appear in the Soviet Union until shortly before we arrived.
Pasternak's son Yevgeny was with me, and as I placed a bouquet of
flowers on his father's grave, I was suddenly aware that Yevgeny
was humming softly. It was, I learned later, a requiem. He also told
me that May 30, the date of my visit, was the twenty-eighth anniversary of his father's death.

Before I left, Yevgeny took me into his father's dacha and showed
me the room where Pasternak wrote *Doctor Zhivago.* Then he
handed me a small book of his own poems. Suddenly, amidst the
birch trees and the lilacs, I was seeing a Russia very different from

the one I had seen in the Kremlin. That was Russian power, but this was the Russian soul.

When I came out of the dacha to drive to my next appointment, I was greeted by four village women holding lilacs. "We're so happy to see you," they said. "We're so glad you came. We've waited for you for so long. All we want is for our children to live under blue skies—and no war."

They hugged and kissed me, but finally I had to leave. I got into the car, and when I looked out the rearview window, they were sobbing. I felt terrible, as if I were deserting them.

My only other spontaneous interaction with regular people came during our ill-fated walk down the Arbat, Moscow's pedestrian mall. Before we left Washington, Ron had said to me, "Try to get out, Mom. Don't let them push you into a car. Get out and walk around. See the Arbat and get a feel for the people."

That was easy for him to say, but I don't think he understood the massive amount of security that such a trip entails. Even so, Ronnie and I remembered his advice, and the afternoon when we had a free moment because our visit with the Ziemans had been canceled, we strolled out onto the Arbat. Everybody recognized us and called to us and seemed excited and happy that we were there.

It was all going beautifully until the KGB suddenly arrived and started roughing people up. They were supposed to be protecting us, but we didn't need any additional protection, and we soon found ourselves in the middle of a mob scene. Some of the reporters who came with us were punched and kicked, and I had to rescue Helen Thomas from the KGB—whom Ron had described as "the kind of lugs who crush walnuts on their foreheads because it feels good." (Afterward, I told Helen she owed me one.) I was frightened—these people hadn't been doing anything; they just wanted to shake hands and welcome us. The whole incident was an ugly reminder that some things in the Soviet Union still hadn't changed.

Even with *glasnost*, this was still a closed and secretive society. Ronnie and I stayed at Spaso House, and it was a strange and uncomfortable experience to be in a place where you can't talk freely because the rooms are almost certainly bugged. I found it frustrating to have my mind and my heart filled with thoughts, impressions, and reactions, and not to be able to talk about any of it with my husband. We were even warned not to write notes because they could be photographed with hidden cameras. And when Ronnie had to read his confidential briefing papers, he went down to a special, secure room in the basement.

On the second day of the summit, I flew off to Leningrad for a quick visit to the famous Hermitage museum. My hostess was Lidiya Gromyko, the wife, and now widow, of President Andrei Gromyko. Raisa was busy with a previously scheduled engagement with Mrs. Papandreou of Greece, which was fine with me.

I was in Leningrad for only a few hours, but it was the most beautiful city I have ever seen, and I can understand why the Russians call it the Venice of the North. And I was overwhelmed by the reception I received from the people. I left Ronnie behind in Moscow—now *there's* a phrase I never expected to write—but even so, tens of thousands of people lined the streets to welcome me on the way in from the airport.

The Hermitage was built by Catherine the Great, as a winter palace, in 1754. It's an enormous building, with 353 rooms and three *million* pieces of art. To see it properly would take weeks, which left me with a dilemma that was all too common in my years as first lady: Either I could take a fast and superficial look at a famous landmark, or I had to skip it entirely. On the principle that something is better than nothing, I had decided to spend eighty minutes at the Hermitage.

I saw only a tiny fraction of the exhibits, of course, and even then I had to walk quickly. Poor Mrs. Gromyko! While I was racing through, one of the reporters asked if she was tired. "Of course I'm tired," she said. "I'm seventy-seven years old!"

I'm glad I saw a little of the Hermitage, but I'm sorry that some Russians took offense at the brevity of my visit. One official was quoted as saying, "It's a crime that she did it so quickly," and in a sense he was right. But at least I was there. The entire summit lasted less than a hundred hours; you do what you can on these trips.

Perhaps in my new life as a private citizen, I'll be able to return to some of the wonderful places all over the world that I saw for only a few minutes as first lady.

It was shortly after leaving the Hermitage that I made the kind of blunder I was most afraid of. I was on a hydrofoil on the Neva River, en route to the summer palace of Peter the Great. My companion was Dmitri Likhachev, an elderly Soviet scholar who is trying to preserve some of his country's historic buildings, and we were talking about how the government was tearing down beautiful structures to make room for ugly concrete high rises. I knew exactly what he meant, because we have the same problem in our country. "What are we going to do about these monstrosities?" I asked.

I thought we were having a private conversation, but a reporter was sitting with us, and soon it was all over the world that I had referred to Soviet buildings as "monstrosities." I hadn't meant it that way, but it was too late to undo the damage.

On the final evening of our visit, Ronnie and I and the Gorbachevs attended a special performance at the magnificent Bolshoi Theater. The royal box was flanked by American and Soviet flags, and as the four of us stood together while the orchestra played our two national anthems, I was just overwhelmed by the pageantry of it all. *This is really happening,* I thought. Here we are in *Moscow,* and they're playing *our* anthem.

As I mentioned before, at our state dinner in Washington, Gorbachev had remarked on how wonderful the Soviet anthem had sounded that morning when it was played by the Marine Corps Band. Listening to "The Star-Spangled Banner" in the Bolshoi Theater I had a similar reaction. During eight years of White House life, I heard our anthem played hundreds, if not thousands, of times. But never did it sound as grand and imposing as it did that night, in that breathtaking setting, just hours after Ronnie and Gorbachev had signed the historic INF treaty. Once again I had a sense of history in the making.

Owing to some minor logistical problem, Ronnie and I had been a little late in getting to the theater. When we arrived, Gorbachev asked if our late arrival had anything to do with a rumor that was circulating in Moscow that Ronnie was going to be assassinated at the Bolshoi. This was the first we had heard of it, and although Gorbachev assured us that there was absolutely nothing to worry about, I wasn't exactly thrilled. But it didn't seem to bother Ronnie, who assumed that Gorbachev wasn't taking any chances when it came to the safety of his American guests.

While this is not normally the sort of worry I can put out of my mind, I still managed to enjoy the ballet, which featured selections from *Sleeping Beauty, Swan Lake, Romeo and Juliet,* and other works. It helped that we were at the end of a long and exciting trip which had obviously been successful. That sense of relief, combined with the warmth and beauty of the Bolshoi Theater, made for a memorable evening.

When the performance was over, we took a thirty-minute drive to the Gorbachevs' dacha for dinner with them, the Shultzes, and the Shevardnadzes. We were only a few miles from Moscow, but the atmosphere was much more casual and relaxed than in the city. We had been led to believe that this was the Gorbachevs' private dacha, but I learned later that it was an official guest house. They also have a private dacha, but we didn't see that.

At dinner, Gorbachev talked at some length about the nuclear accident at Chernobyl. It was obvious to all of us at the table that this tragedy had made a tremendous impression on him; he was clearly disturbed and deeply affected by it. I was already well disposed toward Gorbachev, and I found his concern moving.

Gorbachev also discussed the upcoming Communist party congress. He told us that one of the reforms he wanted to institute was to limit the terms of top Soviet officials to a specific number of years. As soon as he said that, Raisa jumped right in. "Yes," she said, "except for the general secretary. If the people want *him* to stay, of course he should."

Earlier in the evening, I had asked George Shultz for a favor. "Please," I said, "this trip has been wonderful, but Ronnie and I are exhausted, and tomorrow morning we fly to London. Can you speak to Shevardnadze and see to it that we're out of here by ten?"

George said he would, but as the dinner was drawing to a close, he leaned over and whispered to me, "I think I've failed you."

"I think you did too," I replied. It was clear that we were never going to leave by ten.

But George hadn't given up. When dinner finally ended and we moved to the sitting room for coffee, he and Shevardnadze approached our hosts together and said, "It's been a wonderful evening and we want to thank you. But now it's time to go home."

I was already on my feet. But then Raisa said, "No, no, I want everyone to sit down. I have something to say."

Well, when Raisa Gorbachev tells you to sit down, you sit down.

She spoke about the meaning of the summit and the friendship between our two countries. She said some kind things, but, as usual, she went on too long. Then her husband made some very gracious comments about how important this contact was for our two nations, and for the entire world.

I could barely stay awake during the ride home, but when we passed through Red Square, Ronnie insisted that we get out of the car so he could show me the red marble of Lenin's tomb and the painted brick of the Kremlin Wall. I had never seen Red Square, and as tired as I was, I desperately wanted to. So of course we stopped, and it was very impressive. It would have been a shame to go home without seeing it.

Fortunately, there's a happy postscript to my difficult relationship with Raisa. In December 1988, Gorbachev flew to New York to address the United Nations. While he and Ronnie met for lunch, Raisa and I were among the guests at a women's luncheon at the home of Marcela Pérez de Cuéllar, the wife of the secretary general of the U.N.

But something had clearly changed. At the table, Raisa talked with Matilda Cuomo, the governor's wife, and acknowledged that Soviet society had not done a good job in the area of child care. "We could have handled this better," she said. "We always provided day care in the mother's workplace, but now I think it might have made more sense to keep the child at home for the first few years."

Raisa talked, but this time she didn't lecture. The atmosphere was warmer than usual, and I was touched by what she told me. "I will miss you and your husband," she said. "As for the two of us, it was destiny that put us at the place we were, next to our husbands, to help bring about the relationship that our two countries now have. My husband and I hope you will return to the Soviet Union to see us."

"We'd like that very much," I said. "You know, Ronnie has always said that he would love to have you and your husband see the Western states. We would be delighted if you could visit us in California."

Believe it or not, I meant it.

I didn't know this at the time, but just as Raisa was issuing her invitation to me, Mikhail Gorbachev was extending a similar invitation to Ronnie. And Ronnie, who would enjoy nothing better than to show Gorbachev our country, immediately invited them to California, and to the ranch.

If Raisa and I had been left alone, without any press, we probably would have had an easier time of it. But even before our first meeting in Geneva, there had been so much talk about the two of us that we were both enormously self-conscious. In any event, I'm very glad that we saw each other one last time in New York, which was a nice ending to a relationship that had obviously been difficult for both of us.

18

❖❖❖

Coming Home

NOTHING can prepare you for living in the White House—and nothing can prepare you for leaving it. On January 20, 1989, Ronnie and I left under the best of circumstances, and still it was wrenching for both of us. I can only imagine how hard it must be to leave in defeat.

Our final two months were emotionally and physically draining. So much happened, and I have so many memories to hold on to. The Senate honored Ronnie, and Bob Dole, not normally a sentimental man, gave him such a moving tribute that Bob was as teary as everyone else. At the end of the Kennedy Center Honors, Walter Cronkite called the cast back on stage and said, "It's a special time as we salute two people who have sat in that box for the past eight years," whereupon the orchestra played "Auld Lang Syne" and the audience stood and sang to us. When it was over there was a pause, and Ronnie called out, "This is better than an Oscar!"

There was Ronnie's final appearance with the press, when Tom Brokaw said, "So Ronald Wilson Reagan ends his last press conference. He's seventy-eight years old and has never looked better." The Children's Hospital named a room after me because of all my visits there. And we had our last Christmas weekend at Camp David, where Eddie Serrano and the boys had decorated our cabin more beautifully than ever and put in a lovely tree and poinsettias all over. After dinner the enlisted men—most of them so young—came by to serenade us with Christmas carols. The last Christmas at the White House had an old-fashioned theme, and the kids from Second Genesis, a drug rehabilitation program, came to help us decorate, as usual.

The press was there for the party, and Sam Donaldson came up to me and said, "I know reporters aren't supposed to show emotion, but now that you're leaving I want you to know that I was the first to say that Ronald Reagan would go down in history and would leave this place even more popular than when he came in. We'll miss you." I'll miss Sam, too. This may come as a shock, but I always liked him. I think Sam carved out a character for himself and played to that, but underneath there was a soft, sentimental side. I didn't always appreciate the questions he asked, but he's a hardworking journalist who really does his homework.

So many goodbyes! The military aides gave us a tracing of a John Adams saying that is carved on the mantel in the State Dining Room: "May only good and wise men inhabit this house." They said, "As far as we're concerned, that's been true for the past eight years."

Ronnie went to the park police stables to have his picture taken with the men who taught the Secret Service agents how to ride. They said they'd never before had such a warm relationship with a president.

During the many Christmas receptions, there were tears all around and Linda Faulkner had to keep handing me tissues. There was Ronnie's farewell address to the nation on television, and the military tribute to Ronnie. I had a bad cold that day and no voice, so they wouldn't let me go, which I'll always regret. I watched it on television, and when Ronnie inspected the troops, and they turned, faced him, saluted, and sang "Auld Lang Syne," I saw him bend his head. He whispered to the man next to him, "I think I'm going to cry."

At the final Reagan Library dinner in the original family dining room, everything looked so pretty. I remembered when that room was just a pass-through to the kitchen: I had it converted to a place where Ronnie could have lunch with state leaders, in a warm atmosphere, in front of the fire. Sitting there, I thought of all the changes I'd made on the second and third floors, and outside, too—getting them to peel thirty-two coats of paint off the White House even though nobody else wanted to put up with all that inconvenience. I put a lot of myself into that house, and I was leaving a lot of me there.

Ronnie wanted to make one last overnight visit to Camp David, and we did. I had lunch with some of the women from the press who covered me; they all wore red and brought me autographed pictures of themselves, and a fishbowl to symbolize the life I had led. There were so many pictures taken with so many people. And in the East Room farewell ceremony for six hundred members of the White House staff, I had never seen so many people crying. As we left the room and headed for the elevator, John Bourgeois, the leader of the Marine Band, stopped us and said to Ronnie, "We'll miss you. We were always proud to be called the president's band while you were here. We want to give you this harmonica. Even though you won't be here, we want you to play 'Hail to the Chief' every morning."

Our last White House event was the Medal of Freedom luncheon, where we presented awards to Mike Mansfield and George Shultz. We spent the final night quietly with Maureen, Dennis, and Ted Graber, in Ronnie's study with the fire going. The kitchen staff prepared a special dinner, which began with caviar served in a boat with Ronnie's initials on it. Alfredo, the butler, brought in a bottle of champagne as a gift from the staff.

Then the day finally came—the day I had both hoped for and dreaded. It was gray and cold. We ate breakfast early and went downstairs to say goodbye to the household staff in the State Dining Room. Then out to welcome the Bushes and the Quayles. A few other guests had already arrived—Jim Wright, Bob Michel, Tom Foley, Senator George Mitchell, and Senator Ted Stevens, who gave me a pin and Ronnie a pair of cufflinks with a dove motif because, he said, we'd done so much for peace.

We were supposed to have coffee, but I don't remember anybody drinking any. Then it was time to leave for the inauguration. I hugged the butlers and we walked outside; Ronnie and George

Bush got into one car with Jim Wright and Tom Foley; Barbara Bush and I got into another with George Mitchell and Bob Michel. The conversation was a little easier than it had been eight years before, and I managed to say, "I hope the magnolia trees I planted will do well. Maybe my grandchildren will see them one day." But my heart ached as I looked at those beautiful grounds that I was unlikely to see again.

The inaugural ceremony was held on the West Front of the Capitol, and it was a peculiar feeling looking down at the monument where Ronnie had taken his oath that first time, and trying to recall my emotions then. Sandra Day O'Connor looked over at me and I mouthed, "How are you feeling?"—she'd had a mastectomy soon after I did. She swore in Dan Quayle, and William Rehnquist swore in George Bush.

The whole day was like a dream, and then suddenly this part, too, was over. The Bushes and the Quayles walked down the steps with us to see us off in the helicopter. As we started walking toward the helicopter I saw a lone figure standing to one side—George Opfer, from the Secret Service, who was there to say goodbye. I broke away from Ronnie and ran over to give him a big hug. At the steps of the helicopter, Ronnie turned and saluted, which caused a lump in everyone's throat. When we took off, the pilots circled the White House so we could see it once more, and Ronnie leaned over to me and said, "Look, dear, there's our bungalow." This was really good-bye to Washington, and eight wonderful, exciting, frustrating, and sometimes frightening years.

On *Air Force One,* the pilot, who was flying his last trip too, came back to give us a beautiful picture of the White House and a lovely inscription from the crew. Ronnie and I went back to see the press, including Sam Donaldson, Bill Plante, and Lou Cannon, and the crew served cake and champagne.

When we landed in Los Angeles there was a welcome ceremony; the University of Southern California band played, and one of the musicians threw his helmet to Ronnie. As we left the platform to get into the car, Sam Donaldson gave Ronnie a final salute. See what I mean about Sam?

When we got to our house, John Hutton, Ken and Sydney Duberstein, and Tim McCarthy came in to see it, and then we all started to cry. They finally had to leave, and it was just Ronnie and me alone, surrounded by all those boxes—and no support team to help us. It seemed unreal and overwhelming. Ron came over and helped his Dad start to unpack.

A few days earlier, Kay Graham and Meg Greenfield had suggested that we have people over that night, but Ronnie and I were so exhausted that I don't think it would have worked. When we finally fell into bed, I lay there and wondered: If there hadn't been a Twenty-second Amendment, would we still be in Washington? Ronnie had worked as hard as he could to get George Bush elected—harder than any president had ever worked for his successor. But I knew there were things Ronnie would still have liked to accomplish.

George and Barbara have an enormous job ahead of them, and Ronnie and I wish them all the luck in the world. But still, it's sometimes difficult to watch anyone else in Ronnie's old job. The truth is that I didn't know George all that well while Ronnie was president. People may have the impression that the president and the vice president and their wives spend a lot of time together, but in fact the system rarely allows that. The two couples almost invariably attend separate events, and for the most part, we had completely different schedules. During our first year in Washington, the Bushes came to the White House alone for dinner with us, and they had us to their house as well. But after that we were on separate tracks, except for state dinners.

As painful as leaving was for me, I did feel it was time. We'd had twenty years of public life, and I thought we needed to spend more time with family and friends—and with each other.

And so as one door closes and another opens, we enter another phase of our lives. We're both busy giving speeches. I'm still involved with the drug program through the Nancy Reagan Foundation and the Just Say No clubs. Ronnie is busy with his memoirs, and we're getting reacquainted with California.

Ronnie and I were privileged to have an opportunity that is given to very few—to be a part of history, and the shaping of it. We have so many memories of those years. We still feel a tremendous warmth from the public, and we hope our children are proud of us.

Being first lady has taught me so much. Over those eight years in Washington, amid the exaggerated ups and downs of life at the White House, I found out what was really important to me. I learned how to serve. I grew, and I learned how, despite intense scrutiny and criticism, just to go on being myself—to let Nancy be Nancy. And for this, and for so many other things, I'll always be grateful.

Photo Credits

61   Bill Fitz-Patrick, Courtesy Ronald Reagan Presidential Library
62   David Johnson, Courtesy Ronald Reagan Presidential Library
63   Pete Souza, Courtesy Ronald Reagan Presidential Library
64–65 Mary Anne Fackelman-Miner, Courtesy Ronald Reagan
     Presidential Library
66   Bill Fitz-Patrick, Courtesy Ronald Reagan Presidential Library
67–69 Mary Anne Fackelman-Miner, Courtesy Ronald Reagan
     Presidential Library
70   David Valdez, Courtesy Ronald Reagan Presidential Library
71   Pete Souza, Courtesy Ronald Reagan Presidential Library
72   Bill Fitz-Patrick, Courtesy Ronald Reagan Presidential Library
73   Mary Anne Fackelman-Miner, Courtesy Ronald Reagan
     Presidential Library
74–75 Bill Fitz-Patrick, Courtesy Ronald Reagan Presidential Library
76   Mary Anne Fackelman-Miner, Courtesy Ronald Reagan
     Presidential Library
77   Bill Fitz-Patrick, Courtesy Ronald Reagan Presidential Library
78–79 Michael Evans, Courtesy Ronald Reagan Presidential Library
80   Pete Souza, Courtesy Ronald Reagan Presidential Library
81   Mary Anne Fackelman-Miner, Courtesy Ronald Reagan
     Presidential Library
82   Susan Biddle, Courtesy Ronald Reagan Presidential Library
83   © Dirck Halstead

Index